YOU'RE READING THE WRONG WAY!

Nura: Rise of the Yokai Clan reads from right to left, starting in the upper-right corner. Japanese is read from right to left, meaning that action, sound effects, and word-balloon order are completely reversed from English order.

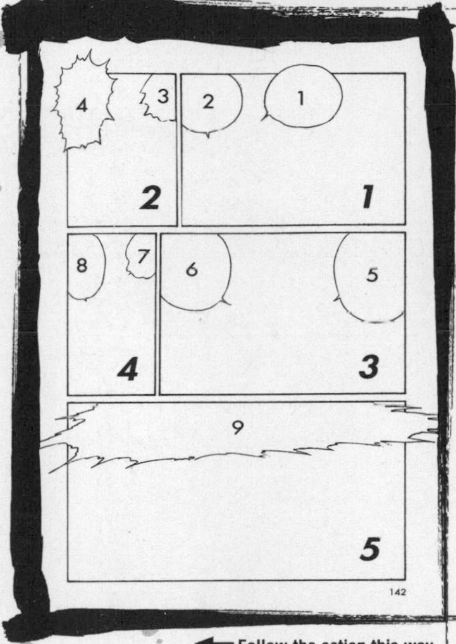
1
2
3
4
5
6
7
8
9
142

← Follow the action this way.

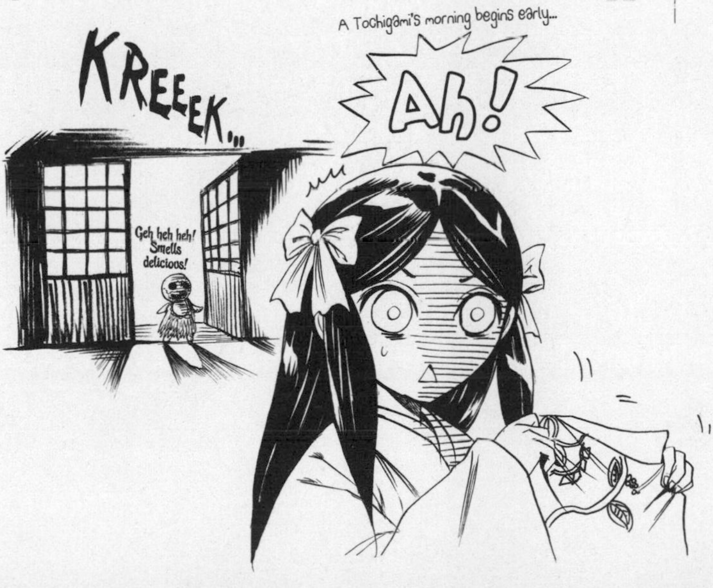
A Tochigami's morning begins early...
Ah!
KREEEK...
Geh heh heh! Smells delicious!

ᐯI∠MᐯNGᐯ

Read manga anytime, anywhere!

n our newest hit series to the classics you know
love, the best manga in the world is now available
ally. Buy a volume* of digital manga for your:

S device (**iPad®**, **iPhone®**, **iPod®** touch)
rough the **VIZ Manga app**

ndroid-powered device (**phone or tablet**)
ith a browser by visiting VIZManga.com

ac or PC computer by visiting VIZManga.com

VIZ Digital has loads to offer:

- 500+ ready-to-read volumes
- New volumes each week
- FREE previews
- Access on multiple devices! Create a log-in through the app
  so you buy a book once, and read it on your device of choice!*

To learn more, visit www.viz.com/apps

* Some series may not be available for multiple devices.
Check the app on your device to find out what's available.

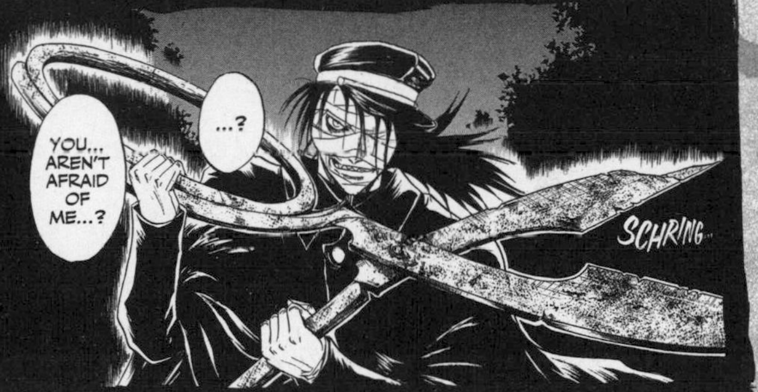
YOU... AREN'T AFRAID OF ME...?
...?
SCHRING...

IN THE NEXT VOLUME...

KIRISAKI TORYANSE, THE RIPPER

Caught in The Ripper's scissors-hold, Rikuo faces off against this terrifying enemy whose Fear feeds on the pain of children. Speaking of eating, brother and sister team Ryuji and Yura travel to the worst tourist destination ever, the Village That Devours People!

AVAILABLE OCTOBER 2013!

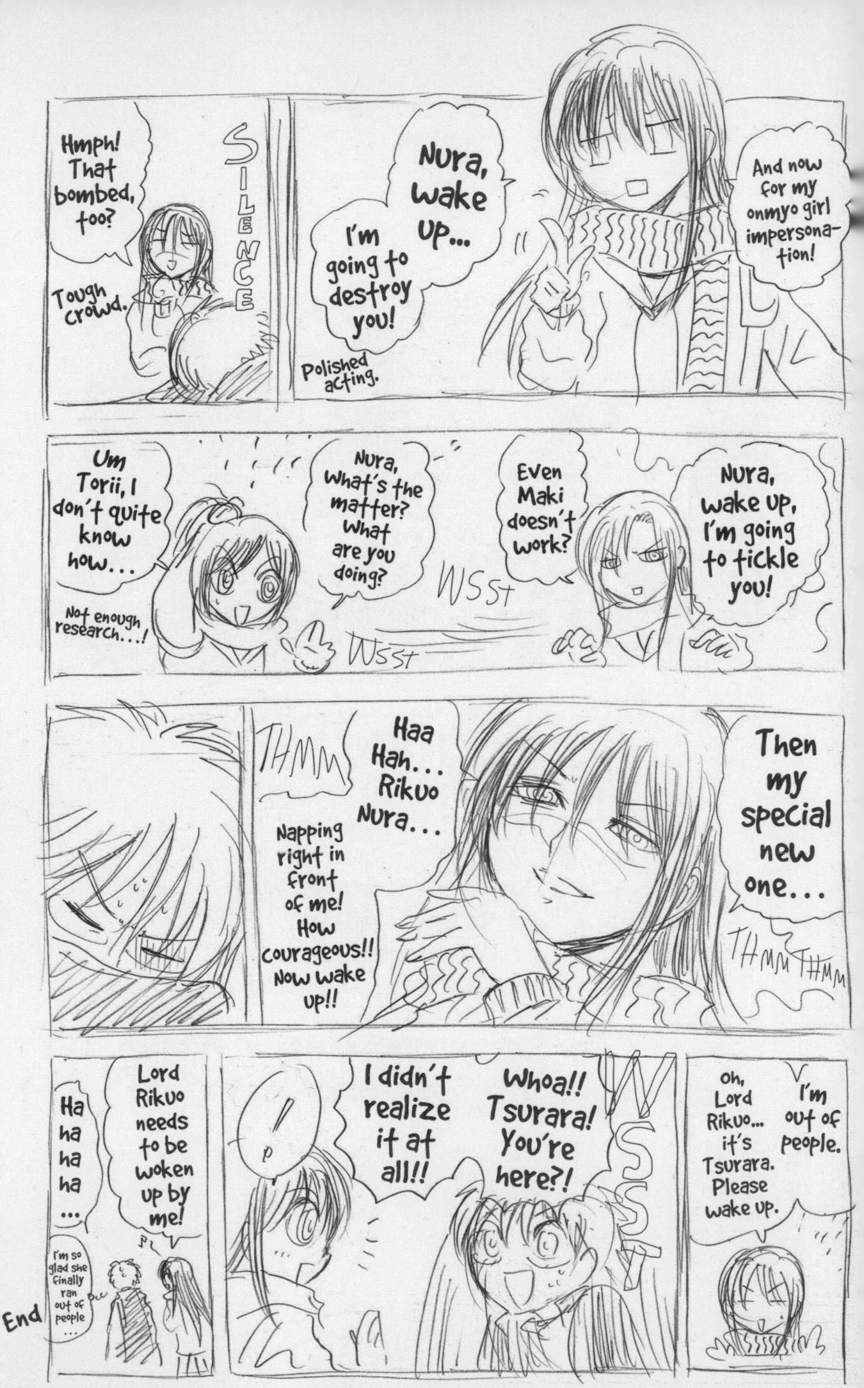
And now for my onmyo girl impersonation!
Nura, wake up... I'm going to destroy you!
Polished acting.
SILENCE
Hmph! That bombed, too?
Tough crowd.
Nura, wake up, I'm going to tickle you!
Even Maki doesn't work?
WSST
Nura, what's the matter? What are you doing?
WSST
Um Torii, I don't quite know how...
Not enough research...!
Then my special new one...
THMM THMM
Haa Hah... Rikuo Nura...
Napping right in front of me! How courageous!! Now wake up!!
THMM
I'm out of people.
Oh, Lord Rikuo... it's Tsurara. Please wake up.
WSST
Whoa!! Tsurara! You're here?!
I didn't realize it at all!!
!
Lord Rikuo needs to be woken up by me!
Ha ha ha ha ...
I'm so glad she finally ran out of people ...
End

After school Tsurara—

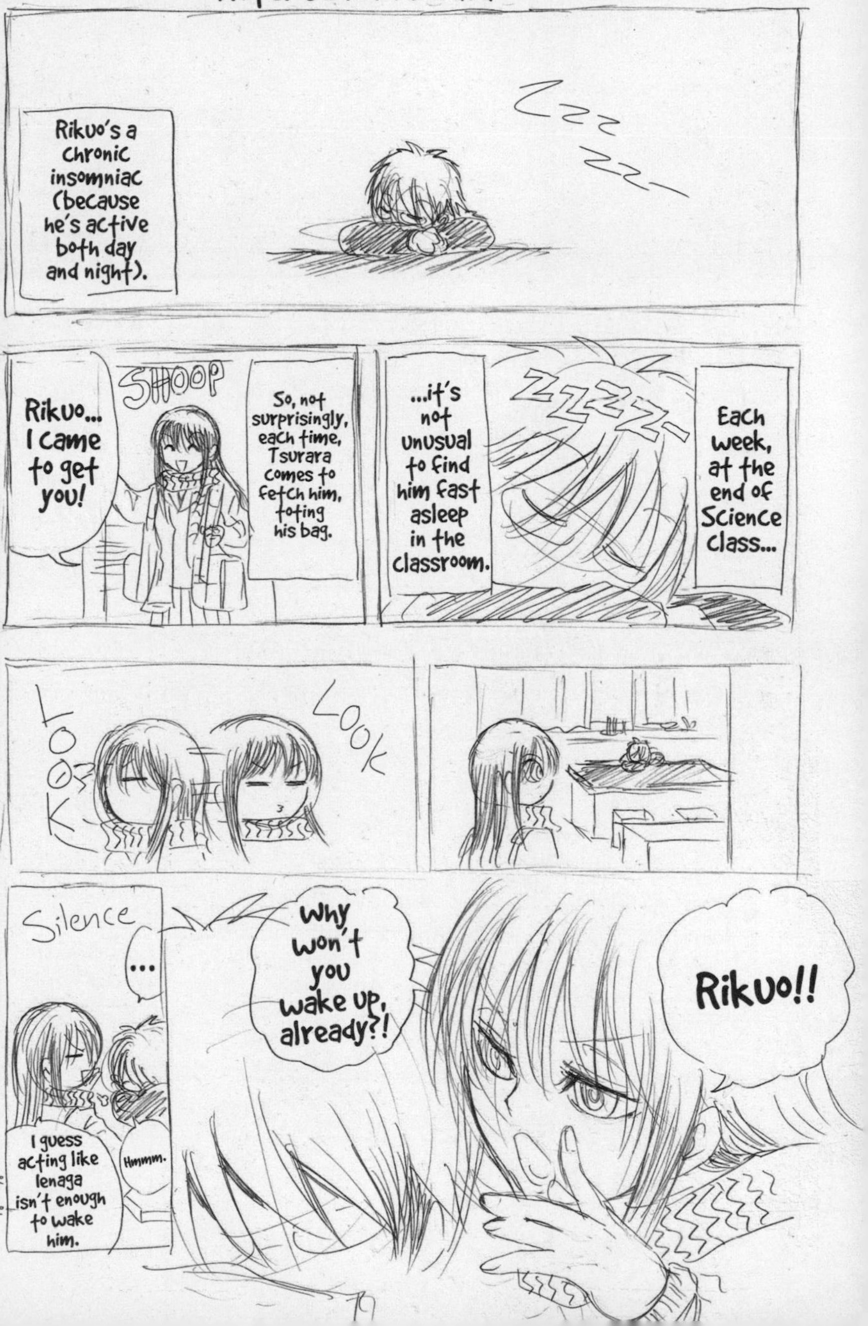
Zzz
Rikuo's a chronic insomniac (because he's active both day and night).
Each week, at the end of Science class...
ZZZZ-
...it's not unusual to find him fast asleep in the classroom.
So, not surprisingly, each time, Tsurara comes to fetch him, toting his bag.
SHOOP
Rikuo... I came to get you!
LOOK
LOOK
Rikuo!!
Why won't you wake up, already?!
Silence
...
Hmmm.
I guess acting like Ienaga isn't enough to wake him.
Hee Hee

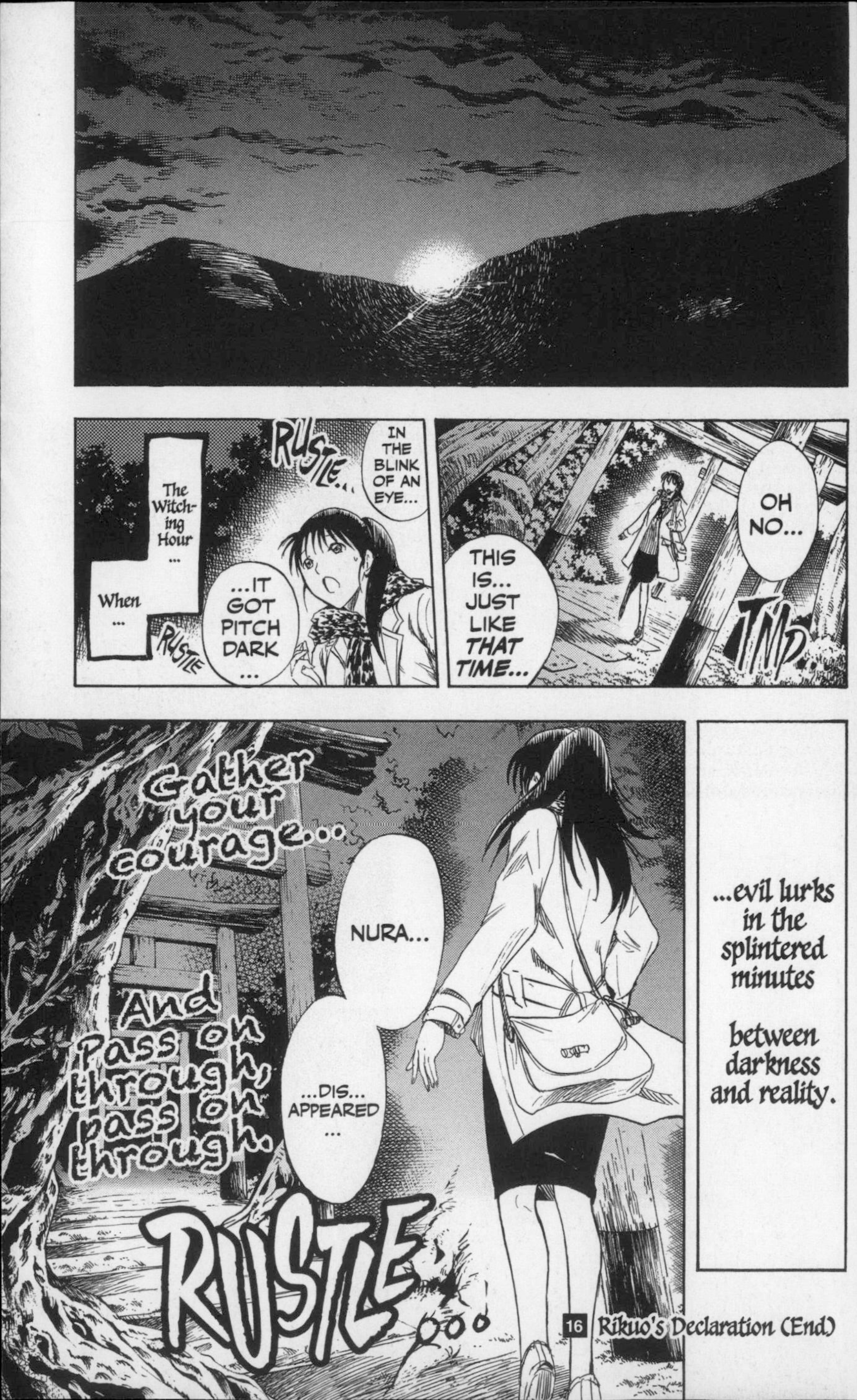
OH NO...
TMP...
THIS IS... JUST LIKE THAT TIME...
IN THE BLINK OF AN EYE...
RUSTLE...
The Witching Hour ...
When ...
...IT GOT PITCH DARK ...
RUSTLE
...evil lurks in the splintered minutes
between darkness and reality.
NURA...
...DIS... APPEARED ...
Gather your courage...
And pass on through, pass on through.
RUSTLE...
16 Rikuo's Declaration (End)

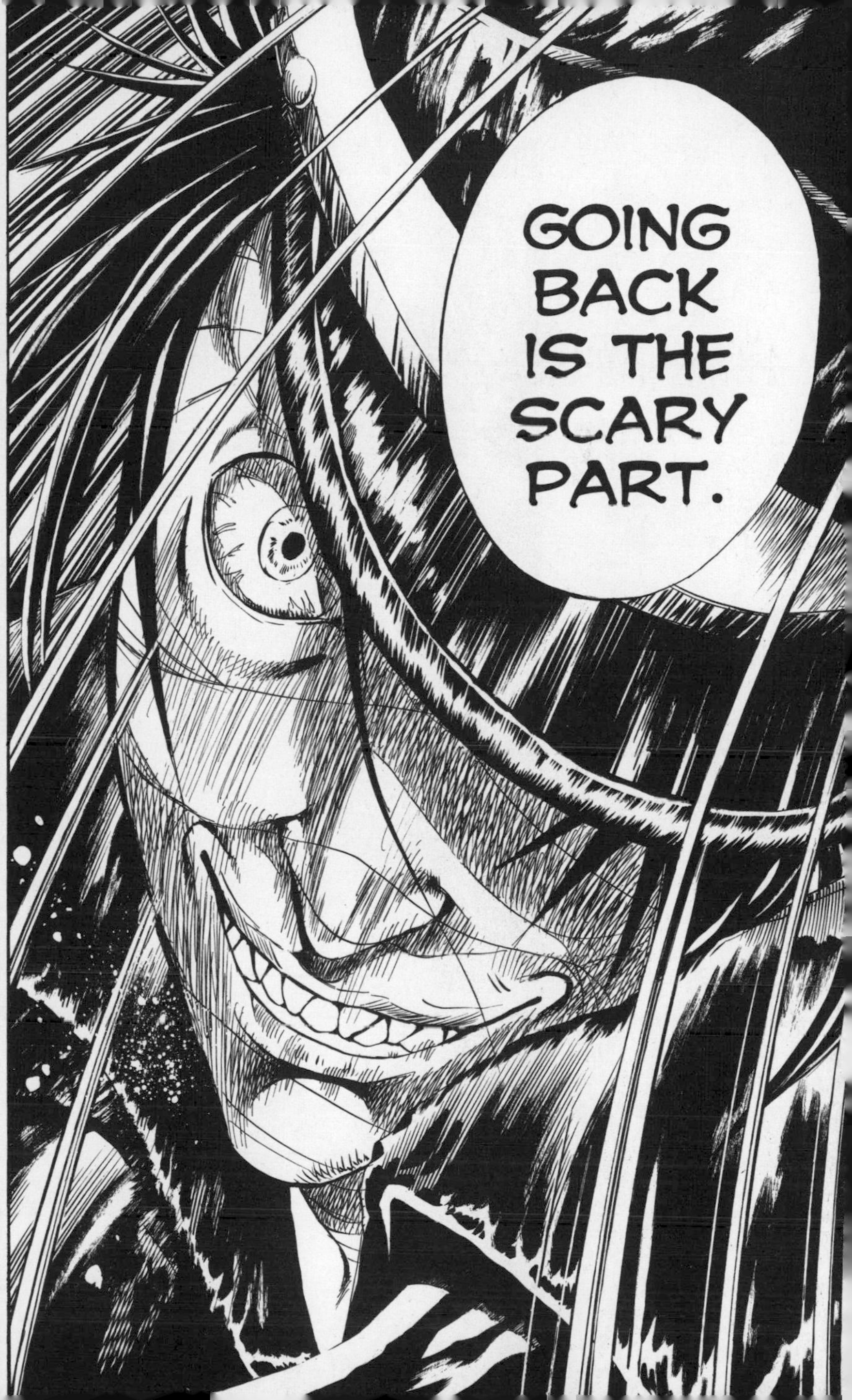
GOING BACK IS THE SCARY PART.

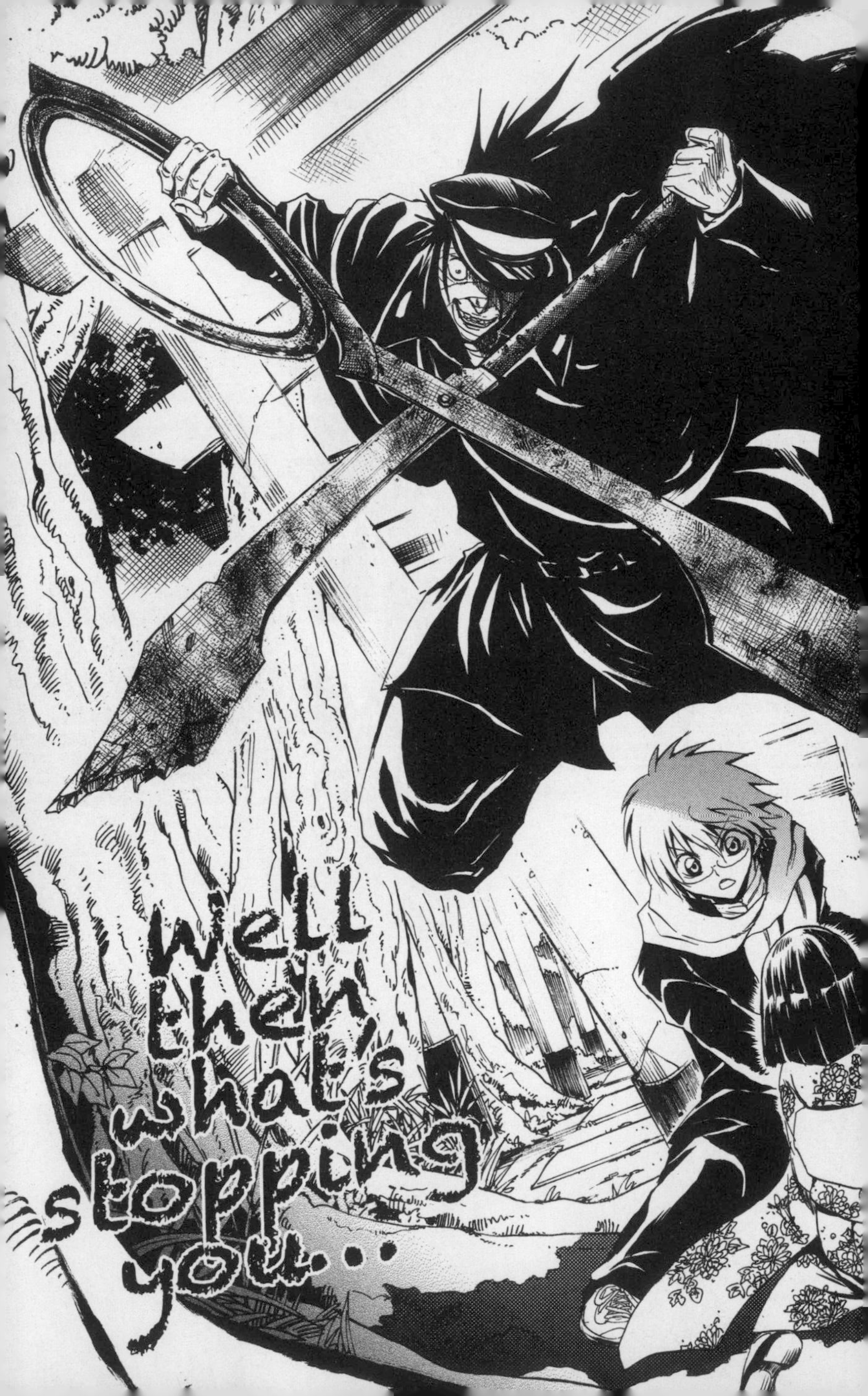
Well then what's stopping you...

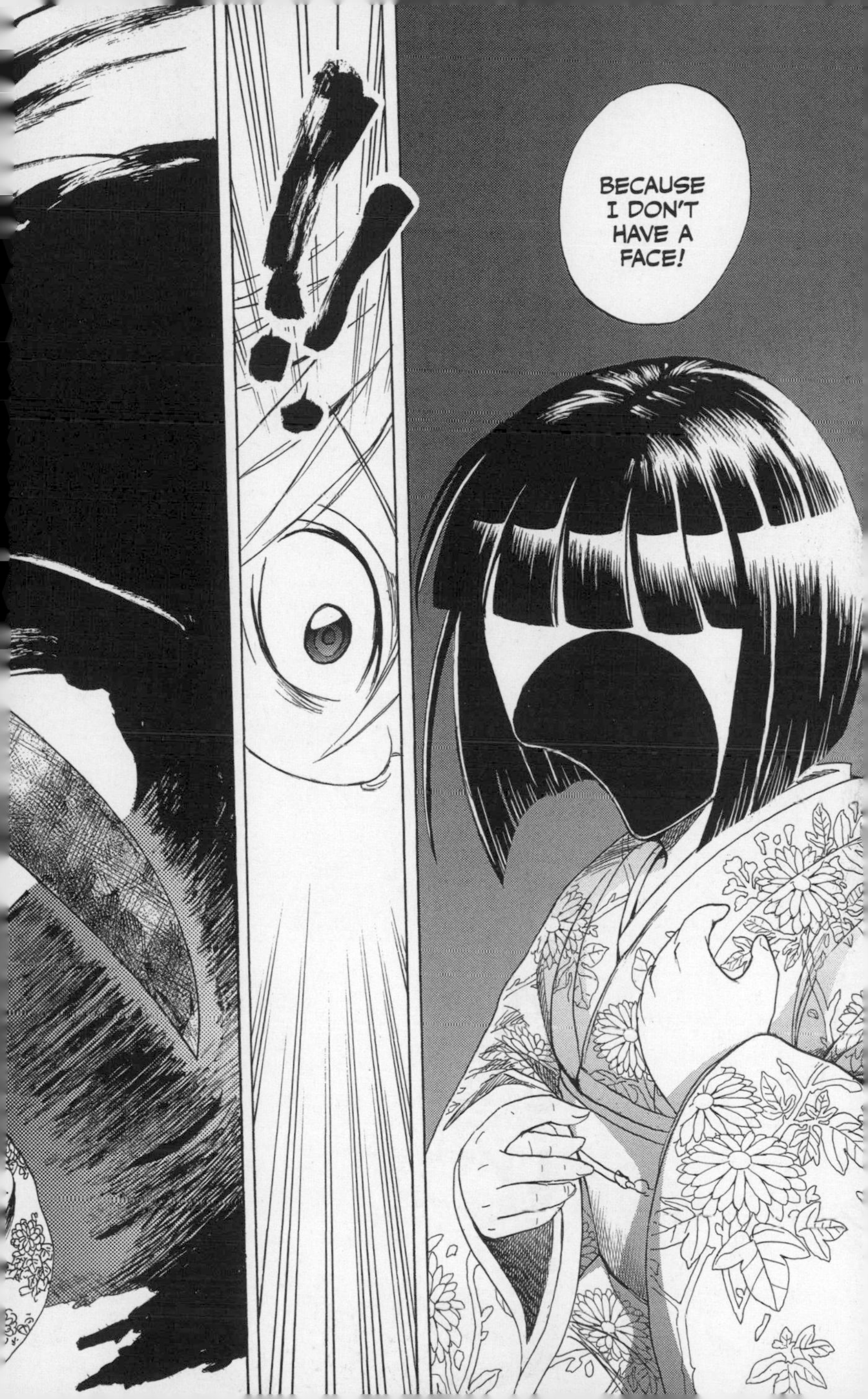
BECAUSE I DON'T HAVE A FACE!

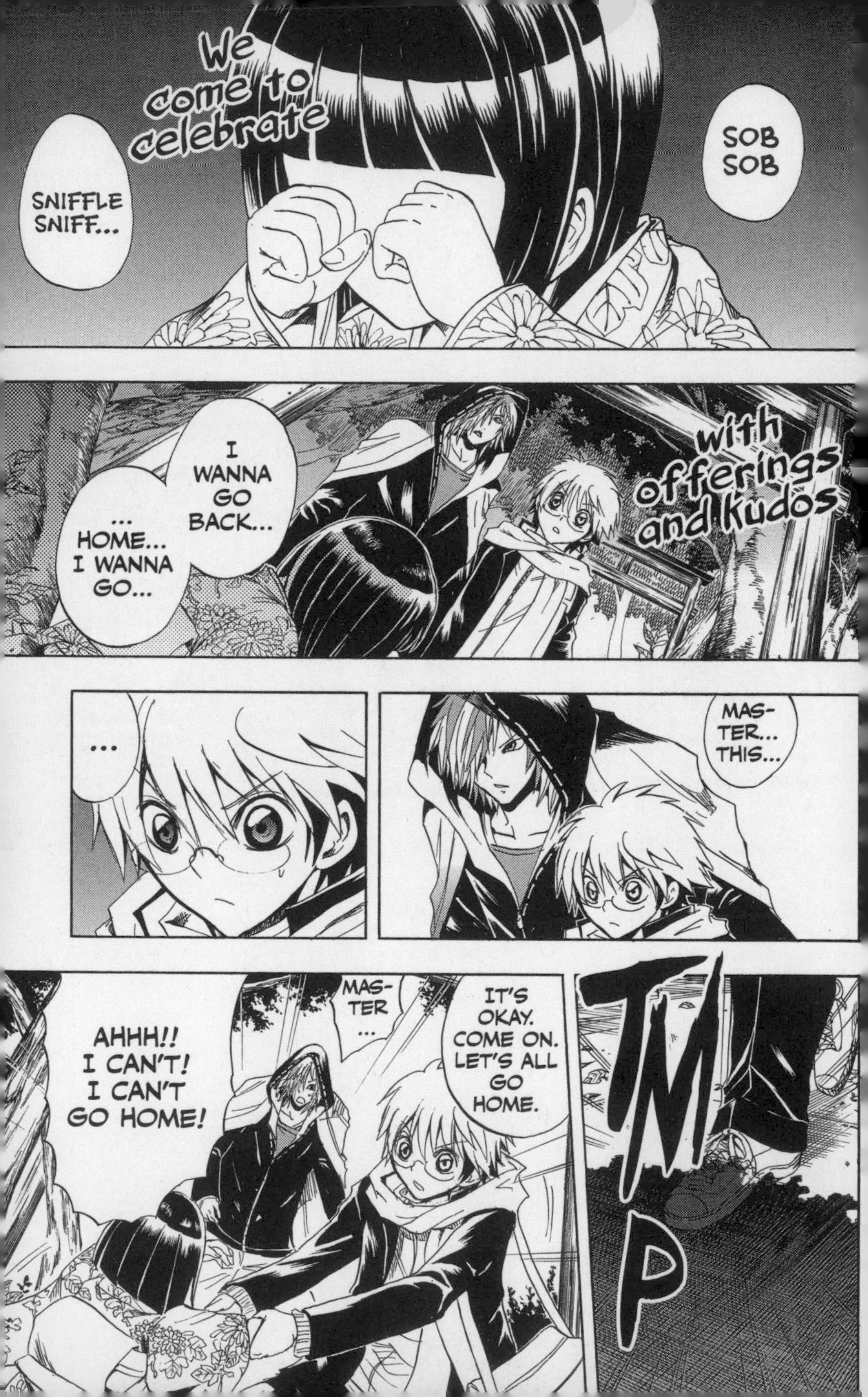
We come to celebrate
SOB SOB
SNIFFLE SNIFF...
with offerings and kudos
I WANNA GO BACK...
... HOME... I WANNA GO...
MAS-TER... THIS...
...
TMP
IT'S OKAY. COME ON. LET'S ALL GO HOME.
MAS-TER ...
AHHH!! I CAN'T! I CAN'T GO HOME!

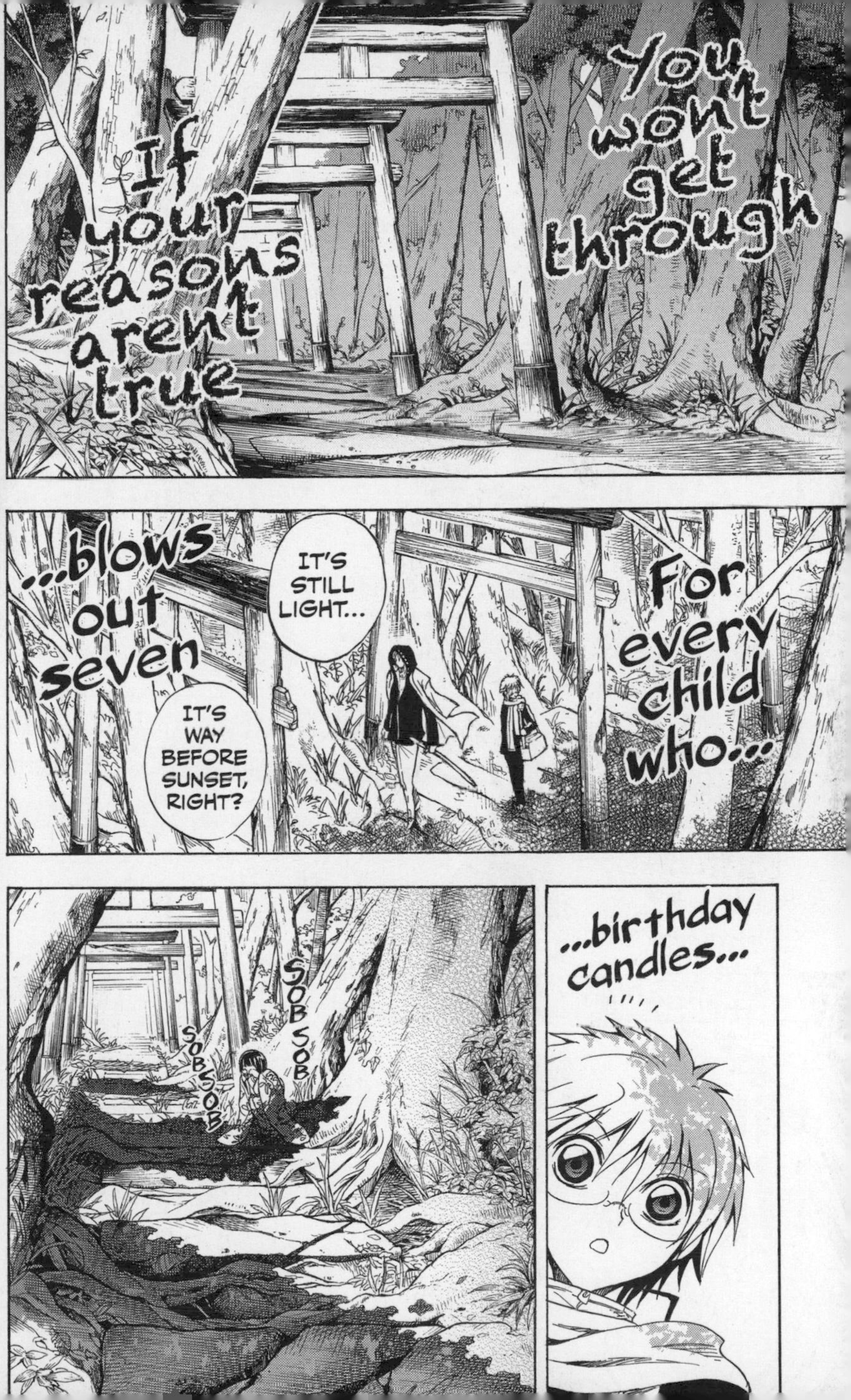
You wont get through
If your reasons arent true
For every child who...
...blows out seven
IT'S STILL LIGHT...
IT'S WAY BEFORE SUNSET, RIGHT?
...birthday candles...
SOB SOB
SOB SOB

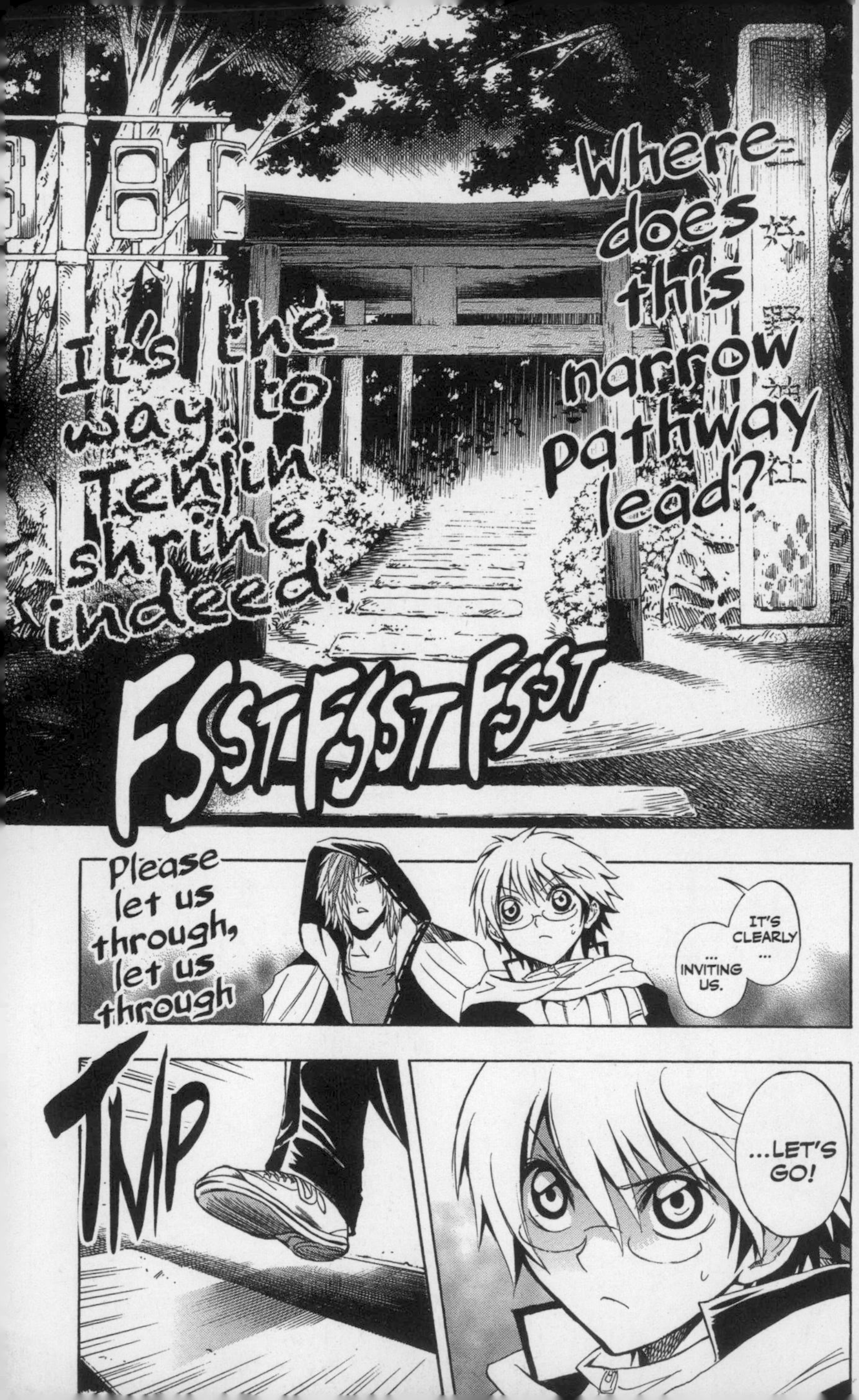
Where does this narrow pathway lead?
It's the way to Tenjin shrine, indeed.
FSST FSST FSST
IT'S CLEARLY ... ... INVITING US.
Please let us through, let us through
...LET'S GO!
TMP

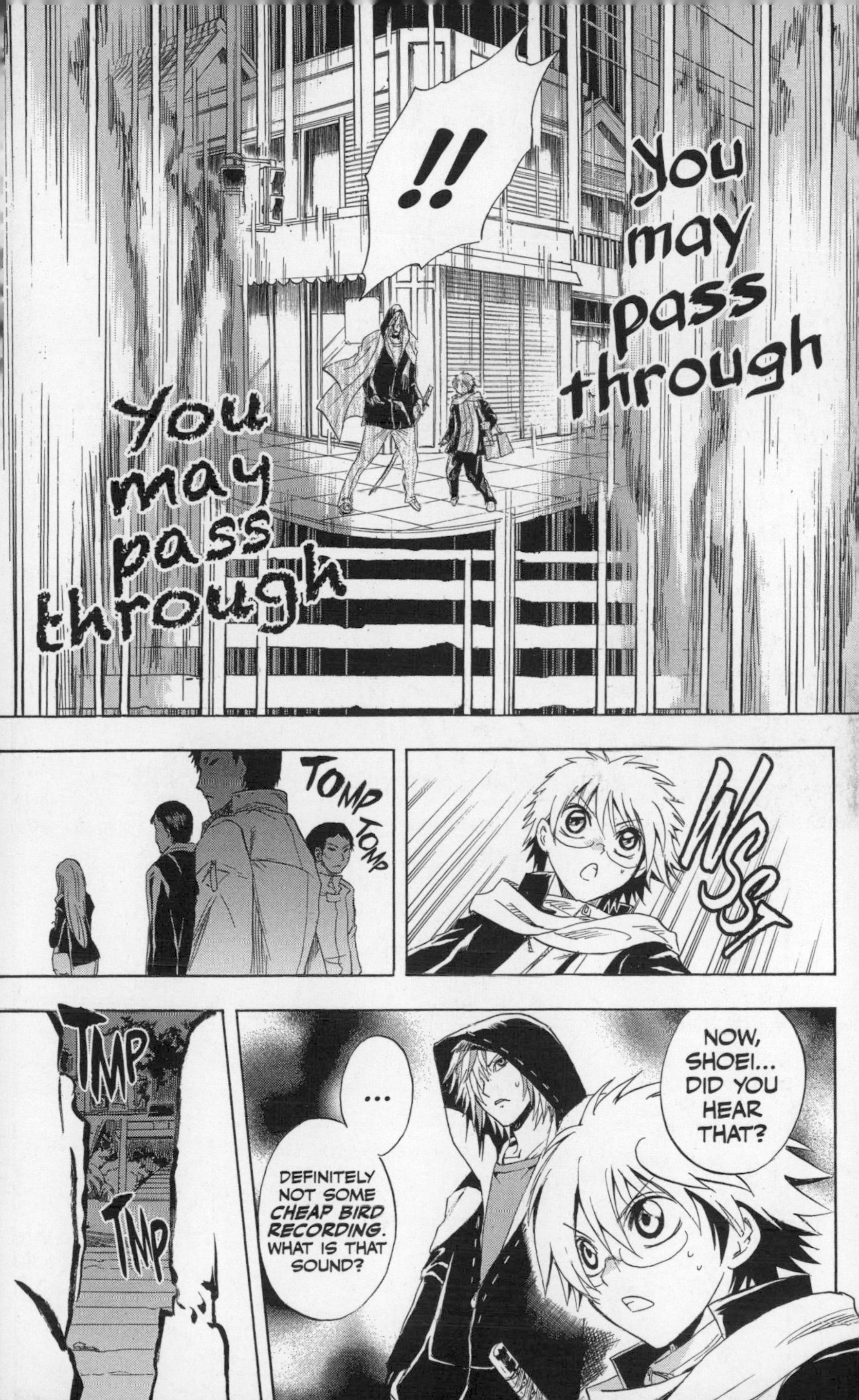
!!
You may pass through
You may pass through
WHSST
TOMP TOMP TOMP
NOW, SHOEI... DID YOU HEAR THAT?
...
DEFINITELY NOT SOME *CHEAP BIRD RECORDING*. WHAT IS THAT SOUND?
TMP
TMP

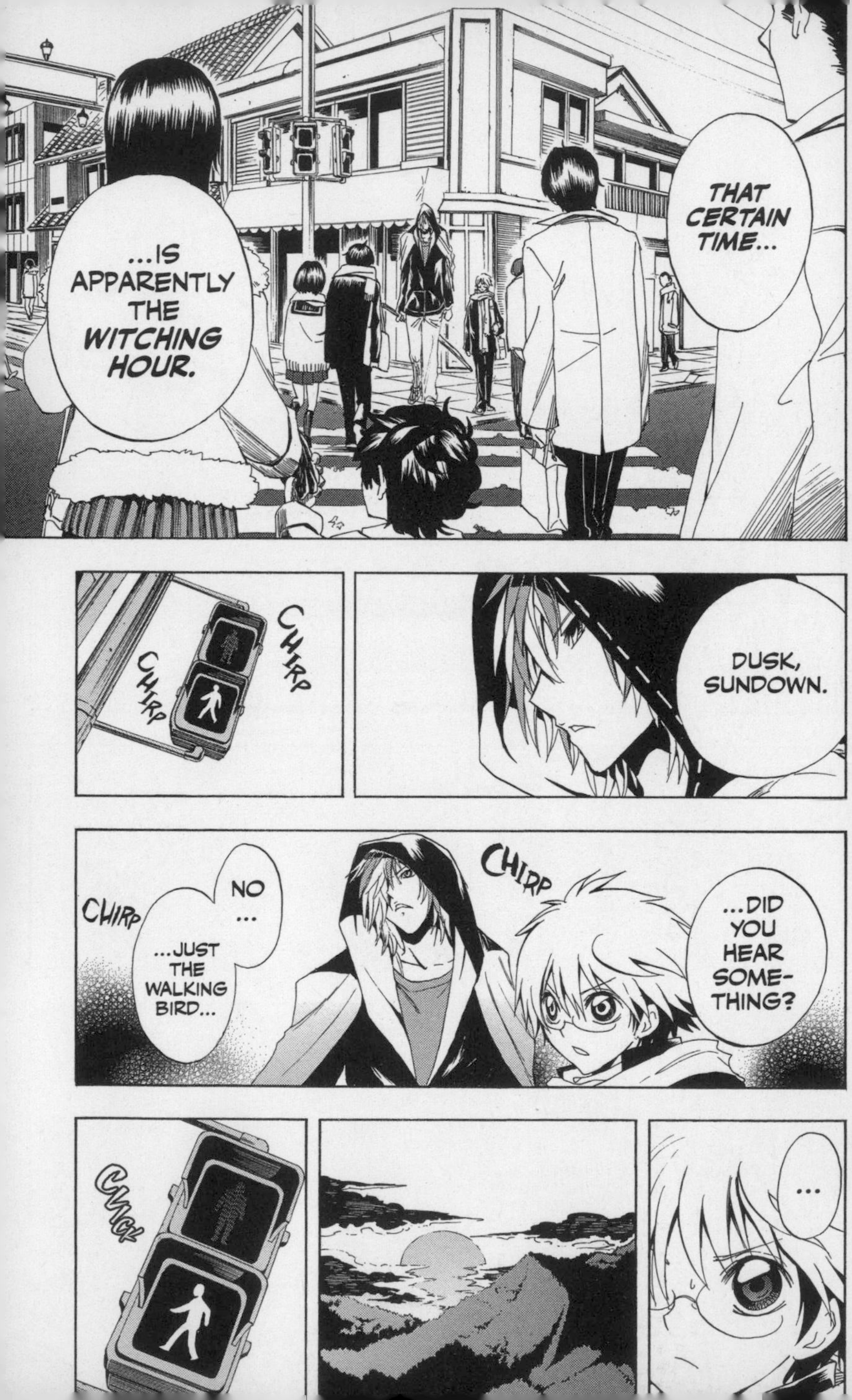
THAT CERTAIN TIME...
...IS APPARENTLY THE WITCHING HOUR.
DUSK, SUNDOWN.
CHIRP
CHIRP
...DID YOU HEAR SOMETHING?
CHIRP
NO ...
...JUST THE WALKING BIRD...
CHIRP
...
CLICK

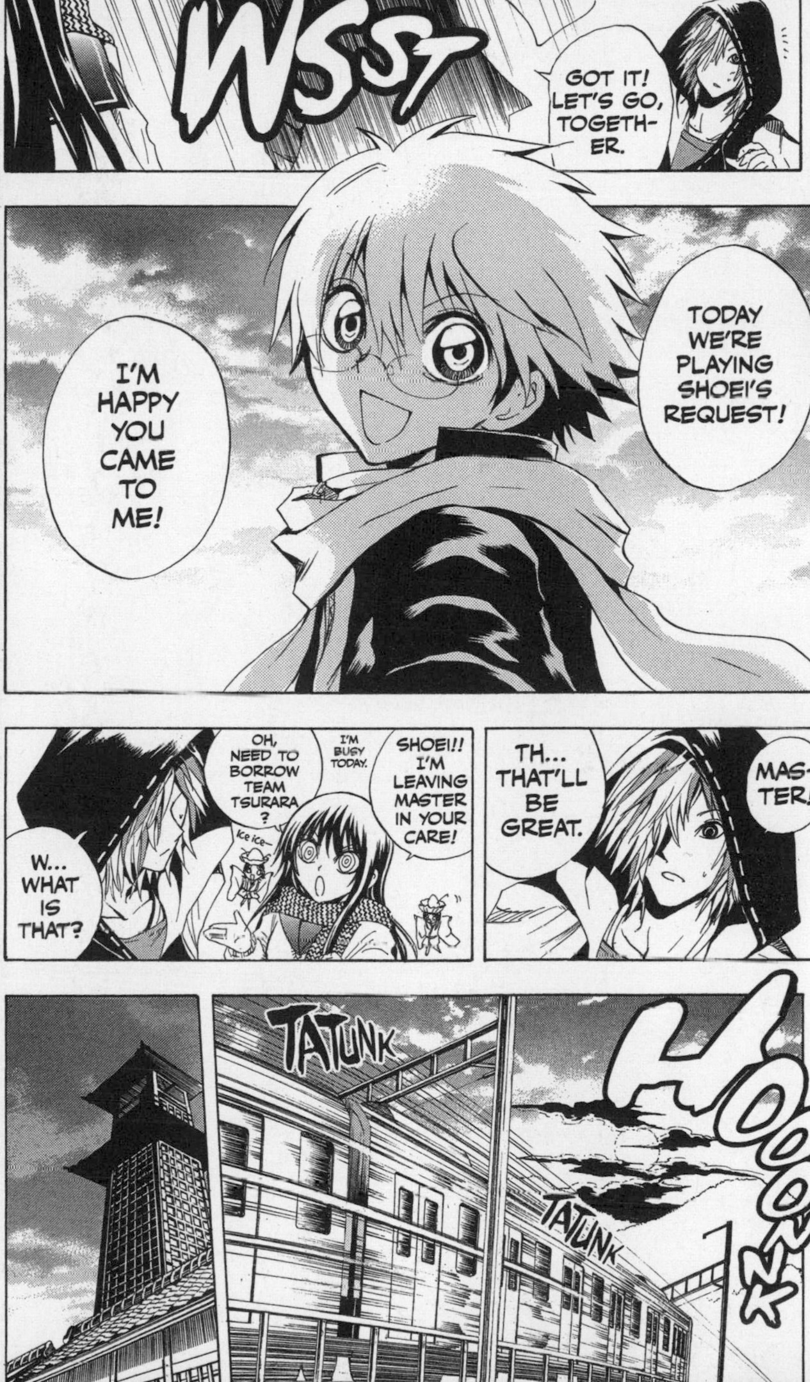
GOT IT! LET'S GO, TOGETH-ER.
WSST
TODAY WE'RE PLAYING SHOEI'S REQUEST!
I'M HAPPY YOU CAME TO ME!
MAS-TER!
TH... THAT'LL BE GREAT.
SHOEI!! I'M LEAVING MASTER IN YOUR CARE!
I'M BUSY TODAY.
OH, NEED TO BORROW TEAM TSURARA?
Ice ice—
W... WHAT IS THAT?
HOOOONK
TATUNK
TATUNK

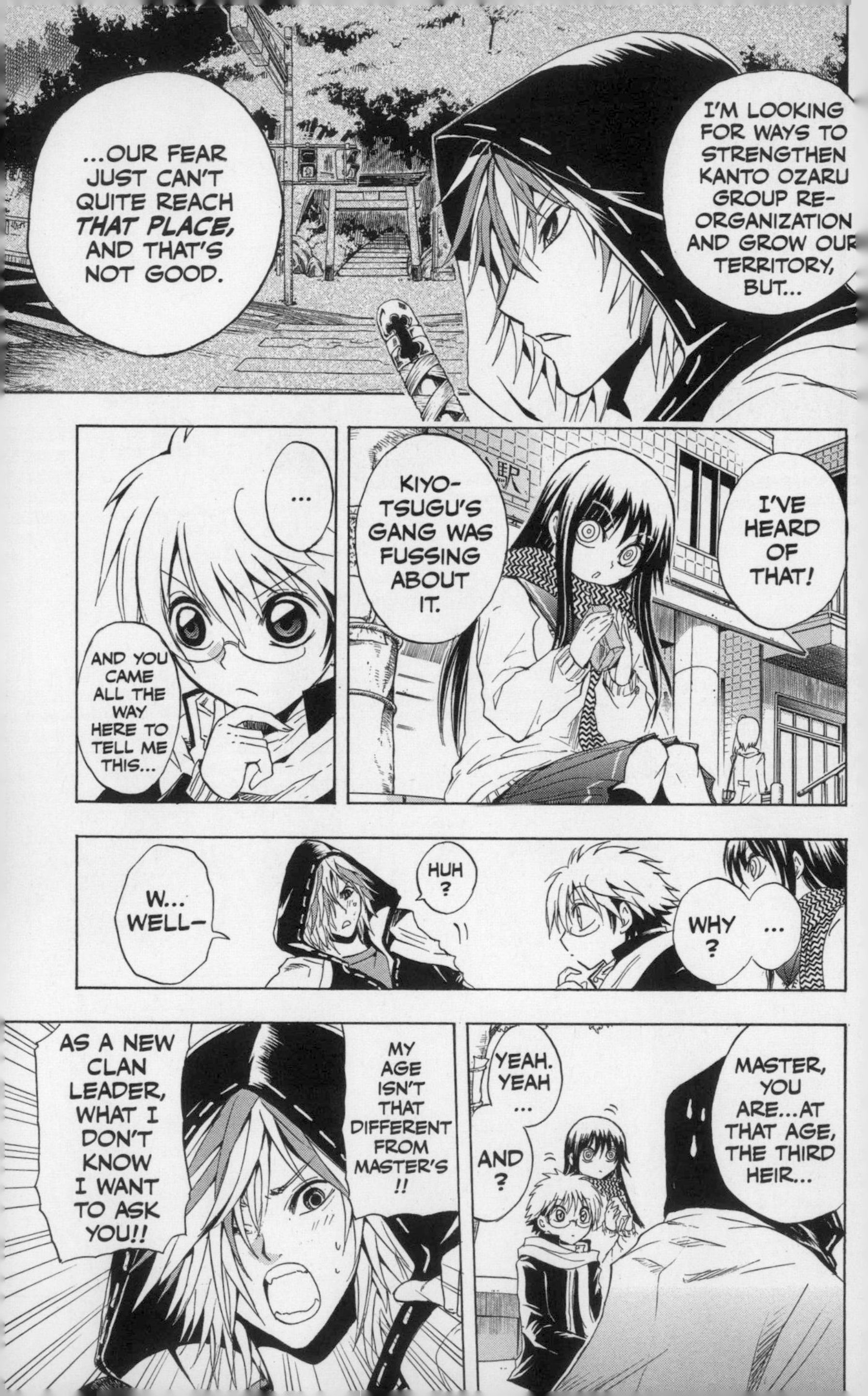

I'M LOOKING FOR WAYS TO STRENGTHEN KANTO OZARU GROUP RE-ORGANIZATION AND GROW OUR TERRITORY, BUT...
...OUR FEAR JUST CAN'T QUITE REACH *THAT PLACE,* AND THAT'S NOT GOOD.
I'VE HEARD OF THAT!
KIYO-TSUGU'S GANG WAS FUSSING ABOUT IT.
...
AND YOU CAME ALL THE WAY HERE TO TELL ME THIS...
...
WHY?
HUH?
W... WELL-
MASTER, YOU ARE...AT THAT AGE, THE THIRD HEIR...
YEAH. YEAH...
AND?
MY AGE ISN'T THAT DIFFERENT FROM MASTER'S!!
AS A NEW CLAN LEADER, WHAT I DON'T KNOW I WANT TO ASK YOU!!

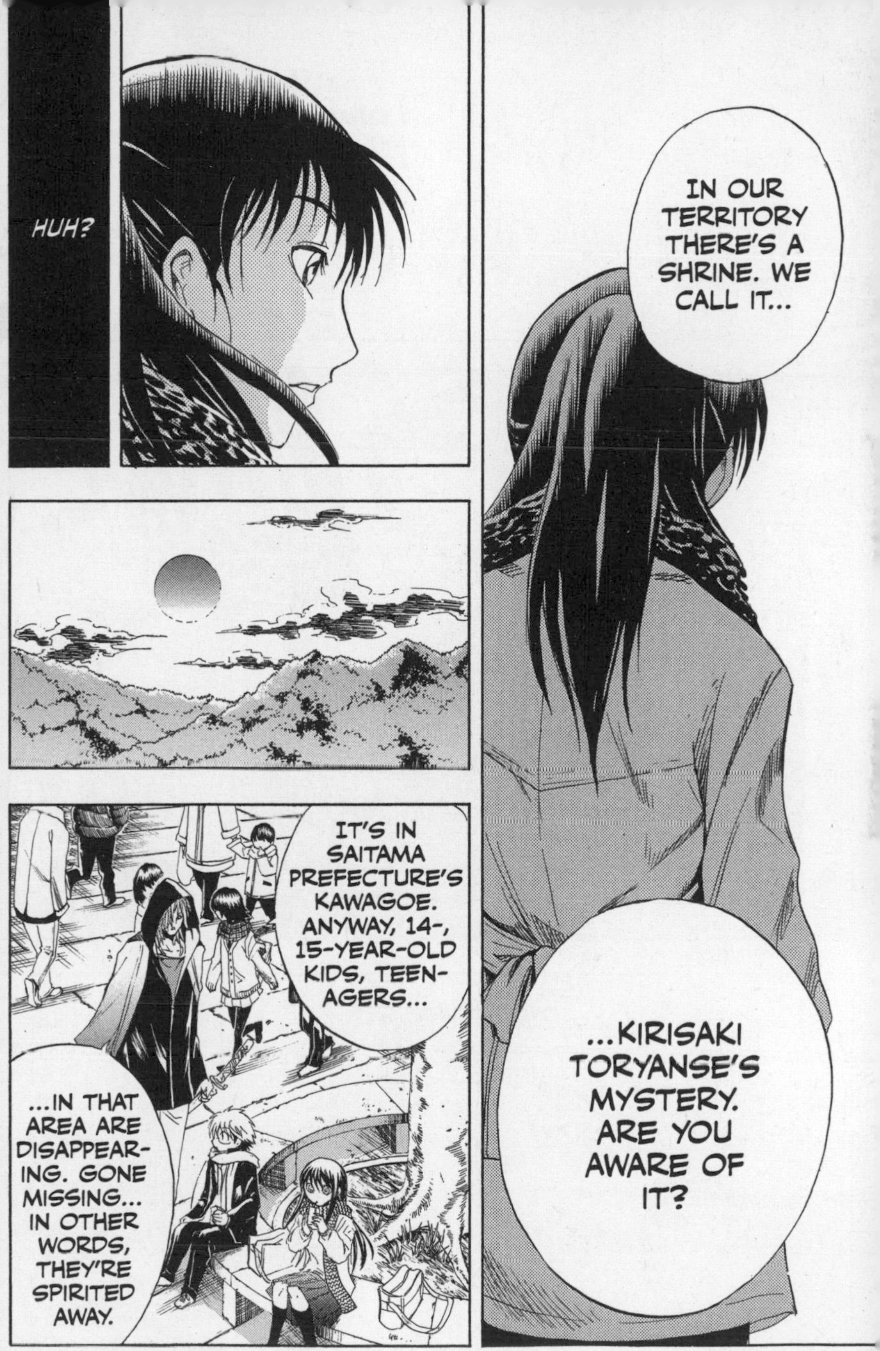
IN OUR TERRITORY THERE'S A SHRINE. WE CALL IT...
...KIRISAKI TORYANSE'S MYSTERY. ARE YOU AWARE OF IT?
HUH?
IT'S IN SAITAMA PREFECTURE'S KAWAGOE. ANYWAY, 14-, 15-YEAR-OLD KIDS, TEEN-AGERS...
...IN THAT AREA ARE DISAPPEAR-ING. GONE MISSING... IN OTHER WORDS, THEY'RE SPIRITED AWAY.

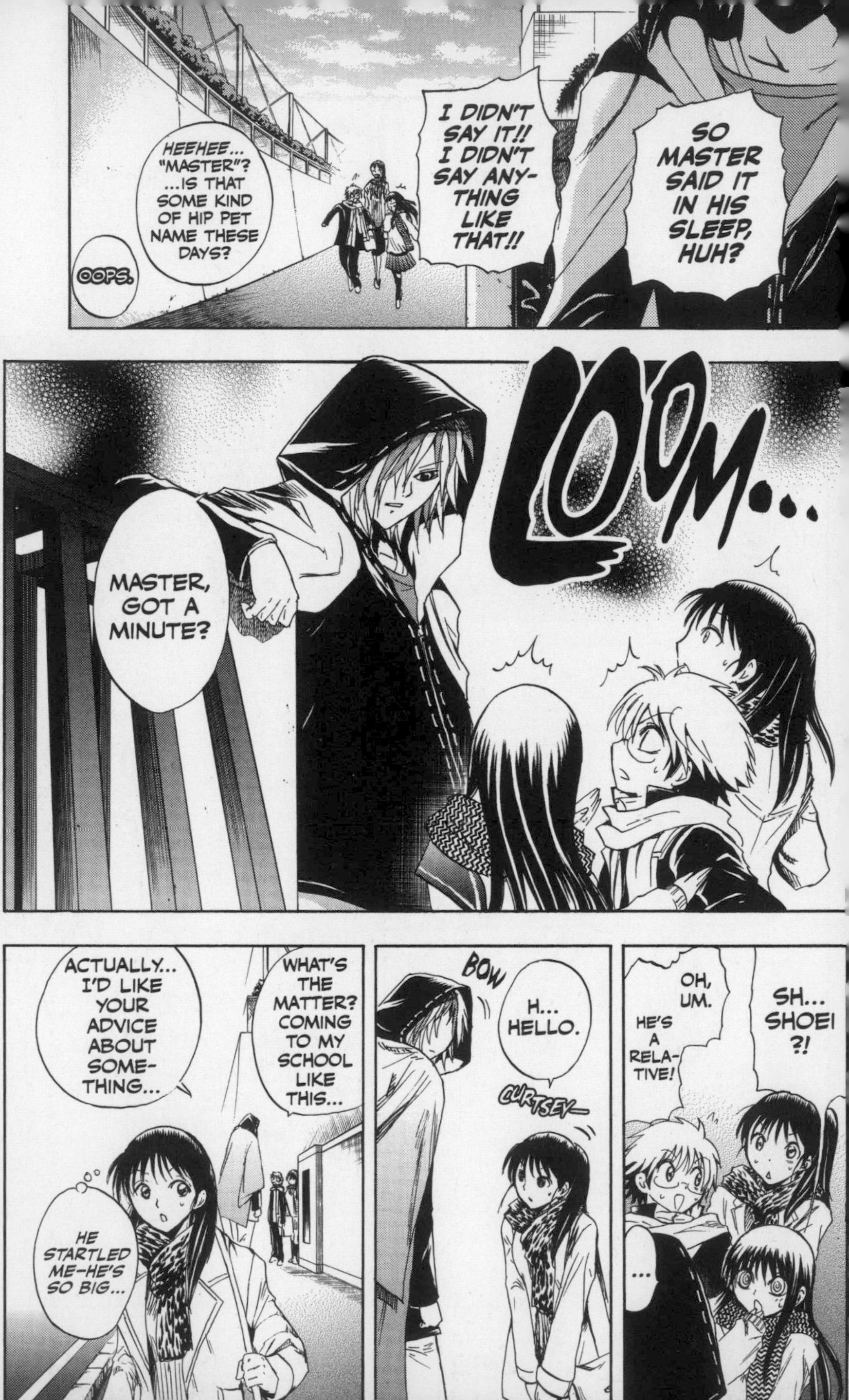
SO MASTER SAID IT IN HIS SLEEP, HUH?
I DIDN'T SAY IT!! I DIDN'T SAY ANY-THING LIKE THAT!!
HEEHEE... "MASTER"? ...IS THAT SOME KIND OF HIP PET NAME THESE DAYS?
OOPS.
LOOM...
MASTER, GOT A MINUTE?
SH... SHOEI ?!
OH, UM.
HE'S A RELA-TIVE!
...
BOW
H... HELLO.
CURTSEY—
WHAT'S THE MATTER? COMING TO MY SCHOOL LIKE THIS...
ACTUALLY... I'D LIKE YOUR ADVICE ABOUT SOME-THING...
HE STARTLED ME—HE'S SO BIG...

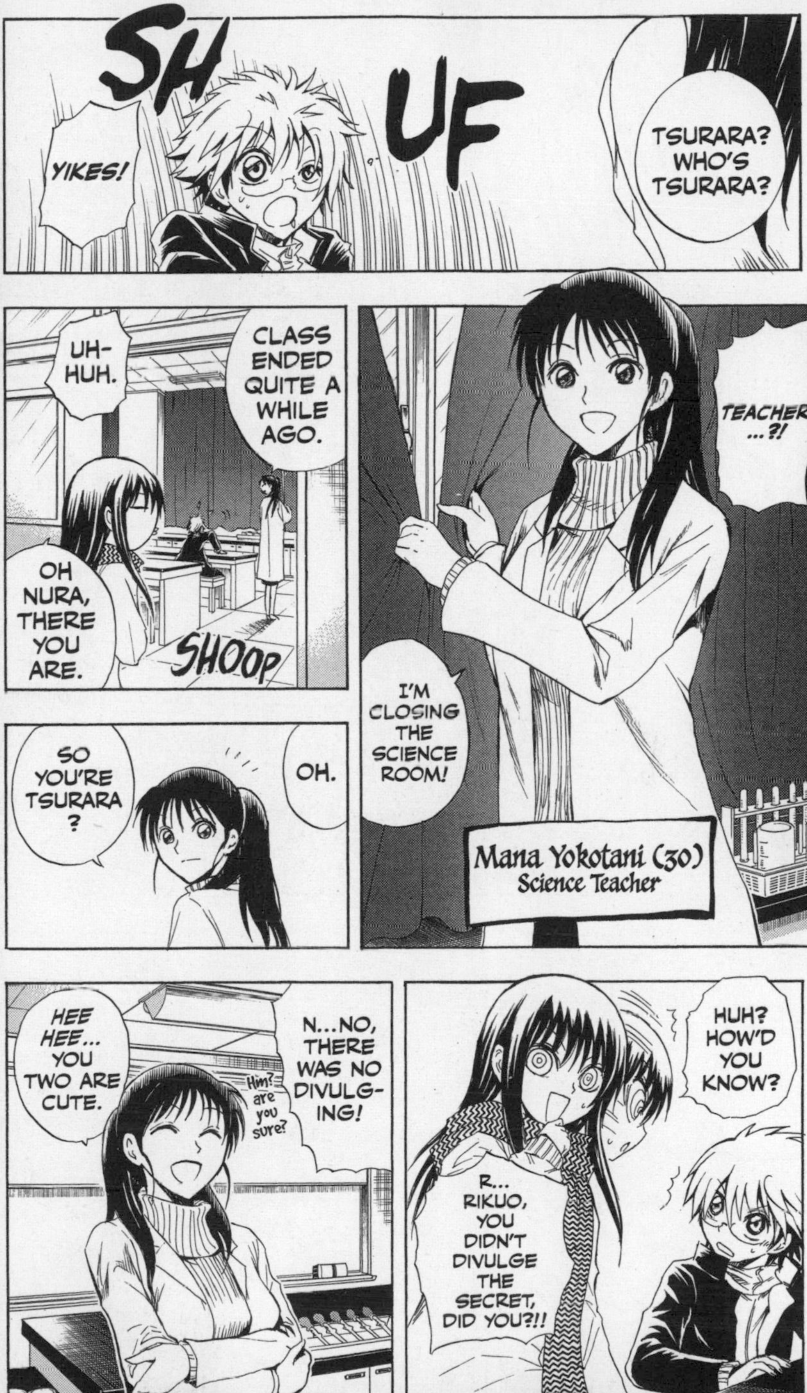
TSURARA? WHO'S TSURARA?
SHUF
YIKES!
TEACHER ...?!
I'M CLOSING THE SCIENCE ROOM!
Mana Yokotani (30)
Science Teacher
CLASS ENDED QUITE A WHILE AGO.
UH-HUH.
OH NURA, THERE YOU ARE.
SHOOP
OH.
SO YOU'RE TSURARA?
HUH? HOW'D YOU KNOW?
R... RIKUO, YOU DIDN'T DIVULGE THE SECRET, DID YOU?!!
N...NO, THERE WAS NO DIVULGING!
Hm? are you sure?
HEE HEE... YOU TWO ARE CUTE.

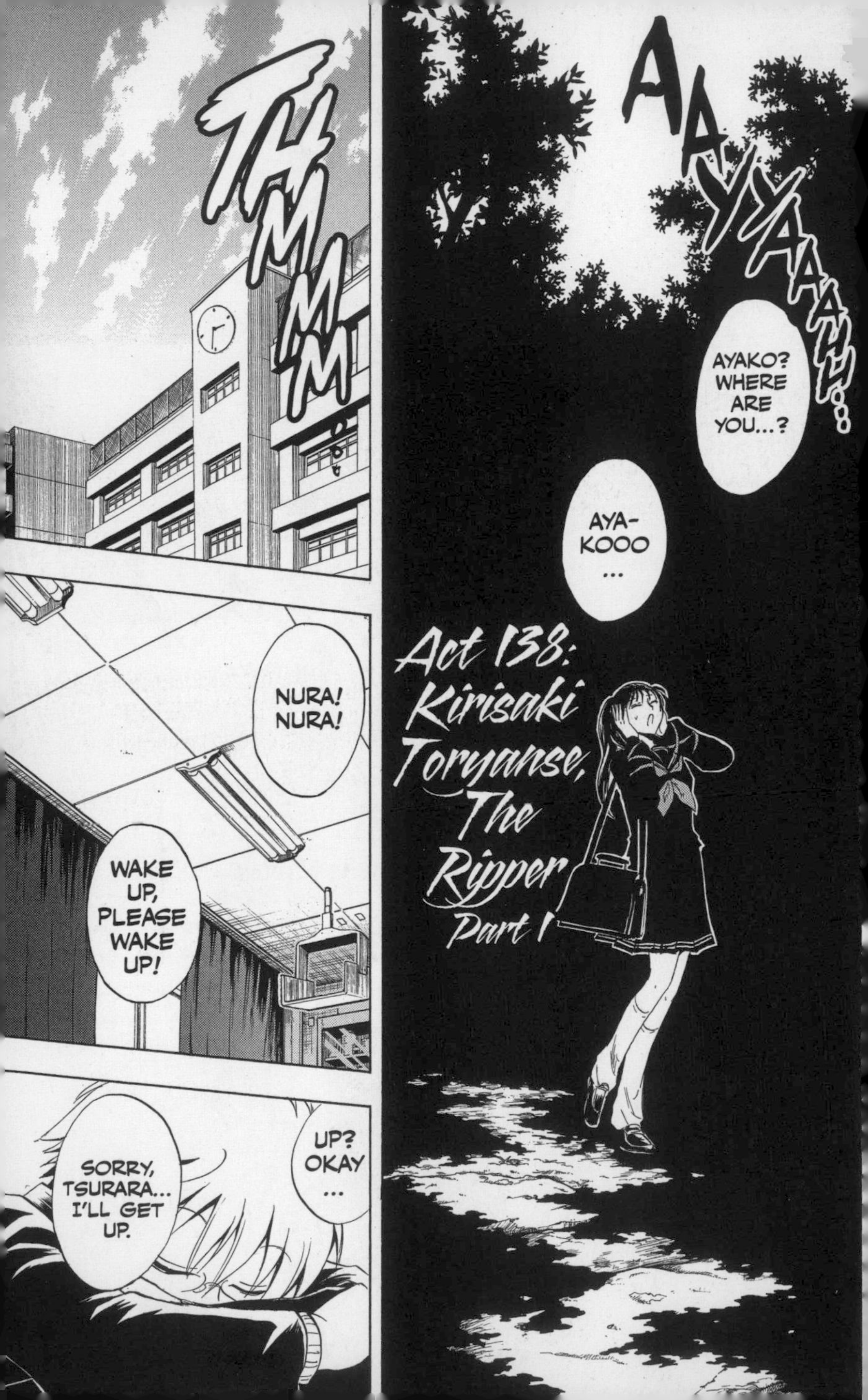
AAYYAAAAH..
AYAKO? WHERE ARE YOU...?
AYA-KOOO ...
Act 138: Kirisaki Toryanse, The Ripper Part 1
THMMM
NURA! NURA!
WAKE UP, PLEASE WAKE UP!
UP? OKAY ...
SORRY, TSURARA... I'LL GET UP.

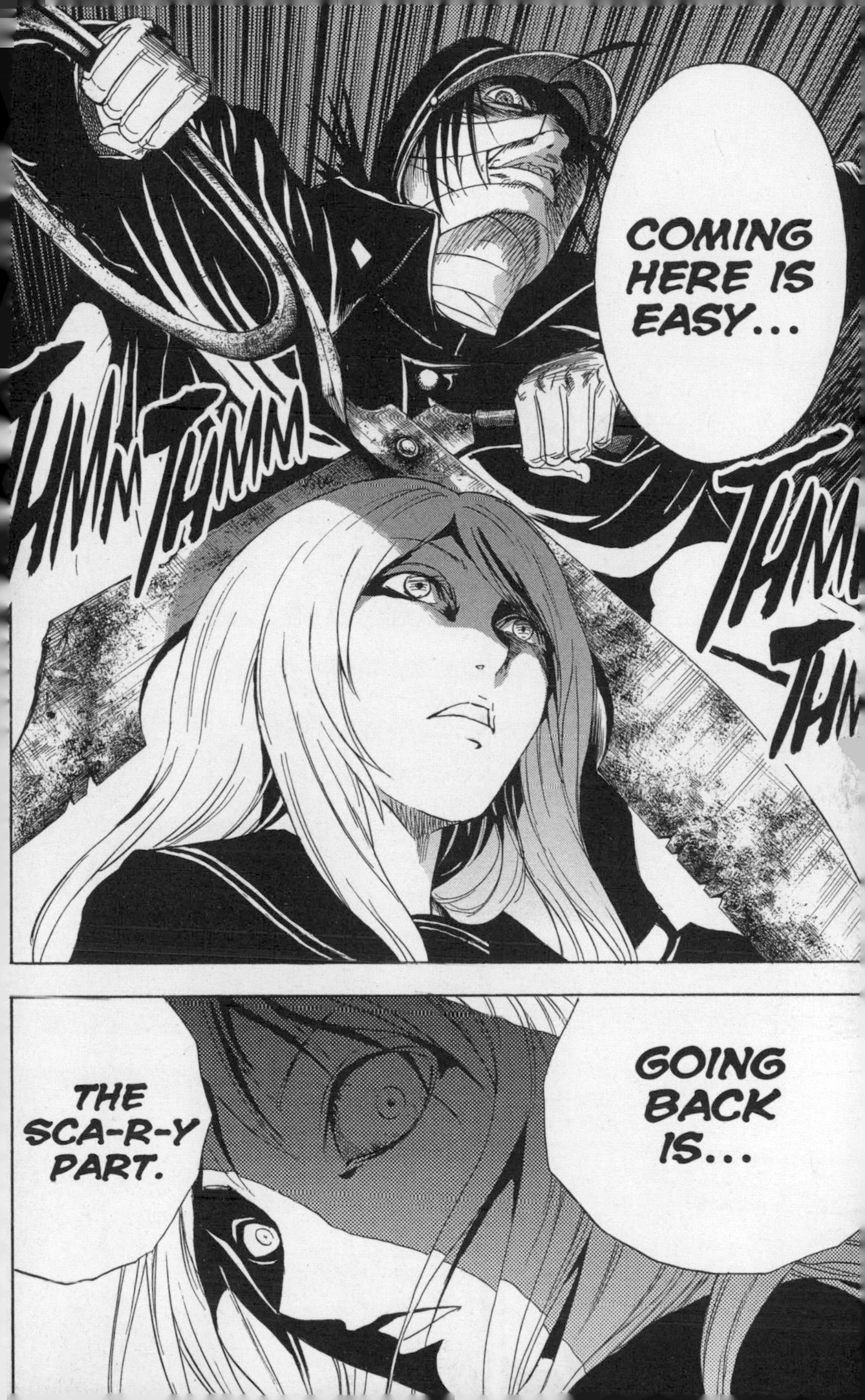
COMING HERE IS EASY...
GOING BACK IS...
THE SCA-R-Y PART.

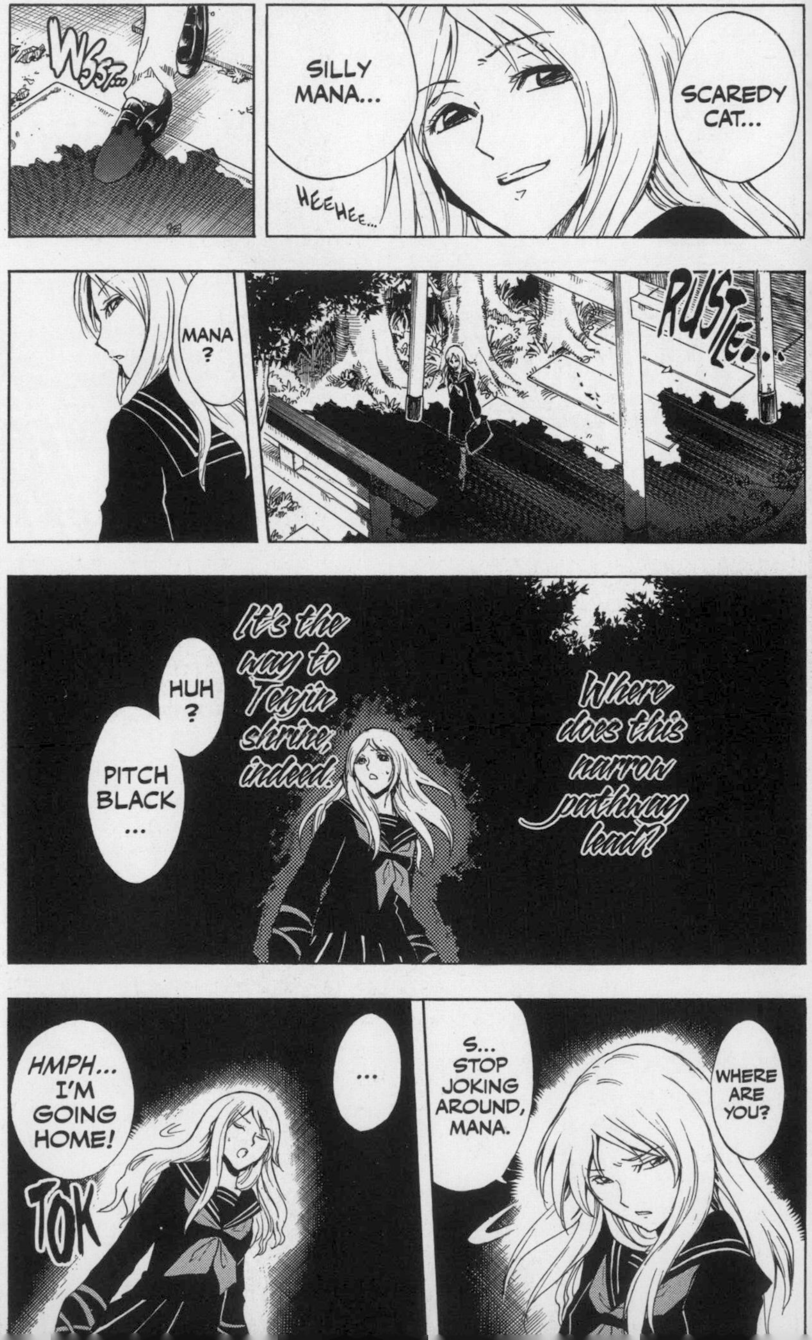
SCAREDY CAT...
SILLY MANA...
HEEHEE...
WSST...
RUSTLE...
MANA?
Where does this narrow pathway lead?
It's the way to Tenjin shrine, indeed.
HUH?
PITCH BLACK...
WHERE ARE YOU?
S... STOP JOKING AROUND, MANA.
...
HMPH... I'M GOING HOME!
TOK

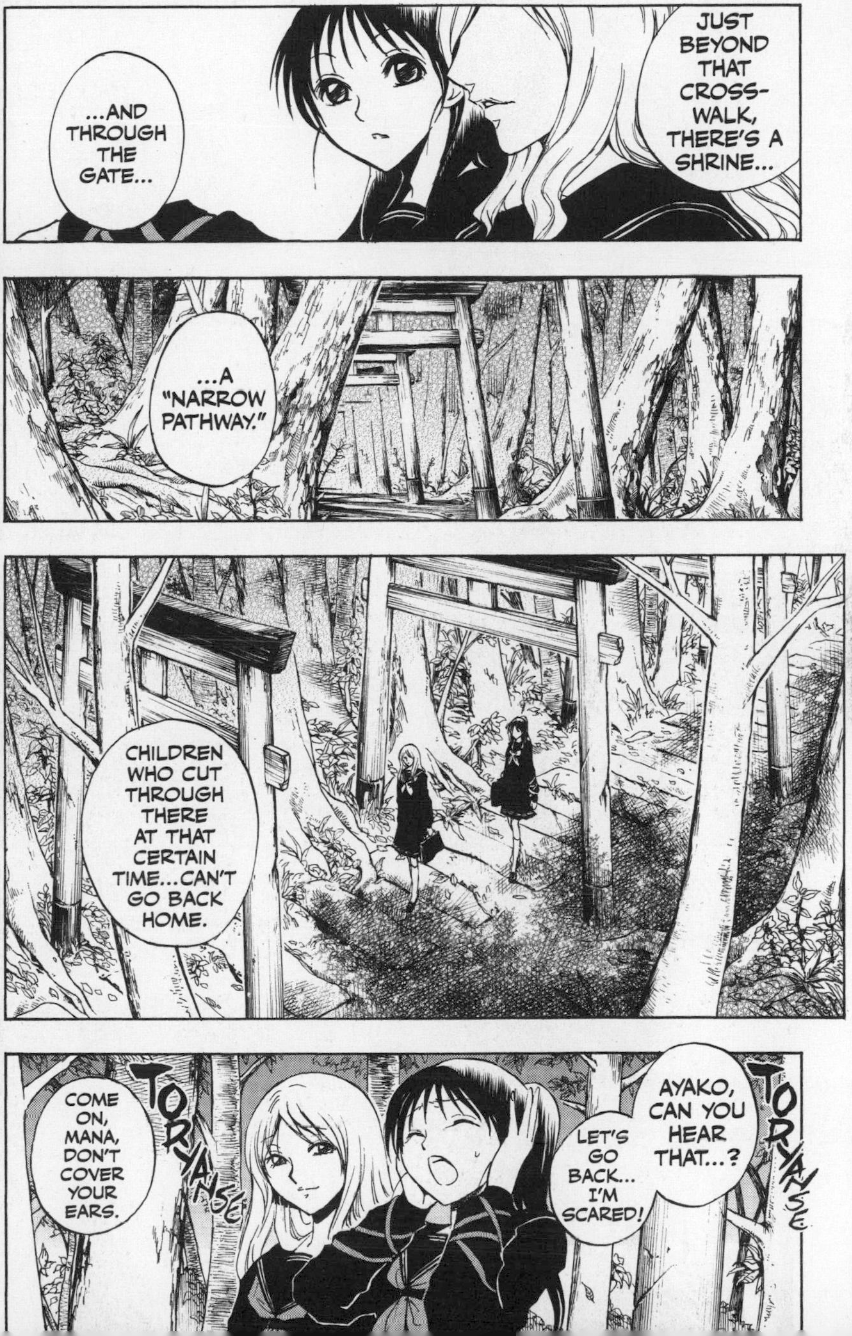
JUST BEYOND THAT CROSS-WALK, THERE'S A SHRINE...
...AND THROUGH THE GATE...
...A "NARROW PATHWAY."
CHILDREN WHO CUT THROUGH THERE AT THAT CERTAIN TIME...CAN'T GO BACK HOME.
TORYANSE
AYAKO, CAN YOU HEAR THAT...?
LET'S GO BACK... I'M SCARED!
TORYANSE
COME ON, MANA, DON'T COVER YOUR EARS.

Act 138: Kirisaki Toryanse, The Ripper Part 1

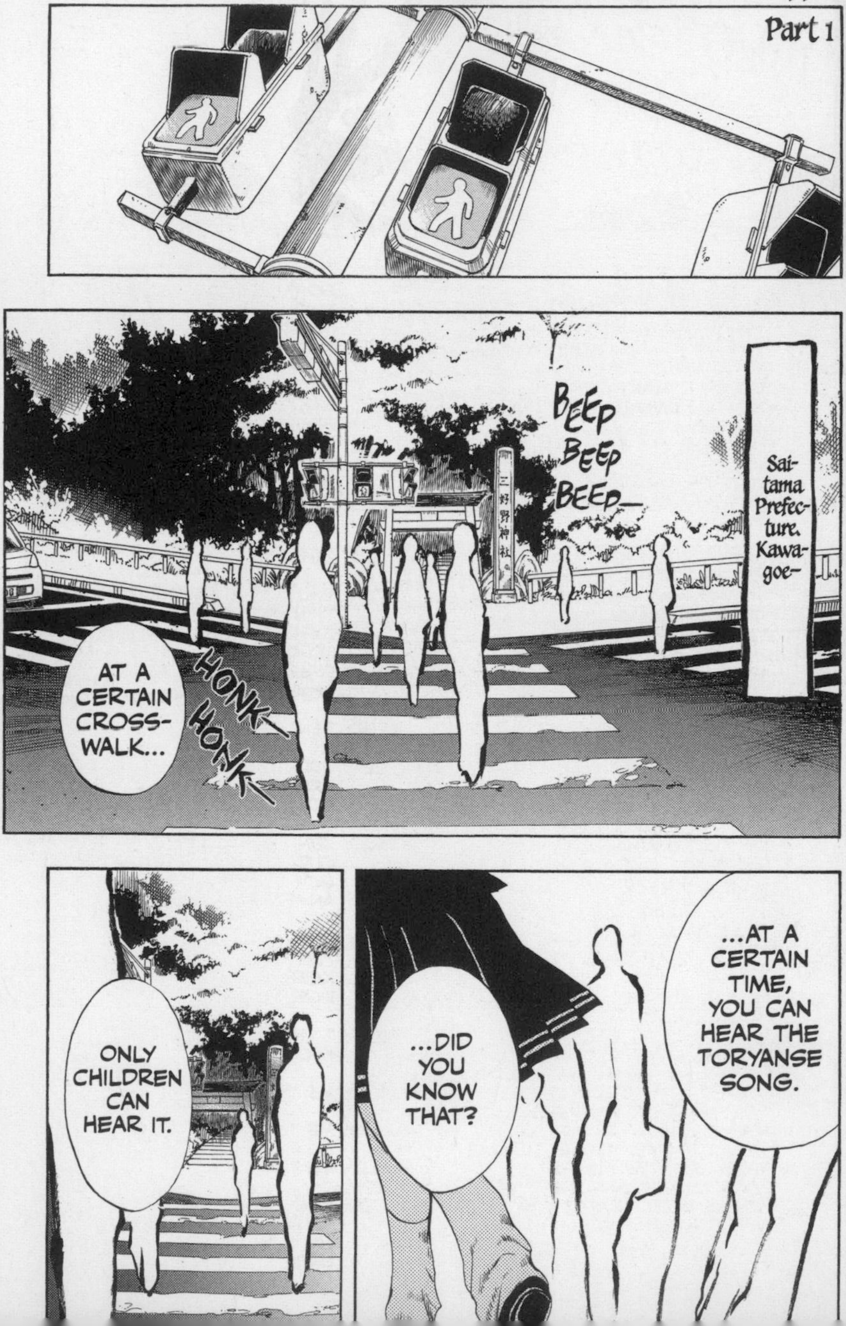

Saitama Prefecture. Kawagoe-
BEEP BEEP BEEP
HONK HONK
AT A CERTAIN CROSSWALK...
...AT A CERTAIN TIME, YOU CAN HEAR THE TORYANSE SONG.
...DID YOU KNOW THAT?
ONLY CHILDREN CAN HEAR IT.

KIYOTSUGU'S YOKAI BRAIN

NO. 15 KIYO

THE VOMIT BLOOD SPECIAL

Q: AT NIGHT, RIKUO'S HAIR...IS IT HARDENED WITH SPRAY AND WAX? —ZENKOKUAKA, HYOGO PREFECTURE

URARA: UM, LORD RIKUO NORMALLY GOES TO SCHOOL WITHOUT ANYTHING APPLIED. NO MATTER WHAT I SAY, HE LEAVES THE HOUSE WITH HIS HAIR STICKING UP (FROM SLEEPING ON IT). THAT BOTHERS ME! ANYWAY, SO AT NIGHT, IT'S LIKELY JUST ANOTHER VARIATION OF THAT...

RIKUO: HMMM?! REALLY?! I NORMALLY DON'T THINK ABOUT IT, BUT NOW THAT YOU BRING IT UP, I FEEL A BIT EMBARASSED FOR THE NIGHT ME!! NO, IT CAN'T BE! LET'S JUST CALL IT A RATHER BOLD FASHION STATEMENT!

Q: QUESTION FOR RYOTA-NEKO. DO YOU WEAR FUNDOSHI? OR DO YOU WEAR UNDERPANTS? —UBUME, ANONYMOUS ADDRESS

RYOTA-NEKO: WELL, I'M A MAN, SO, IN A WORD: FUNDOSHI!! UNDERPANTS?! UHG. WAY TOO DRAFTY. ...SO, WHY IN THE WORLD ARE YOU ASKING SUCH A THING?!

Q: DO YOKAI HEAL RIGHT AWAY AFTER GETTING INJURED? —SHIGURE HIIRAGI-SAMA, IWATE PREFECTURE

ZEN: OH. I'LL ANSWER THIS ONE. YOKAI'S INJURIES ARE MANY. USUALLY WE DON'T GET HURT. BUT IF THERE'S A SPIRIT SWORD OR A FIGHT AMONGST AYAKASHI INVOLVED, THE STRENGTH THAT GOES AGAINST AYAKASHI WILL INJURE US. AND IF IT'S FATAL, WELL THEN, WE DIE, OF COURSE. BECOME EXTINCT, I GUESS... FOR YOKAI "DEATH" SIMPLY MEANS LOSING ONES FEAR. EXTINGUISHED, AS IT WERE.

SO IF WE DON'T LOSE OUR FEAR THEN NO MATTER HOW BAD THE INJURY IS, IT'LL HEAL. KEJORO AND THE GUYS FROM TONO WERE INJURED TO THE EXTENT THAT IF THEY WERE HUMANS THEY WOULD'VE DIED, BUT THEY GOT BETTER. WHAT I DON'T GET IS RIKUO. HIS INJURIES, EVEN FOR A YOKAI, HEAL REALLY FAST. IT SEEMS THAT HIS GRANDMOTHER'S BLOOD HAS SOMETHING TO DO WITH IT...

RIKUO: ZEN, THAT WAS LONGWINDED.

ZEN: SHUT UP!! IT'S AN IMPORTANT THING!! THIS MANGA FAILED TO EXPLAIN IT! SO, I TOOK THE TIME TO CLARIFY IT RIGHT HERE AND— PUKE-PUKE-BLOW-BLOODY-CHUNKS—(VOMITS BLOOD)

RIKUO: ZEN! CHILL OUT!!

ZEN: DUDE...RIKUO, THAT QUICK-RECOVERY MOJO YOU'VE GOT. GIVE ME... SOME...OF...THAT...(COUGH)

RIKUO: ZEN, SORRY MAN, WITH THAT INCURABLE SICKNESS THING YOU'VE GOT GOING, I JUST CAN'T DO ANYTHING ABOUT IT!!

YUKARI: UHM, BUT, DID ANYONE ELSE HAPPEN TO NOTICE, THIS PERSON KEEPS VOMITING BLOOD BUT DOESN'T SEEM TO DIE?

REIRA: I THOUGHT HE WOULD DIE IN KYOTO.

DOHIKO: ME TOO.

AMEZO: ME TOO.

RIKUO: ME TOO.

ZEN: YOU GUYS!! WHAAT?!! DID YOU REALLY JUST SAY THAT? I'M GONNA MAKE YOU ALL UNRECOVERABLE!!

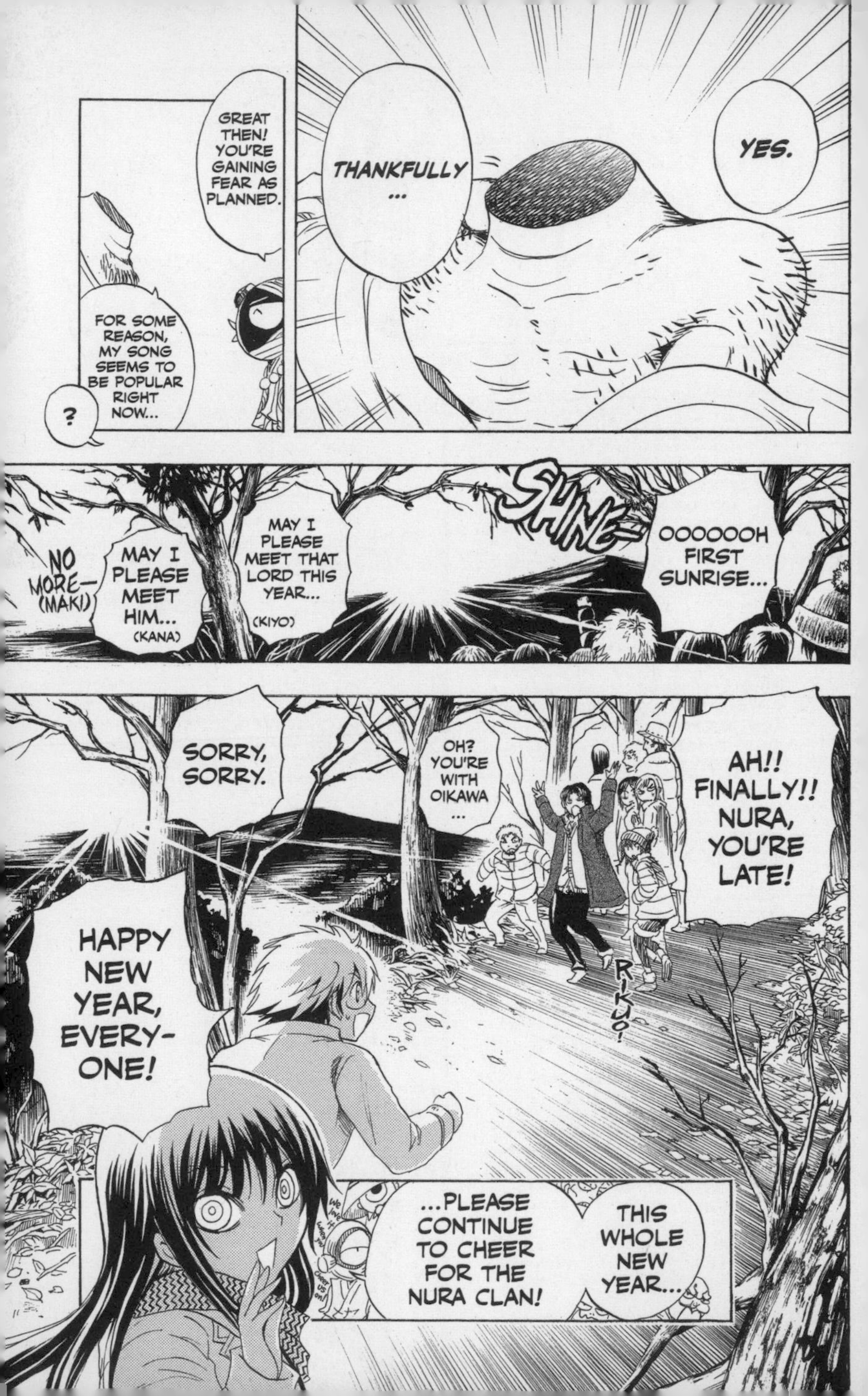
YES.
THANKFULLY...
GREAT THEN! YOU'RE GAINING FEAR AS PLANNED.
FOR SOME REASON, MY SONG SEEMS TO BE POPULAR RIGHT NOW...
?
SHINE
OOOOOOH FIRST SUNRISE...
MAY I PLEASE MEET THAT LORD THIS YEAR... (KIYO)
MAY I PLEASE MEET HIM... (KANA)
NO MORE— (MAKI)
AH!! FINALLY!! NURA, YOU'RE LATE!
OH? YOU'RE WITH OIKAWA...
SORRY, SORRY.
RIKUO!
HAPPY NEW YEAR, EVERY-ONE!
THIS WHOLE NEW YEAR...
...PLEASE CONTINUE TO CHEER FOR THE NURA CLAN!

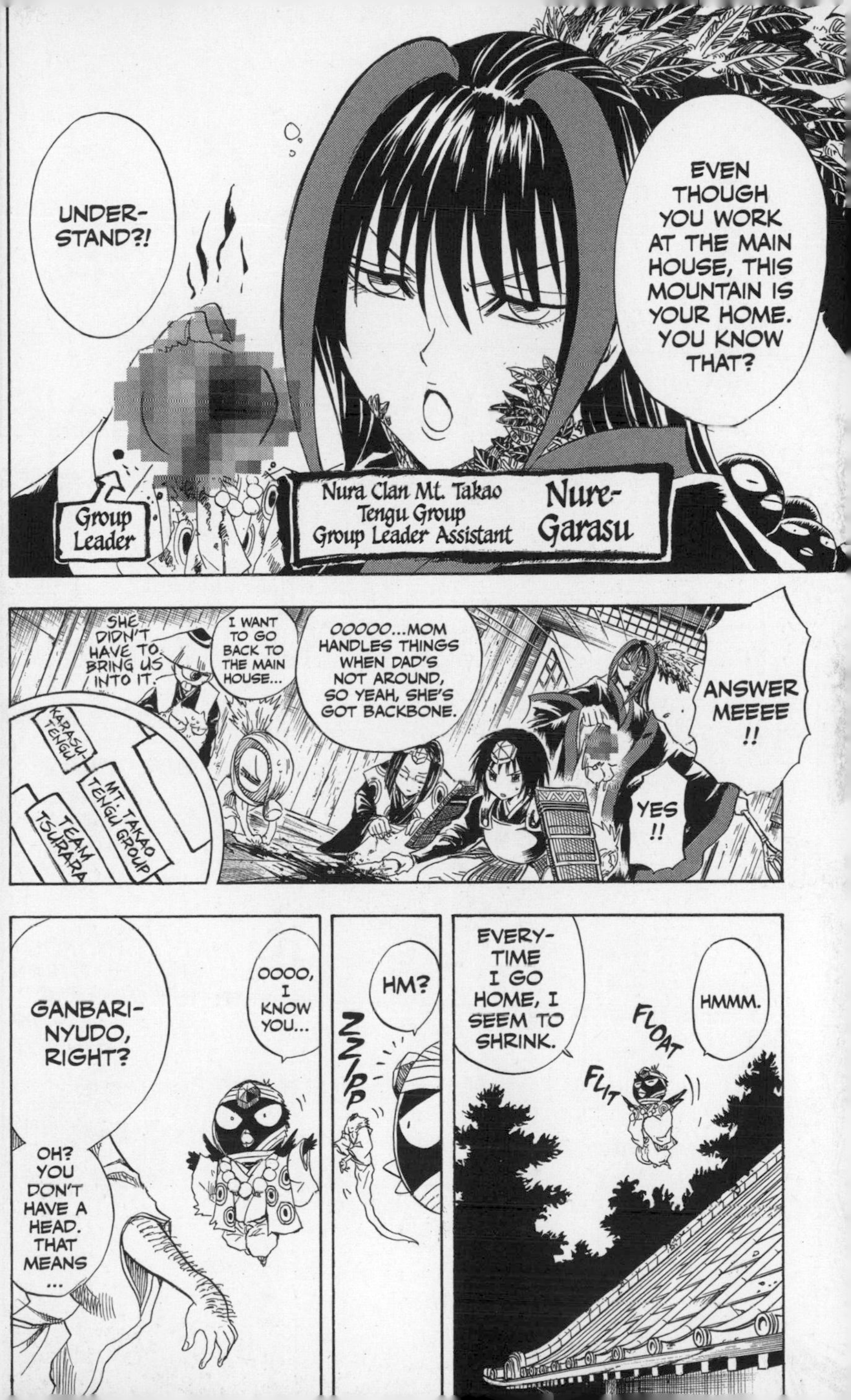
EVEN THOUGH YOU WORK AT THE MAIN HOUSE, THIS MOUNTAIN IS YOUR HOME. YOU KNOW THAT?
Nura Clan Mt. Takao Tengu Group Group Leader Assistant
Nure-Garasu
UNDER-STAND?!
Group Leader
ANSWER MEEEE!!
YES!!
OOOOO...MOM HANDLES THINGS WHEN DAD'S NOT AROUND, SO YEAH, SHE'S GOT BACKBONE.
I WANT TO GO BACK TO THE MAIN HOUSE...
SHE DIDN'T HAVE TO BRING US INTO IT.
KARASU-TENGU
MT. TAKAO TENGU GROUP
TEAM TSURARA
HMMM.
FLOAT
FLIT
EVERY-TIME I GO HOME, I SEEM TO SHRINK.
HM?
ZZIPP
OOOO, I KNOW YOU...
GANBARI-NYUDO, RIGHT?
OH? YOU DON'T HAVE A HEAD. THAT MEANS ...

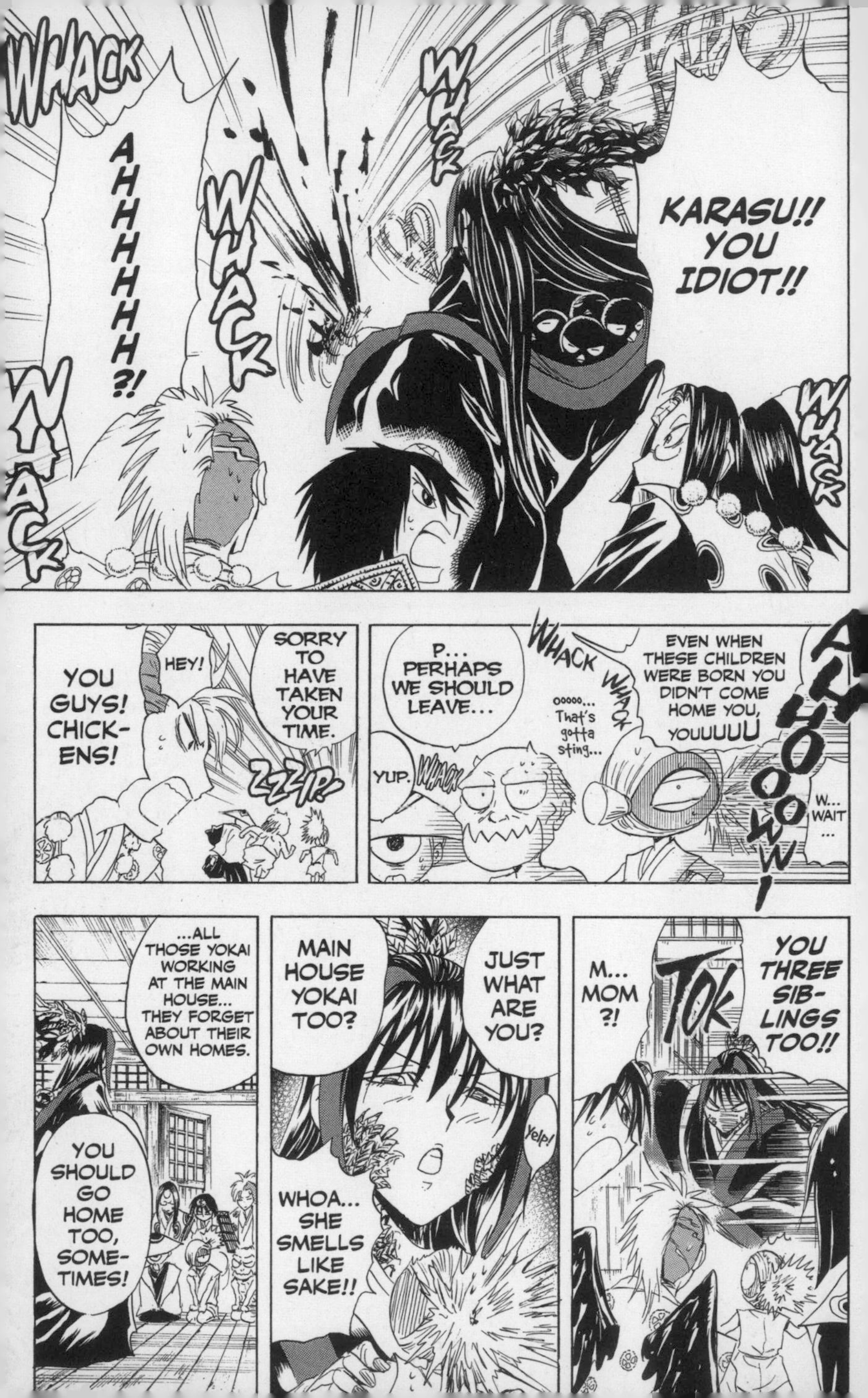
KARASU!! YOU IDIOT!!
WHACK
WHACK
WHACK
AHHHHHHH?!
WHACK
WHACK
AHHOOOOWW!
EVEN WHEN THESE CHILDREN WERE BORN YOU DIDN'T COME HOME YOU, YOUUUUU
W... WAIT ...
WHACK WHACK
Ooooo... That's gotta sting...
P... PERHAPS WE SHOULD LEAVE...
YUP.
WHACK
SORRY TO HAVE TAKEN YOUR TIME.
HEY!
YOU GUYS! CHICK-ENS!
ZZZIP!
YOU THREE SIB-LINGS TOO!!
TOK
M... MOM ?!
JUST WHAT ARE YOU?
MAIN HOUSE YOKAI TOO?
Yelp!
WHOA... SHE SMELLS LIKE SAKE!!
...ALL THOSE YOKAI WORKING AT THE MAIN HOUSE... THEY FORGET ABOUT THEIR OWN HOMES.
YOU SHOULD GO HOME TOO, SOME-TIMES!

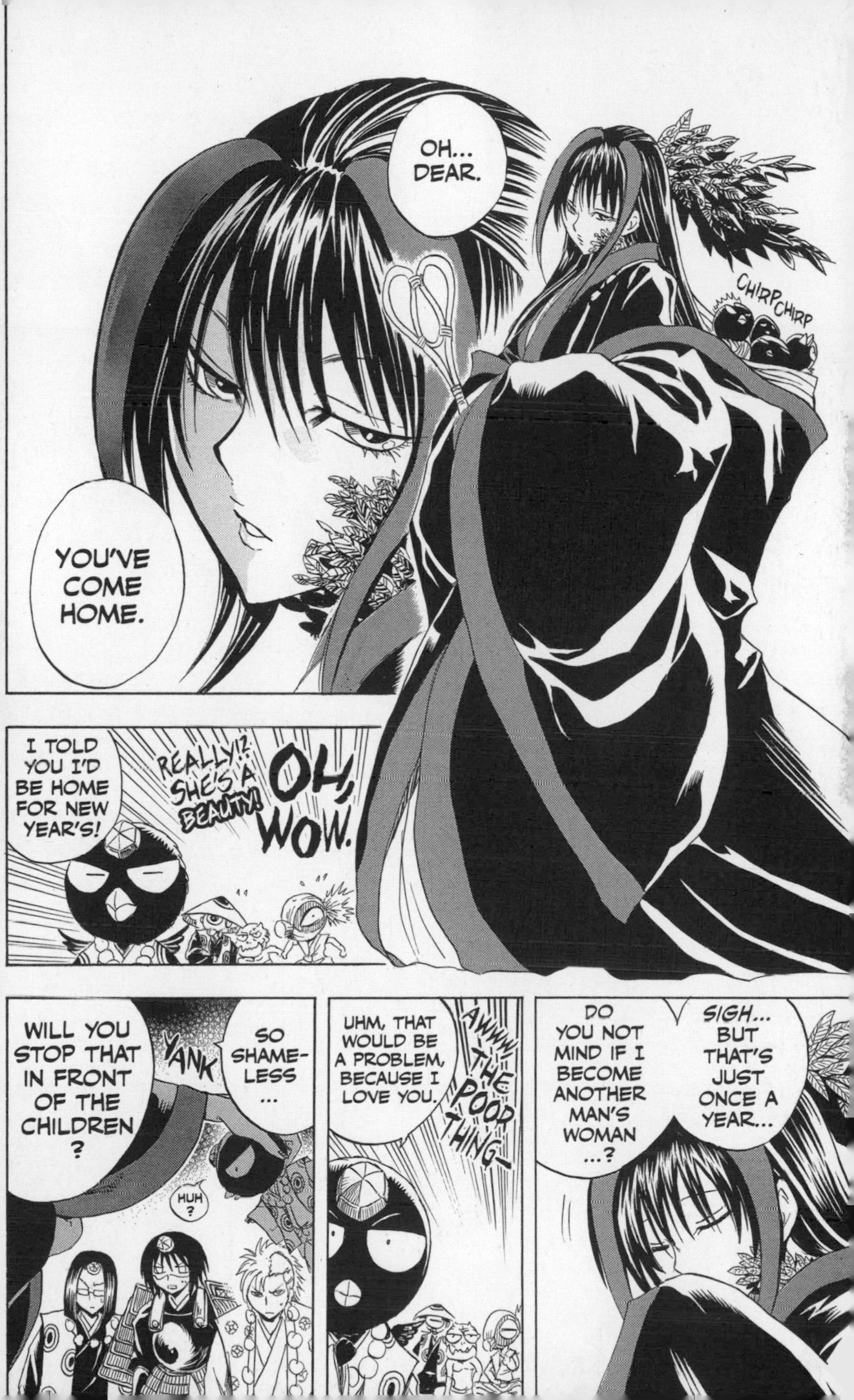
OH... DEAR.
CHIRP CHIRP
YOU'VE COME HOME.
OH, WOW.
REALLY!? SHE'S A BEAUTY!
I TOLD YOU I'D BE HOME FOR NEW YEAR'S!
SIGH... BUT THAT'S JUST ONCE A YEAR...
DO YOU NOT MIND IF I BECOME ANOTHER MAN'S WOMAN ...?
AWWW THE POOR THING~
UHM, THAT WOULD BE A PROBLEM, BECAUSE I LOVE YOU.
SO SHAME-LESS ...
YANK
WILL YOU STOP THAT IN FRONT OF THE CHILDREN ?
HUH ?

READ THIS WAY

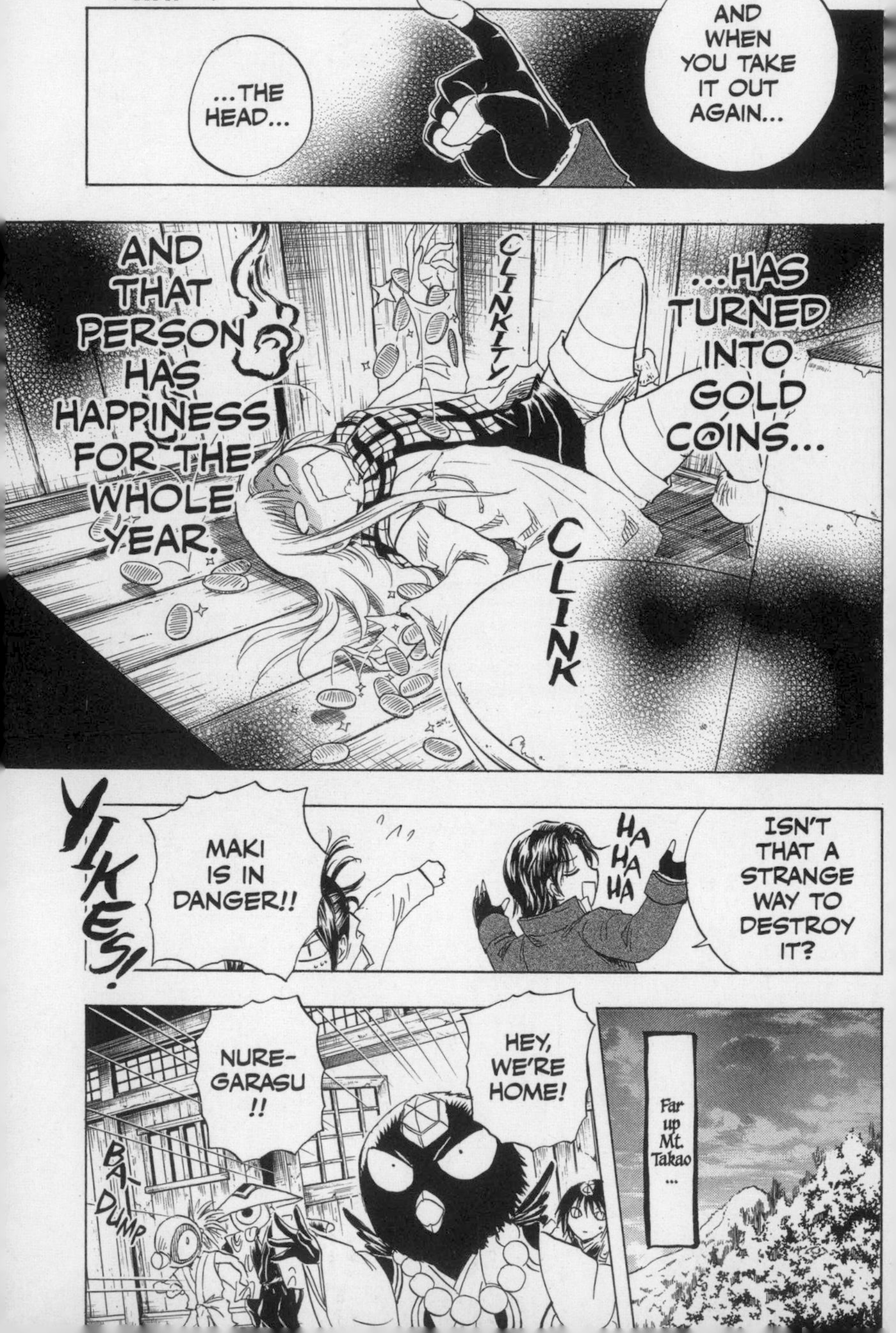
AND WHEN YOU TAKE IT OUT AGAIN...
...THE HEAD...
...HAS TURNED INTO GOLD COINS...
CLINKITY
CLINK
AND THAT PERSON HAS HAPPINESS FOR THE WHOLE YEAR.
ISN'T THAT A STRANGE WAY TO DESTROY IT?
HA HA HA HA
MAKI IS IN DANGER!!
YIKES!
Far up Mt. Takao...
HEY, WE'RE HOME!
NURE-GARASU!!
BA-DUMP

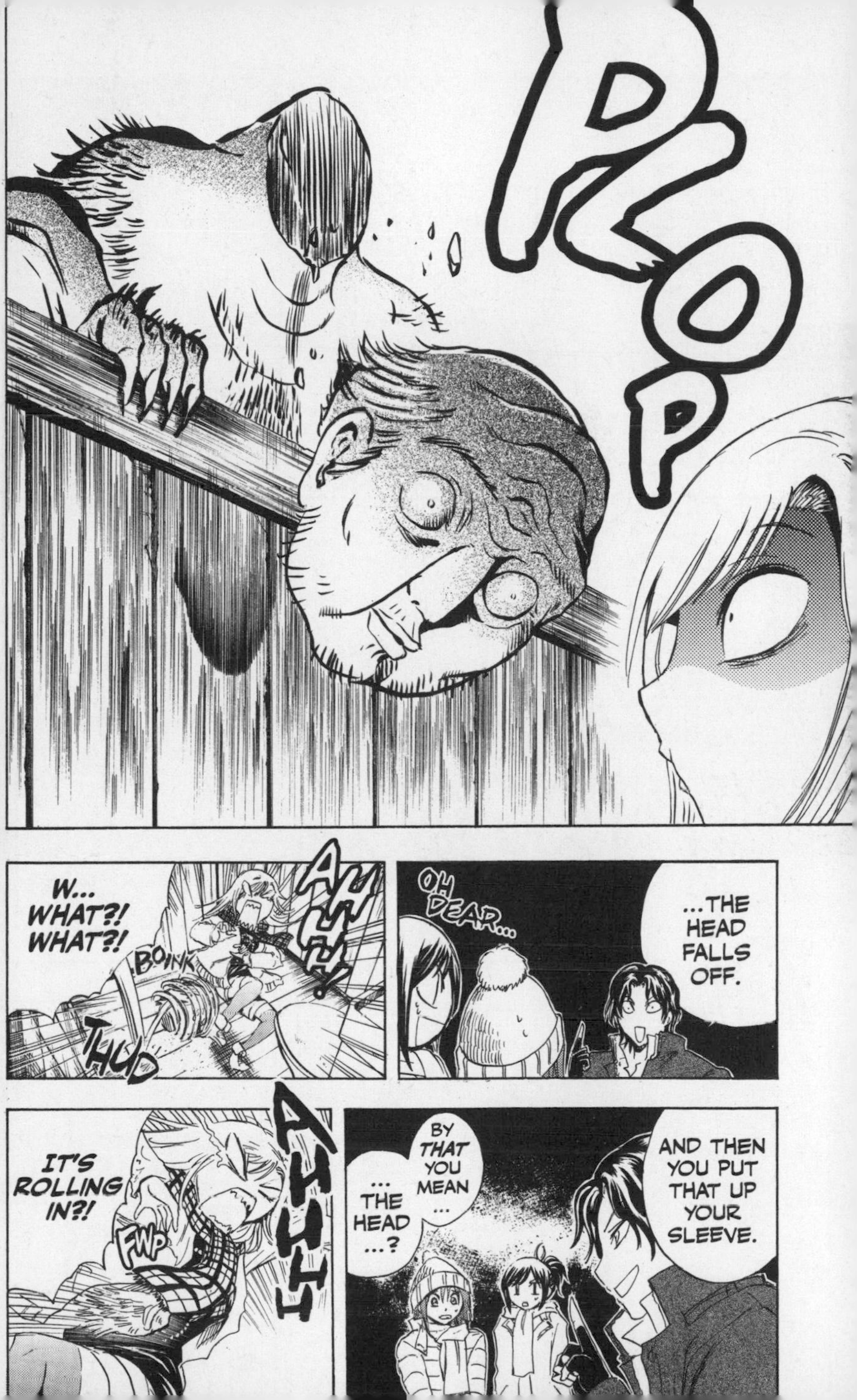
PLOP
...THE HEAD FALLS OFF.
OH DEAR...
AHHH!
W... WHAT?! WHAT?!
BOINK
THUD
AND THEN YOU PUT THAT UP YOUR SLEEVE.
BY THAT YOU MEAN ...
... THE HEAD ...?
AHHH!
IT'S ROLLING IN?!
FWP

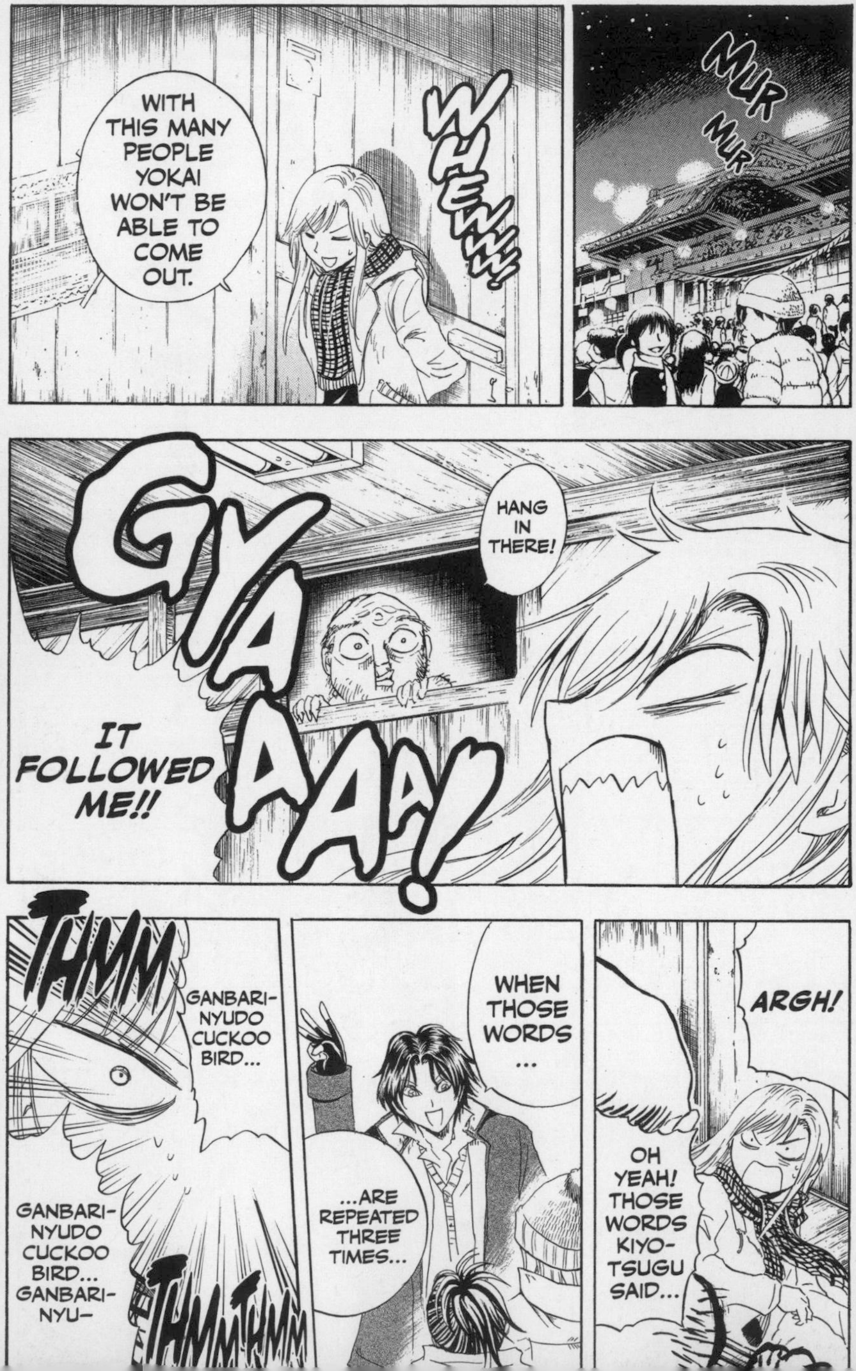
MUR MUR
WHEWW!
WITH THIS MANY PEOPLE YOKAI WON'T BE ABLE TO COME OUT.
HANG IN THERE!
GYAAAA!
IT FOLLOWED ME!!
ARGH!
OH YEAH! THOSE WORDS KIYO-TSUGU SAID...
WHEN THOSE WORDS ...
...ARE REPEATED THREE TIMES...
THMM
GANBARI-NYUDO CUCKOO BIRD...
GANBARI-NYUDO CUCKOO BIRD... GANBARI-NYU–
THMMTHMM

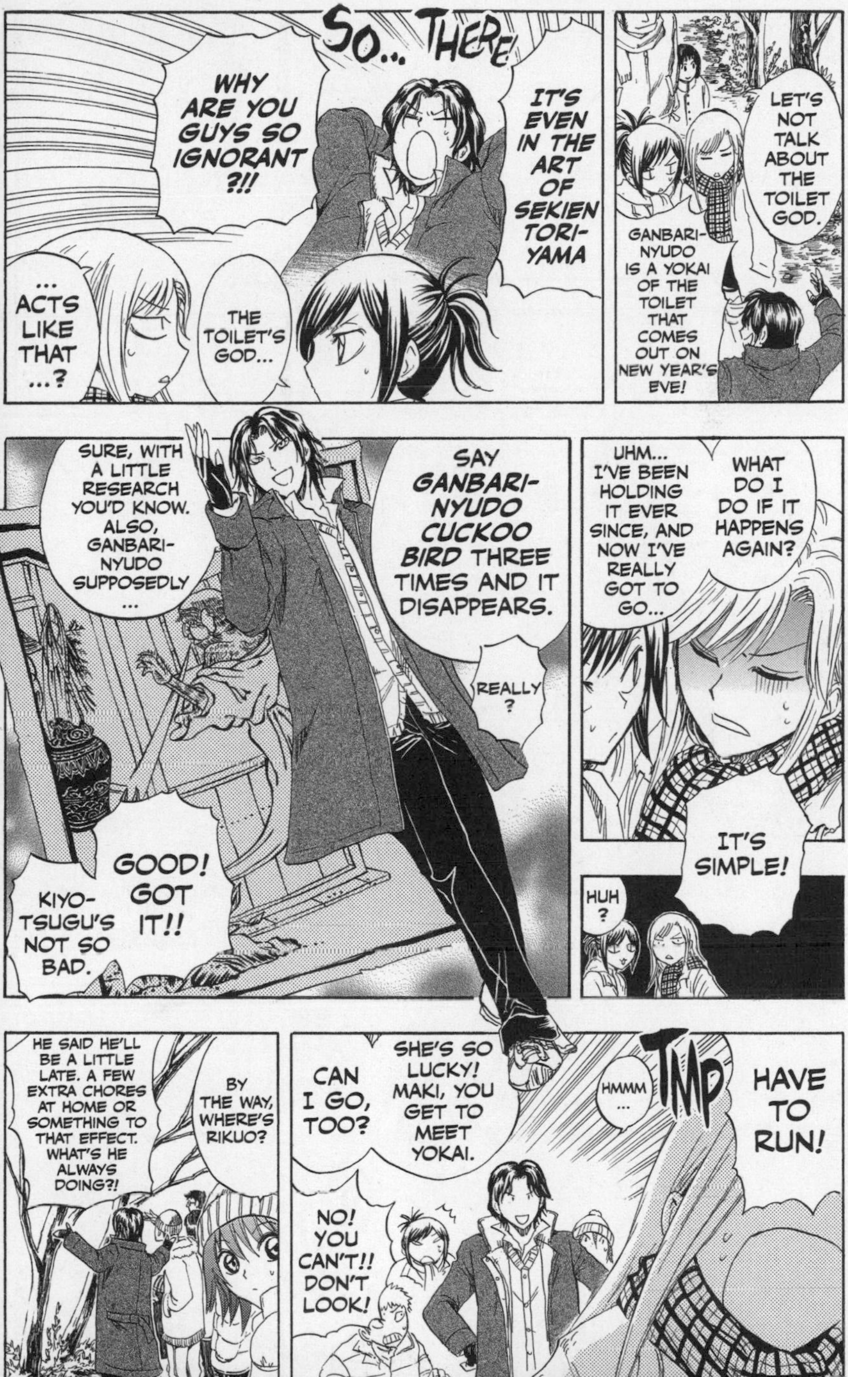
LET'S NOT TALK ABOUT THE TOILET GOD.
GANBARI-NYUDO IS A YOKAI OF THE TOILET THAT COMES OUT ON NEW YEAR'S EVE!
SO... THERE!
IT'S EVEN IN THE ART OF SEKIEN TORI-YAMA
WHY ARE YOU GUYS SO IGNORANT?!!
THE TOILET'S GOD...
... ACTS LIKE THAT ...?
WHAT DO I DO IF IT HAPPENS AGAIN?
UHM... I'VE BEEN HOLDING IT EVER SINCE, AND NOW I'VE REALLY GOT TO GO...
IT'S SIMPLE!
HUH?
SAY GANBARI-NYUDO CUCKOO BIRD THREE TIMES AND IT DISAPPEARS.
SURE, WITH A LITTLE RESEARCH YOU'D KNOW. ALSO, GANBARI-NYUDO SUPPOSEDLY ...
REALLY?
GOOD! GOT IT!!
KIYO-TSUGU'S NOT SO BAD.
HAVE TO RUN!
TMP
HMMM ...
SHE'S SO LUCKY! MAKI, YOU GET TO MEET YOKAI.
CAN I GO, TOO?
NO! YOU CAN'T!! DON'T LOOK!
BY THE WAY, WHERE'S RIKUO?
HE SAID HE'LL BE A LITTLE LATE. A FEW EXTRA CHORES AT HOME OR SOMETHING TO THAT EFFECT. WHAT'S HE ALWAYS DOING?!

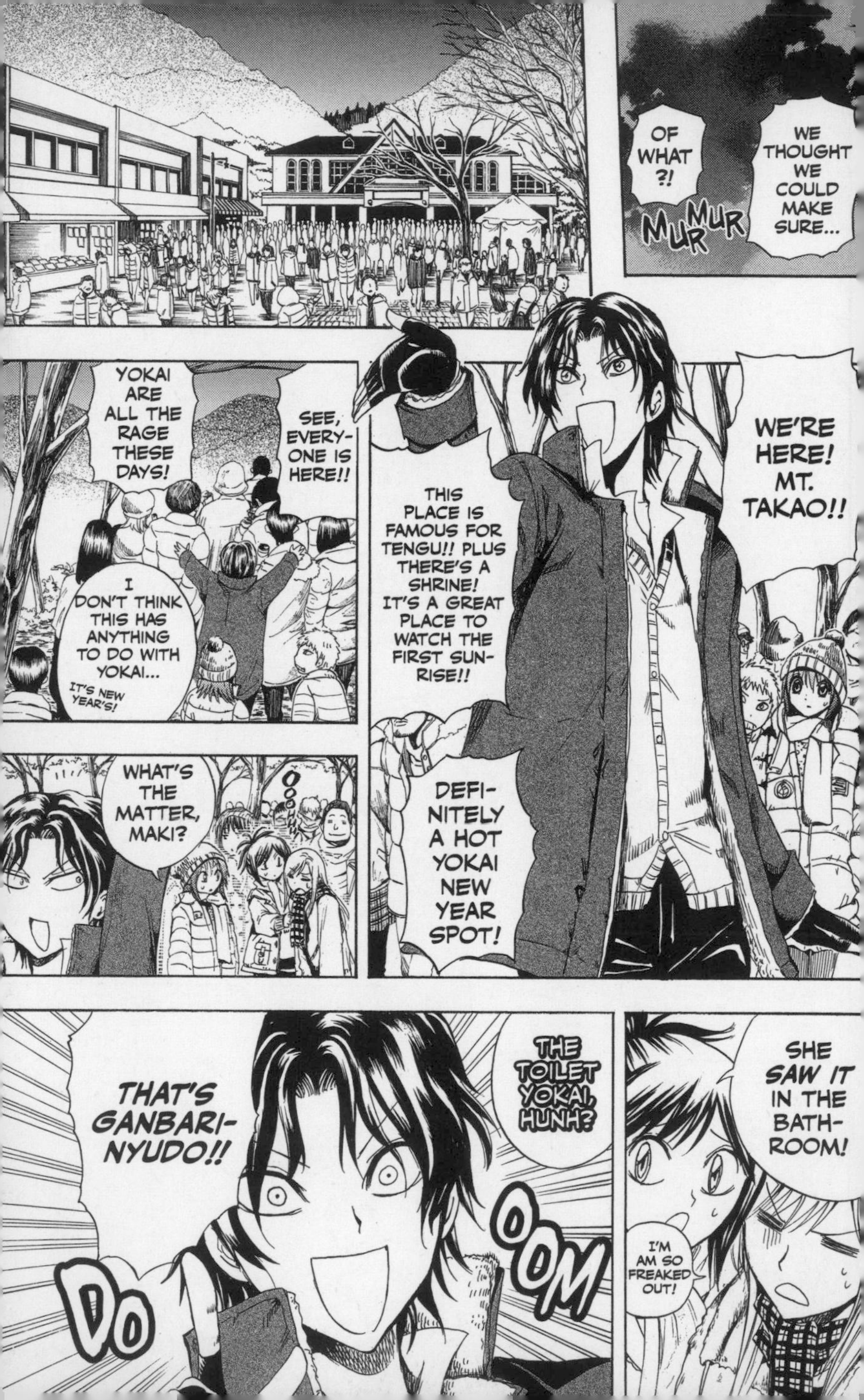
WE THOUGHT WE COULD MAKE SURE...
OF WHAT?!
MUR MUR MUR
WE'RE HERE! MT. TAKAO!!
THIS PLACE IS FAMOUS FOR TENGU!! PLUS THERE'S A SHRINE! IT'S A GREAT PLACE TO WATCH THE FIRST SUN-RISE!!
DEFI-NITELY A HOT YOKAI NEW YEAR SPOT!
SEE, EVERY-ONE IS HERE!!
YOKAI ARE ALL THE RAGE THESE DAYS!
I DON'T THINK THIS HAS ANYTHING TO DO WITH YOKAI...
IT'S NEW YEAR'S!
OOOHH
WHAT'S THE MATTER, MAKI?
SHE SAW IT IN THE BATH-ROOM!
I'M AM SO FREAKED OUT!
THE TOILET YOKAI, HUNH?
THAT'S GANBARI-NYUDO!!
DOOM

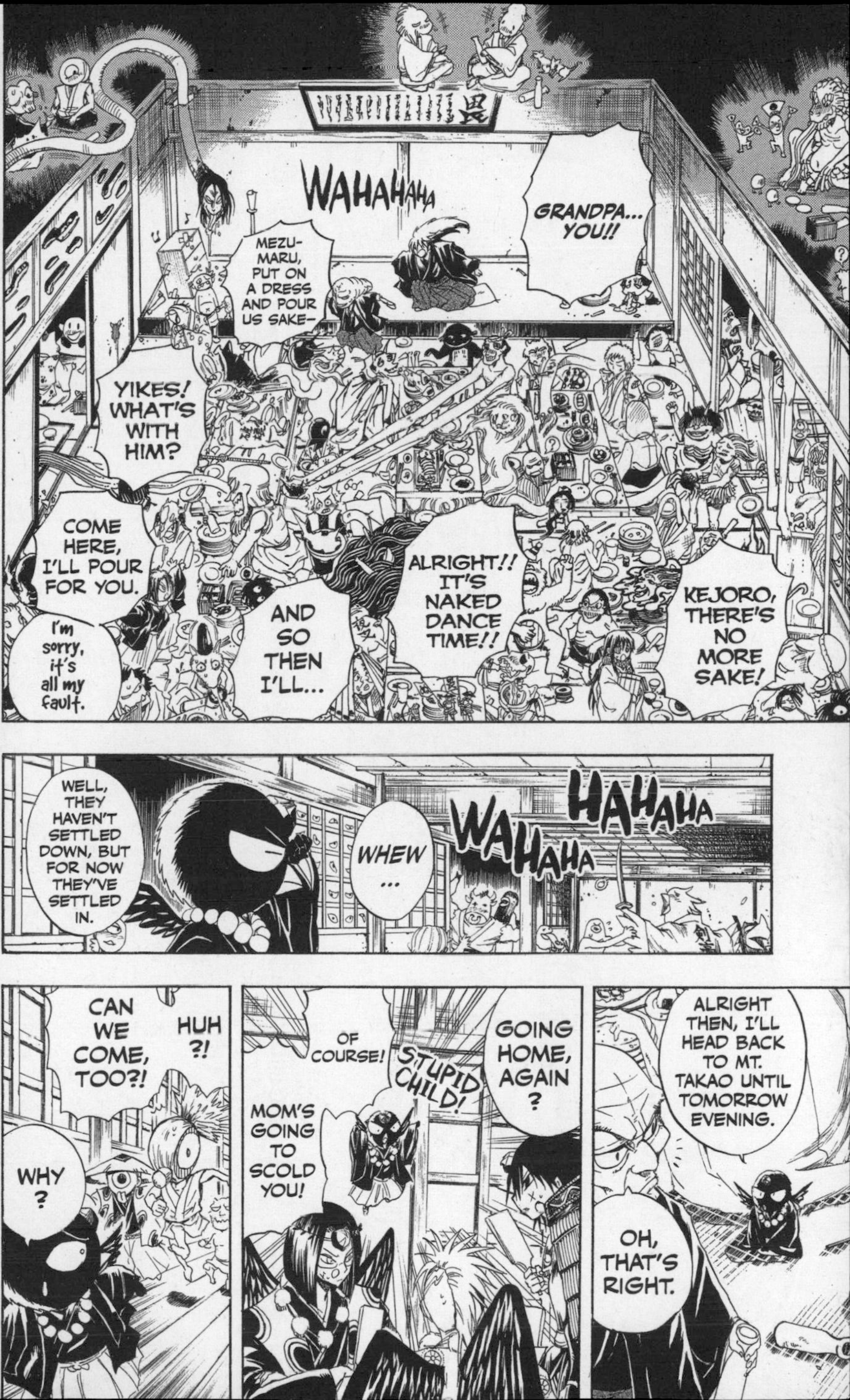
GRANDPA... YOU!!
WAHAHAHAHA
MEZU-MARU, PUT ON A DRESS AND POUR US SAKE–
KEJORO, THERE'S NO MORE SAKE!
ALRIGHT!! IT'S NAKED DANCE TIME!!
YIKES! WHAT'S WITH HIM?
AND SO THEN I'LL...
COME HERE, I'LL POUR FOR YOU.
I'm sorry, it's all my fault.
HAHAHA
WAHAHAHA
WHEW ...
WELL, THEY HAVEN'T SETTLED DOWN, BUT FOR NOW THEY'VE SETTLED IN.
ALRIGHT THEN, I'LL HEAD BACK TO MT. TAKAO UNTIL TOMORROW EVENING.
OH, THAT'S RIGHT.
GOING HOME, AGAIN ?
STUPID CHILD!
OF COURSE!
MOM'S GOING TO SCOLD YOU!
HUH ?!
CAN WE COME, TOO?!
WHY ?

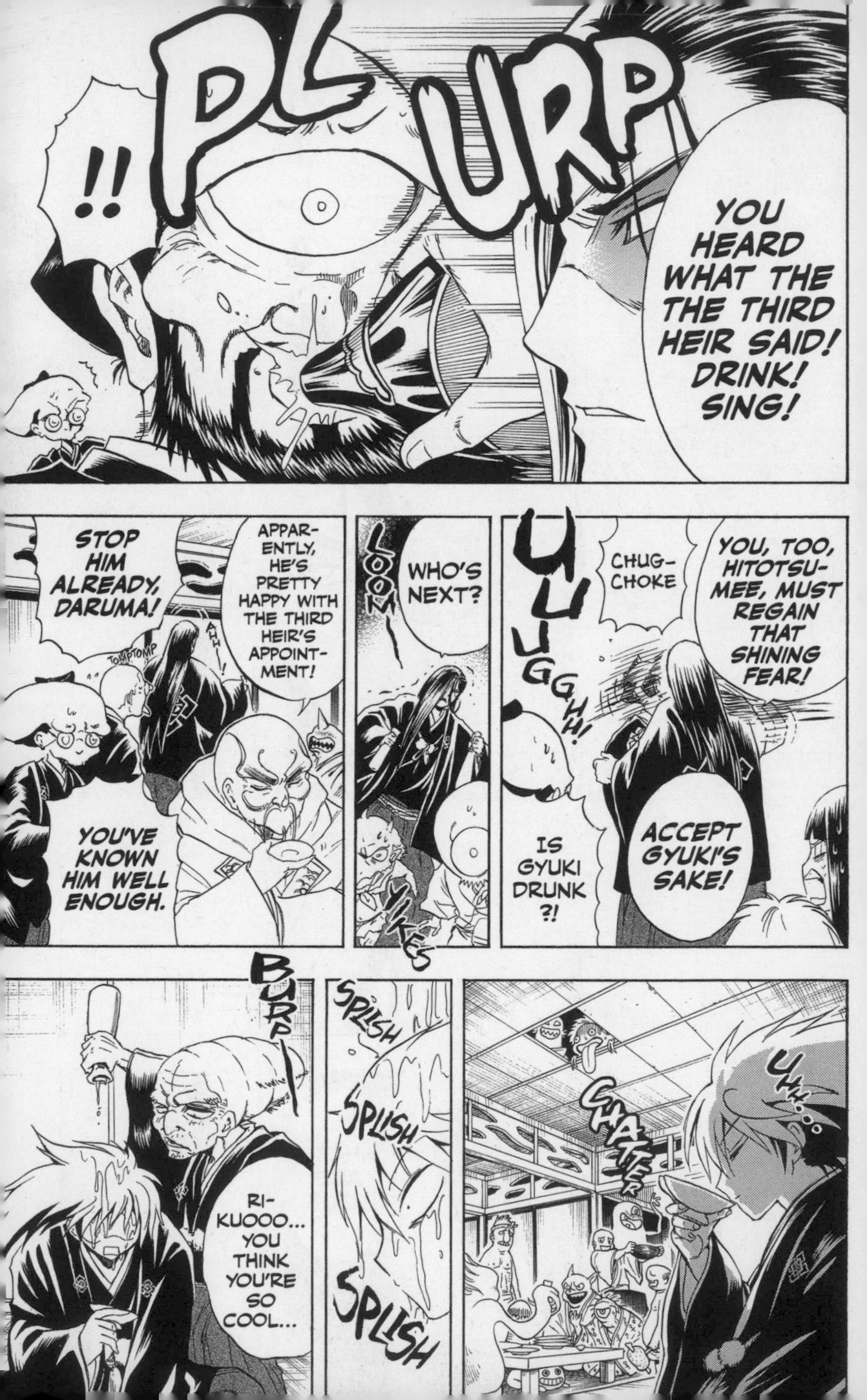
PLURP
YOU HEARD WHAT THE THE THIRD HEIR SAID! DRINK! SING!
!!
YOU, TOO, HITOTSU-MEE, MUST REGAIN THAT SHINING FEAR!
CHUG-CHOKE
UUUUGGHH!
ACCEPT GYUKI'S SAKE!
IS GYUKI DRUNK?!
WHO'S NEXT?
LOOM
YIKES
APPAR-ENTLY, HE'S PRETTY HAPPY WITH THE THIRD HEIR'S APPOINT-MENT!
STOP HIM ALREADY, DARUMA!
AHH-!
TOMP TOMP
YOU'VE KNOWN HIM WELL ENOUGH.
UHH...
CHATTER
SPLISH
SPLISH
SPLISH
BURP
RI-KUOOO... YOU THINK YOU'RE SO COOL...

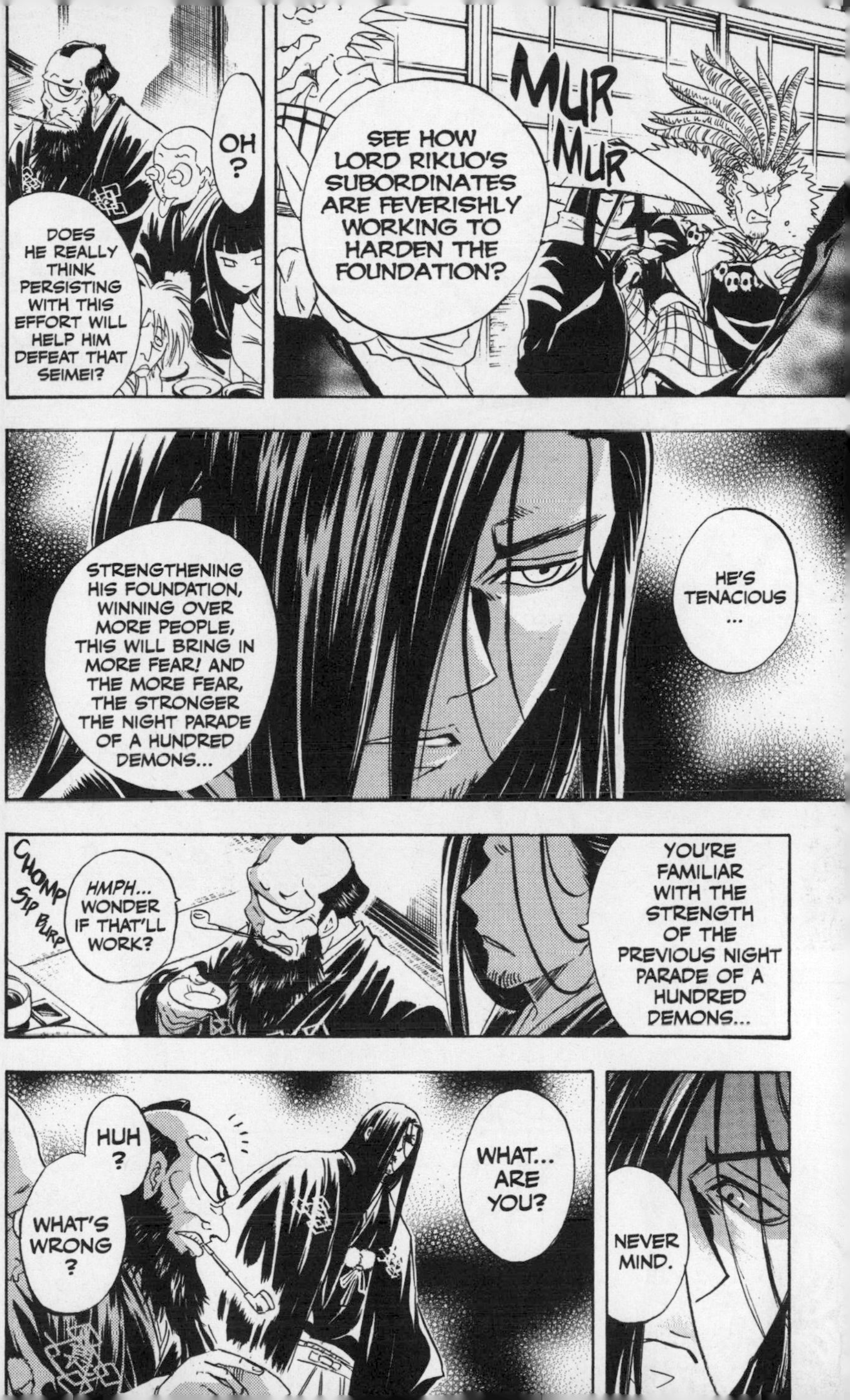
MUR MUR
SEE HOW LORD RIKUO'S SUBORDINATES ARE FEVERISHLY WORKING TO HARDEN THE FOUNDATION?
OH?
DOES HE REALLY THINK PERSISTING WITH THIS EFFORT WILL HELP HIM DEFEAT THAT SEIMEI?
HE'S TENACIOUS...
STRENGTHENING HIS FOUNDATION, WINNING OVER MORE PEOPLE, THIS WILL BRING IN MORE FEAR! AND THE MORE FEAR, THE STRONGER THE NIGHT PARADE OF A HUNDRED DEMONS...
YOU'RE FAMILIAR WITH THE STRENGTH OF THE PREVIOUS NIGHT PARADE OF A HUNDRED DEMONS...
HMPH... WONDER IF THAT'LL WORK?
CHOMP SIP BURP
NEVER MIND.
WHAT... ARE YOU?
HUH?
WHAT'S WRONG?

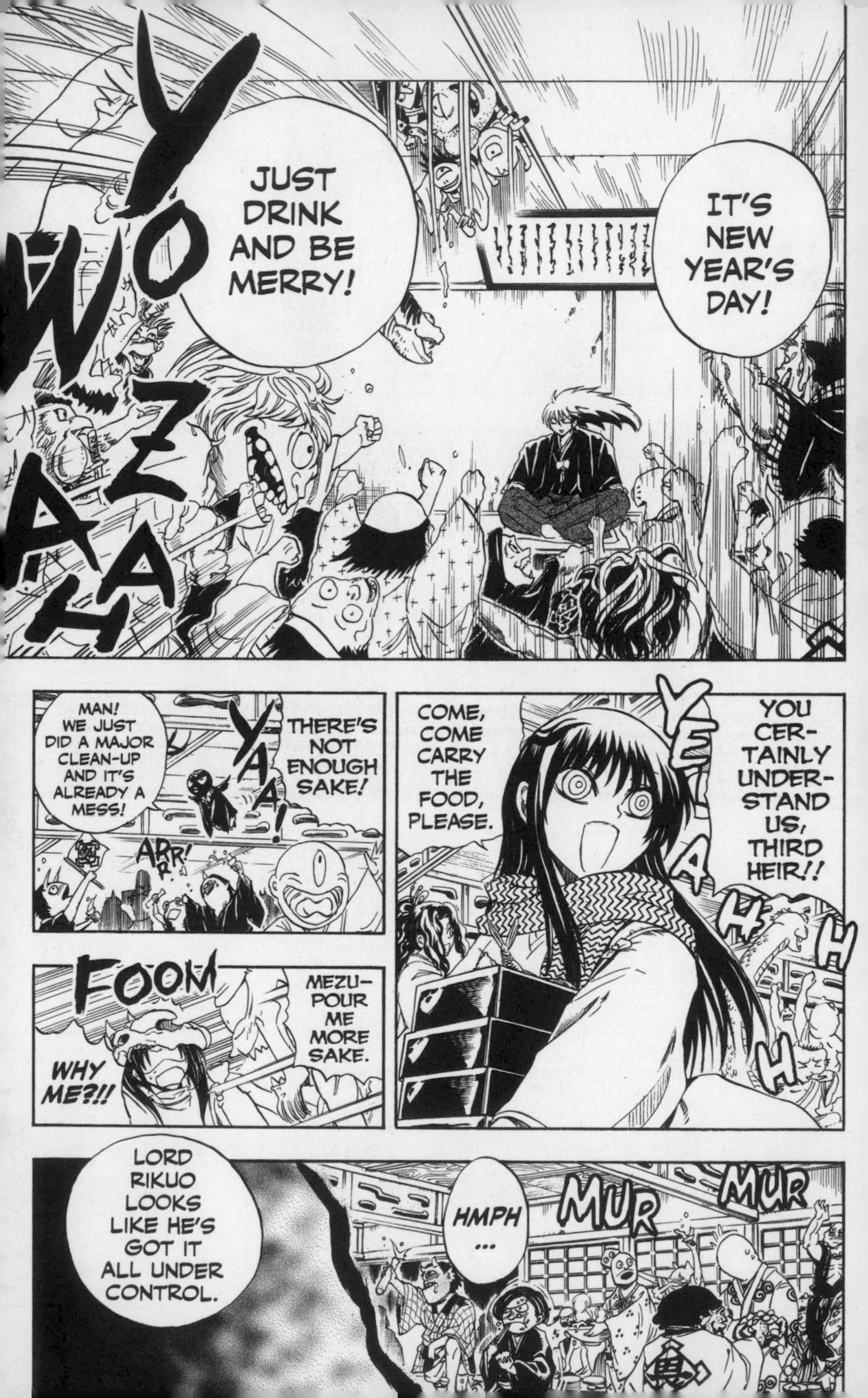
IT'S NEW YEAR'S DAY!
JUST DRINK AND BE MERRY!
YOWZAAH
YOU CER-TAINLY UNDER-STAND US, THIRD HEIR!!
YEAHHHH
COME, COME CARRY THE FOOD, PLEASE.
THERE'S NOT ENOUGH SAKE!
YAAA!
MAN! WE JUST DID A MAJOR CLEAN-UP AND IT'S ALREADY A MESS!
ARRR!
MEZU-POUR ME MORE SAKE.
FOOM
WHY ME?!!
MUR
MUR
HMPH ...
LORD RIKUO LOOKS LIKE HE'S GOT IT ALL UNDER CONTROL.

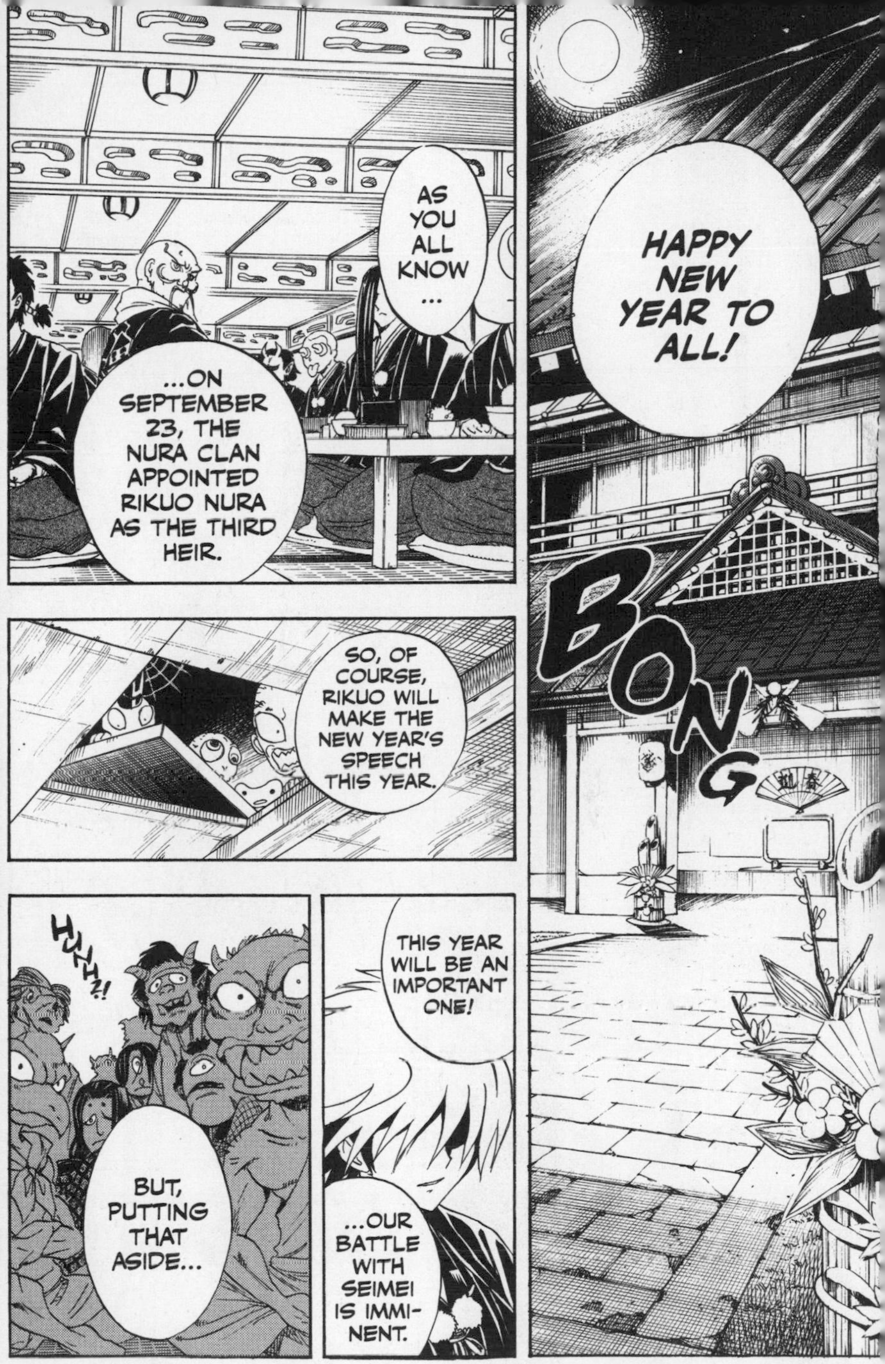
HAPPY NEW YEAR TO ALL!
BONG
AS YOU ALL KNOW...
...ON SEPTEMBER 23, THE NURA CLAN APPOINTED RIKUO NURA AS THE THIRD HEIR.
SO, OF COURSE, RIKUO WILL MAKE THE NEW YEAR'S SPEECH THIS YEAR.
THIS YEAR WILL BE AN IMPORTANT ONE!
...OUR BATTLE WITH SEIMEI IS IMMINENT.
HUHH?!
BUT, PUTTING THAT ASIDE...

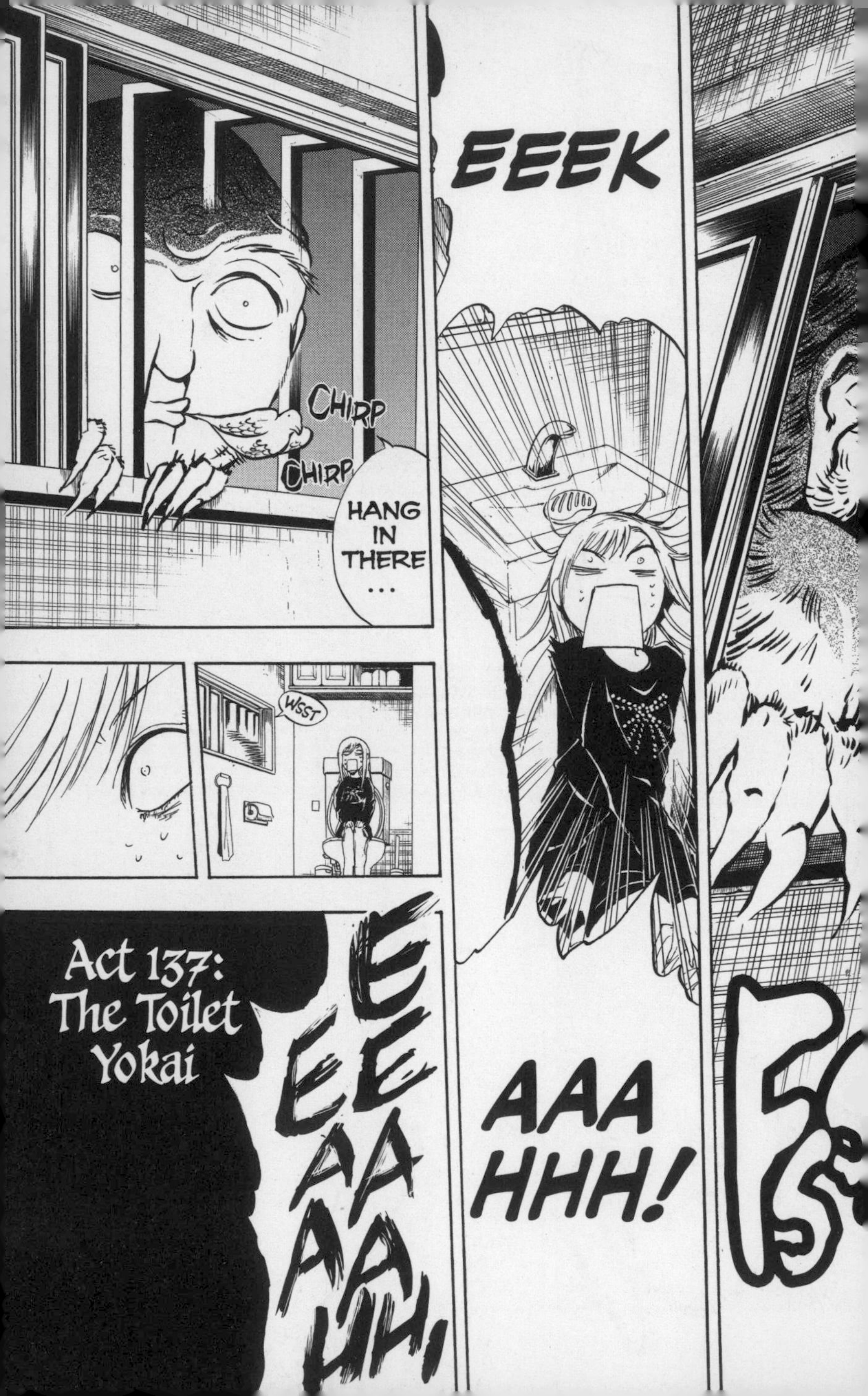
EEEK
AAA HHH!
CHIRP
CHIRP
HANG IN THERE ...
WSST
Act 137: The Toilet Yokai
EEEEAAAAAAH!

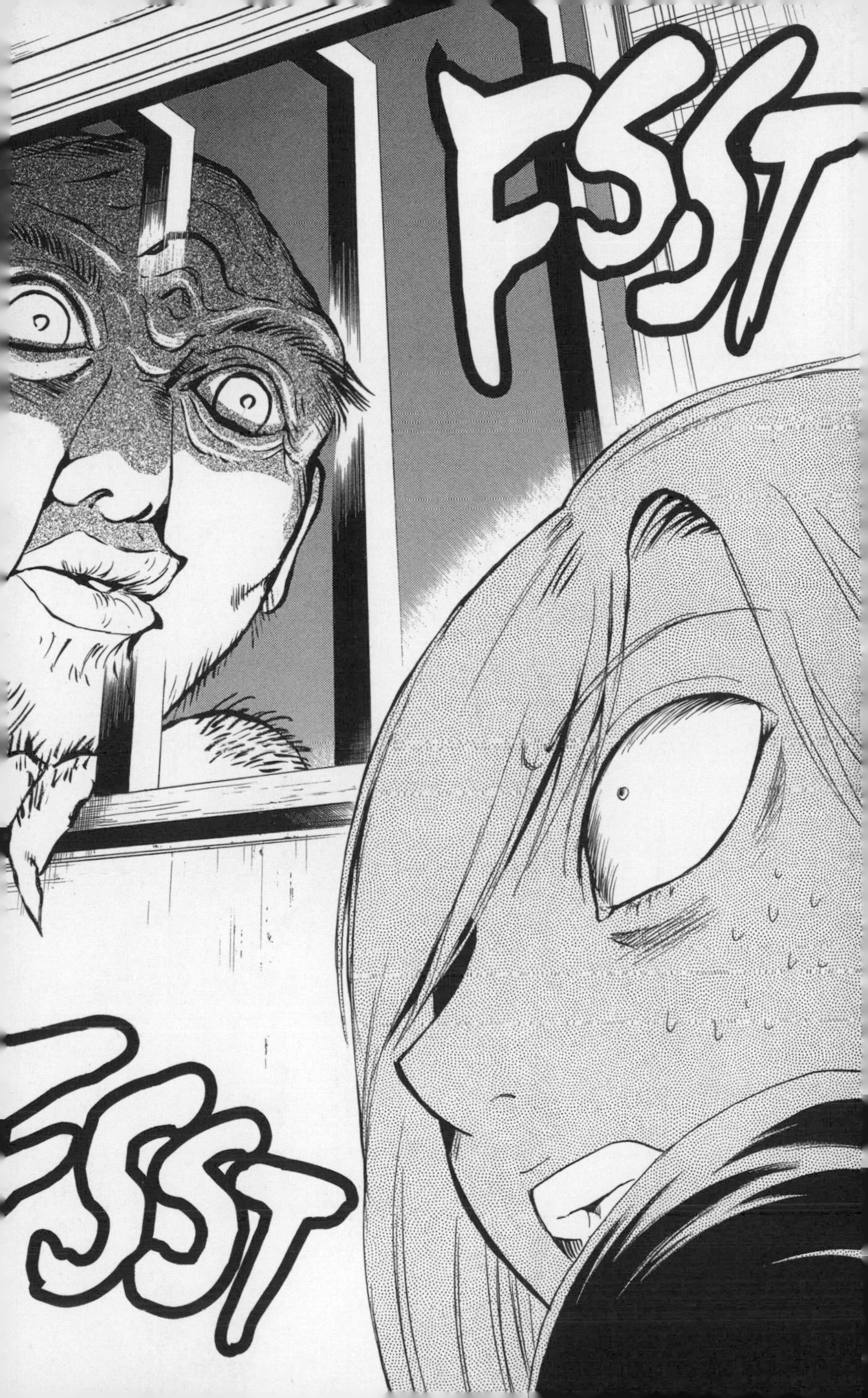
FSST
FSSST

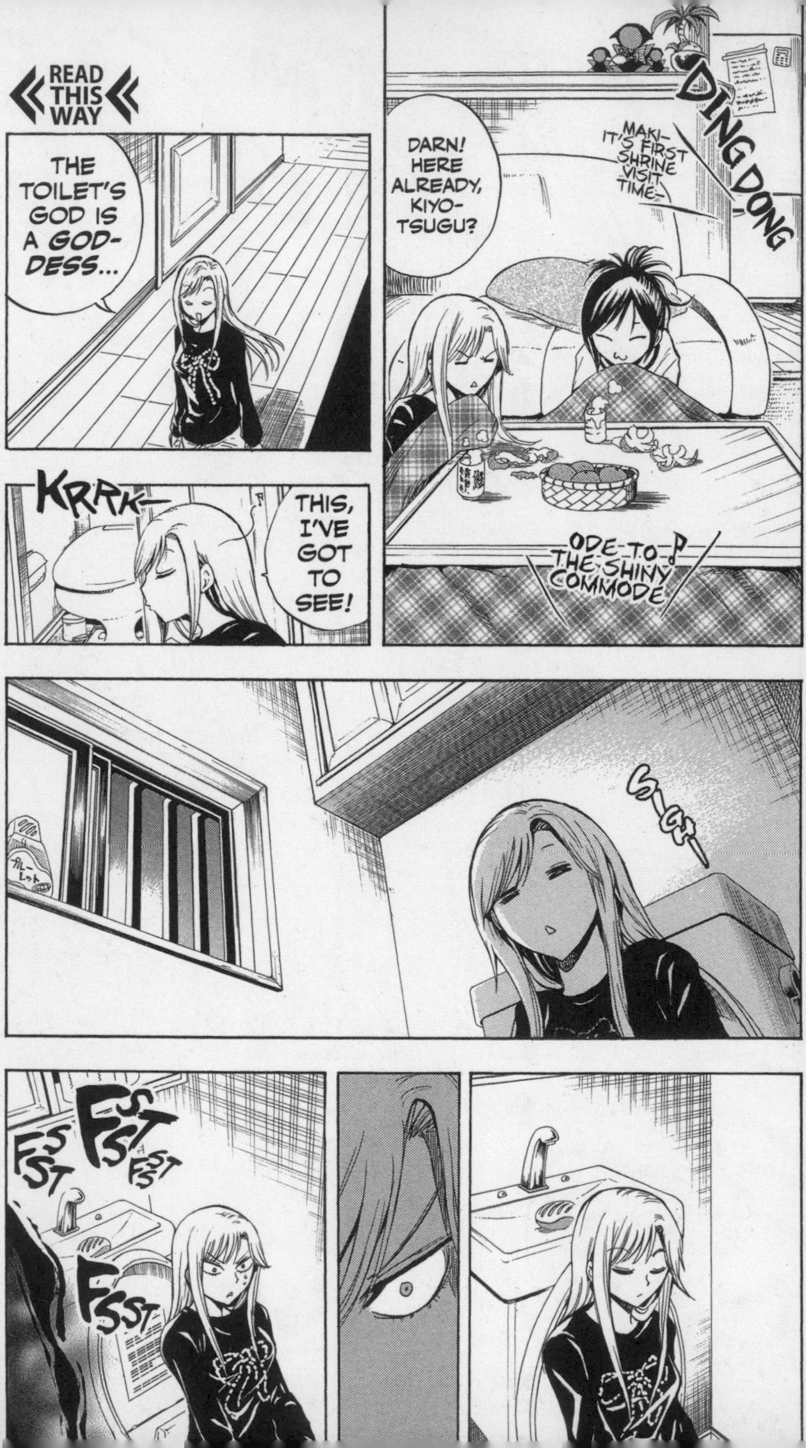
READ THIS WAY
DING DONG
MAKI— IT'S FIRST SHRINE VISIT TIME—
DARN! HERE ALREADY, KIYOTSUGU?
ODE TO THE SHINY COMMODE
THE TOILET'S GOD IS A GODDESS...
KRRK—
THIS, I'VE GOT TO SEE!
FST FST
FSST FST FST
FSST

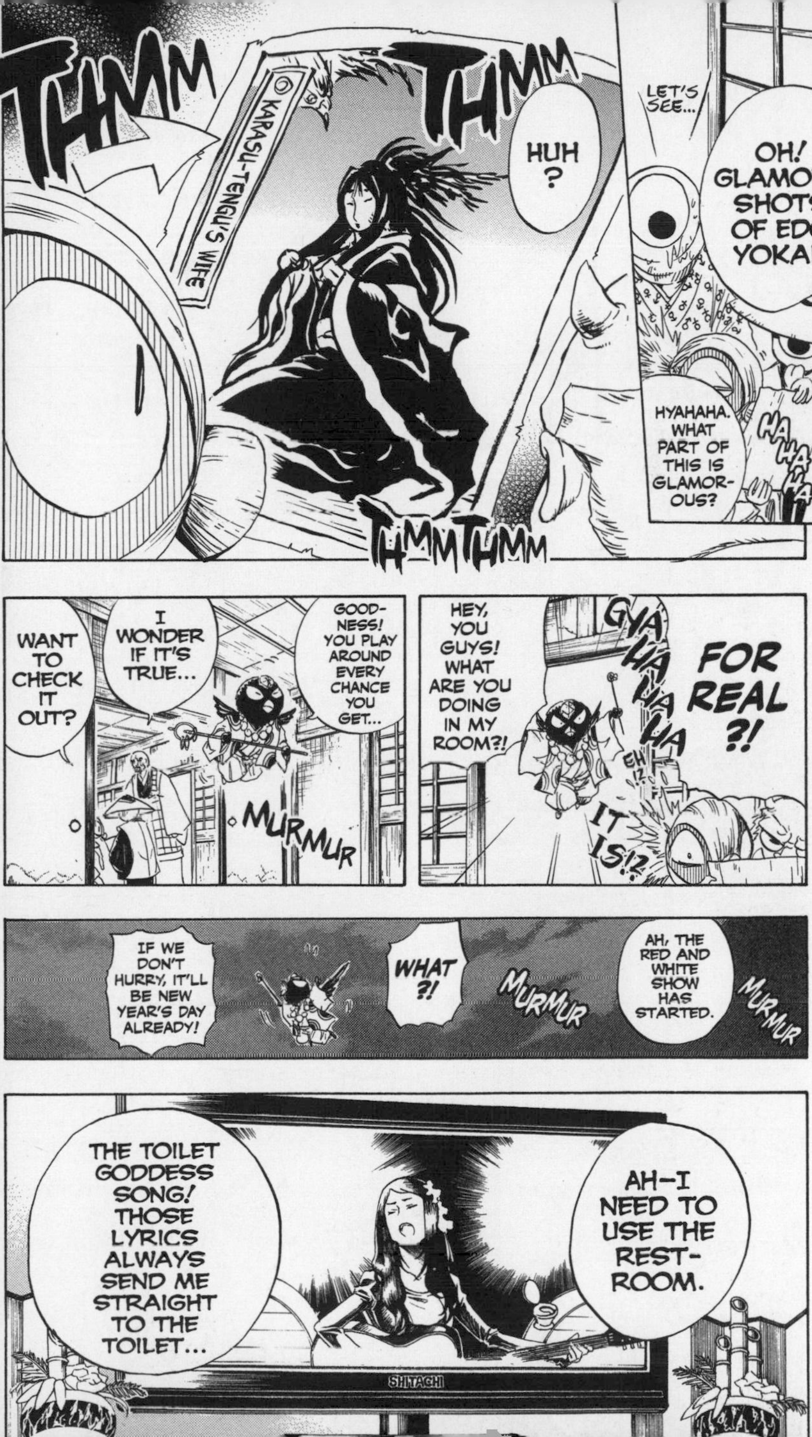
LET'S SEE...
OH! GLAMOUR SHOTS OF EDO YOKAI!
HYAHAHA. WHAT PART OF THIS IS GLAMOROUS?
HAHAHA
THMM
HUH?
KARASU-TENGU'S WIFE
THMM
THMMTHMM
GYAHAHAHA
FOR REAL?!
HEY, YOU GUYS! WHAT ARE YOU DOING IN MY ROOM?!
EH!?
IT IS!?
GOODNESS! YOU PLAY AROUND EVERY CHANCE YOU GET...
I WONDER IF IT'S TRUE...
WANT TO CHECK IT OUT?
MURMUR
MURMUR
AH, THE RED AND WHITE SHOW HAS STARTED.
MURMUR
WHAT?!
IF WE DON'T HURRY, IT'LL BE NEW YEAR'S DAY ALREADY!
AH—I NEED TO USE THE REST-ROOM.
THE TOILET GODDESS SONG! THOSE LYRICS ALWAYS SEND ME STRAIGHT TO THE TOILET...
SHITACHI

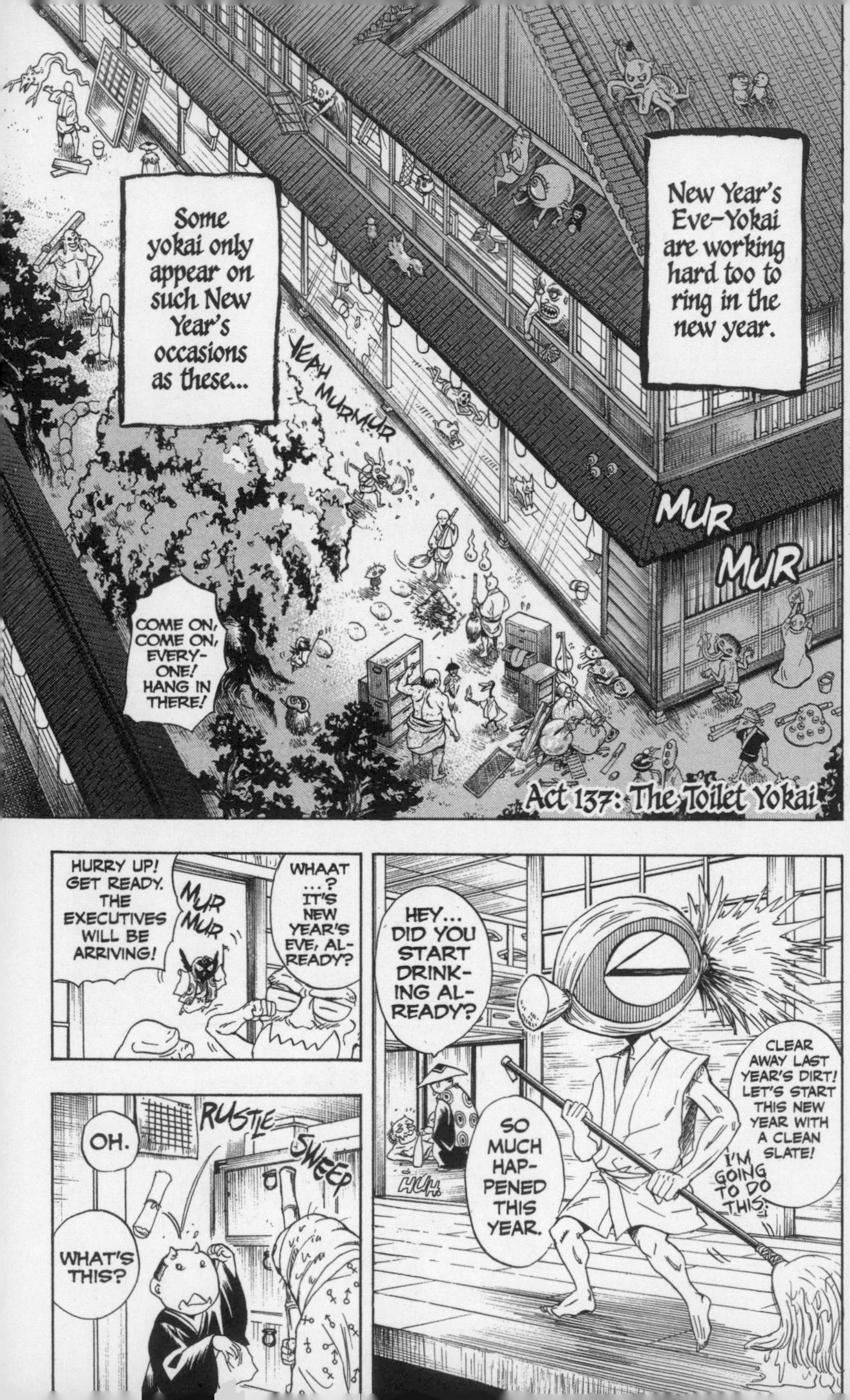
New Year's Eve-Yokai are working hard too to ring in the new year.
Some yokai only appear on such New Year's occasions as these...
MUR MUR
YEAH MURMUR
COME ON, COME ON, EVERYONE! HANG IN THERE!
Act 137: The Toilet Yokai
CLEAR AWAY LAST YEAR'S DIRT! LET'S START THIS NEW YEAR WITH A CLEAN SLATE!
HEY... DID YOU START DRINKING ALREADY?
I'M GOING TO DO THIS.
SO MUCH HAPPENED THIS YEAR.
HUH.
WHAAT ...? IT'S NEW YEAR'S EVE, ALREADY?
MUR MUR
HURRY UP! GET READY. THE EXECUTIVES WILL BE ARRIVING!
RUSTLE
SWEEP
OH.
WHAT'S THIS?

BONUS EVENT!
LAUGH WHILE CLEANING UP
WITH THIS 4-FRAME MANGA!!

AFTER THE PARTY...

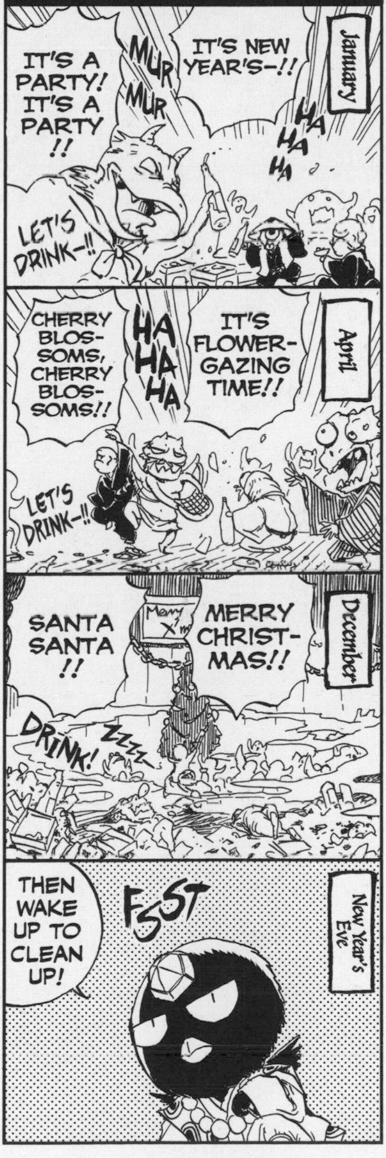
January
IT'S NEW YEAR'S—!!
HA HA HA HA
MUR MUR
IT'S A PARTY! IT'S A PARTY !!
LET'S DRINK—!!
April
IT'S FLOWER-GAZING TIME!!
HA HA HA
CHERRY BLOSSOMS, CHERRY BLOSSOMS!!
LET'S DRINK—!!
December
MERRY CHRISTMAS!!
Merry X'mas
SANTA SANTA !!
ZZZZ
DRINK!
New Year's Eve
FSST
THEN WAKE UP TO CLEAN UP!

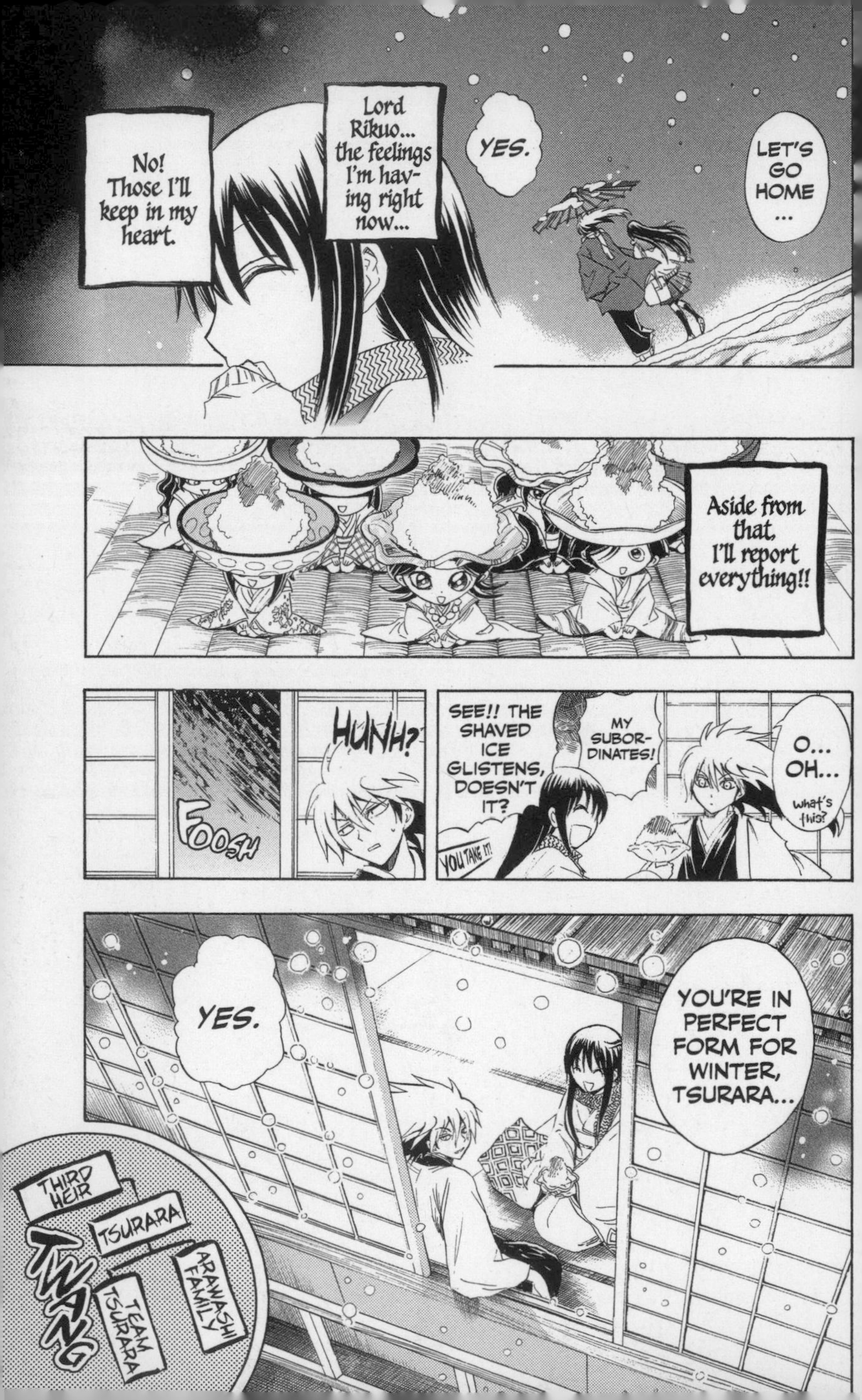
LET'S GO HOME ...
YES.
Lord Riku0... the feelings I'm having right now...
No! Those I'll keep in my heart.
Aside from that, I'll report everything!!
O... OH...
what's this?
MY SUBORDINATES!
SEE!! THE SHAVED ICE GLISTENS, DOESN'T IT?
YOU TAKE IT!
HUNH?
FOOSH
YOU'RE IN PERFECT FORM FOR WINTER, TSURARA...
YES.
THIRD HEIR
TSURARA
ARAWASHI FAMILY
TEAM TSURARA
TWANG

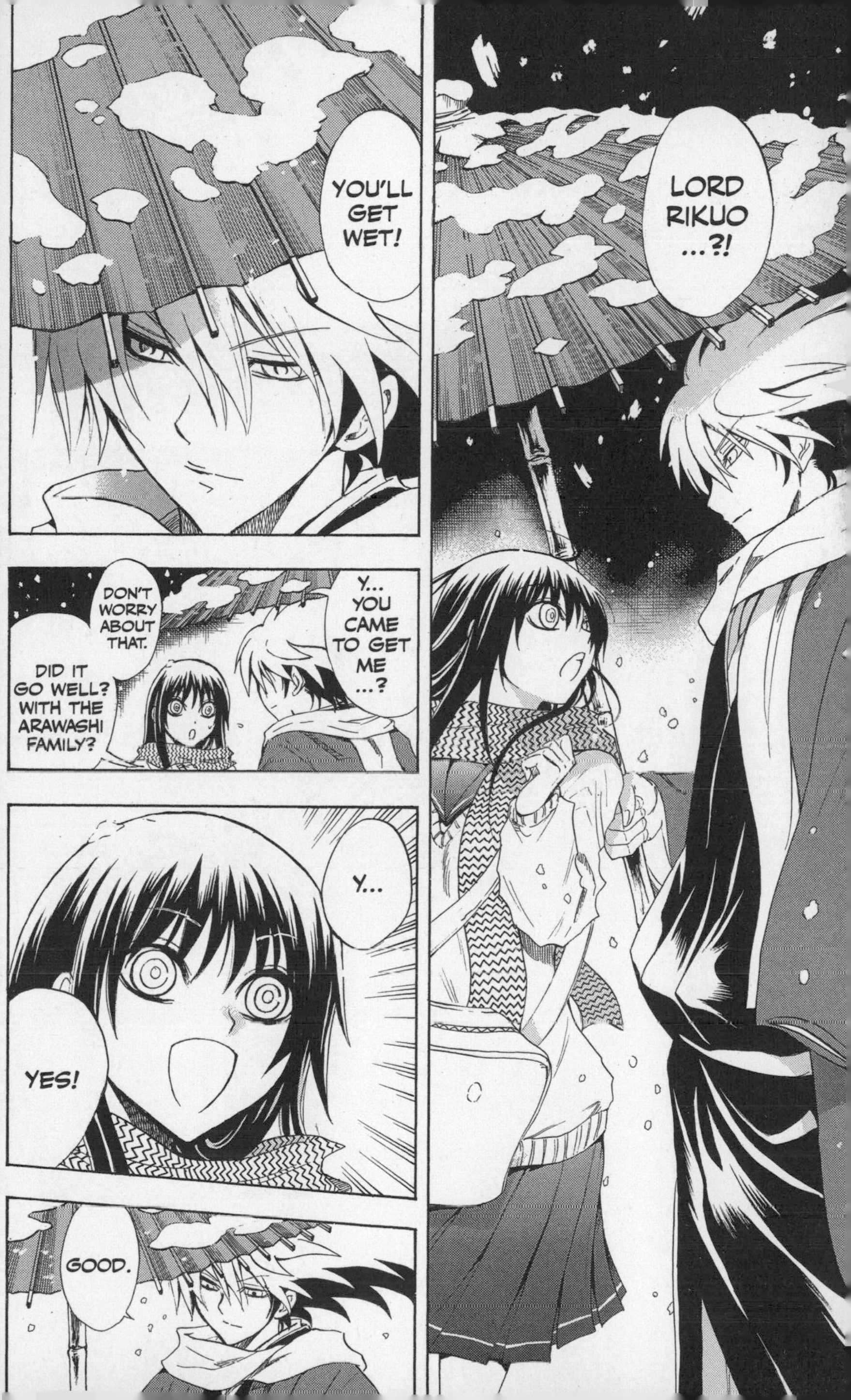
LORD RIKUO ...?!
YOU'LL GET WET!
Y... YOU CAME TO GET ME ...?
DON'T WORRY ABOUT THAT.
DID IT GO WELL? WITH THE ARAWASHI FAMILY?
Y...
YES!
GOOD.

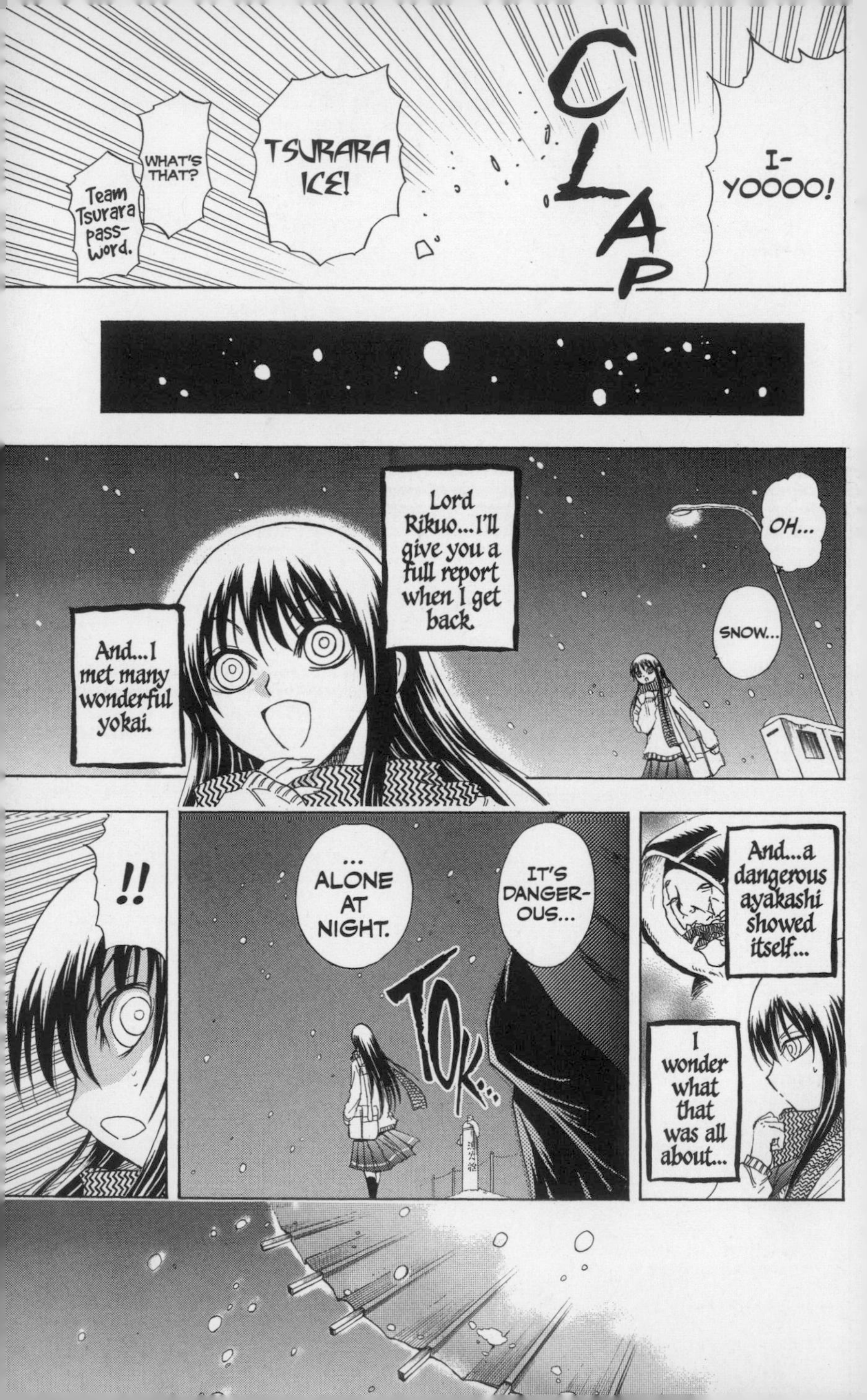
I-YOOOO!
CLAP
TSURARA ICE!
WHAT'S THAT?
Team Tsurara password.
OH...
SNOW...
Lord Rikuo...I'll give you a full report when I get back.
And...I met many wonderful yokai.
And...a dangerous ayakashi showed itself...
I wonder what that was all about...
IT'S DANGEROUS...
...ALONE AT NIGHT.
TOK...
!!

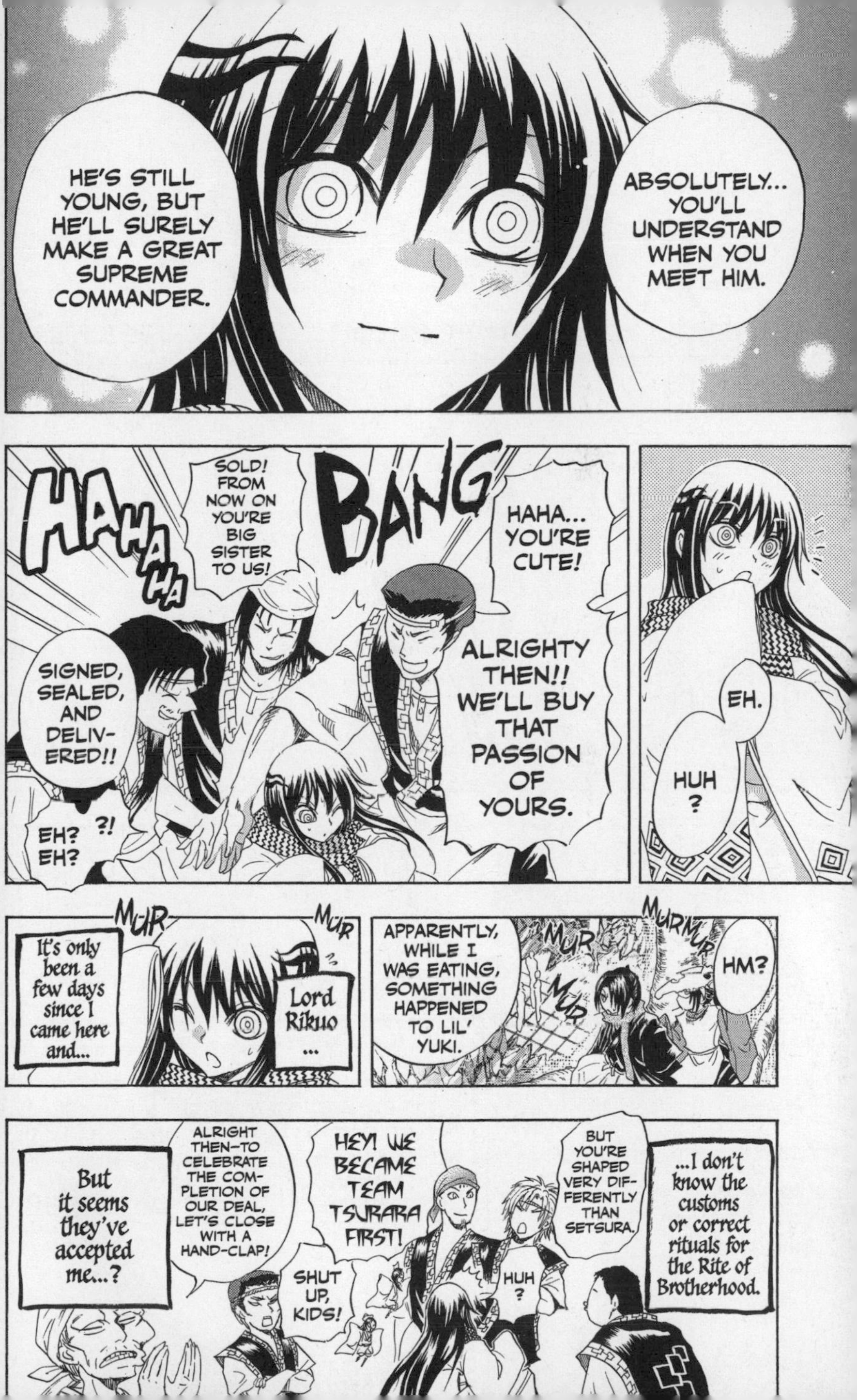
ABSOLUTELY... YOU'LL UNDERSTAND WHEN YOU MEET HIM.
HE'S STILL YOUNG, BUT HE'LL SURELY MAKE A GREAT SUPREME COMMANDER.
EH.
HUH ?
HAHA... YOU'RE CUTE!
BANG
SOLD! FROM NOW ON YOU'RE BIG SISTER TO US!
HAHAHAHA
ALRIGHTY THEN!! WE'LL BUY THAT PASSION OF YOURS.
SIGNED, SEALED, AND DELIV-ERED!!
?!
EH? EH?
MURMUR
HM?
MUR
MUR
APPARENTLY, WHILE I WAS EATING, SOMETHING HAPPENED TO LIL' YUKI.
MUR
Lord Rikuo ...
MUR
It's only been a few days since I came here and...
...I don't know the customs or correct rituals for the Rite of Brotherhood.
BUT YOU'RE SHAPED VERY DIF-FERENTLY THAN SETSURA.
HUH ?
HEY! WE BECAME TEAM TSURARA FIRST!
SHUT UP, KIDS!
ALRIGHT THEN—TO CELEBRATE THE COM-PLETION OF OUR DEAL, LET'S CLOSE WITH A HAND-CLAP!
But it seems they've accepted me...?

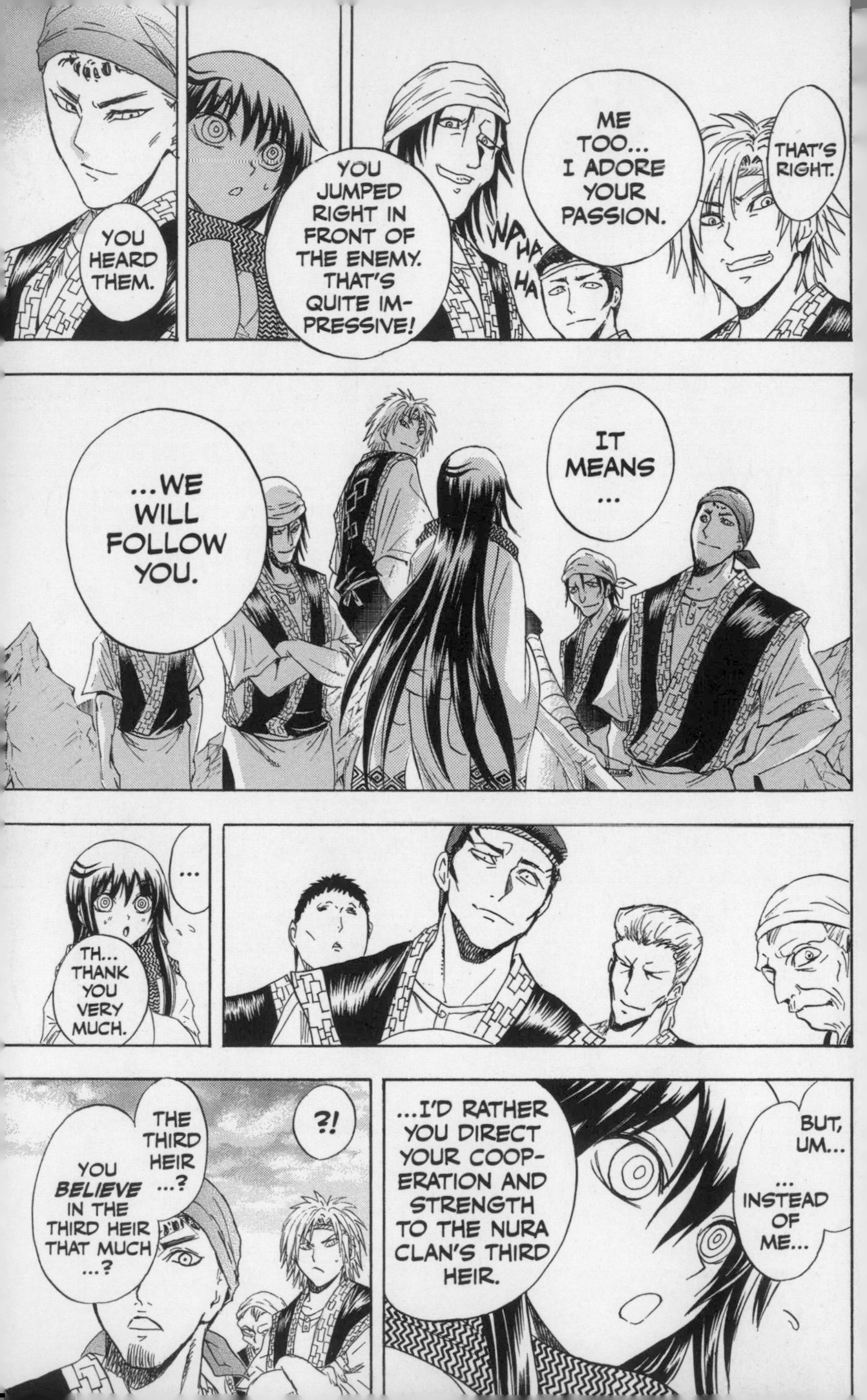
THAT'S RIGHT.
ME TOO... I ADORE YOUR PASSION.
YOU JUMPED RIGHT IN FRONT OF THE ENEMY. THAT'S QUITE IM-PRESSIVE!
WAHAHA
YOU HEARD THEM.
IT MEANS...
...WE WILL FOLLOW YOU.
...
TH... THANK YOU VERY MUCH.
BUT, UM...
... INSTEAD OF ME...
...I'D RATHER YOU DIRECT YOUR COOP-ERATION AND STRENGTH TO THE NURA CLAN'S THIRD HEIR.
?!
THE THIRD HEIR ...?
YOU *BELIEVE* IN THE THIRD HEIR THAT MUCH ...?

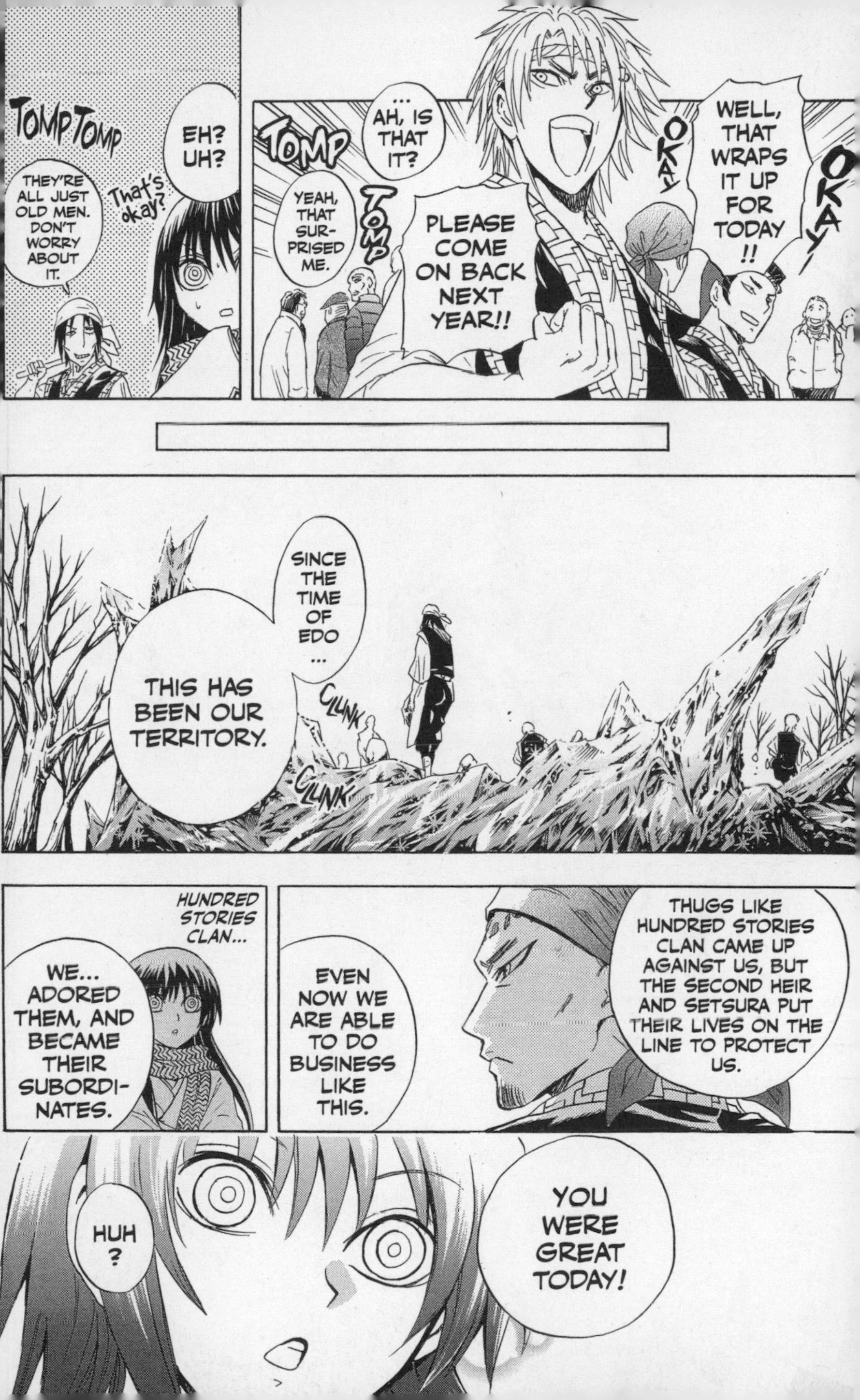
WELL, THAT WRAPS IT UP FOR TODAY!!
OKAY
OKAY
PLEASE COME ON BACK NEXT YEAR!!
... AH, IS THAT IT?
TOMP
TOMP
YEAH, THAT SUR-PRISED ME.
EH? UH?
TOMP TOMP
That's okay?
THEY'RE ALL JUST OLD MEN. DON'T WORRY ABOUT IT.
SINCE THE TIME OF EDO ...
THIS HAS BEEN OUR TERRITORY.
CLUNK
CLUNK
THUGS LIKE HUNDRED STORIES CLAN CAME UP AGAINST US, BUT THE SECOND HEIR AND SETSURA PUT THEIR LIVES ON THE LINE TO PROTECT US.
EVEN NOW WE ARE ABLE TO DO BUSINESS LIKE THIS.
HUNDRED STORIES CLAN...
WE... ADORED THEM, AND BECAME THEIR SUBORDI-NATES.
YOU WERE GREAT TODAY!
HUH ?

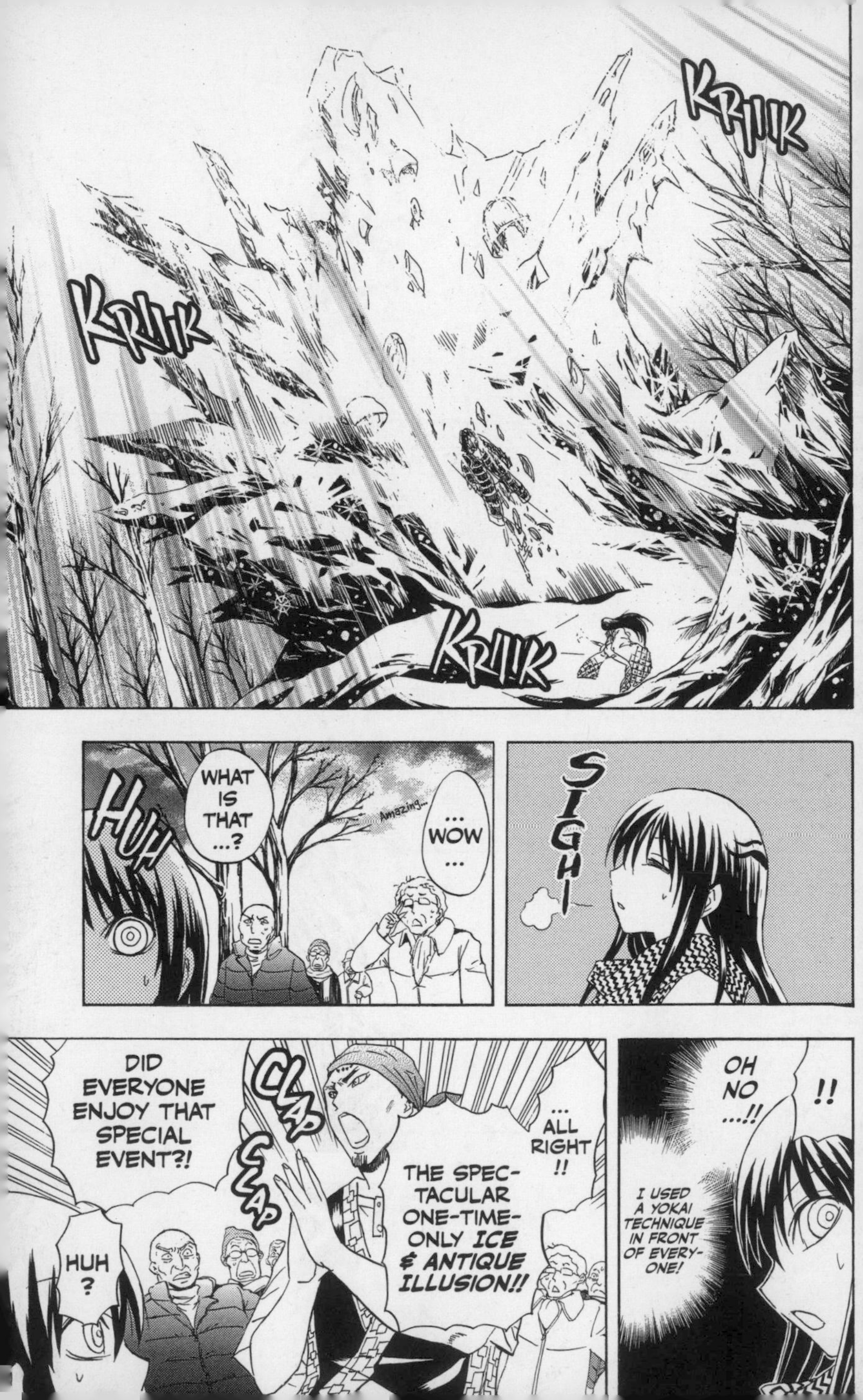
KRIIIK
KRIIIK
KRIIIK
SIGH
... WOW ...
Amazing...
WHAT IS THAT ...?
HUH
!!
OH NO ...!!
I USED A YOKAI TECHNIQUE IN FRONT OF EVERYONE!
... ALL RIGHT !!
THE SPECTACULAR ONE-TIME-ONLY ICE & ANTIQUE ILLUSION!!
CLAP
CLAP
DID EVERYONE ENJOY THAT SPECIAL EVENT?!
HUH ?

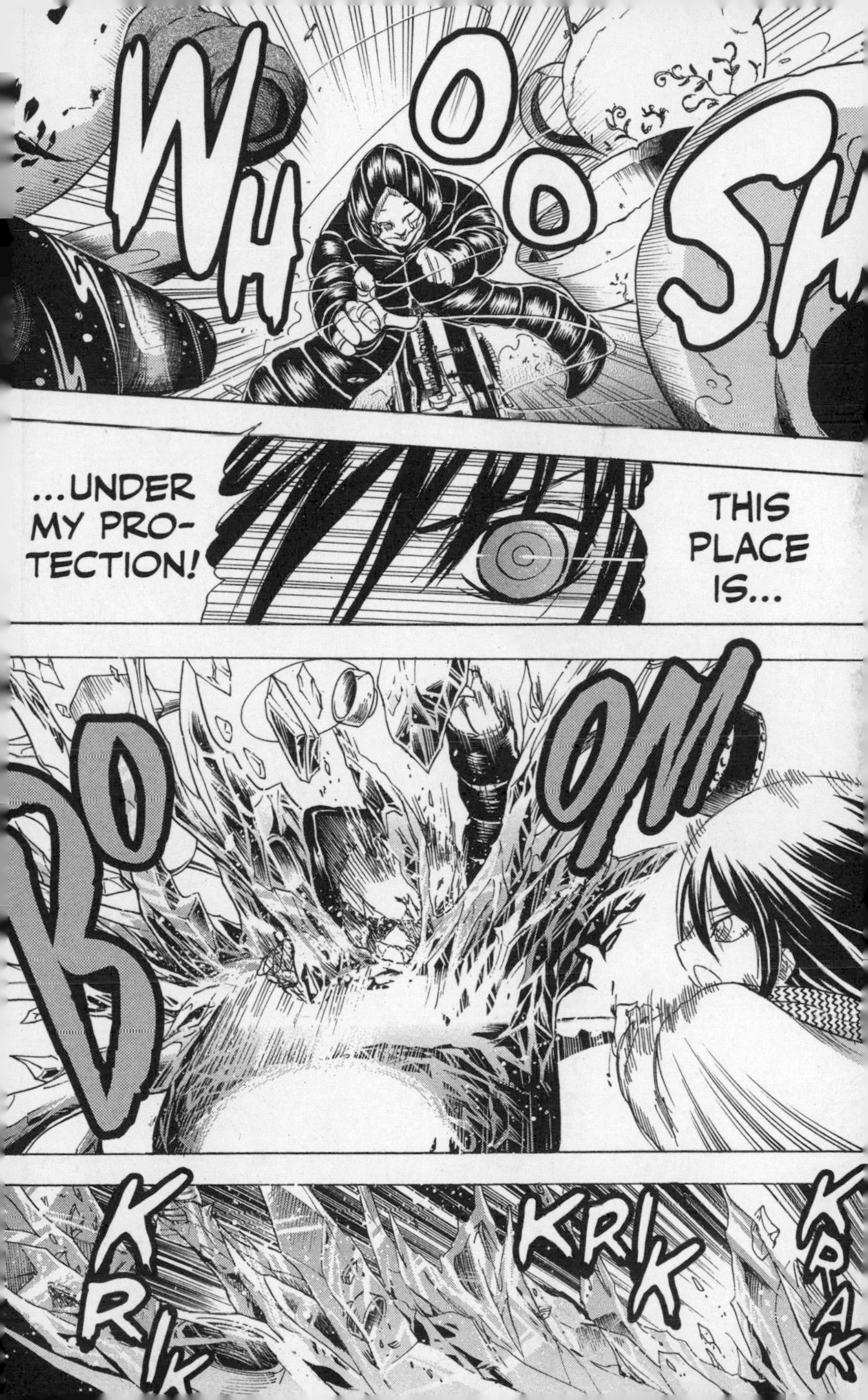
WHOOSH
THIS PLACE IS...
...UNDER MY PRO-TECTION!
BOOM
KRAK
KRK
KRIK

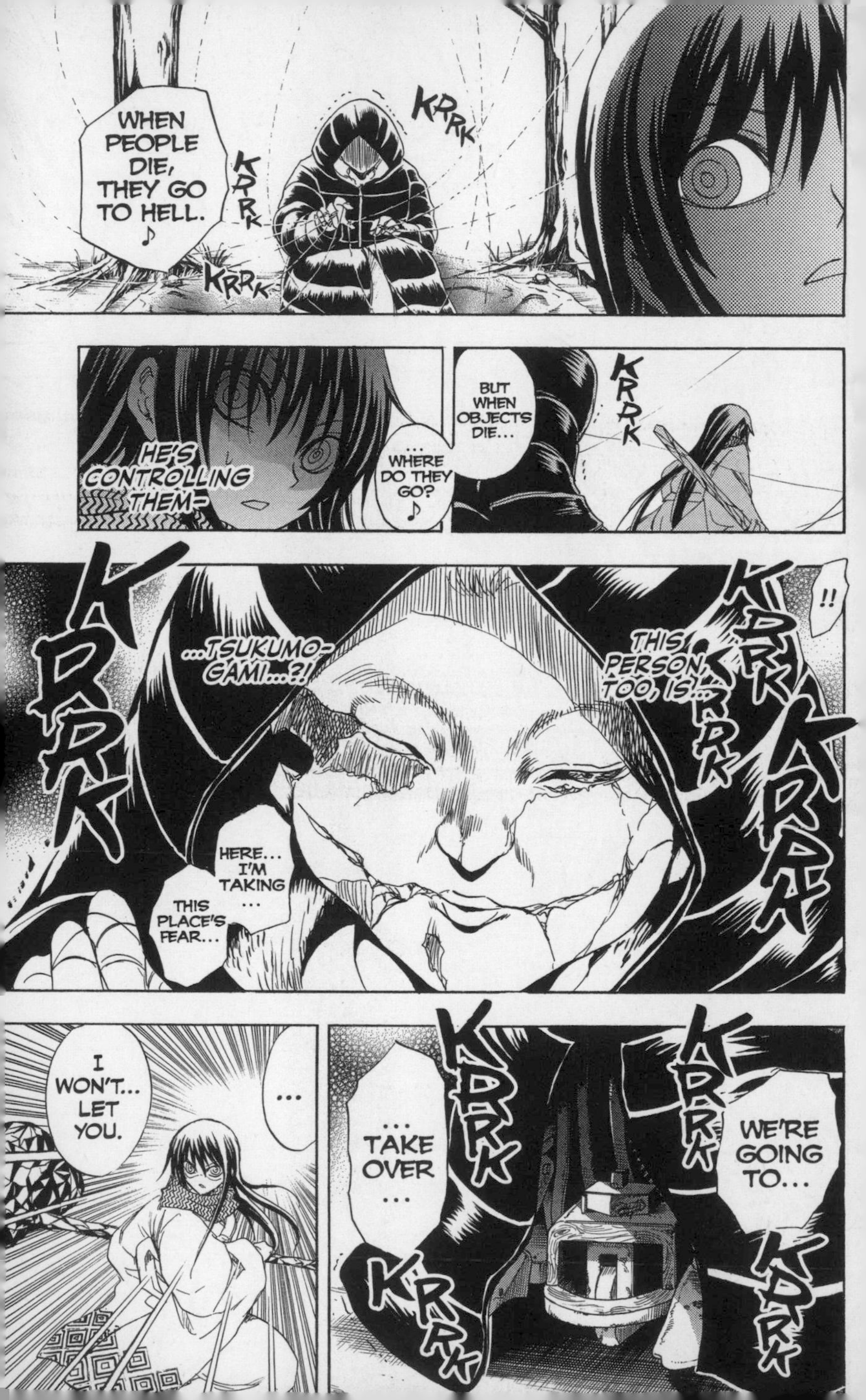
KRRK
WHEN PEOPLE DIE, THEY GO TO HELL. ♪
KRRK
KRRK
KRRK
BUT WHEN OBJECTS DIE...
...WHERE DO THEY GO? ♪
HE'S CONTROLLING THEM-
!!
KRRK
THIS PERSON, TOO, IS...
KRRK
KRRK
KRRK
...TSUKUMO-GAMI...?!
HERE... I'M TAKING...
THIS PLACE'S FEAR...
KRRK
WE'RE GOING TO...
KRRK
KRRK
...TAKE OVER...
KRRK
...
I WON'T... LET YOU.

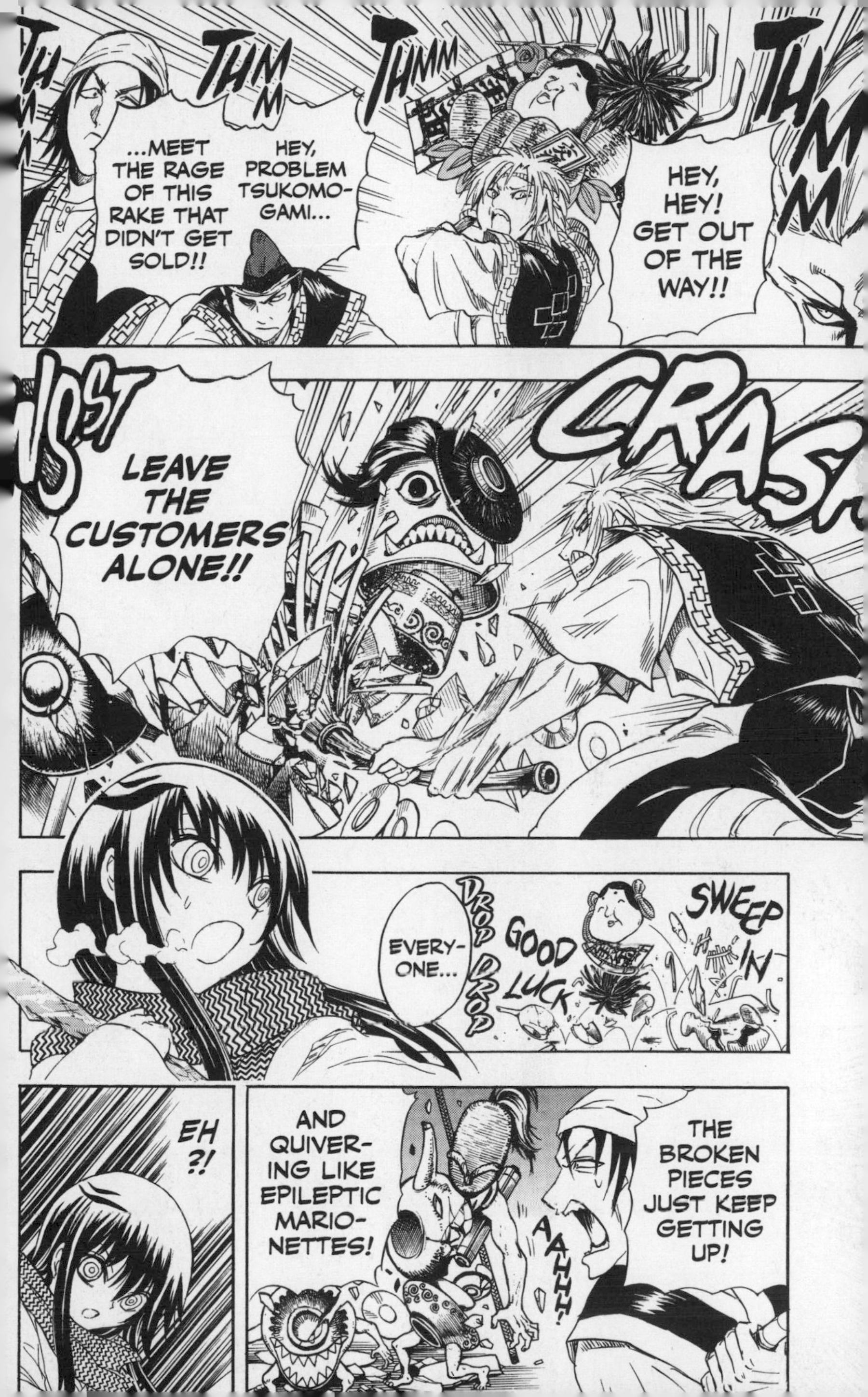
THUMM
HEY, HEY! GET OUT OF THE WAY!!
THMM
HEY, PROBLEM TSUKOMO-GAMI...
THUM M
...MEET THE RAGE OF THIS RAKE THAT DIDN'T GET SOLD!!
LEAVE THE CUSTOMERS ALONE!!
SWEEP IN
GOOD LUCK
DROP DROP
EVERY-ONE...
THE BROKEN PIECES JUST KEEP GETTING UP!
AAHHH!
AND QUIVER-ING LIKE EPILEPTIC MARIO-NETTES!
EH ?!

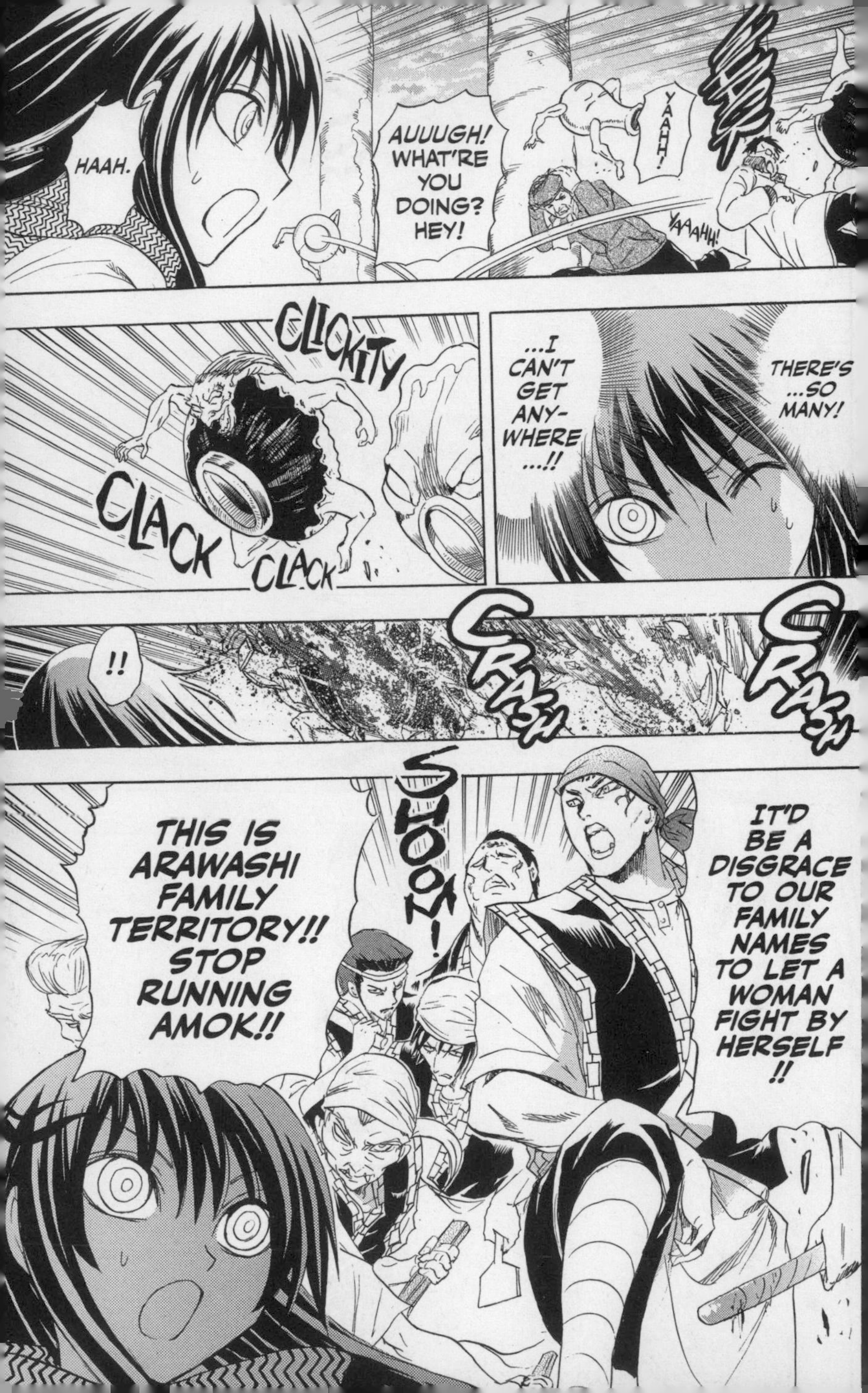
YAAHH!
YAAAHH!
AUUUGH! WHAT'RE YOU DOING? HEY!
HAAH.
THERE'S ...SO MANY!
...I CAN'T GET ANY-WHERE ...!!
CLICKITY
CLACK
CLACK
CRASH
CRASH
!!
IT'D BE A DISGRACE TO OUR FAMILY NAMES TO LET A WOMAN FIGHT BY HERSELF !!
SHOOM!
THIS IS ARAWASHI FAMILY TERRITORY!! STOP RUNNING AMOK!!

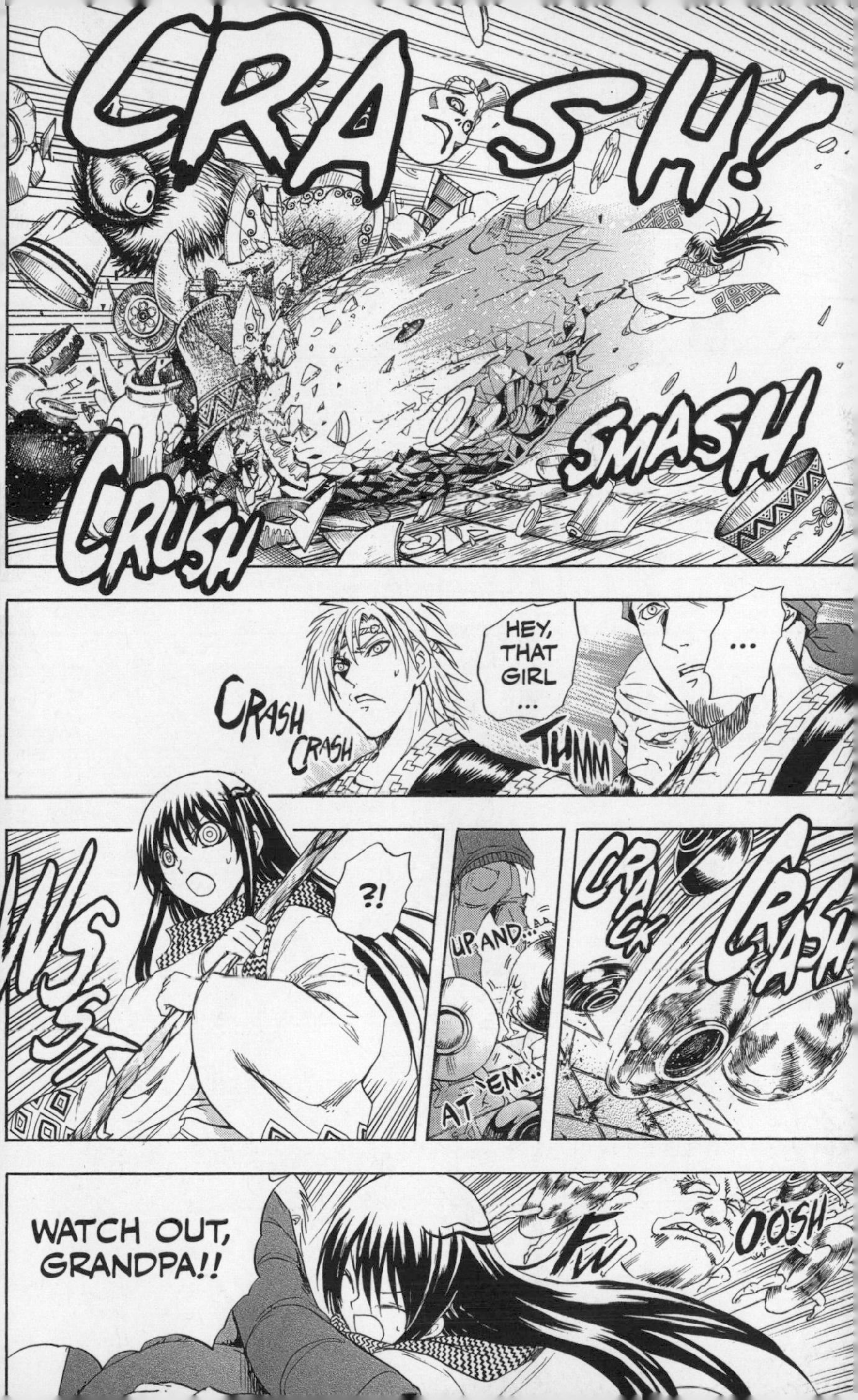
CRASH!
SMASH
CRUSH
...
HEY, THAT GIRL ...
THMM
CRASH CRASH
CRACK
CRASH
UP AND... AT 'EM...
?!
FWOOSH
WATCH OUT, GRANDPA!!

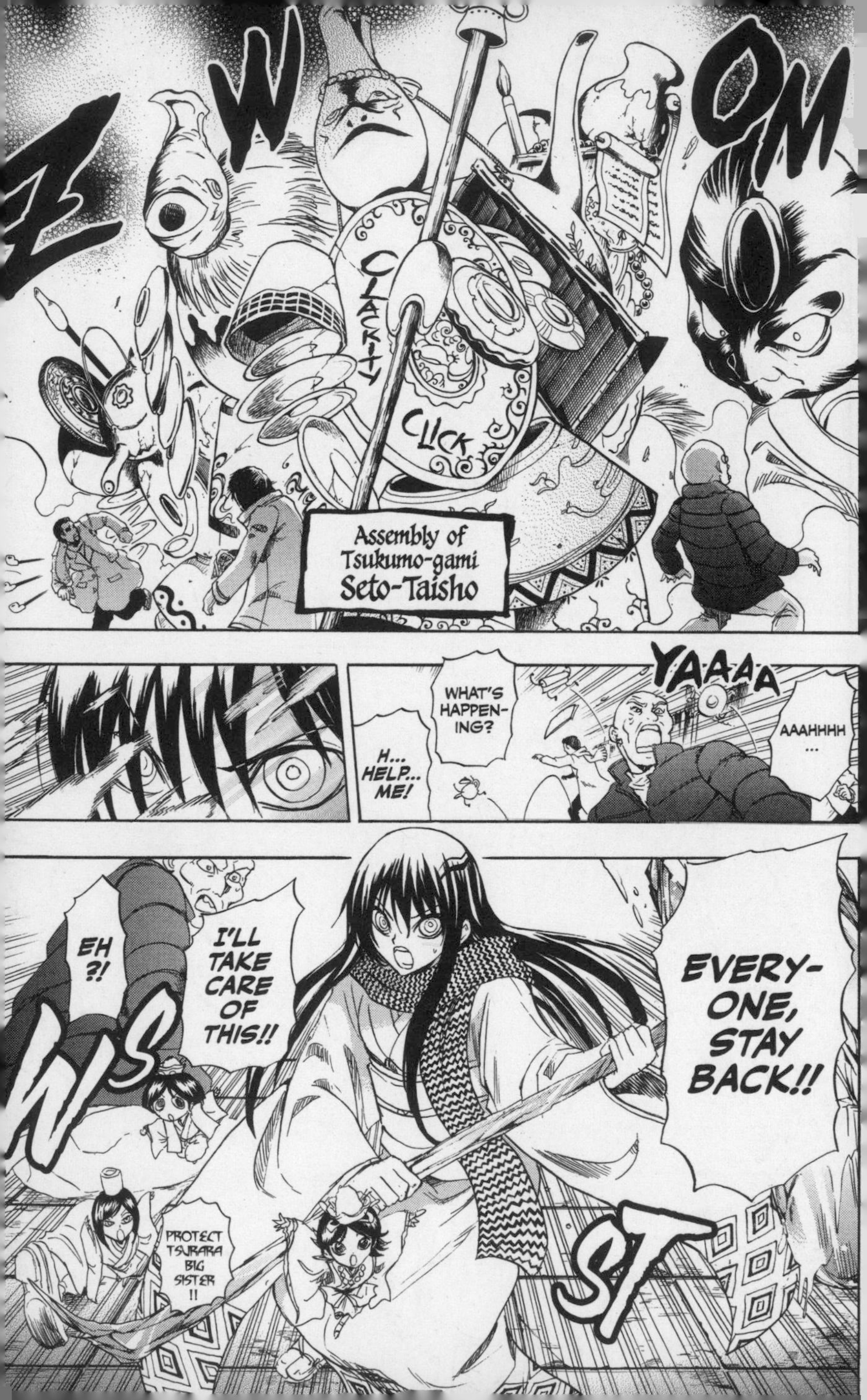
ZWOOM
CLACKITY
CLICK
Assembly of Tsukumo-gami Seto-Taisho
YAAAA
AAAHHHH ...
WHAT'S HAPPEN-ING?
H... HELP... ME!
EVERY-ONE, STAY BACK!!
I'LL TAKE CARE OF THIS!!
EH ?!
PROTECT TSURARA BIG SISTER !!

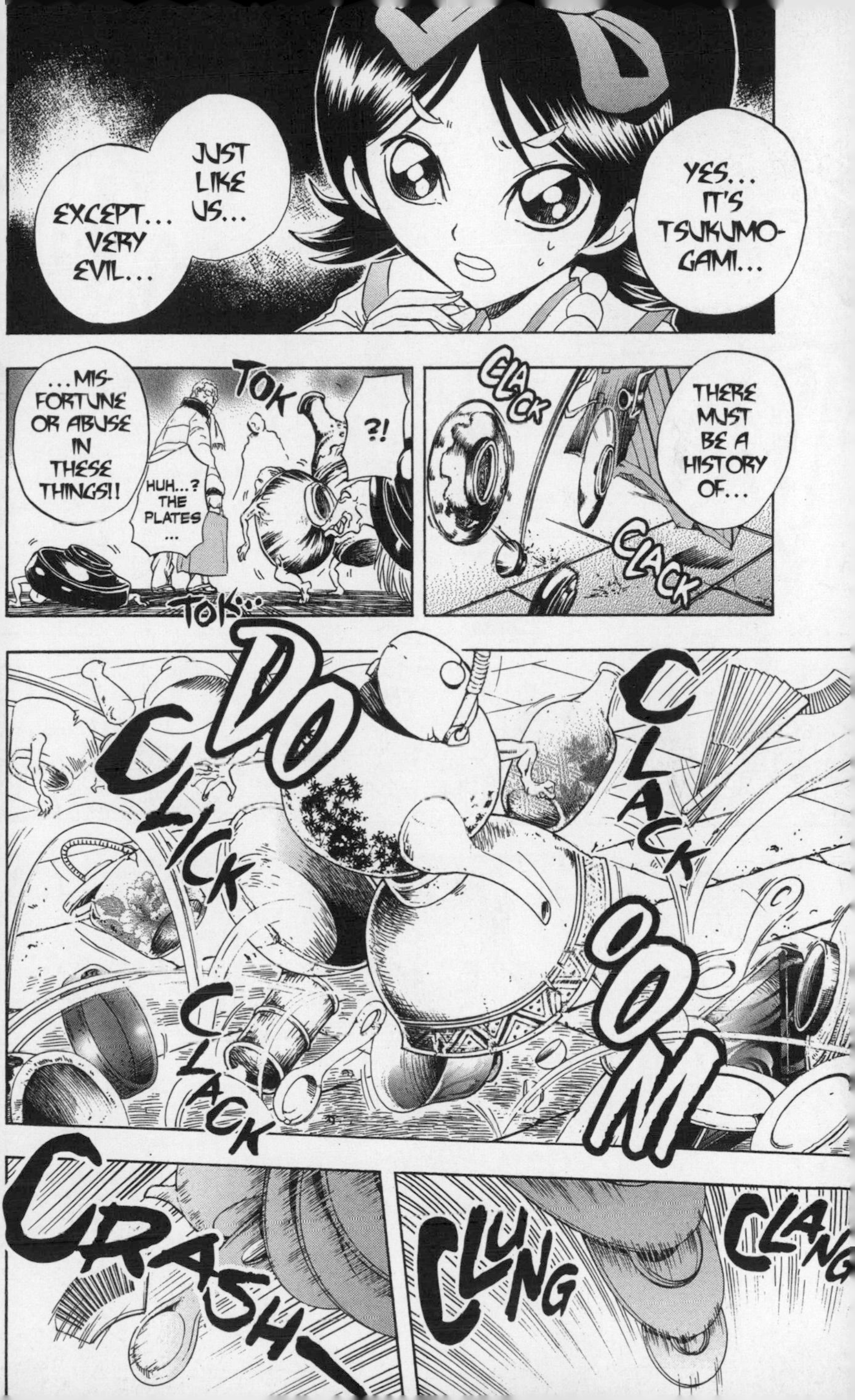
YES... IT'S TSUKUMO-GAMI...
JUST LIKE US...
EXCEPT... VERY EVIL...
CLACK
THERE MUST BE A HISTORY OF...
CLACK
TOK
?!
...MIS-FORTUNE OR ABUSE IN THESE THINGS!!
HUH...? THE PLATES ...
TOK...
DOOOM
CLACK
CLICK
CLACK
CLANG
CLUNG
CRASH

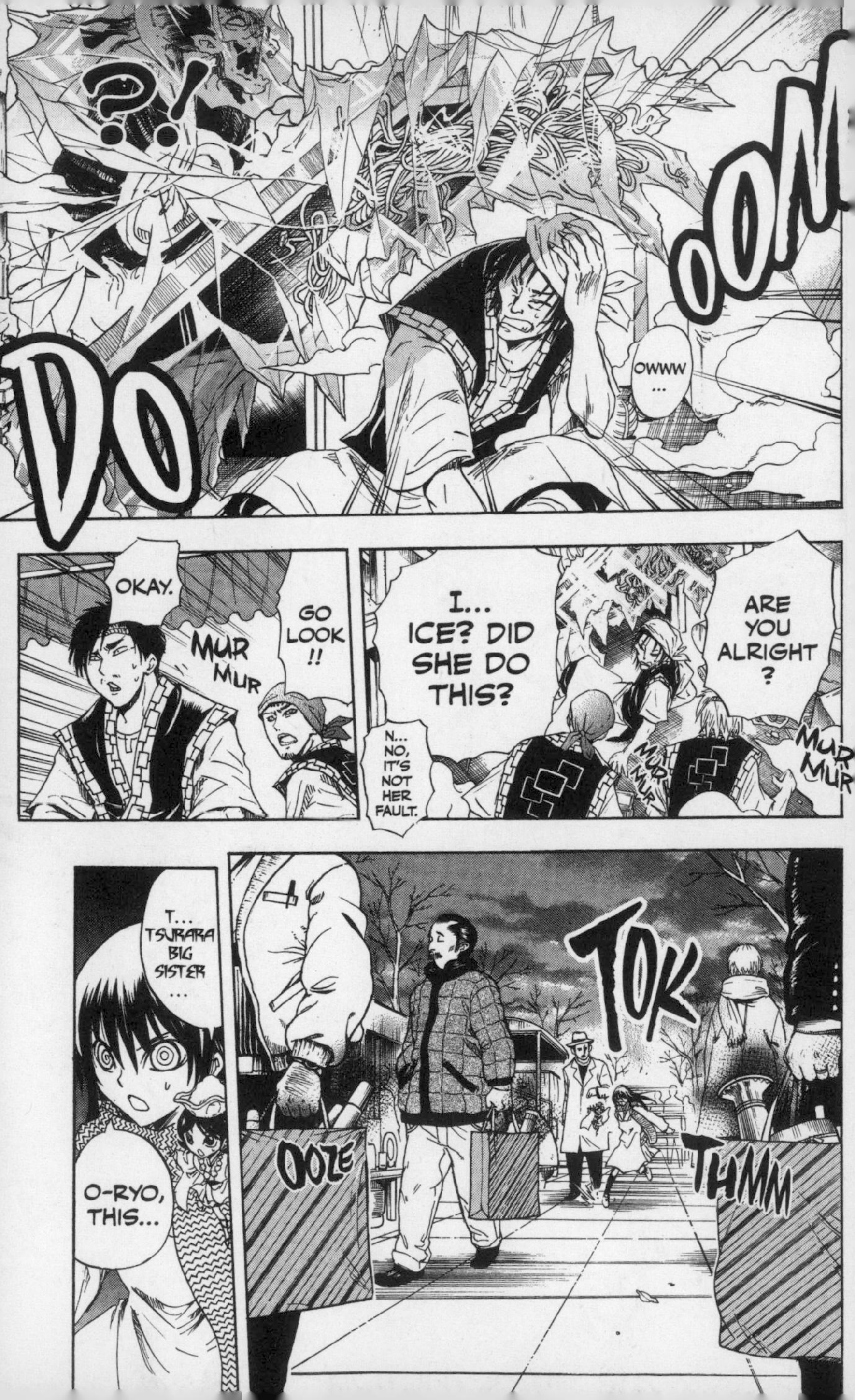
?!
OWWW ...
DO
OON
ARE YOU ALRIGHT ?
MUR MUR
MUR MUR
I... ICE? DID SHE DO THIS?
N... NO, IT'S NOT HER FAULT.
GO LOOK !!
MUR MUR
OKAY.
TOK
THMM
OOZE
T... TSURARA BIG SISTER ...
O-RYO, THIS...

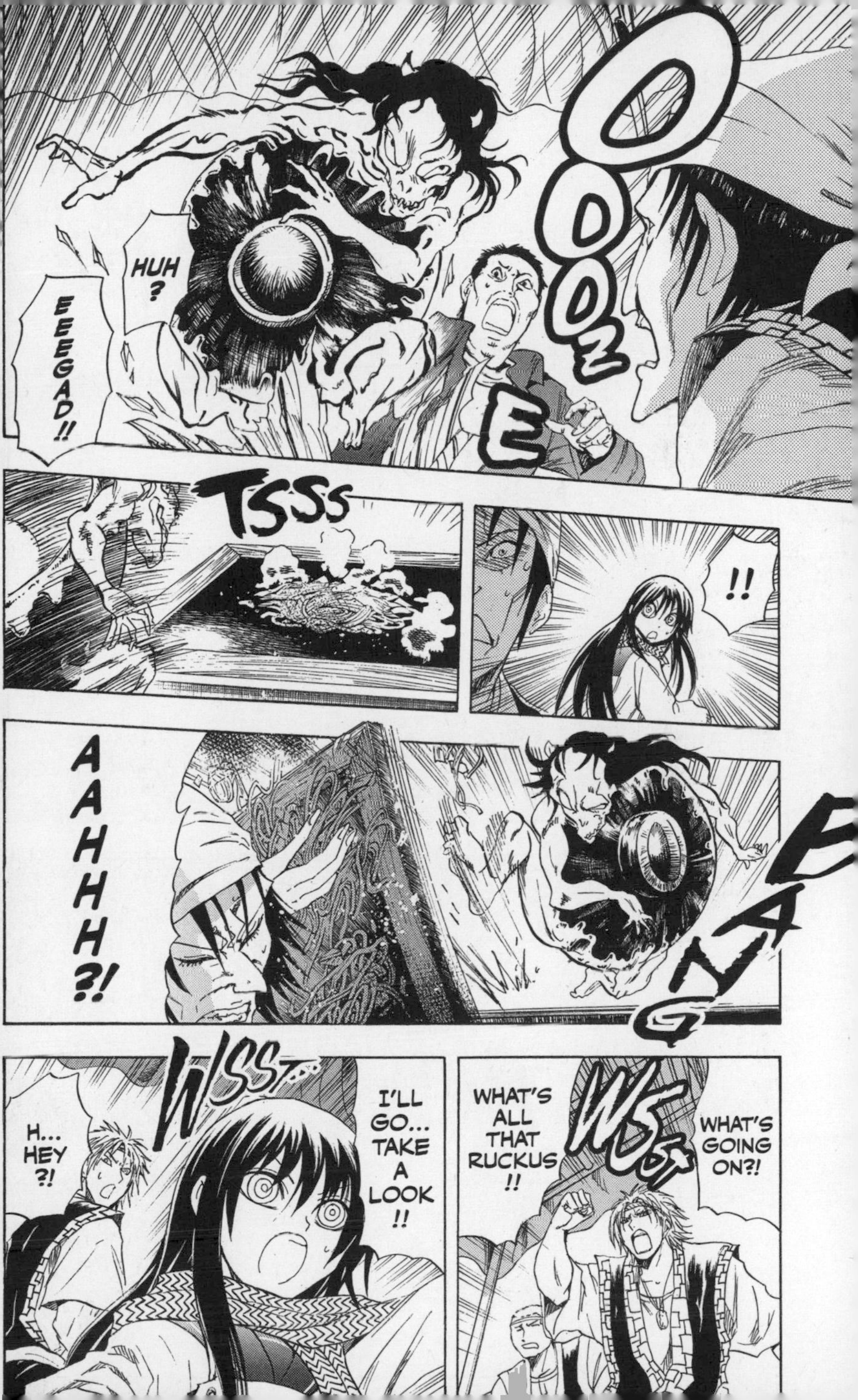
OOOZE
HUH?
EEEGAD!!
!!
TSSS
BANG
AAHHHH?!
WHAT'S GOING ON?!
WS
WHAT'S ALL THAT RUCKUS!!
I'LL GO... TAKE A LOOK!!
WSST...
H... HEY?!

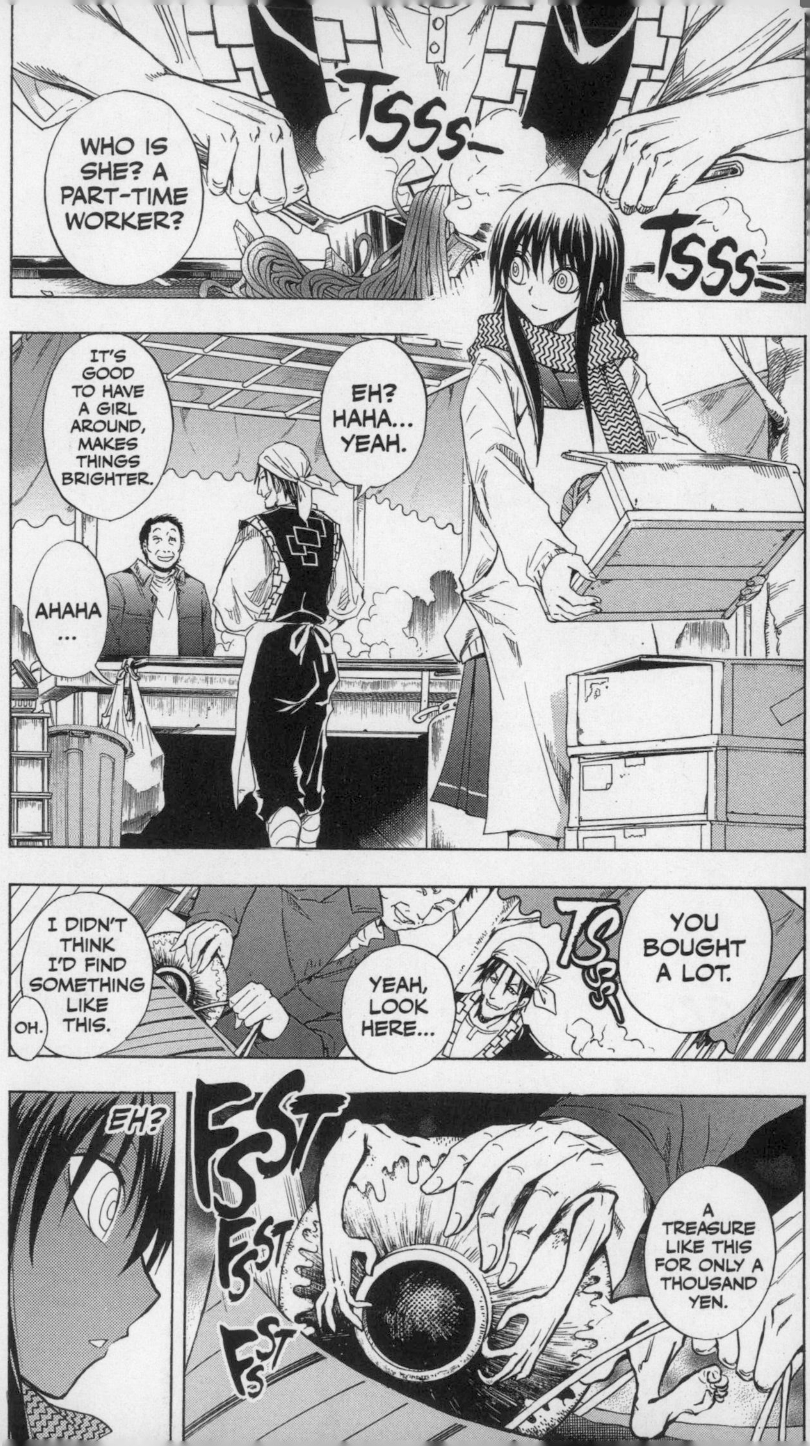
TSSS-
TSSS-
WHO IS SHE? A PART-TIME WORKER?
IT'S GOOD TO HAVE A GIRL AROUND, MAKES THINGS BRIGHTER.
EH? HAHA... YEAH.
AHAHA...
YOU BOUGHT A LOT.
TSSS
YEAH, LOOK HERE...
I DIDN'T THINK I'D FIND SOMETHING LIKE THIS.
OH.
A TREASURE LIKE THIS FOR ONLY A THOUSAND YEN.
FSST
FSST
FSST
EH?

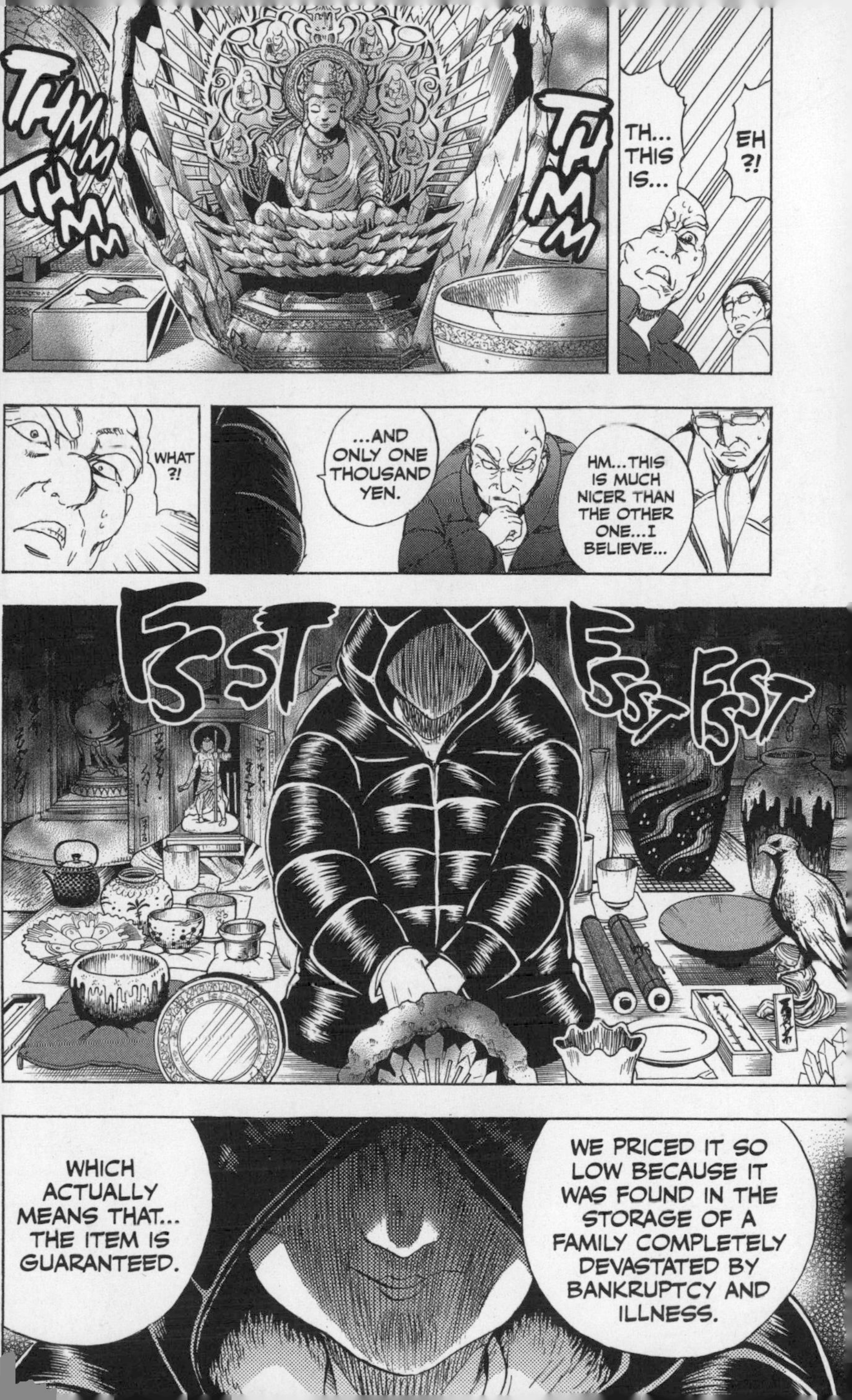
EH ?!
TH... THIS IS...
THMM
THMM THMM
HM...THIS IS MUCH NICER THAN THE OTHER ONE...I BELIEVE...
...AND ONLY ONE THOUSAND YEN.
WHAT ?!
FSST FSST
FSST
WE PRICED IT SO LOW BECAUSE IT WAS FOUND IN THE STORAGE OF A FAMILY COMPLETELY DEVASTATED BY BANKRUPTCY AND ILLNESS.
WHICH ACTUALLY MEANS THAT... THE ITEM IS GUARANTEED.

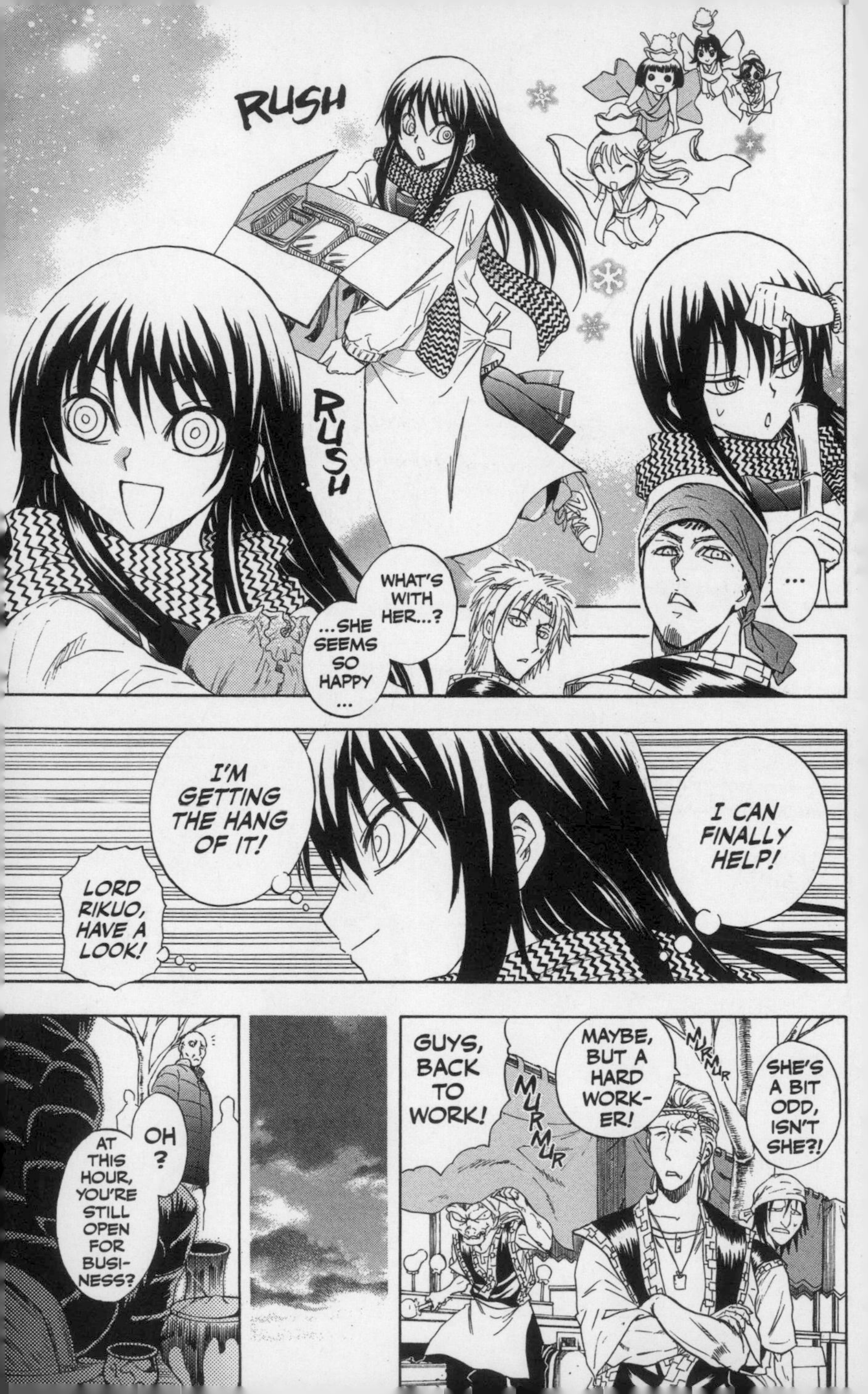
RUSH
RUSH
...
WHAT'S WITH HER...?
...SHE SEEMS SO HAPPY ...
I CAN FINALLY HELP!
I'M GETTING THE HANG OF IT!
LORD RIKUO, HAVE A LOOK!
SHE'S A BIT ODD, ISN'T SHE?!
MURMUR
MAYBE, BUT A HARD WORK-ER!
MURMUR
GUYS, BACK TO WORK!
OH?
AT THIS HOUR, YOU'RE STILL OPEN FOR BUSI-NESS?

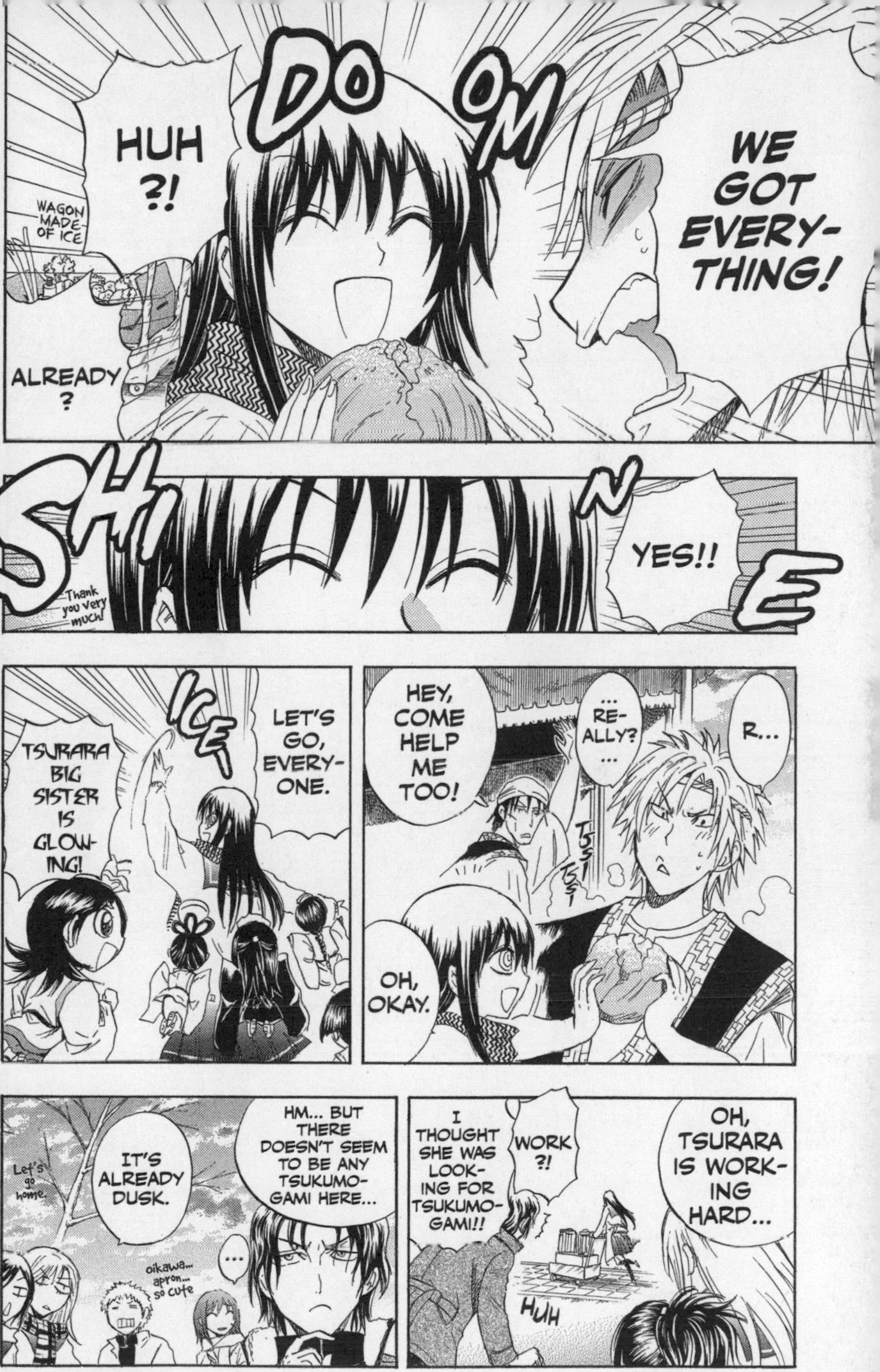
WE GOT EVERYTHING!
DOOM
HUH ?!
WAGON MADE OF ICE
ALREADY ?
YES!!
SHIIN E
Thank you very much!
R...
...REALLY? ...
HEY, COME HELP ME TOO!
TSI TSI
OH, OKAY.
LET'S GO, EVERYONE.
ICE
TSURARA BIG SISTER IS GLOWING!
OH, TSURARA IS WORKING HARD...
WORK ?!
I THOUGHT SHE WAS LOOKING FOR TSUKUMOGAMI!!
HUH
HM... BUT THERE DOESN'T SEEM TO BE ANY TSUKUMOGAMI HERE...
IT'S ALREADY DUSK.
Let's go home.
...
oikawa... apron... so cute

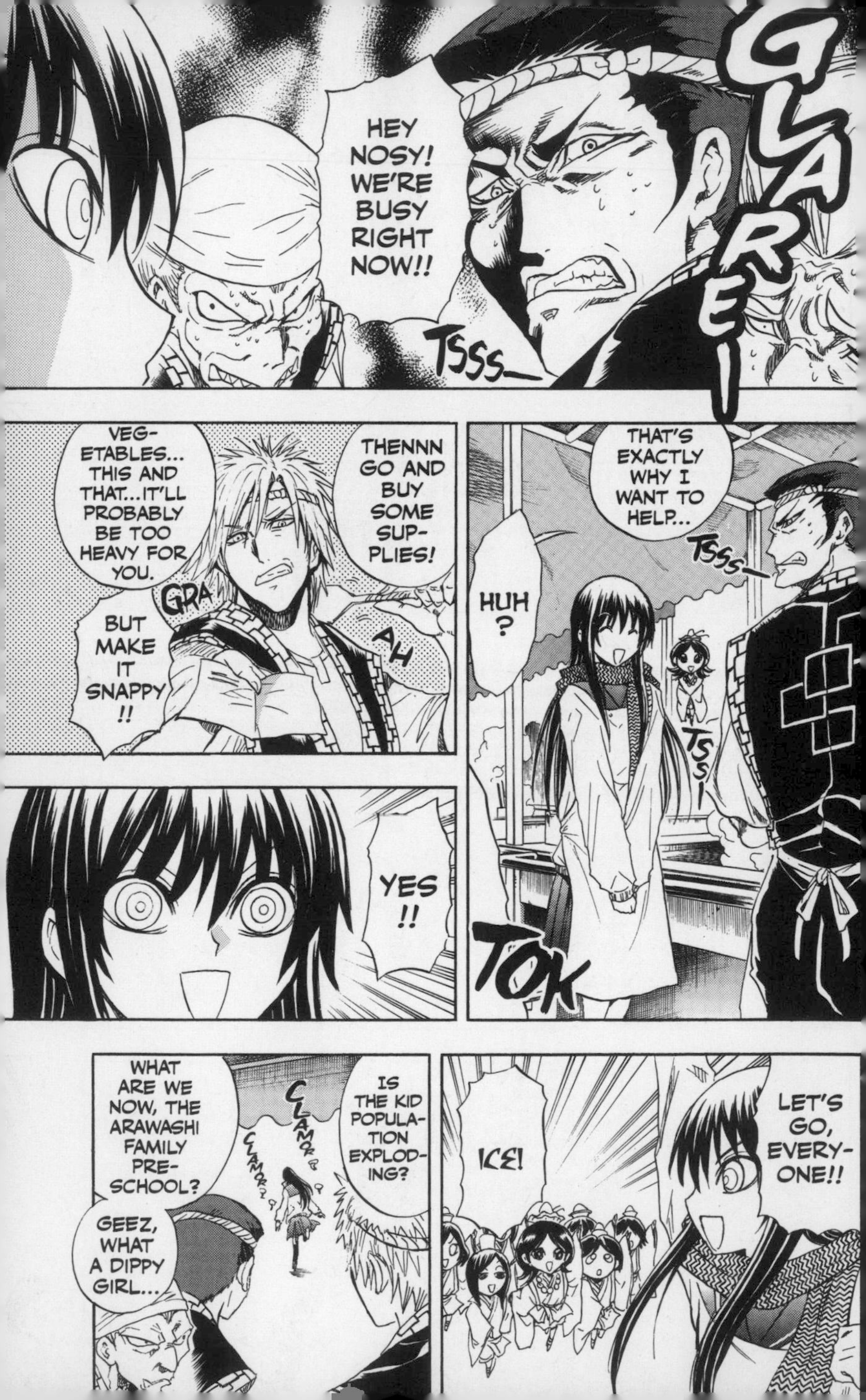
GLARE!
HEY NOSY! WE'RE BUSY RIGHT NOW!!
TSSS
THAT'S EXACTLY WHY I WANT TO HELP...
TSSS
HUH?
TSS!
TOK
THENNN GO AND BUY SOME SUP-PLIES!
VEG-ETABLES... THIS AND THAT...IT'LL PROBABLY BE TOO HEAVY FOR YOU.
GRA
AH
BUT MAKE IT SNAPPY!!
YES!!
LET'S GO, EVERY-ONE!!
ICE!
IS THE KID POPULA-TION EXPLOD-ING?
CLAMOR
CLAMOR
WHAT ARE WE NOW, THE ARAWASHI FAMILY PRE-SCHOOL?
GEEZ, WHAT A DIPPY GIRL...

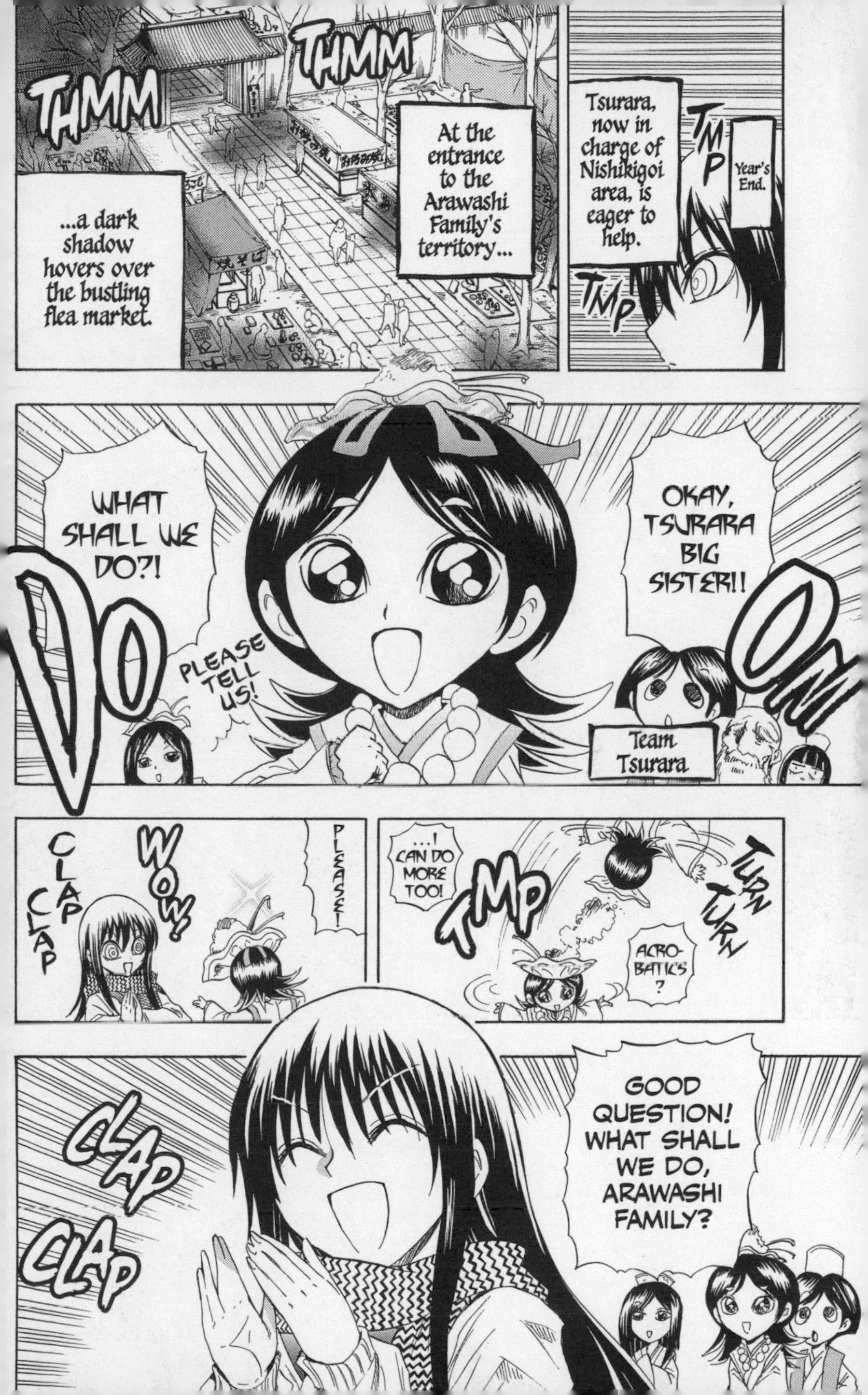
Year's End.
Tsurara, now in charge of Nishikigoi area, is eager to help.
TMP
TMP
THMM
THMM
At the entrance to the Arawashi Family's territory...
...a dark shadow hovers over the bustling flea market.
OKAY, TSURARA BIG SISTER!!
OM
WHAT SHALL WE DO?!
DO
PLEASE TELL US!
Team Tsurara
TURN
TURN
...I CAN DO MORE TOO!
TMP
ACRO-BATIC'S?
PLEASE!
WOW!
CLAP
CLAP
GOOD QUESTION! WHAT SHALL WE DO, ARAWASHI FAMILY?
CLAP
CLAP

Act 136: Tsurara and the Arawashi Clan

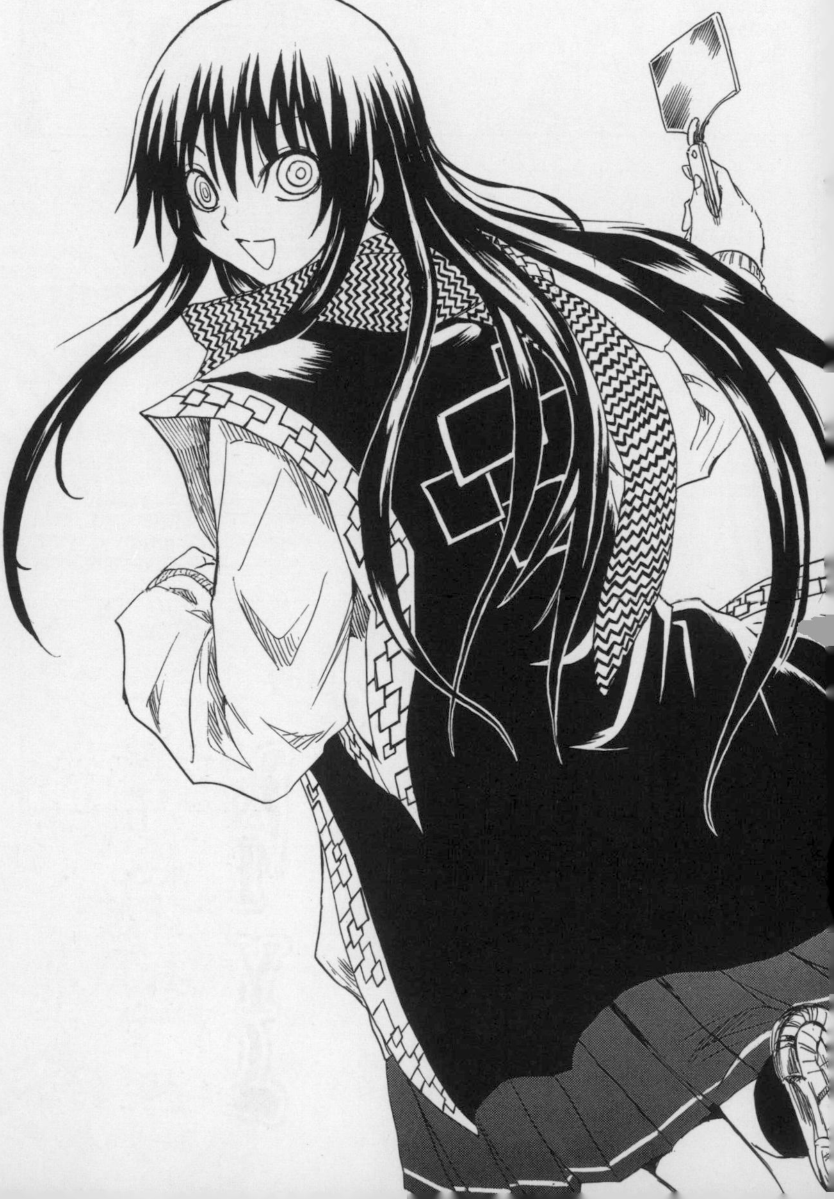

NURA: RISE OF THE YOKAI CLAN

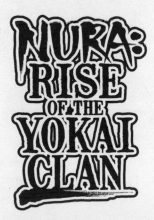

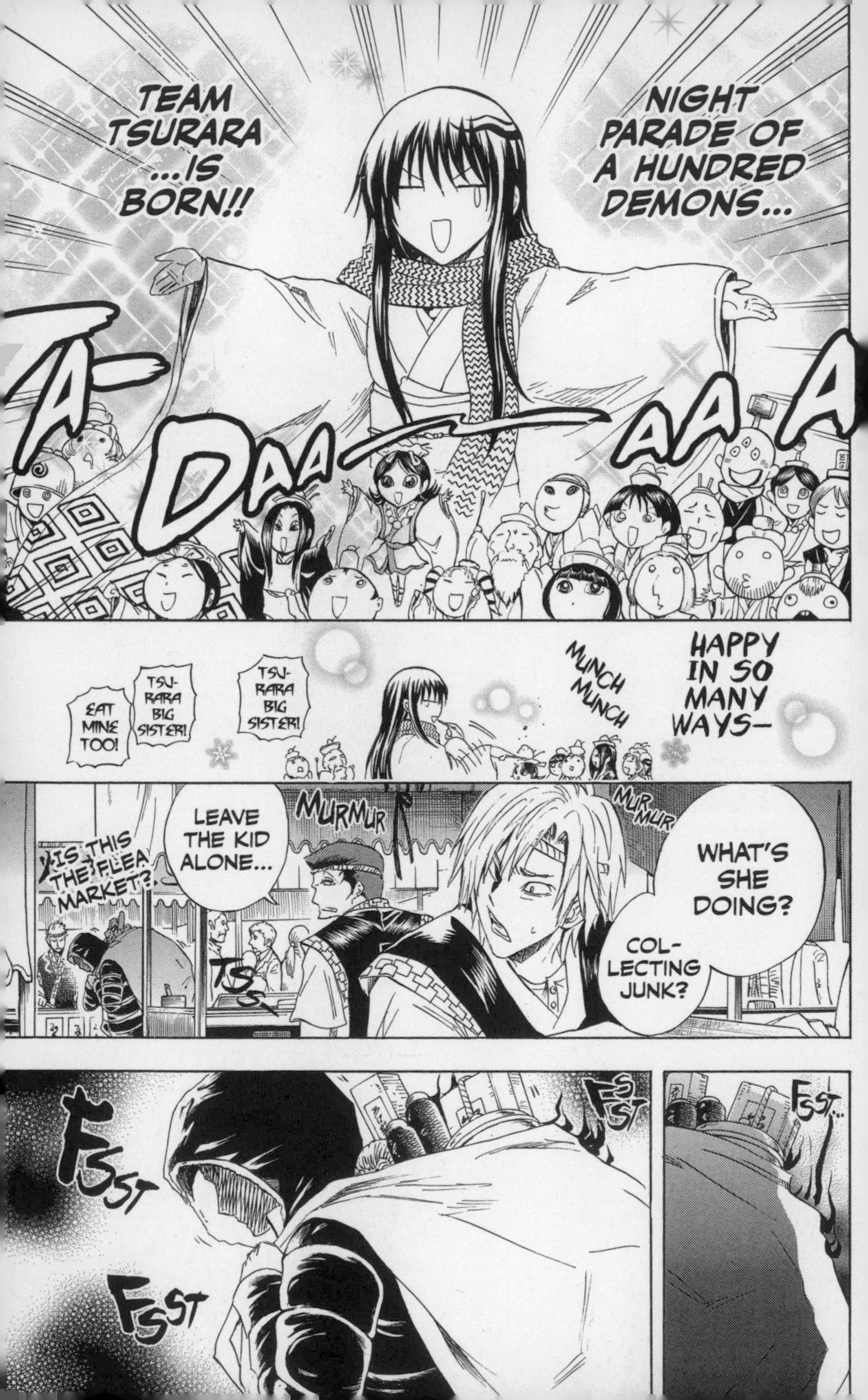
NIGHT PARADE OF A HUNDRED DEMONS...
TEAM TSURARA ...IS BORN!!
TA-DAA—AAA
HAPPY IN SO MANY WAYS—
MUNCH MUNCH
TSU-RARA BIG SISTER!
TSU-RARA BIG SISTER!
EAT MINE TOO!
MUR MUR
WHAT'S SHE DOING?
COL-LECTING JUNK?
MURMUR
LEAVE THE KID ALONE...
IS THIS THE FLEA MARKET?
TSSS
FSST...
FSST
FSST
FSST

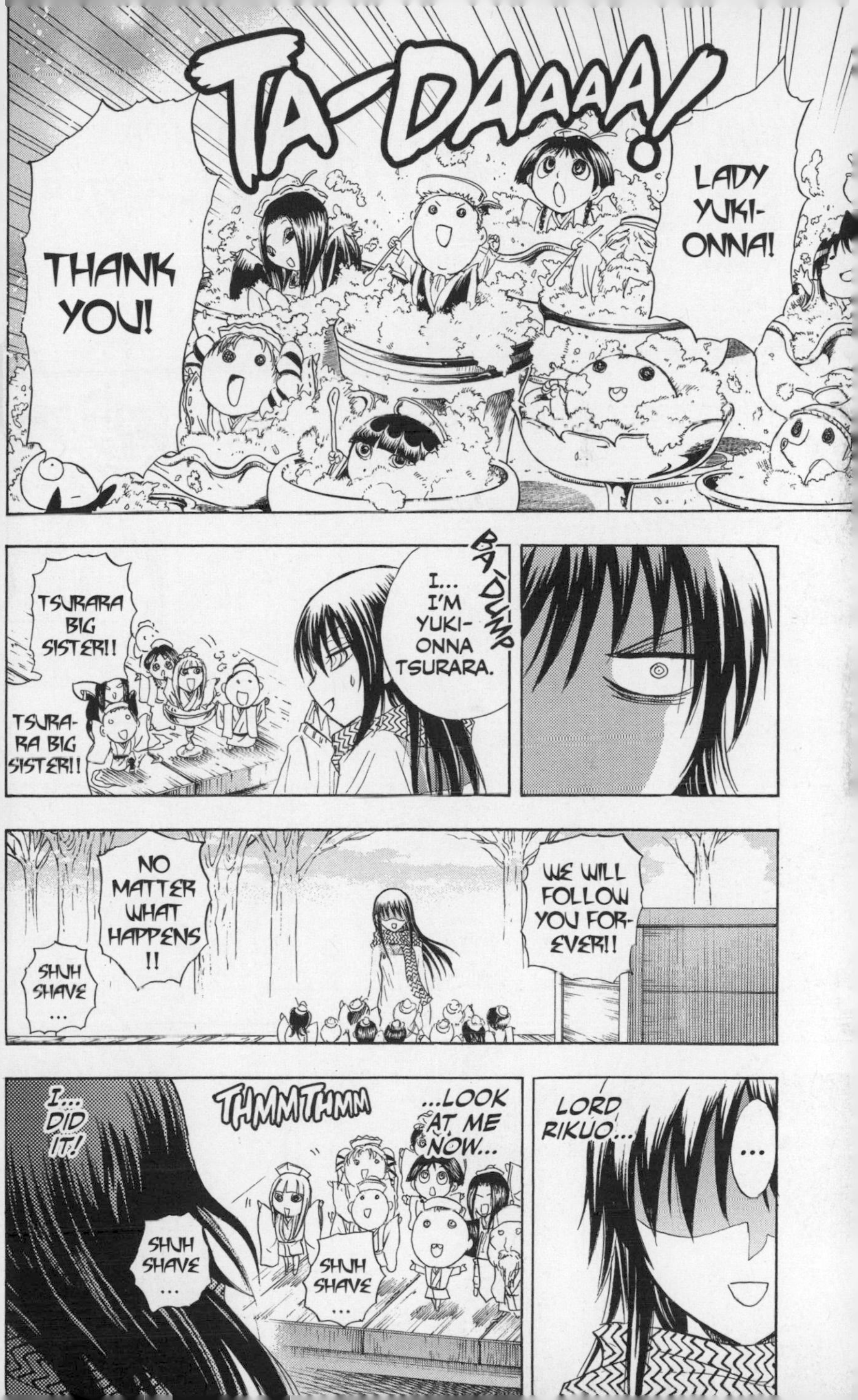
TA-DAAAA!
LADY YUKI-ONNA!
THANK YOU!
BA-DUMP
I... I'M YUKI-ONNA TSURARA.
TSURARA BIG SISTER!!
TSURA-RA BIG SISTER!!
WE WILL FOLLOW YOU FOR-EVER!!
NO MATTER WHAT HAPPENS!!
SHUH SHAVE...
LORD RIKUO...
...
...LOOK AT ME NOW...
THMMTHMM
I... DID IT!
SHUH SHAVE...
SHUH SHAVE...

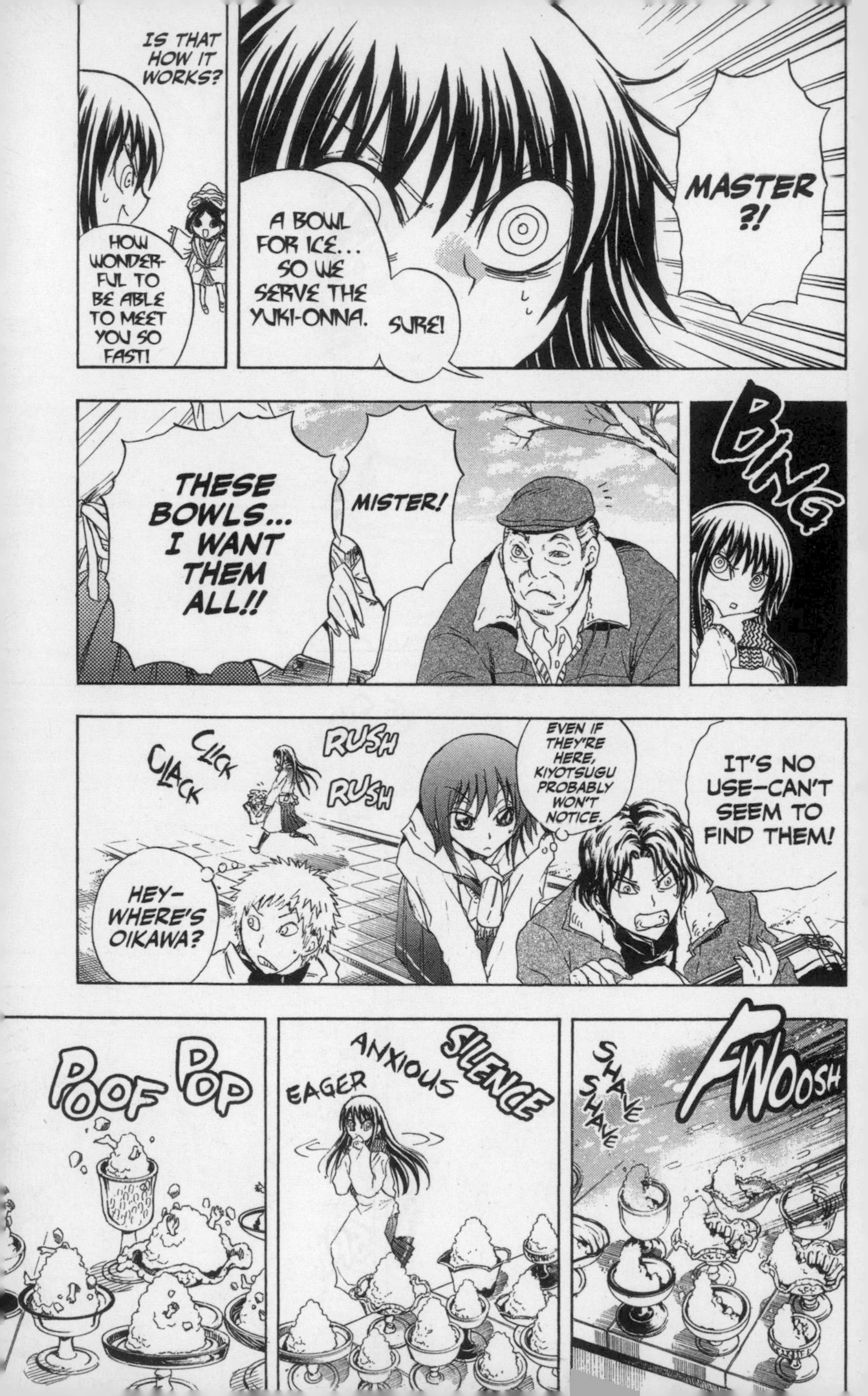
MASTER ?!
A BOWL FOR ICE... SO WE SERVE THE YUKI-ONNA.
SURE!
IS THAT HOW IT WORKS?
HOW WONDERFUL TO BE ABLE TO MEET YOU SO FAST!
BING
MISTER!
THESE BOWLS... I WANT THEM ALL!!
IT'S NO USE—CAN'T SEEM TO FIND THEM!
EVEN IF THEY'RE HERE, KIYOTSUGU PROBABLY WON'T NOTICE.
RUSH
RUSH
CLICK
CLACK
HEY—WHERE'S OIKAWA?
FWOOSH
SHAVE
SHAVE
SHAVE
SILENCE
ANXIOUS
EAGER
POP
POOF

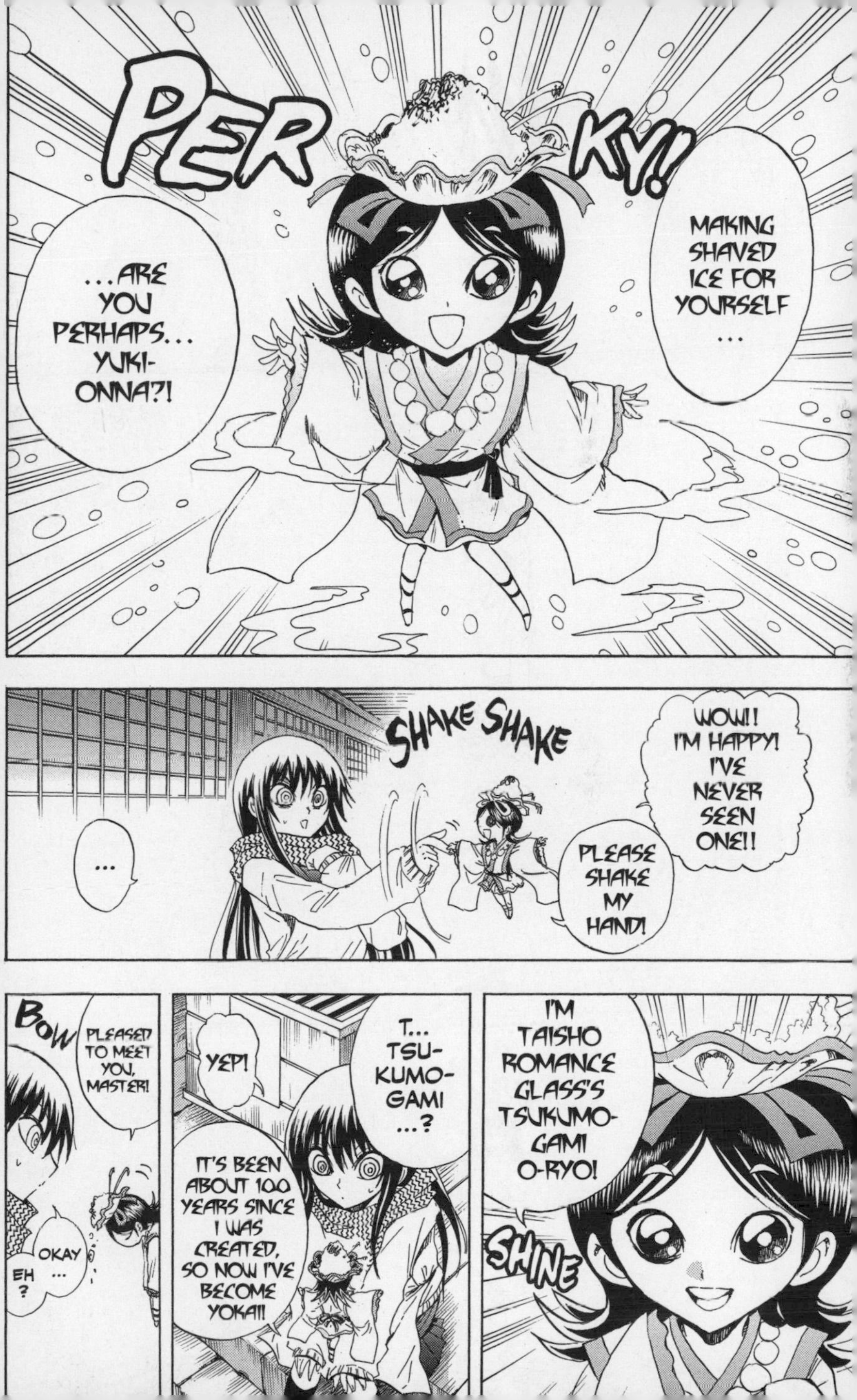
PERKY!
MAKING SHAVED ICE FOR YOURSELF ...
...ARE YOU PERHAPS... YUKI-ONNA?!
WOW!! I'M HAPPY! I'VE NEVER SEEN ONE!!
PLEASE SHAKE MY HAND!
SHAKE SHAKE
...
I'M TAISHO ROMANCE GLASS'S TSUKUMO-GAMI O-RYO!
SHINE
T... TSU-KUMO-GAMI ...?
YEP!
IT'S BEEN ABOUT 100 YEARS SINCE I WAS CREATED, SO NOW I'VE BECOME YOKAI!!
BOW
PLEASED TO MEET YOU, MASTER!
OKAY ...
EH ?

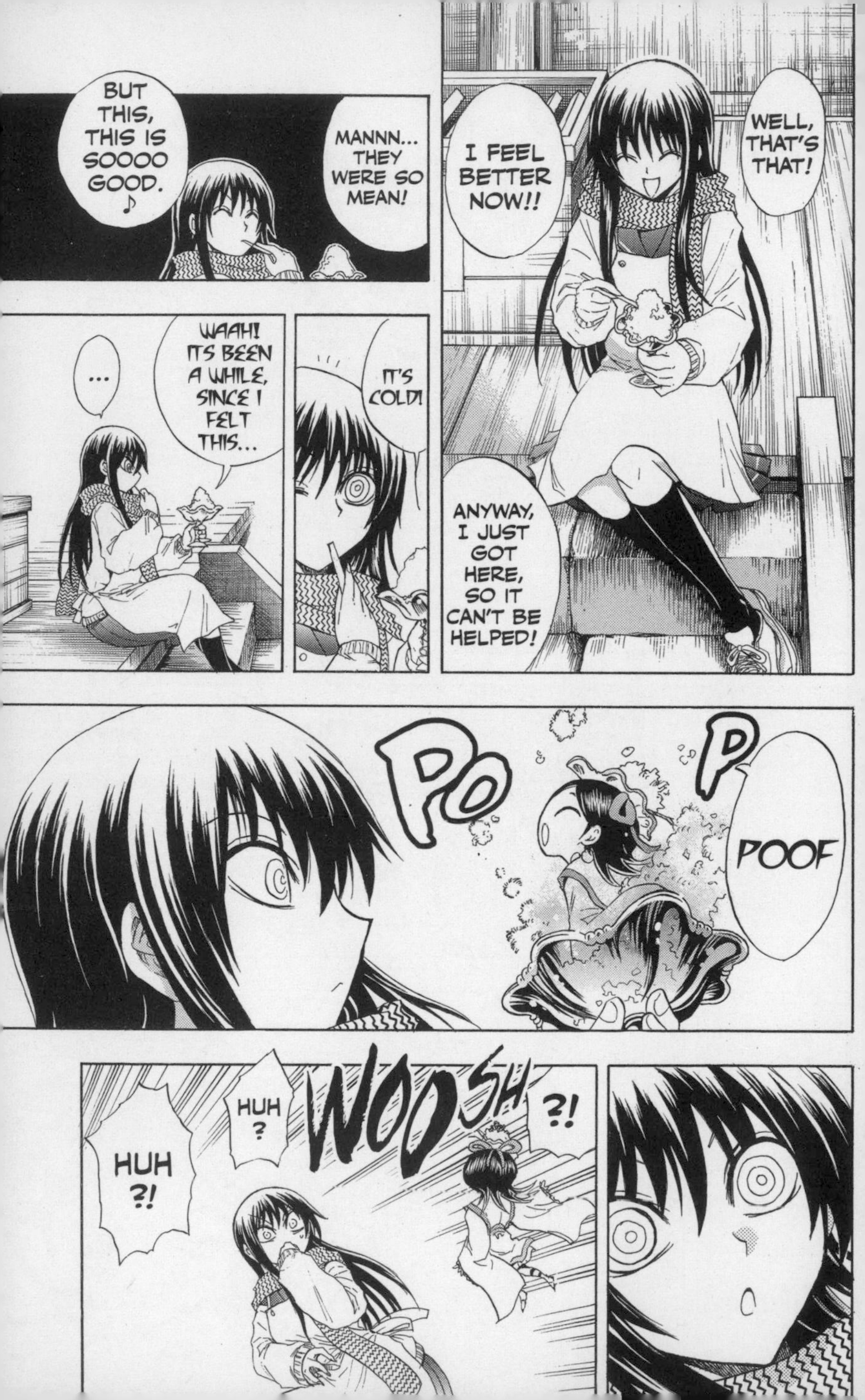
WELL, THAT'S THAT!
I FEEL BETTER NOW!!
ANYWAY, I JUST GOT HERE, SO IT CAN'T BE HELPED!
MANNN... THEY WERE SO MEAN!
BUT THIS, THIS IS SOOOO GOOD. ♪
IT'S COLD!
WAAH! IT'S BEEN A WHILE, SINCE I FELT THIS...
...
PO
P
POOF
?!
WOOSH
HUH ?
HUH ?!

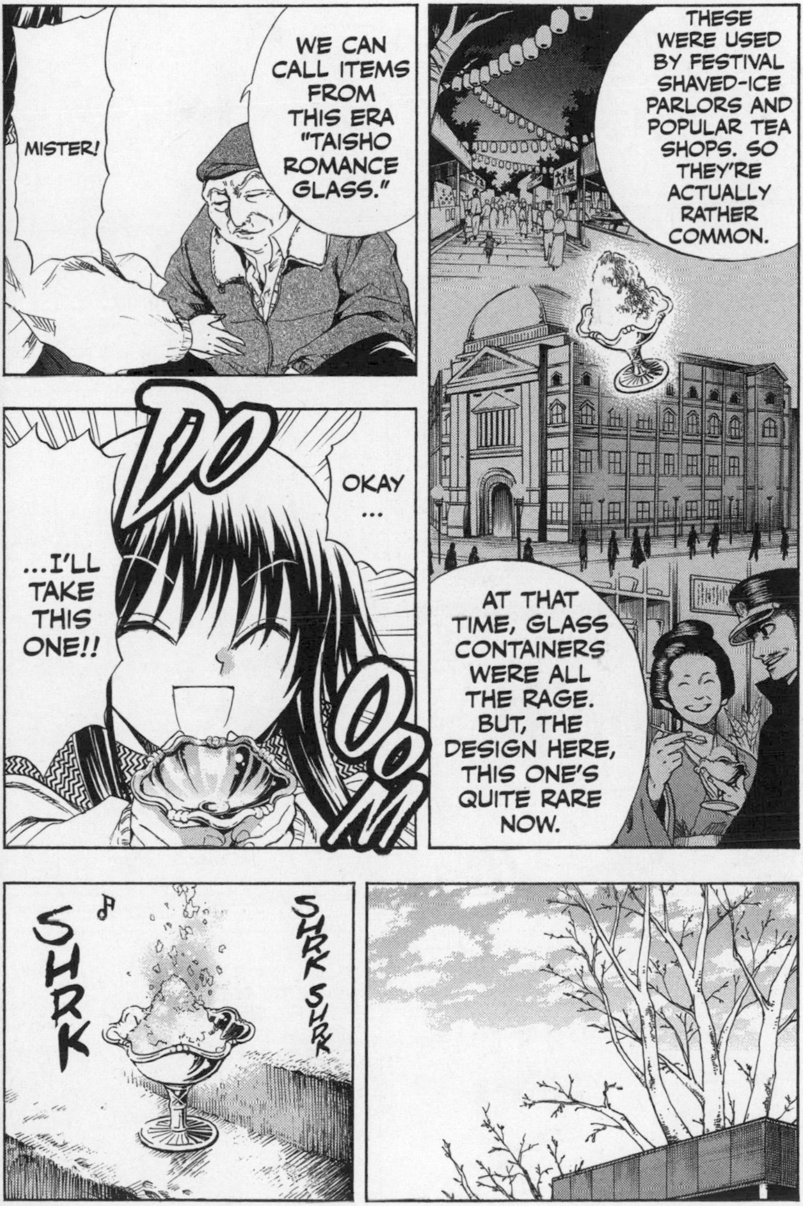
MISTER!
WE CAN CALL ITEMS FROM THIS ERA "TAISHO ROMANCE GLASS."
THESE WERE USED BY FESTIVAL SHAVED-ICE PARLORS AND POPULAR TEA SHOPS. SO THEY'RE ACTUALLY RATHER COMMON.
AT THAT TIME, GLASS CONTAINERS WERE ALL THE RAGE. BUT, THE DESIGN HERE, THIS ONE'S QUITE RARE NOW.
DOOOM
OKAY ...
...I'LL TAKE THIS ONE!!
SHRK
SHRK SHRK

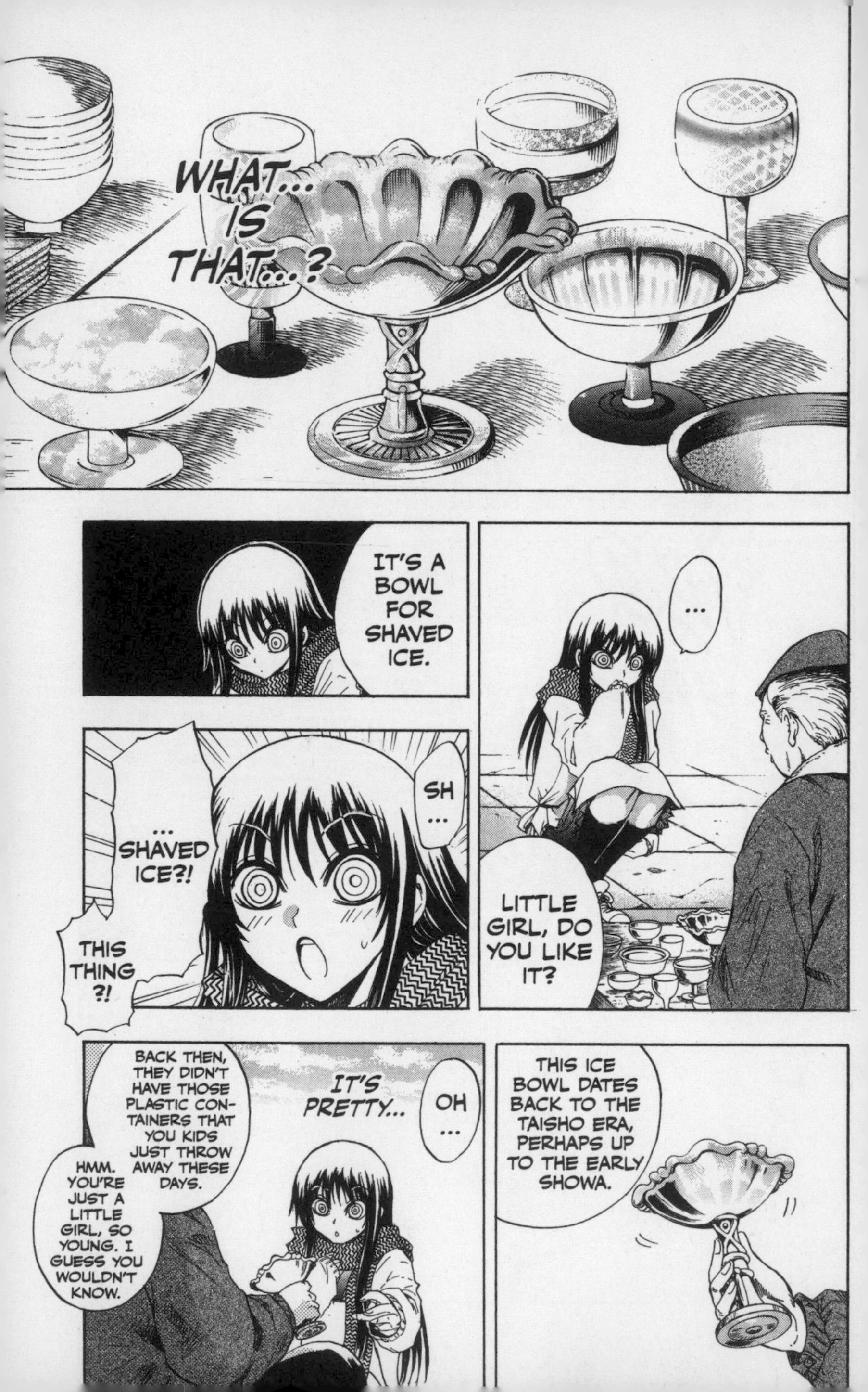
WHAT... IS THAT...?
...
LITTLE GIRL, DO YOU LIKE IT?
IT'S A BOWL FOR SHAVED ICE.
SH...
...SHAVED ICE?!
THIS THING?!
THIS ICE BOWL DATES BACK TO THE TAISHO ERA, PERHAPS UP TO THE EARLY SHOWA.
OH...
IT'S PRETTY...
BACK THEN, THEY DIDN'T HAVE THOSE PLASTIC CONTAINERS THAT YOU KIDS JUST THROW AWAY THESE DAYS.
HMM. YOU'RE JUST A LITTLE GIRL, SO YOUNG. I GUESS YOU WOULDN'T KNOW.

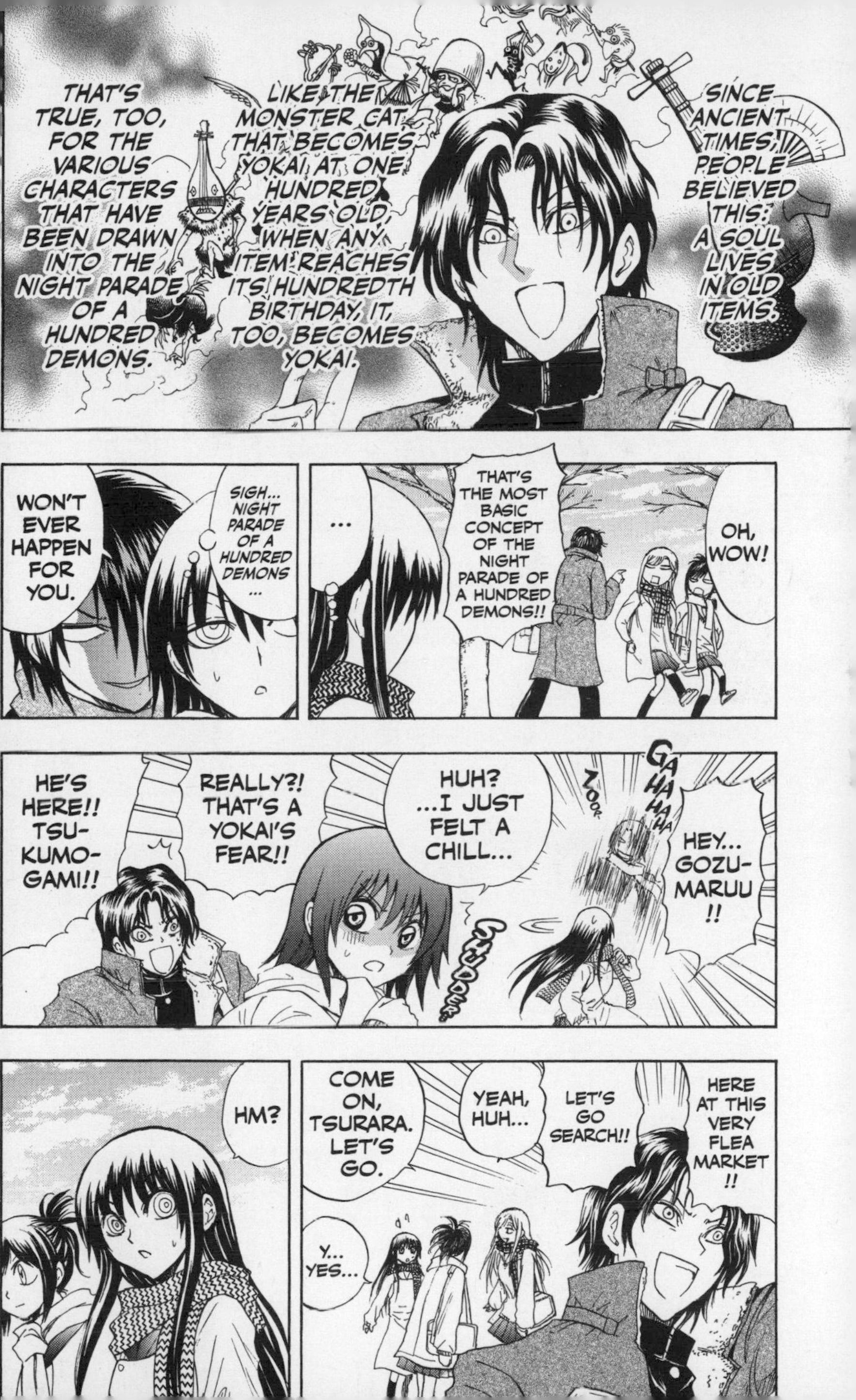
SINCE ANCIENT TIMES, PEOPLE BELIEVED THIS: A SOUL LIVES IN OLD ITEMS.
LIKE THE MONSTER CAT THAT BECOMES YOKAI AT ONE HUNDRED YEARS OLD, WHEN ANY ITEM REACHES ITS HUNDREDTH BIRTHDAY, IT, TOO, BECOMES YOKAI.
THAT'S TRUE, TOO, FOR THE VARIOUS CHARACTERS THAT HAVE BEEN DRAWN INTO THE NIGHT PARADE OF A HUNDRED DEMONS.
OH, WOW!
THAT'S THE MOST BASIC CONCEPT OF THE NIGHT PARADE OF A HUNDRED DEMONS!!
...
SIGH... NIGHT PARADE OF A HUNDRED DEMONS ...
WON'T EVER HAPPEN FOR YOU.
GAHAHAHAHA
HEY... GOZUMARUU !!
HUH? ...I JUST FELT A CHILL...
SHUDDER
REALLY?! THAT'S A YOKAI'S FEAR!!
HE'S HERE!! TSUKUMOGAMI!!
HERE AT THIS VERY FLEA MARKET !!
LET'S GO SEARCH!!
YEAH, HUH...
COME ON, TSURARA. LET'S GO.
Y... YES...
HM?

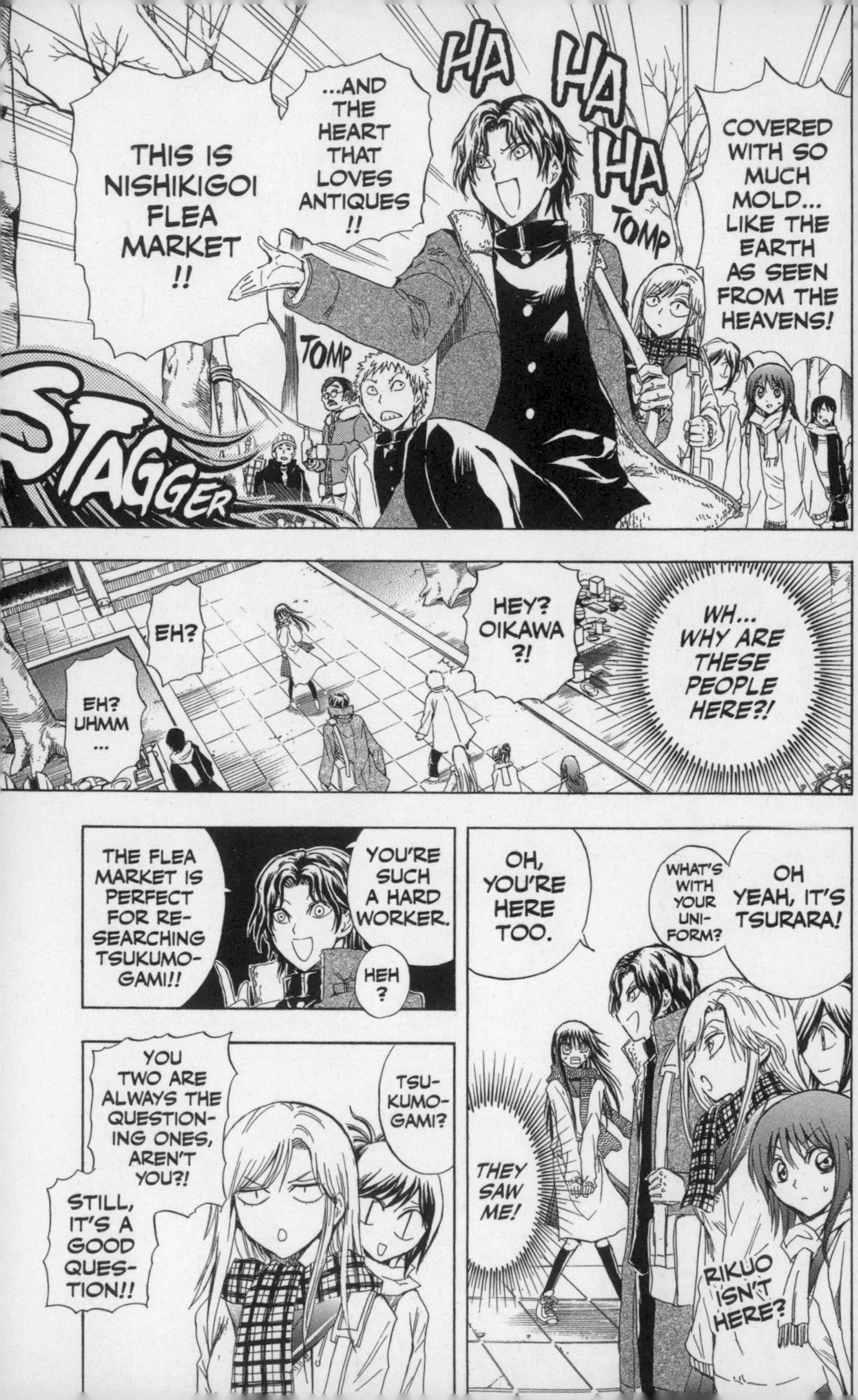
HA HA HA HA
COVERED WITH SO MUCH MOLD... LIKE THE EARTH AS SEEN FROM THE HEAVENS!
TOMP
...AND THE HEART THAT LOVES ANTIQUES!!
THIS IS NISHIKIGOI FLEA MARKET!!
TOMP
STAGGER
WH... WHY ARE THESE PEOPLE HERE?!
HEY? OIKAWA?!
EH?
EH? UHMM...
OH YEAH, IT'S TSURARA!
WHAT'S WITH YOUR UNIFORM?
OH, YOU'RE HERE TOO.
THEY SAW ME!
RIKUO ISN'T HERE?
YOU'RE SUCH A HARD WORKER.
HEH?
THE FLEA MARKET IS PERFECT FOR RESEARCHING TSUKUMOGAMI!!
TSUKUMOGAMI?
YOU TWO ARE ALWAYS THE QUESTIONING ONES, AREN'T YOU?!
STILL, IT'S A GOOD QUESTION!!

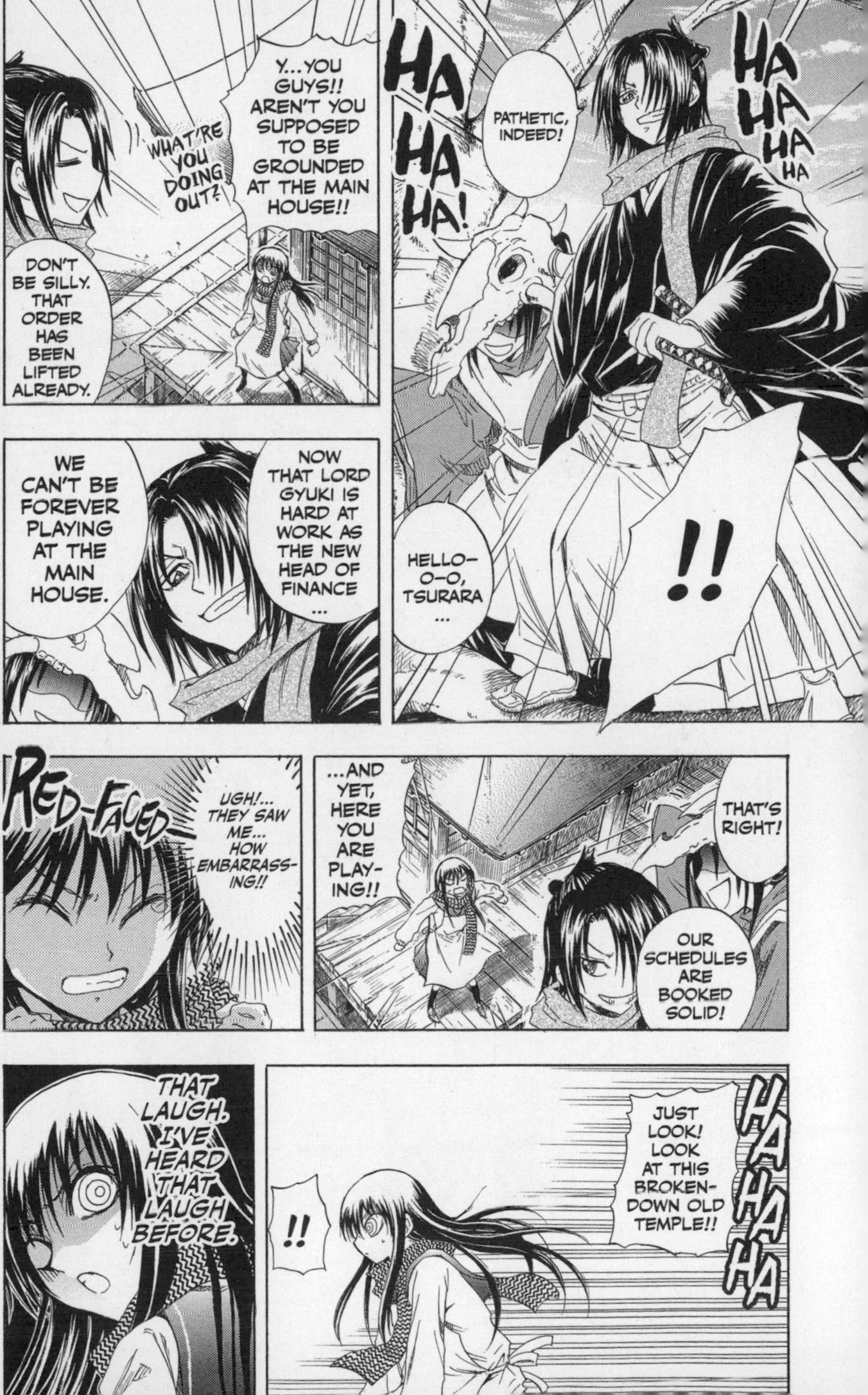
HA HA HA HA HA
PATHETIC, INDEED!
HA HA HA HA!
!!
HELLO-O-O, TSURARA...
Y...YOU GUYS!! AREN'T YOU SUPPOSED TO BE GROUNDED AT THE MAIN HOUSE!!
WHAT'RE YOU DOING OUT?
DON'T BE SILLY. THAT ORDER HAS BEEN LIFTED ALREADY.
NOW THAT LORD GYUKI IS HARD AT WORK AS THE NEW HEAD OF FINANCE...
WE CAN'T BE FOREVER PLAYING AT THE MAIN HOUSE.
...AND YET, HERE YOU ARE PLAYING!!
THAT'S RIGHT!
OUR SCHEDULES ARE BOOKED SOLID!
RED-FACED
UGH!... THEY SAW ME... HOW EMBARRASSING!!
HA HA HA HA HA
JUST LOOK! LOOK AT THIS BROKEN-DOWN OLD TEMPLE!!
!!
THAT LAUGH. I'VE HEARD THAT LAUGH BEFORE.

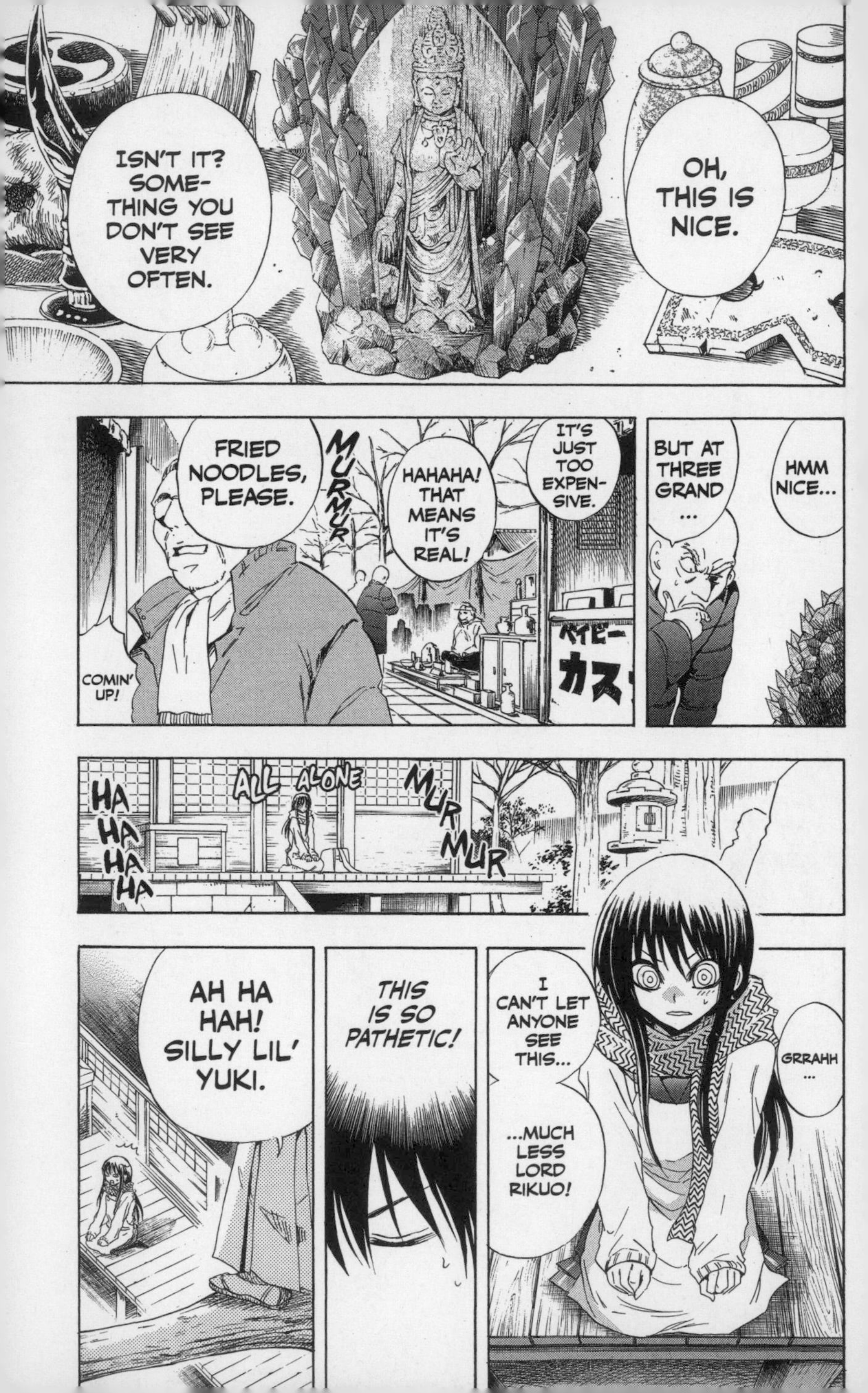

OH, THIS IS NICE.
ISN'T IT? SOMETHING YOU DON'T SEE VERY OFTEN.
HMM NICE...
BUT AT THREE GRAND ...
IT'S JUST TOO EXPENSIVE.
HAHAHA! THAT MEANS IT'S REAL!
MURMUR
FRIED NOODLES, PLEASE.
ベイビー
カス
COMIN' UP!
MUR MUR MUR
ALL ALONE
HA HA HA HA HA HA
GRRAHH ...
I CAN'T LET ANYONE SEE THIS...
...MUCH LESS LORD RIKUO!
THIS IS SO PATHETIC!
AH HA HAH! SILLY LIL' YUKI.

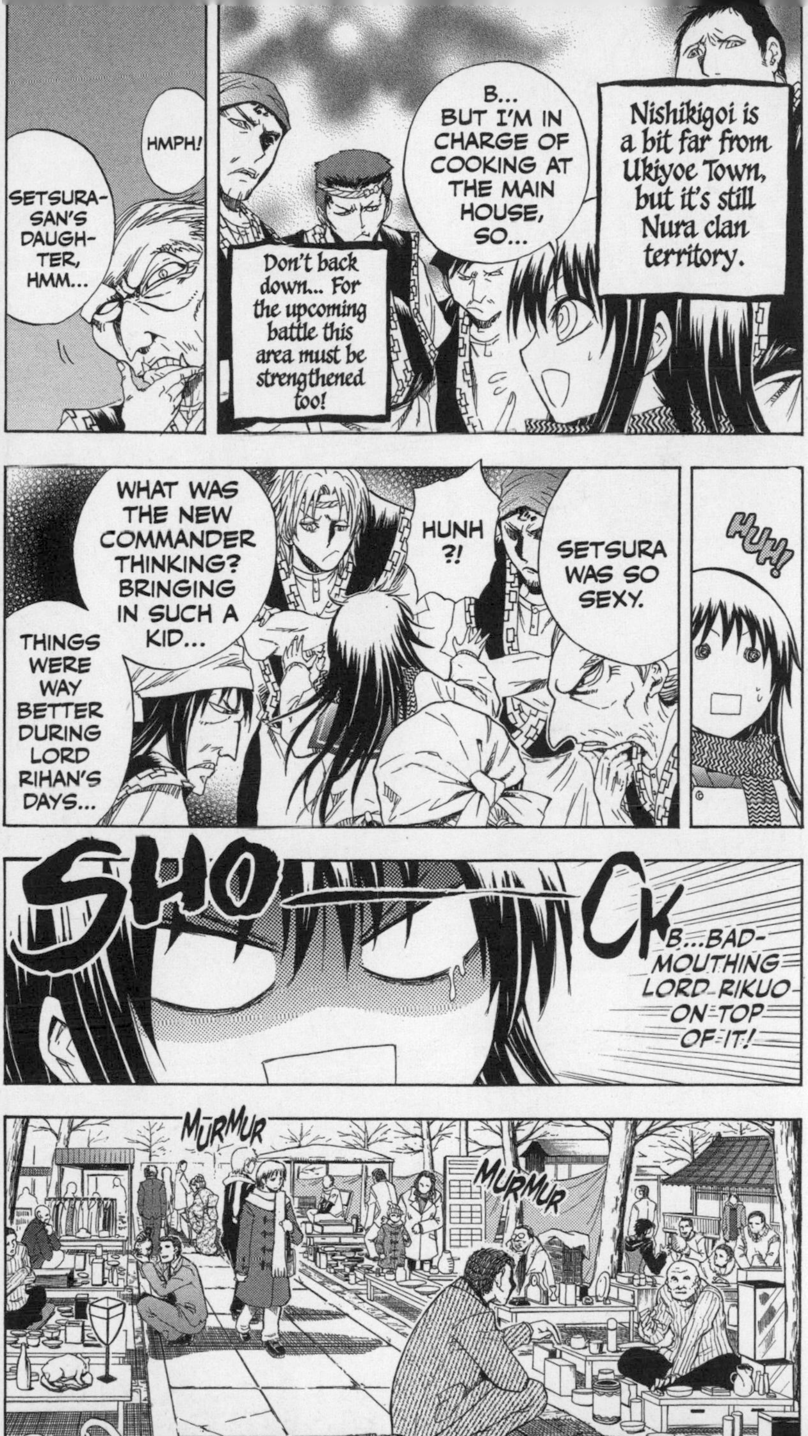
Nishikigoi is a bit far from Ukiyoe Town, but it's still Nura clan territory.
B... BUT I'M IN CHARGE OF COOKING AT THE MAIN HOUSE, SO...
Don't back down... For the upcoming battle this area must be strengthened too!
HMPH!
SETSURA-SAN'S DAUGHTER, HMM...
HUH!
SETSURA WAS SO SEXY.
HUNH ?!
WHAT WAS THE NEW COMMANDER THINKING? BRINGING IN SUCH A KID...
THINGS WERE WAY BETTER DURING LORD RIHAN'S DAYS...
SHOCK
B...BAD-MOUTHING LORD RIKUO ON TOP OF IT!
MURMUR
MURMUR

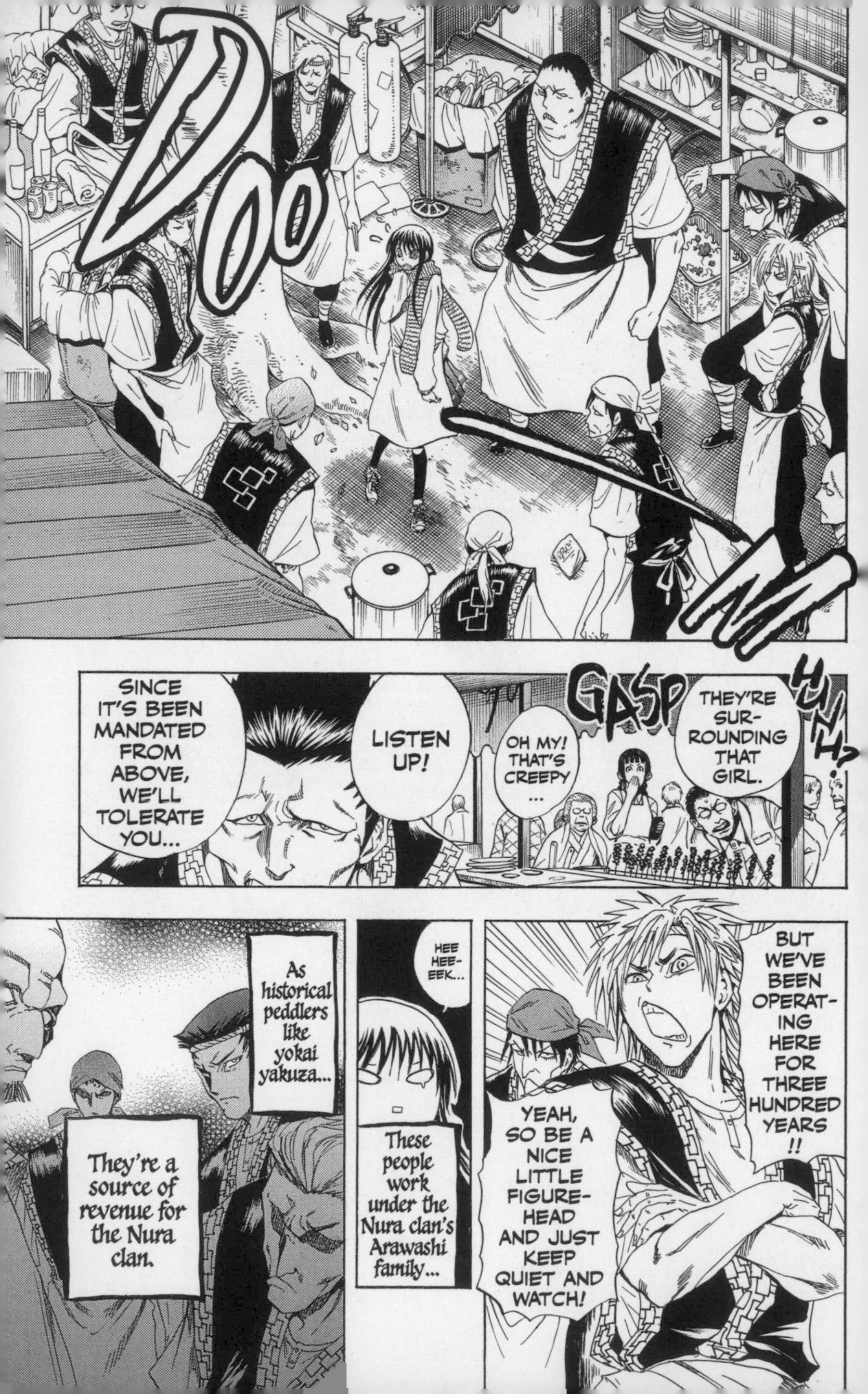
DOO
MM
HUHH?
GASP
THEY'RE SURROUNDING THAT GIRL.
OH MY! THAT'S CREEPY...
LISTEN UP!
SINCE IT'S BEEN MANDATED FROM ABOVE, WE'LL TOLERATE YOU...
BUT WE'VE BEEN OPERATING HERE FOR THREE HUNDRED YEARS!!
YEAH, SO BE A NICE LITTLE FIGUREHEAD AND JUST KEEP QUIET AND WATCH!
HEE HEEEEK...
These people work under the Nura clan's Arawashi family...
As historical peddlers like yokai yakuza...
They're a source of revenue for the Nura clan.

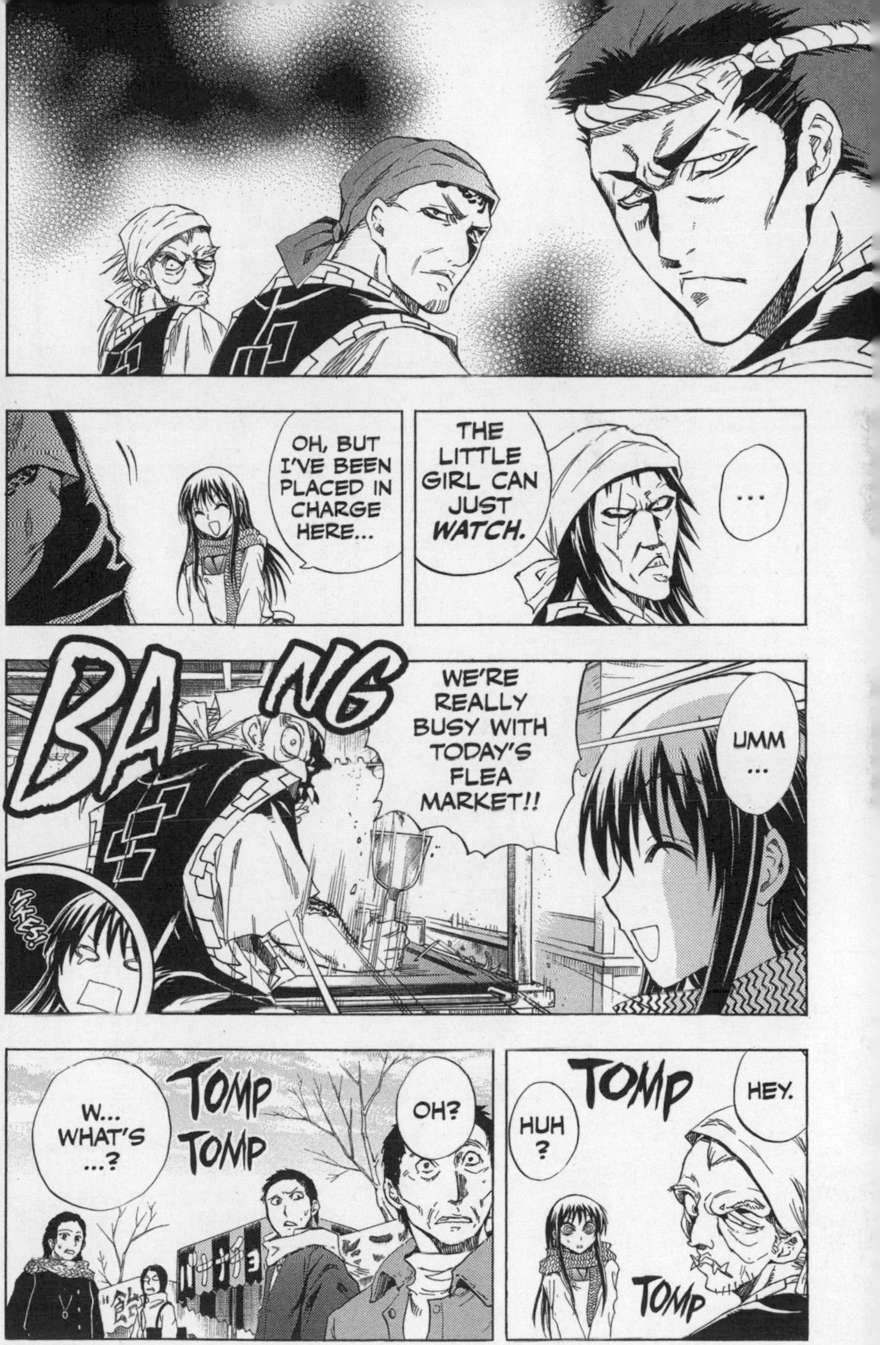
...
THE LITTLE GIRL CAN JUST *WATCH.*
OH, BUT I'VE BEEN PLACED IN CHARGE HERE...
UMM ...
WE'RE REALLY BUSY WITH TODAY'S FLEA MARKET!!
BANG
YIKES!
HEY.
TOMP
HUH ?
TOMP
OH?
TOMP TOMP
W... WHAT'S ...?

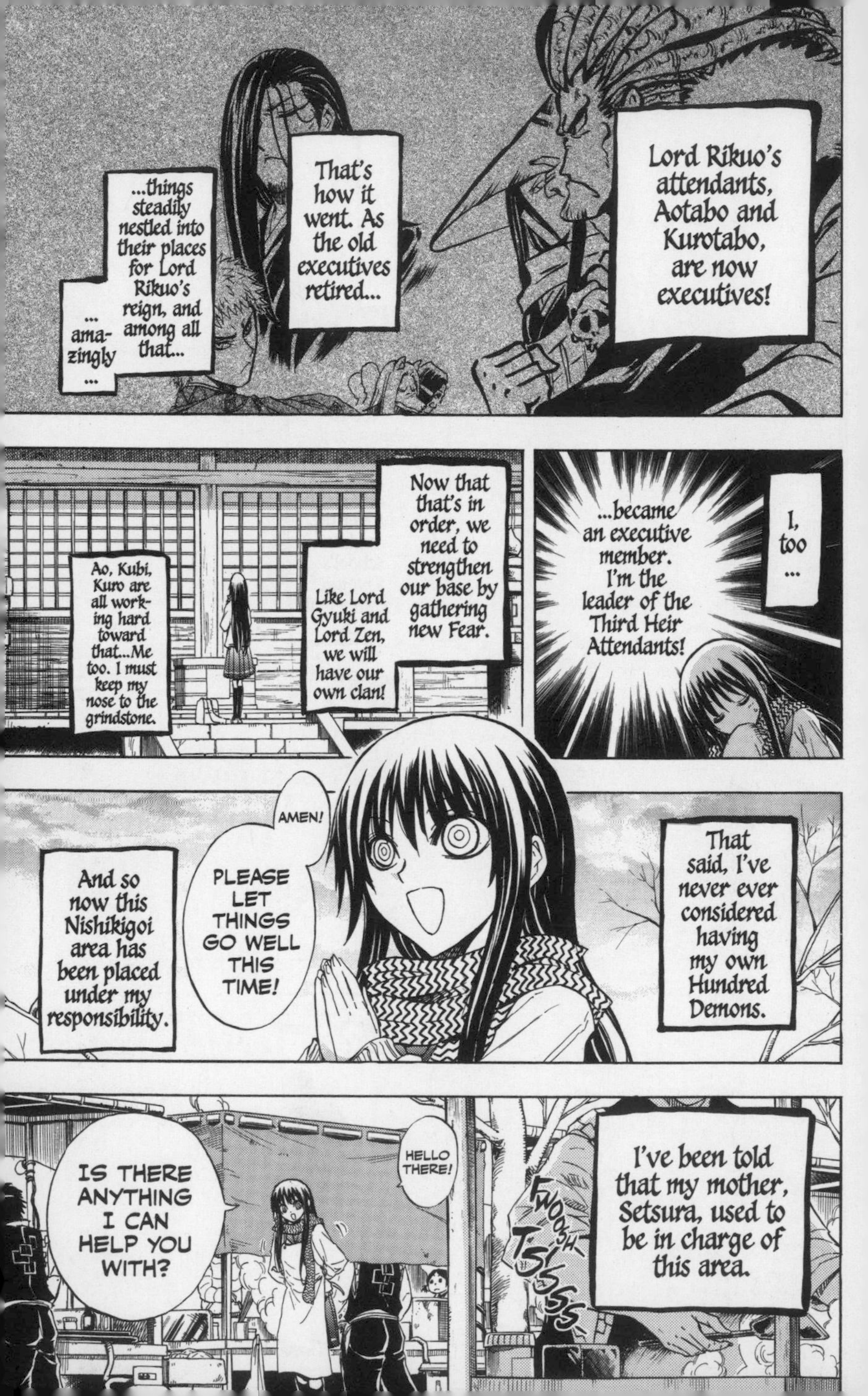

Lord Rikuo's attendants, Aotabo and Kurotabo, are now executives!
That's how it went. As the old executives retired...
...things steadily nestled into their places for Lord Rikuo's reign, and among all that...
...amazingly...
I, too...
...became an executive member. I'm the leader of the Third Heir Attendants!
Now that that's in order, we need to strengthen our base by gathering new Fear.
Like Lord Gyuki and Lord Zen, we will have our own clan!
Ao, Kubi, Kuro are all working hard toward that...Me too. I must keep my nose to the grindstone.
That said, I've never ever considered having my own Hundred Demons.
AMEN!
PLEASE LET THINGS GO WELL THIS TIME!
And so now this Nishikigoi area has been placed under my responsibility.
I've been told that my mother, Setsura, used to be in charge of this area.
FWOOSH
TSSSSS
HELLO THERE!
IS THERE ANYTHING I CAN HELP YOU WITH?

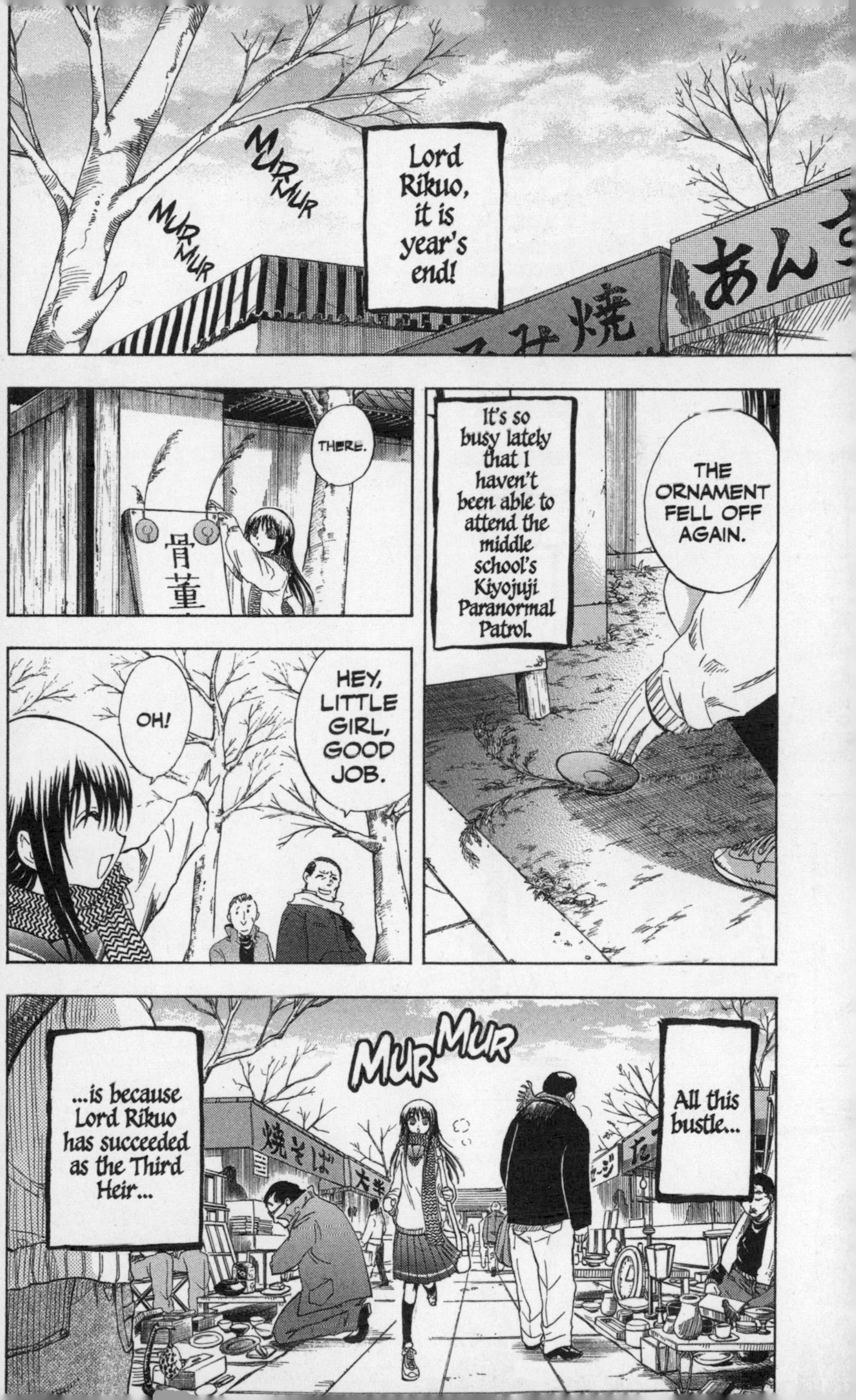
Lord Rikuo, it is year's end!
MURMUR
MURMUR
It's so busy lately that I haven't been able to attend the middle school's Kiyojuji Paranormal Patrol.
THE ORNAMENT FELL OFF AGAIN.
THERE.
HEY, LITTLE GIRL, GOOD JOB.
OH!
All this bustle...
MURMUR
...is because Lord Rikuo has succeeded as the Third Heir...

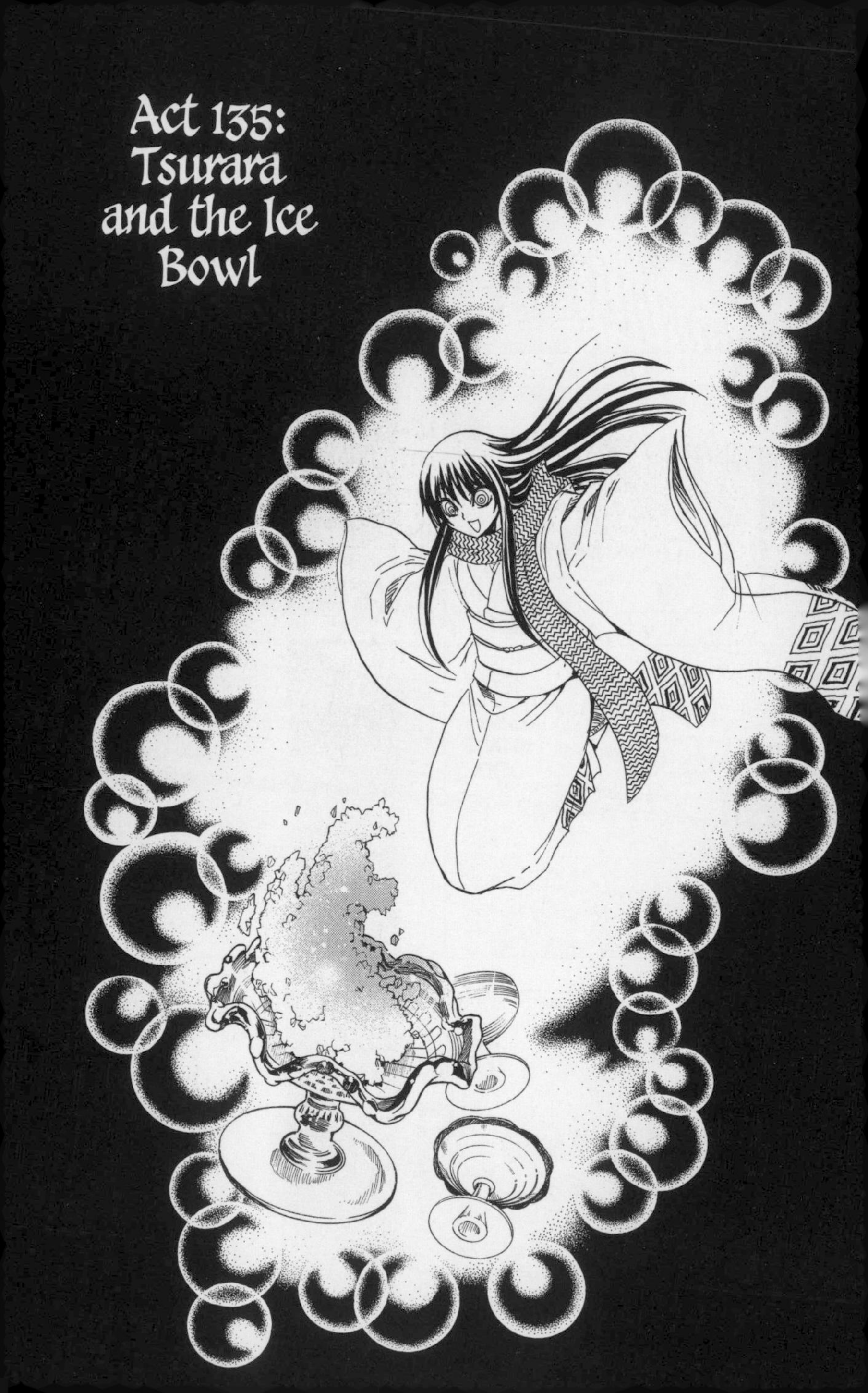
Act 135: Tsurara and the Ice Bowl

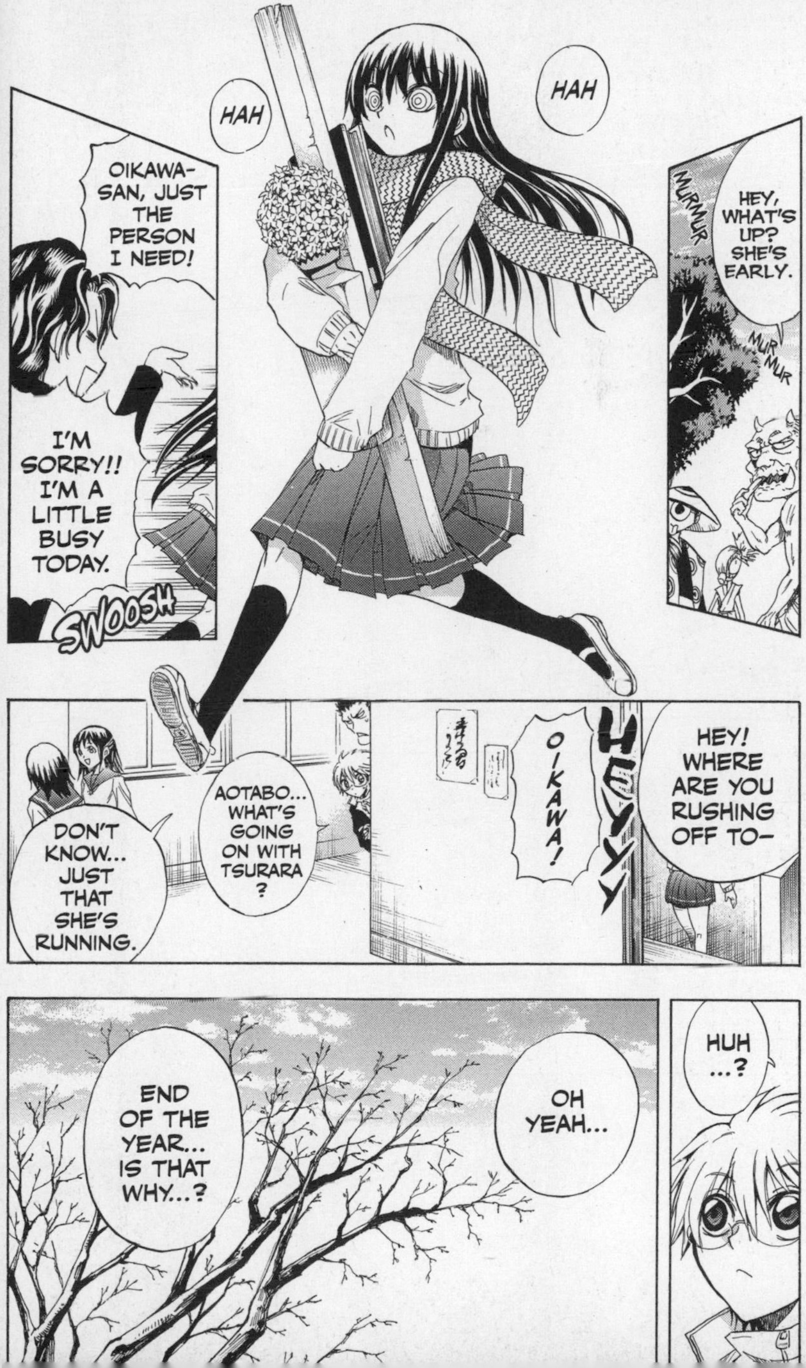
HAH
HAH
HEY, WHAT'S UP? SHE'S EARLY.
MURMUR
MUR MUR
OIKAWA-SAN, JUST THE PERSON I NEED!
I'M SORRY!! I'M A LITTLE BUSY TODAY.
SWOOSH
HEY! WHERE ARE YOU RUSHING OFF TO-
HEYYY
OIKAWA!
AOTABO... WHAT'S GOING ON WITH TSURARA?
DON'T KNOW... JUST THAT SHE'S RUNNING.
HUH ...?
OH YEAH...
END OF THE YEAR... IS THAT WHY...?

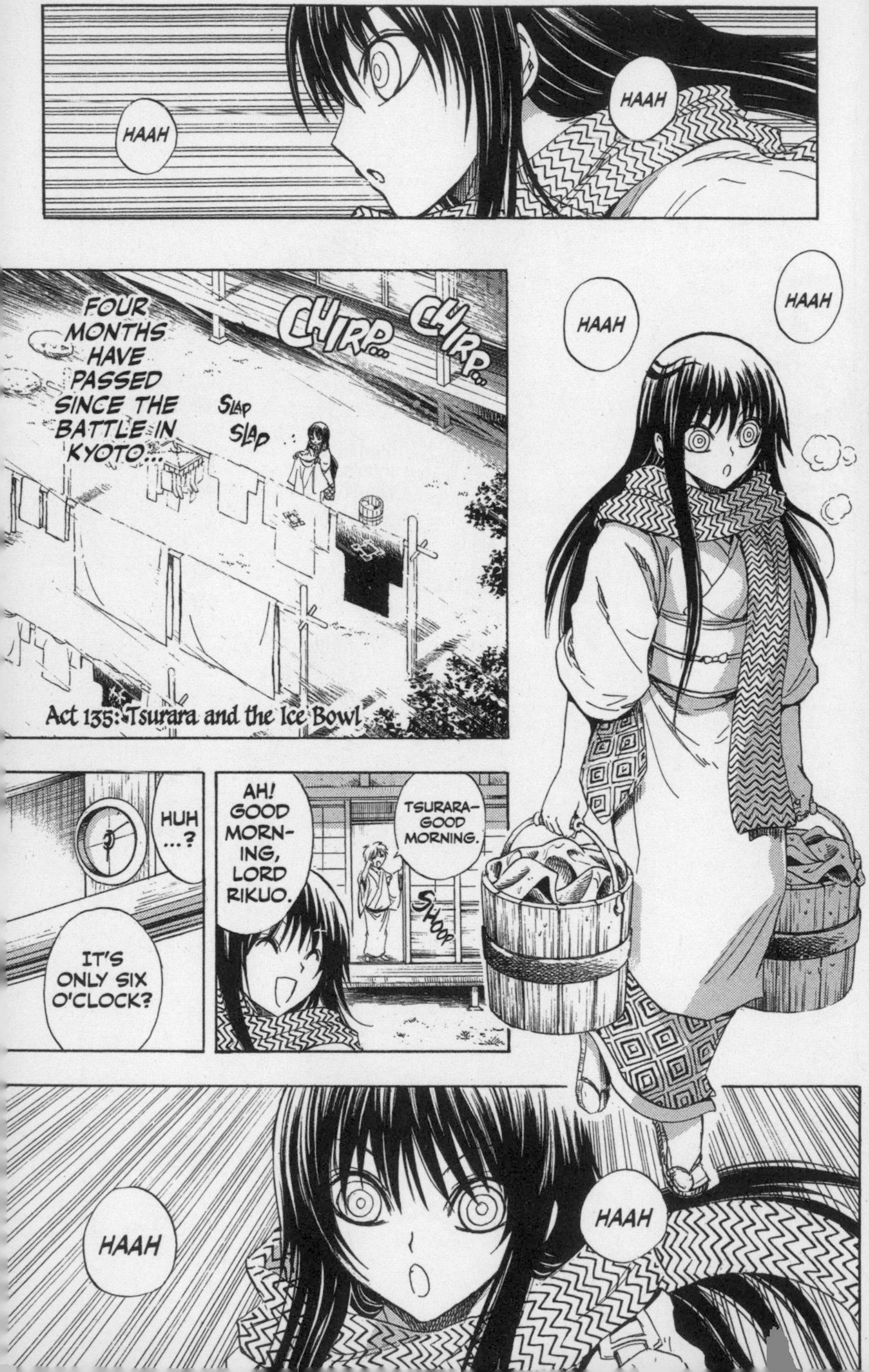
HAAH
HAAH
HAAH
HAAH
CHIRP...
CHIRP...
FOUR MONTHS HAVE PASSED SINCE THE BATTLE IN KYOTO...
SLAP SLAP
Act 135: Tsurara and the Ice Bowl
TSURARA- GOOD MORNING.
AH! GOOD MORN-ING, LORD RIKUO.
SHOOP
HUH ...?
IT'S ONLY SIX O'CLOCK?
HAAH
HAAH

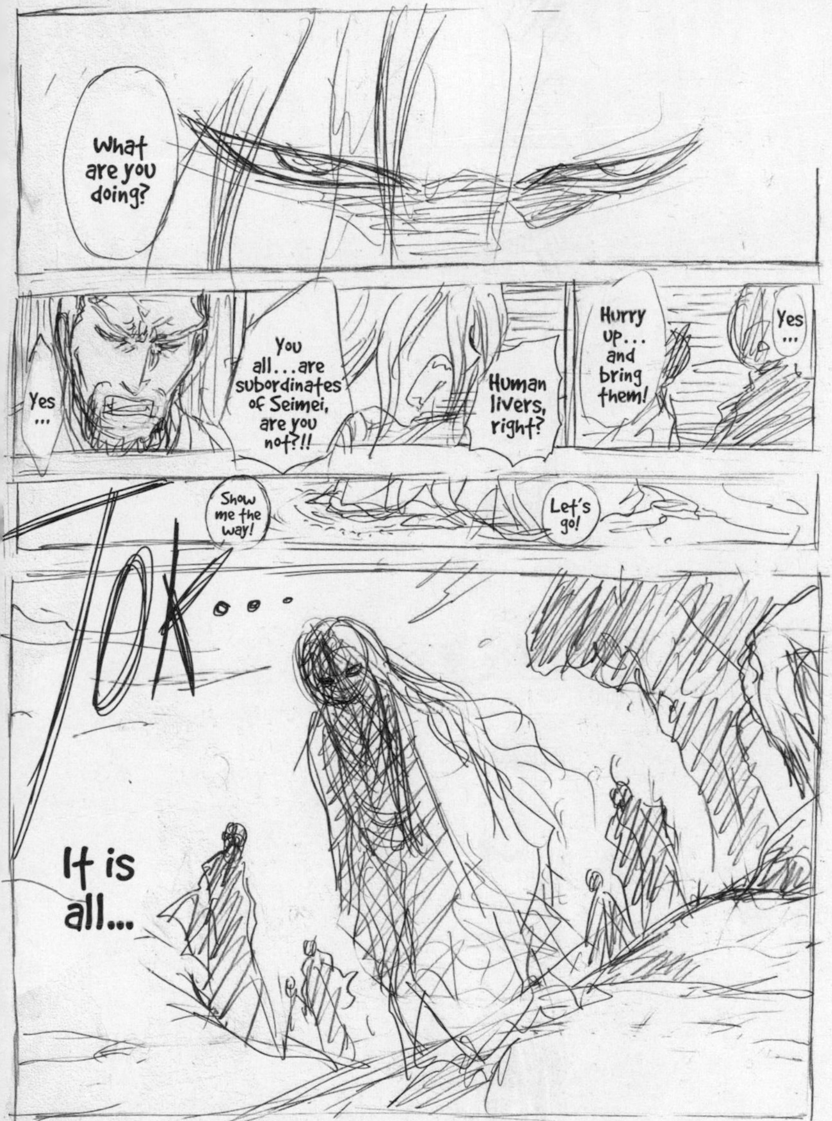
What are you doing?
Yes...
Hurry up... and bring them!
Human livers, right?
You all...are subordinates of Seimei, are you not?!!
Yes...
Let's go!
Show me the way!
TOK...
It is all...

For the love of her son Seimei...

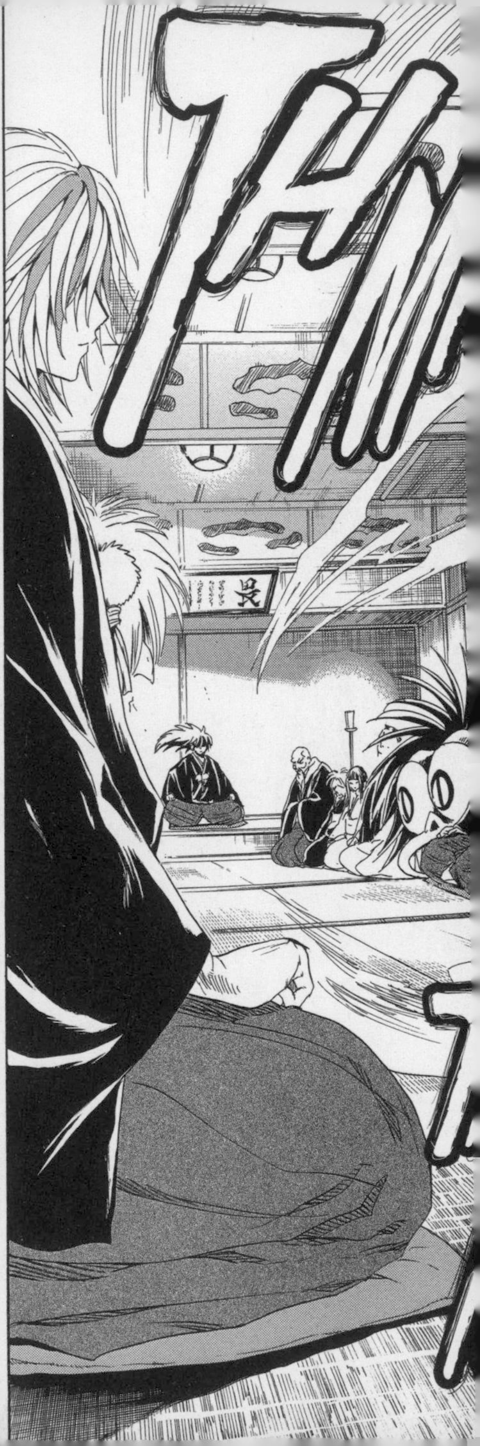

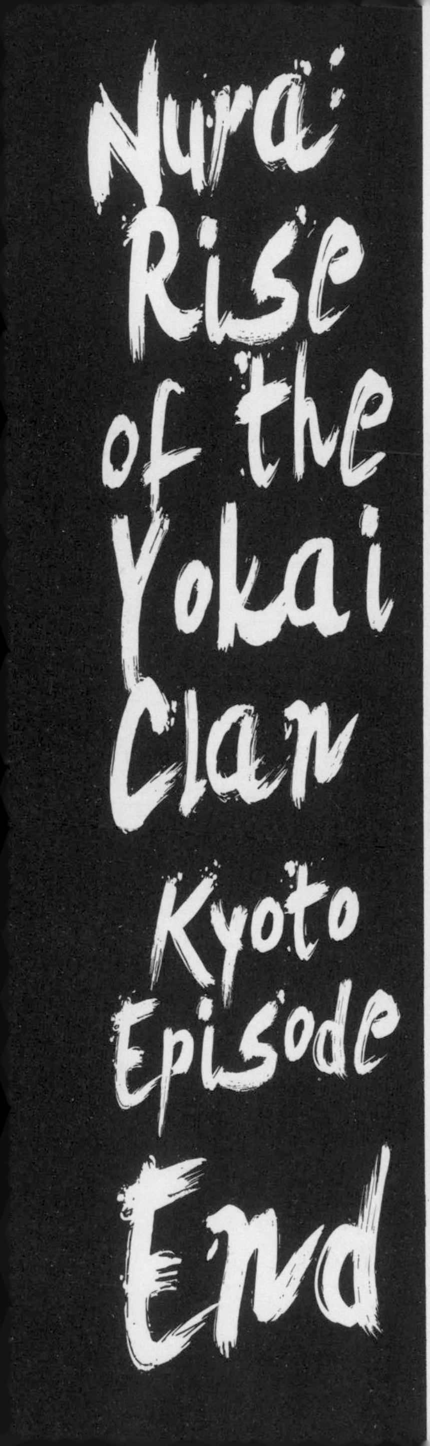
Nura: Rise of the Yokai Clan
Kyoto Episode
End

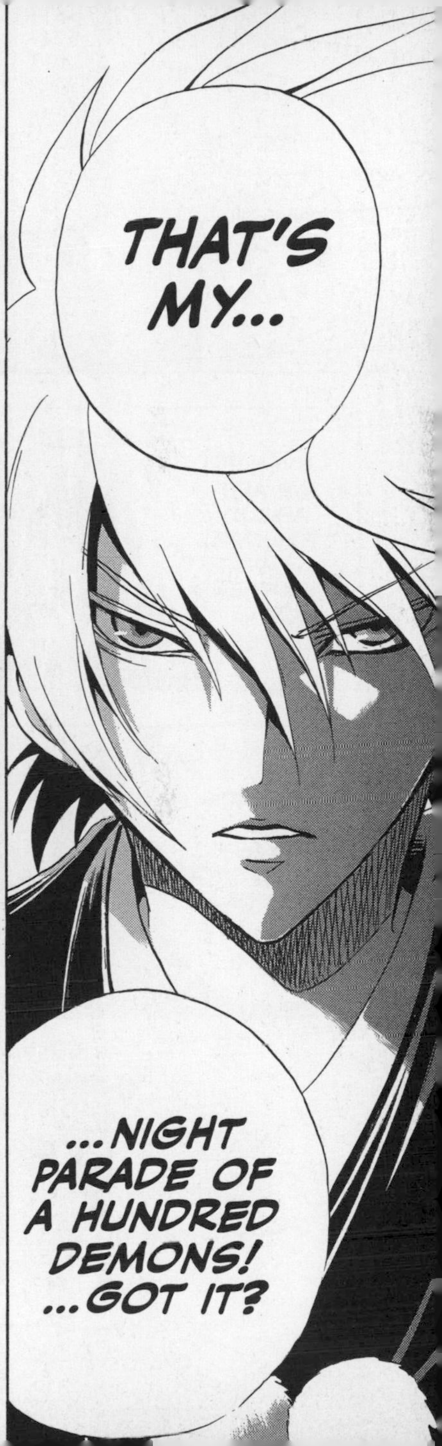
THAT'S MY...
...NIGHT PARADE OF A HUNDRED DEMONS! ...GOT IT?
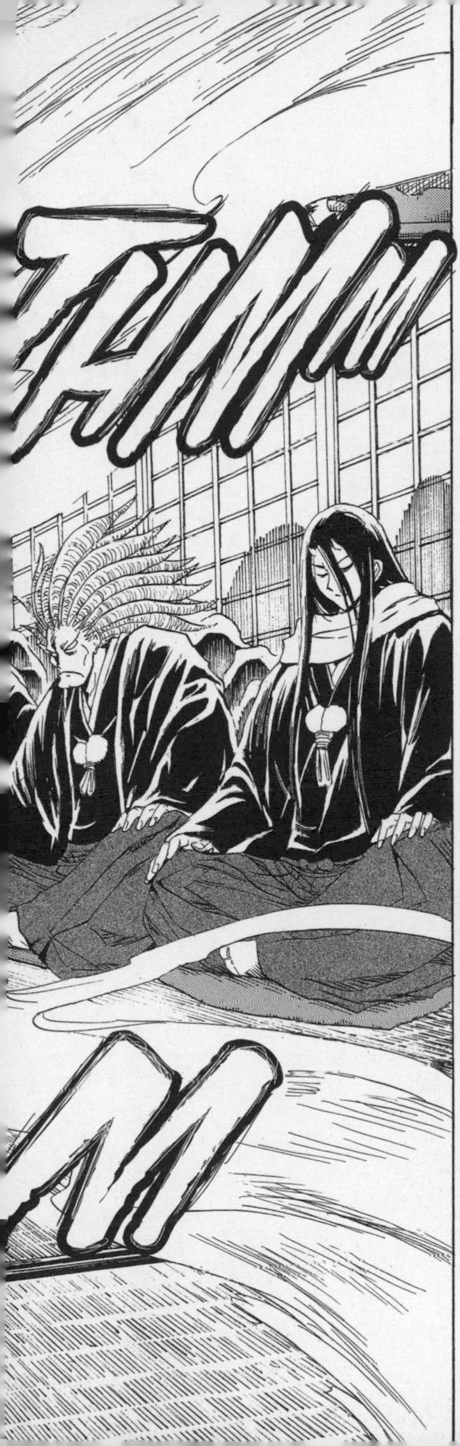

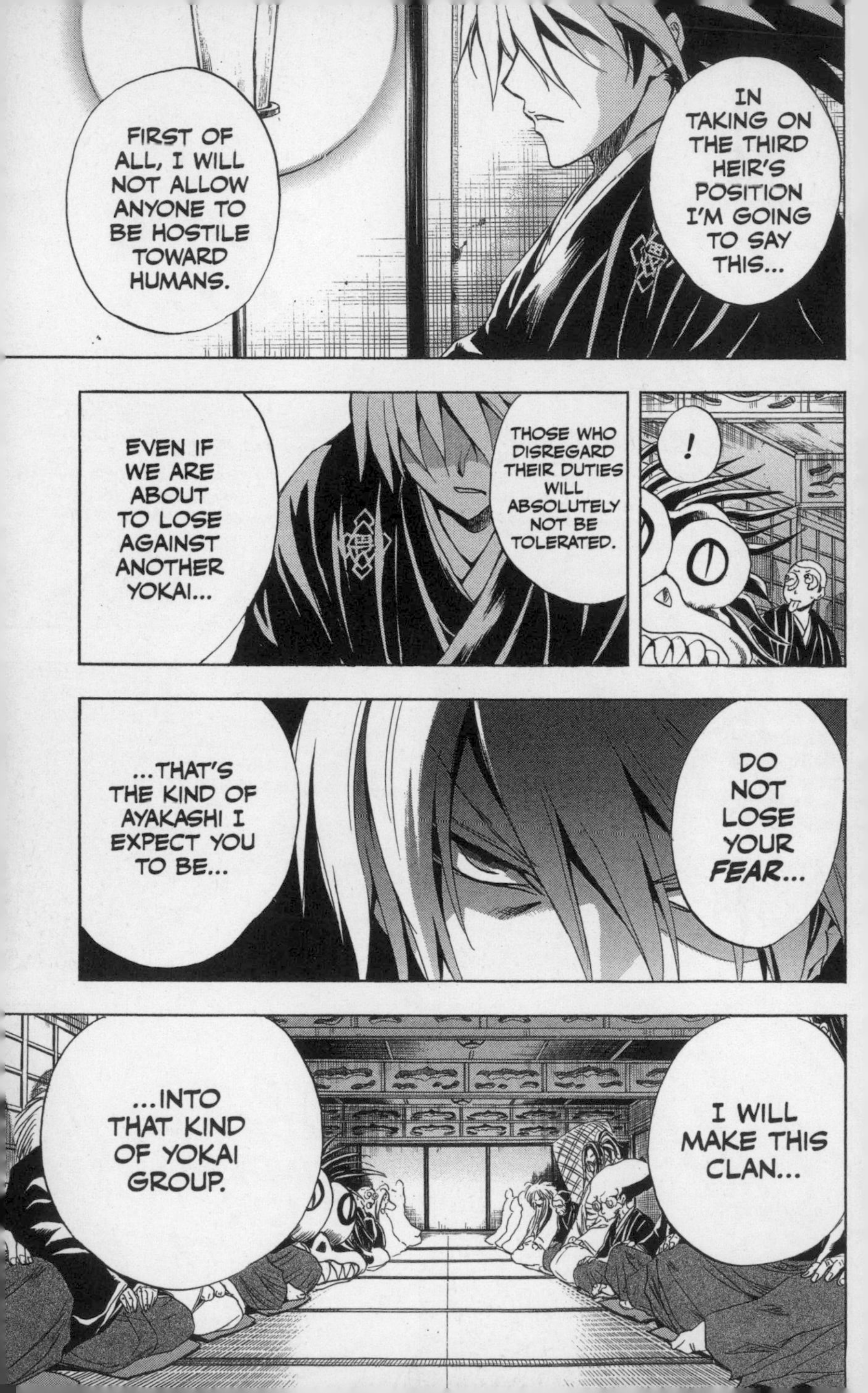
IN TAKING ON THE THIRD HEIR'S POSITION I'M GOING TO SAY THIS...
FIRST OF ALL, I WILL NOT ALLOW ANYONE TO BE HOSTILE TOWARD HUMANS.
!
THOSE WHO DISREGARD THEIR DUTIES WILL ABSOLUTELY NOT BE TOLERATED.
EVEN IF WE ARE ABOUT TO LOSE AGAINST ANOTHER YOKAI...
DO NOT LOSE YOUR *FEAR*...
...THAT'S THE KIND OF AYAKASHI I EXPECT YOU TO BE...
I WILL MAKE THIS CLAN...
...INTO THAT KIND OF YOKAI GROUP.

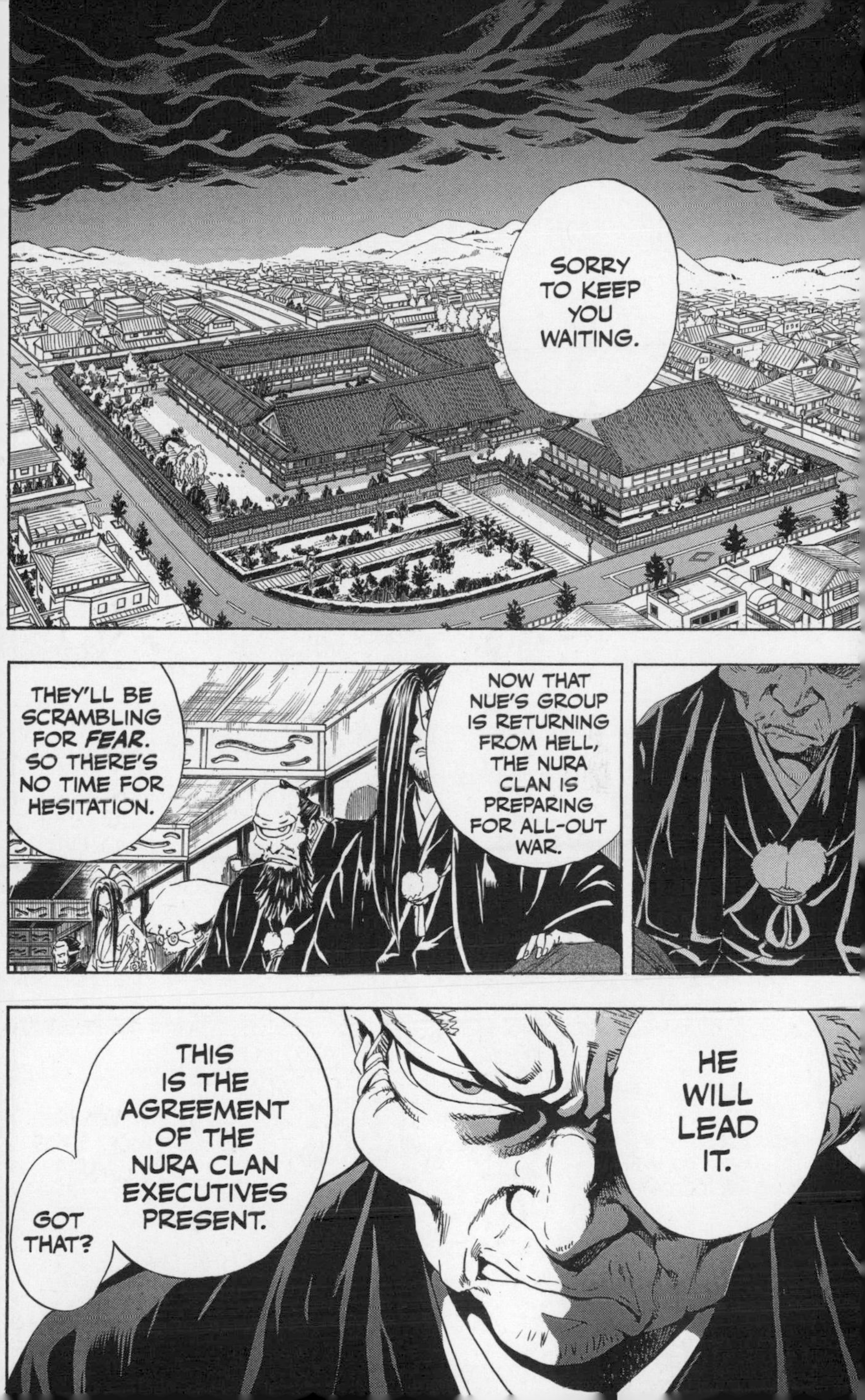
SORRY TO KEEP YOU WAITING.
NOW THAT NUE'S GROUP IS RETURNING FROM HELL, THE NURA CLAN IS PREPARING FOR ALL-OUT WAR.
THEY'LL BE SCRAMBLING FOR *FEAR*. SO THERE'S NO TIME FOR HESITATION.
HE WILL LEAD IT.
THIS IS THE AGREEMENT OF THE NURA CLAN EXECUTIVES PRESENT.
GOT THAT?

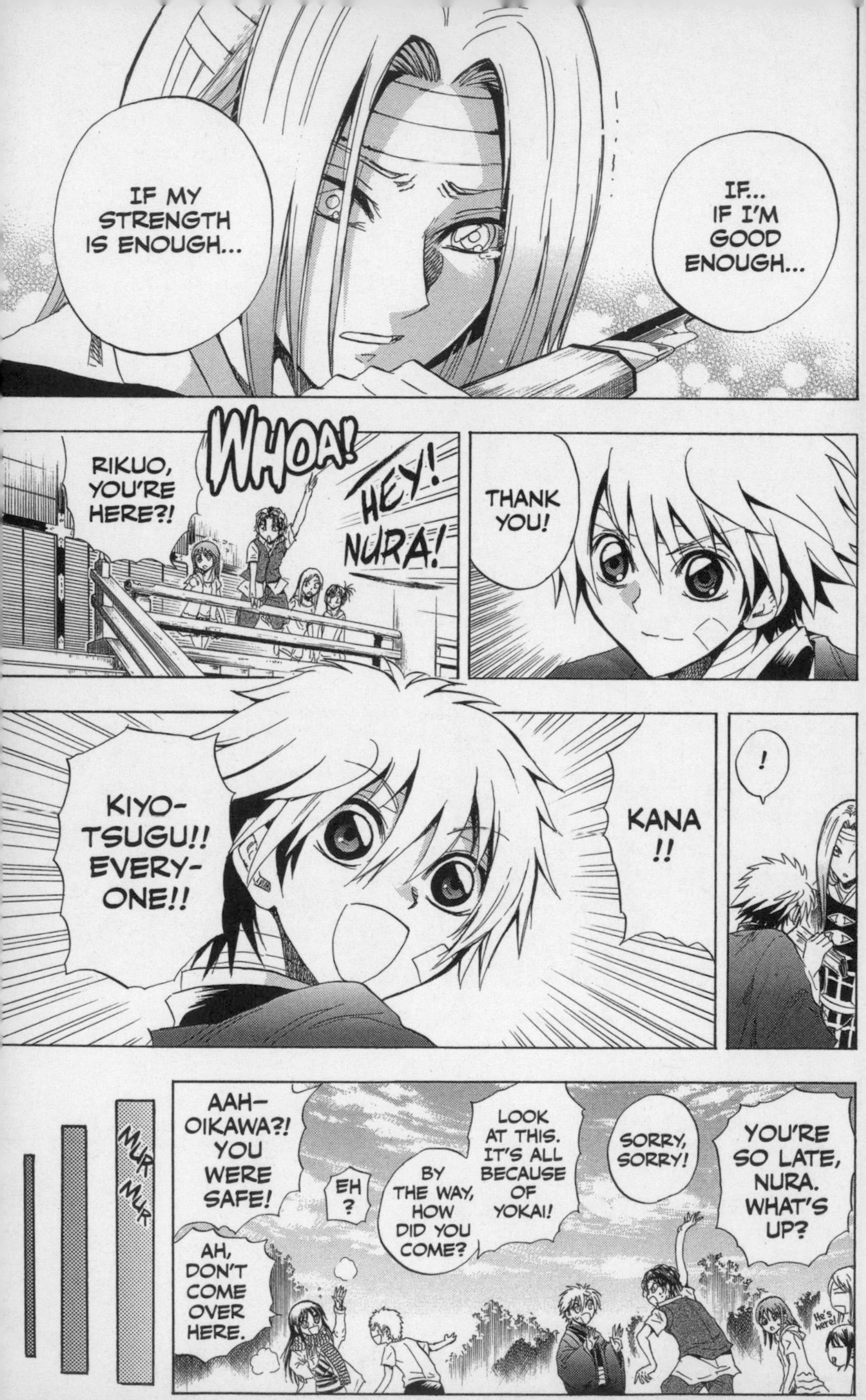
IF... IF I'M GOOD ENOUGH...
IF MY STRENGTH IS ENOUGH...
THANK YOU!
HEY! NURA!
WHOA!
RIKUO, YOU'RE HERE?!
!
KANA !!
KIYO-TSUGU!! EVERY-ONE!!
YOU'RE SO LATE, NURA. WHAT'S UP?
He's here!
SORRY, SORRY!
LOOK AT THIS. IT'S ALL BECAUSE OF YOKAI!
BY THE WAY, HOW DID YOU COME?
EH?
AAH- OIKAWA?! YOU WERE SAFE!
AH, DON'T COME OVER HERE.
MUR MUR

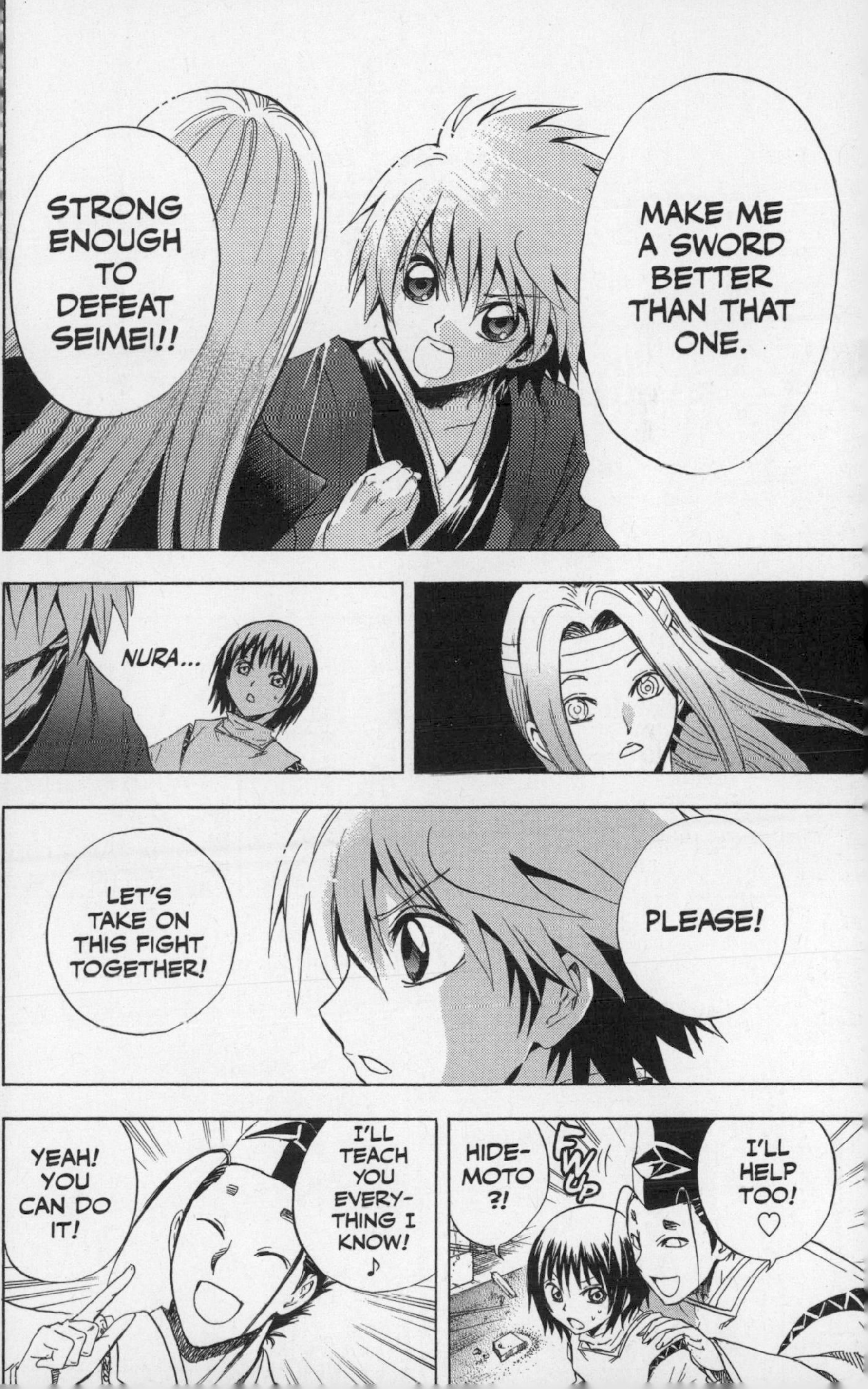
MAKE ME A SWORD BETTER THAN THAT ONE.
STRONG ENOUGH TO DEFEAT SEIMEI!!
NURA...
PLEASE!
LET'S TAKE ON THIS FIGHT TOGETHER!
I'LL HELP TOO! ♡
FWUP
HIDE-MOTO ?!
I'LL TEACH YOU EVERY-THING I KNOW! ♪
YEAH! YOU CAN DO IT!

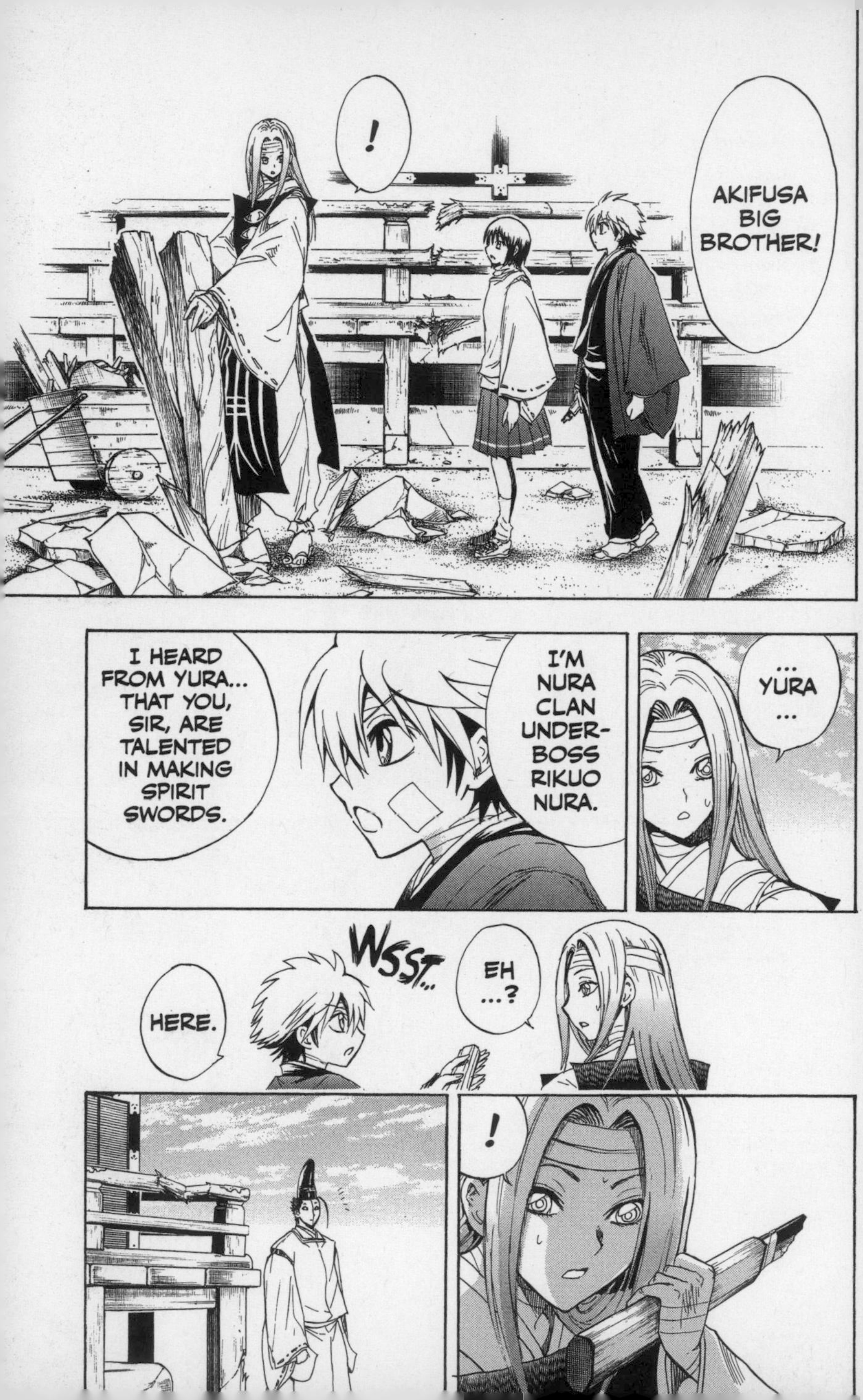
AKIFUSA BIG BROTHER!
!
... YURA ...
I'M NURA CLAN UNDER-BOSS RIKUO NURA.
I HEARD FROM YURA... THAT YOU, SIR, ARE TALENTED IN MAKING SPIRIT SWORDS.
EH ...?
WSST...
HERE.
!

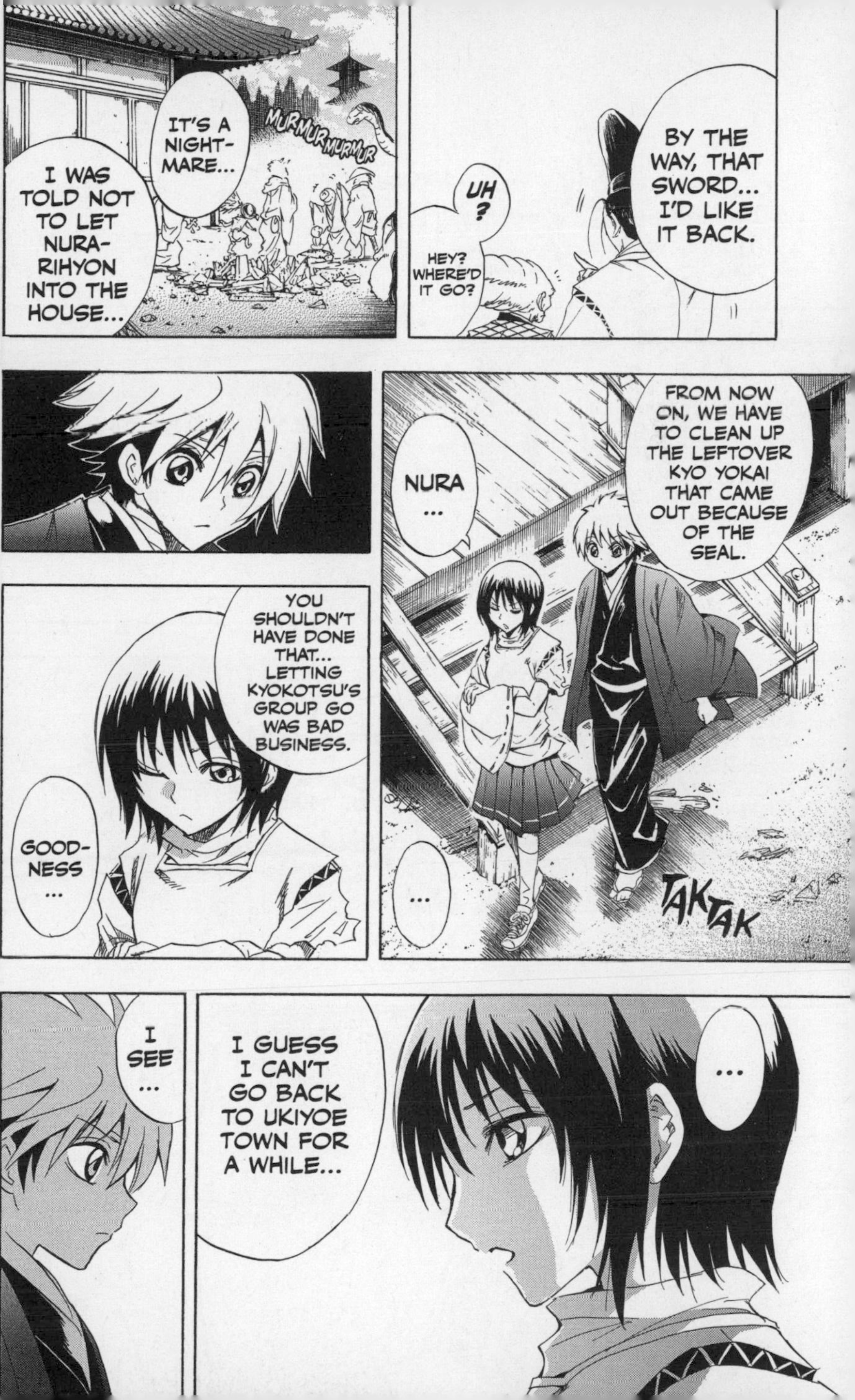
BY THE WAY, THAT SWORD... I'D LIKE IT BACK.
UH?
HEY? WHERE'D IT GO?
MURMURMURMUR
IT'S A NIGHT-MARE...
I WAS TOLD NOT TO LET NURA-RIHYON INTO THE HOUSE...
FROM NOW ON, WE HAVE TO CLEAN UP THE LEFTOVER KYO YOKAI THAT CAME OUT BECAUSE OF THE SEAL.
NURA...
...
TAKTAK
YOU SHOULDN'T HAVE DONE THAT... LETTING KYOKOTSU'S GROUP GO WAS BAD BUSINESS.
GOOD-NESS...
...
I GUESS I CAN'T GO BACK TO UKIYOE TOWN FOR A WHILE...
I SEE...

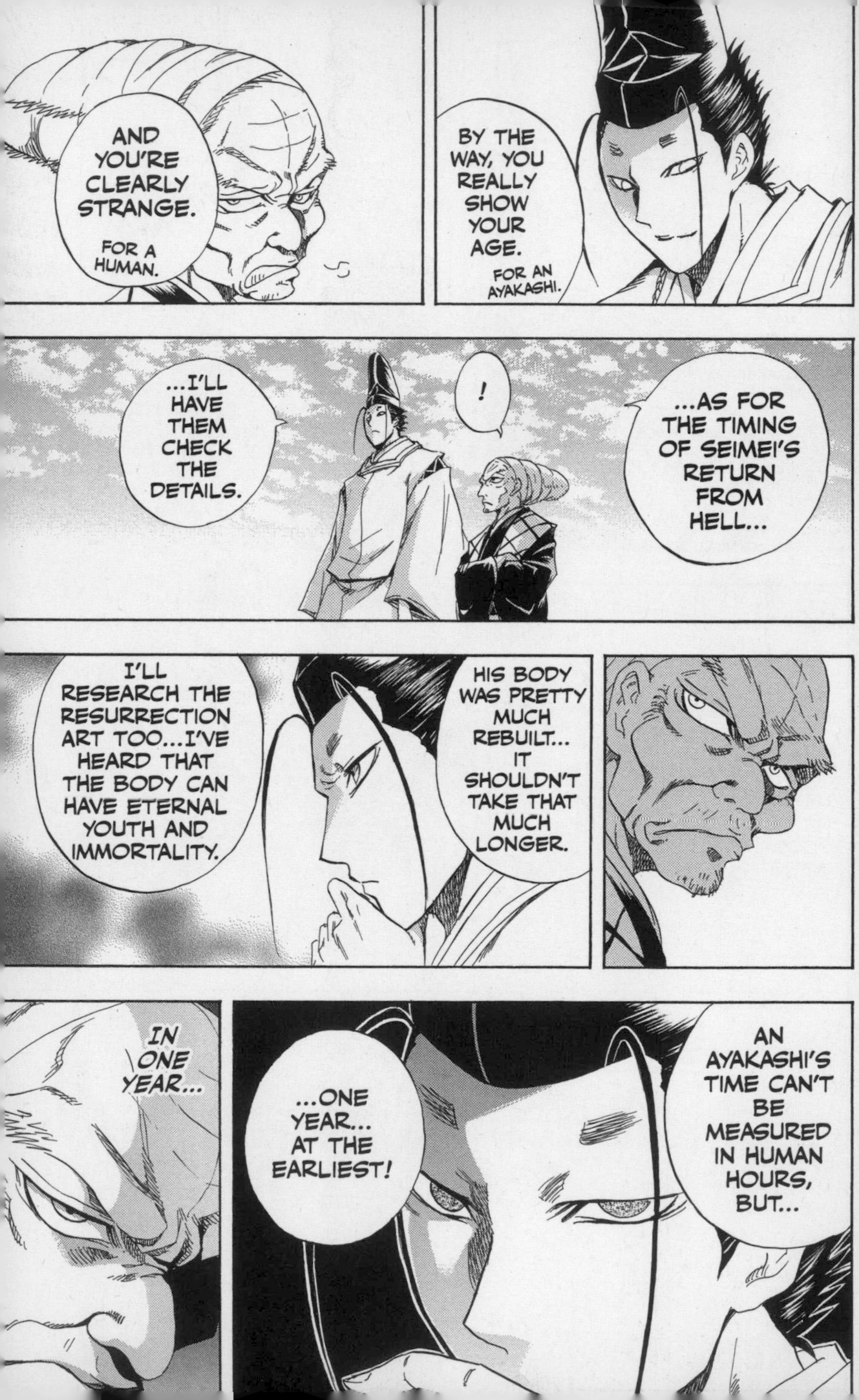
BY THE WAY, YOU REALLY SHOW YOUR AGE.
FOR AN AYAKASHI.
AND YOU'RE CLEARLY STRANGE.
FOR A HUMAN.
...AS FOR THE TIMING OF SEIMEI'S RETURN FROM HELL...
!
...I'LL HAVE THEM CHECK THE DETAILS.
HIS BODY WAS PRETTY MUCH REBUILT... IT SHOULDN'T TAKE THAT MUCH LONGER.
I'LL RESEARCH THE RESURRECTION ART TOO...I'VE HEARD THAT THE BODY CAN HAVE ETERNAL YOUTH AND IMMORTALITY.
AN AYAKASHI'S TIME CAN'T BE MEASURED IN HUMAN HOURS, BUT...
...ONE YEAR... AT THE EARLIEST!
IN ONE YEAR...

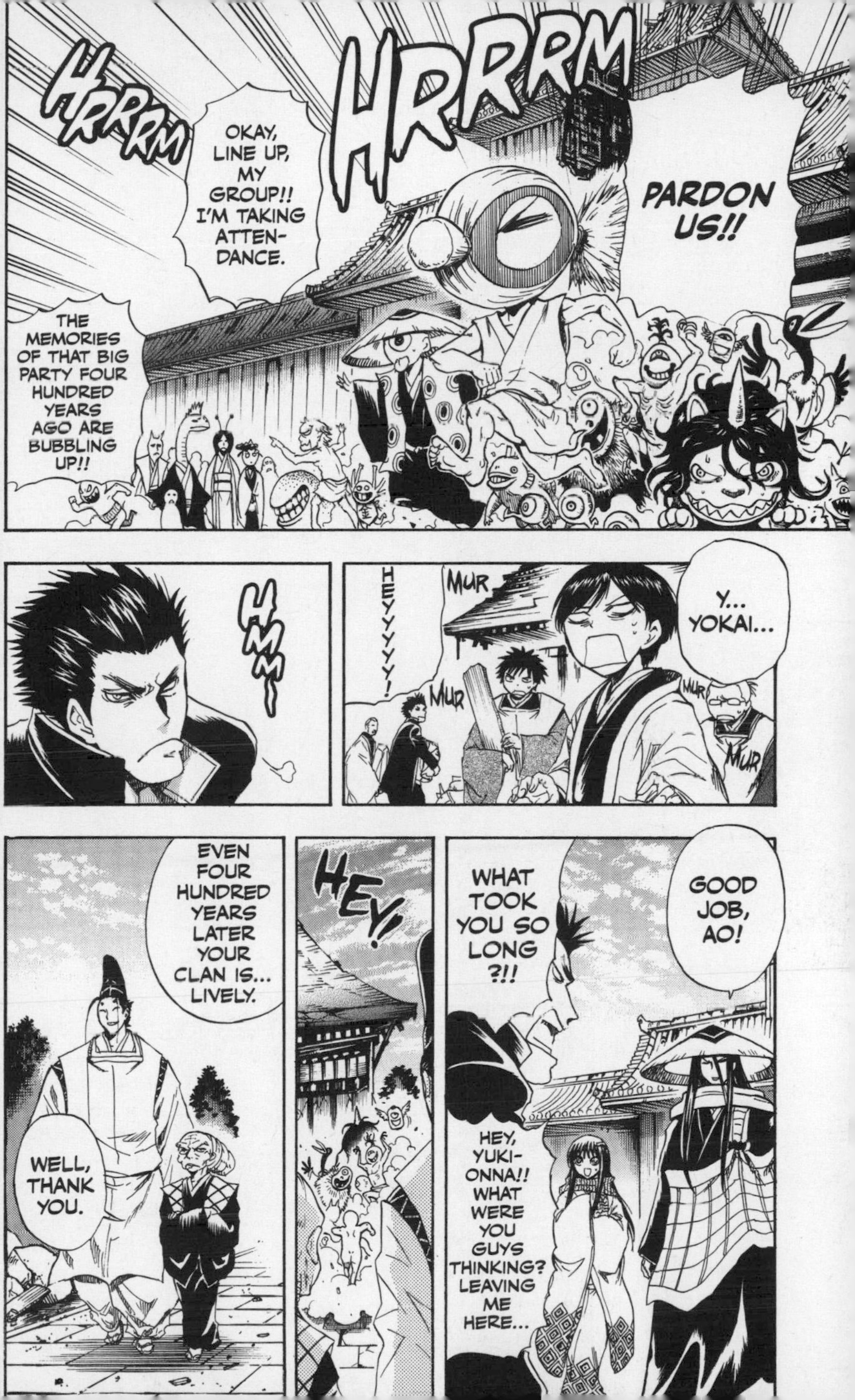
HRRRM
PARDON US!!
OKAY, LINE UP, MY GROUP!! I'M TAKING ATTEN-DANCE.
HRRRM
THE MEMORIES OF THAT BIG PARTY FOUR HUNDRED YEARS AGO ARE BUBBLING UP!!
Y... YOKAI...
MUR
HEYYYYY!
MUR
MUR
MUR
MUR
HMM
GOOD JOB, AO!
WHAT TOOK YOU SO LONG?!!
HEY, YUKI-ONNA!! WHAT WERE YOU GUYS THINKING? LEAVING ME HERE...
HEY!
EVEN FOUR HUNDRED YEARS LATER YOUR CLAN IS... LIVELY.
WELL, THANK YOU.

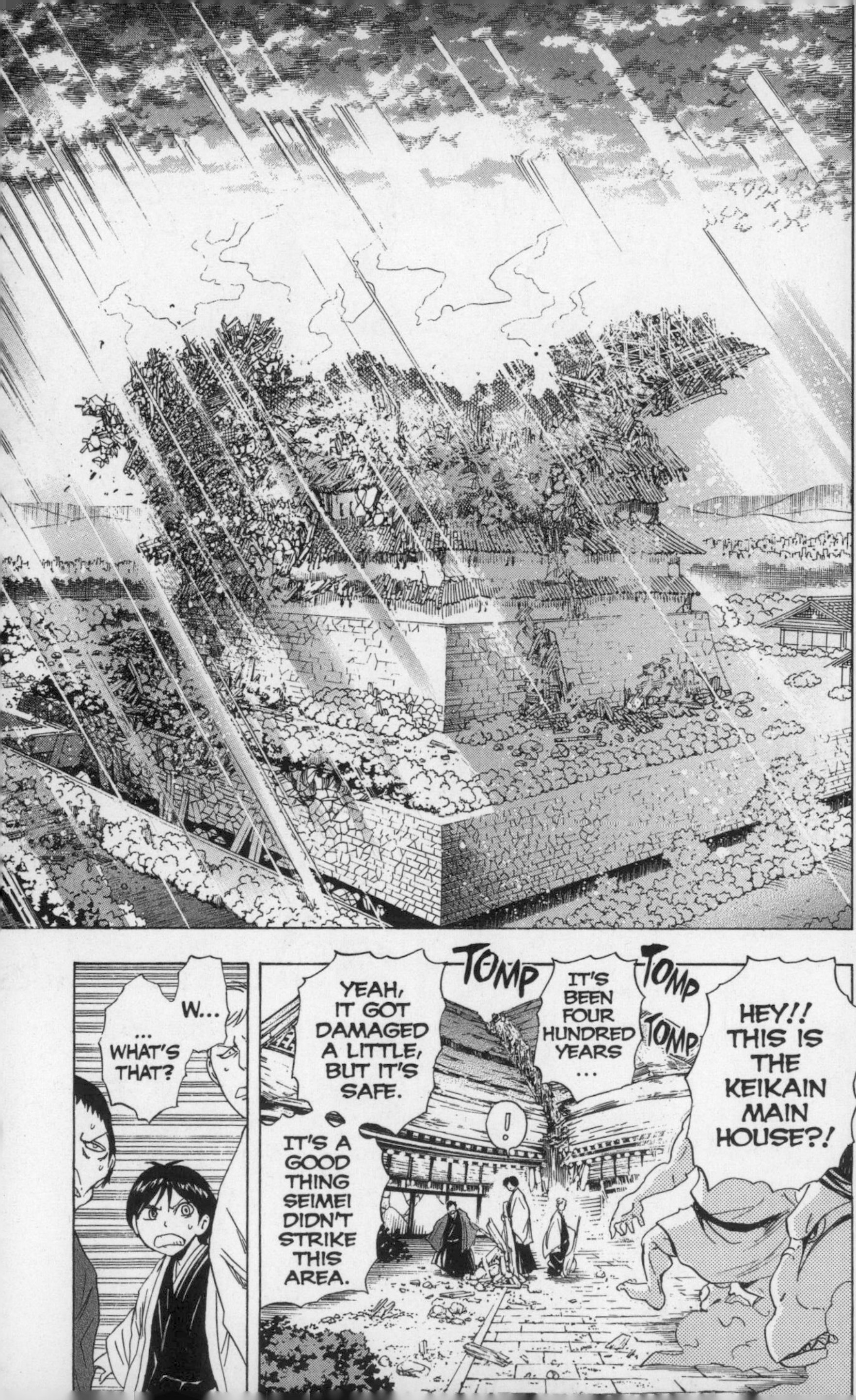
HEY!! THIS IS THE KEIKAIN MAIN HOUSE?!
TOMP
TOMP
TOMP
IT'S BEEN FOUR HUNDRED YEARS ...
TOMP
YEAH, IT GOT DAMAGED A LITTLE, BUT IT'S SAFE.
!
IT'S A GOOD THING SEIMEI DIDN'T STRIKE THIS AREA.
W... ...WHAT'S THAT?

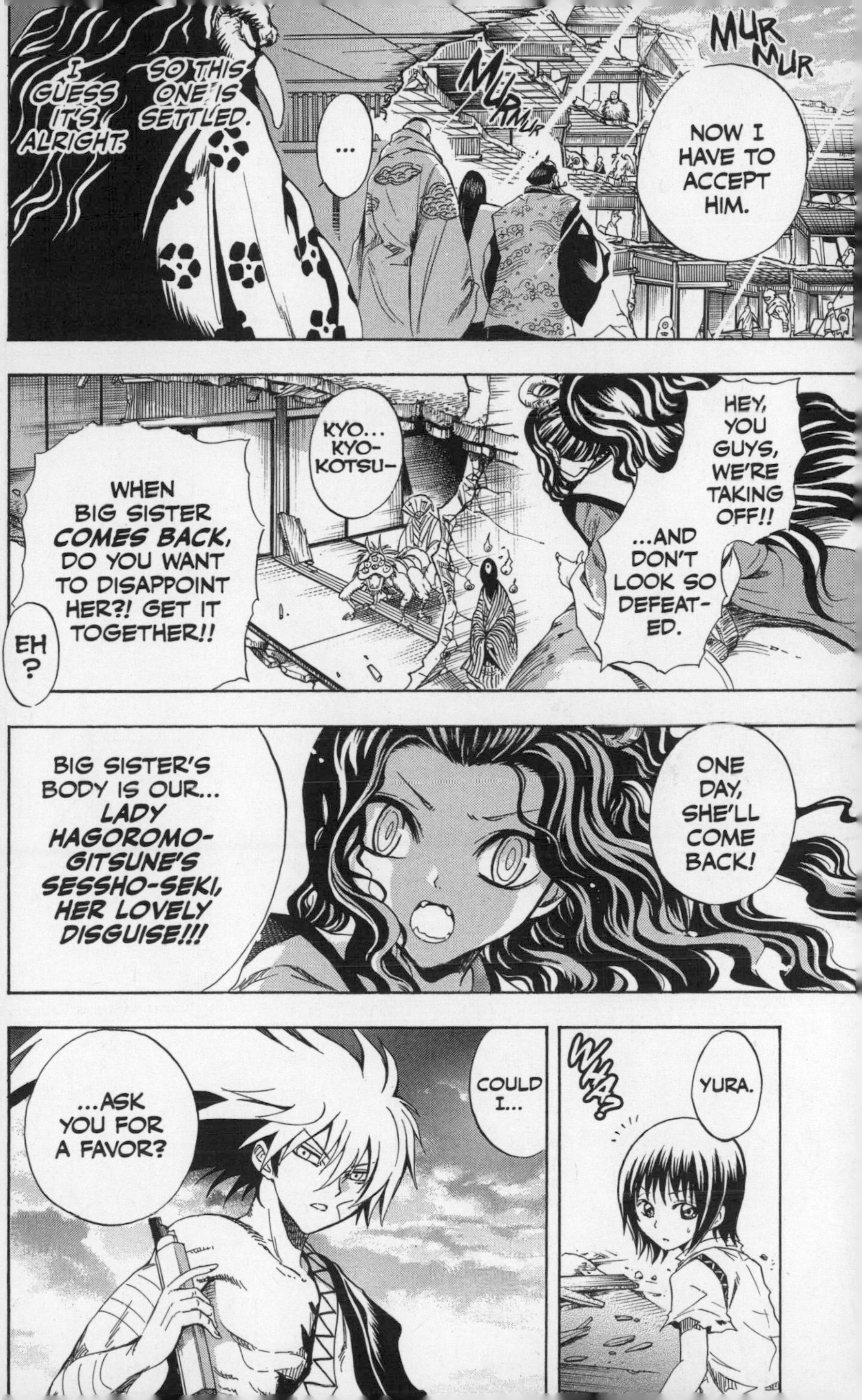
MUR MUR
NOW I HAVE TO ACCEPT HIM.
MUR MUR
...
SO THIS ONE IS SETTLED.
I GUESS IT'S ALRIGHT.
HEY, YOU GUYS, WE'RE TAKING OFF!!
...AND DON'T LOOK SO DEFEAT-ED.
KYO... KYO-KOTSU-
WHEN BIG SISTER *COMES BACK*, DO YOU WANT TO DISAPPOINT HER?! GET IT TOGETHER!!
EH?
ONE DAY, SHE'LL COME BACK!
BIG SISTER'S BODY IS OUR... ***LADY HAGOROMO-GITSUNE'S SESSHO-SEKI, HER LOVELY DISGUISE!!!***
YURA.
WHA?
COULD I...
...ASK YOU FOR A FAVOR?

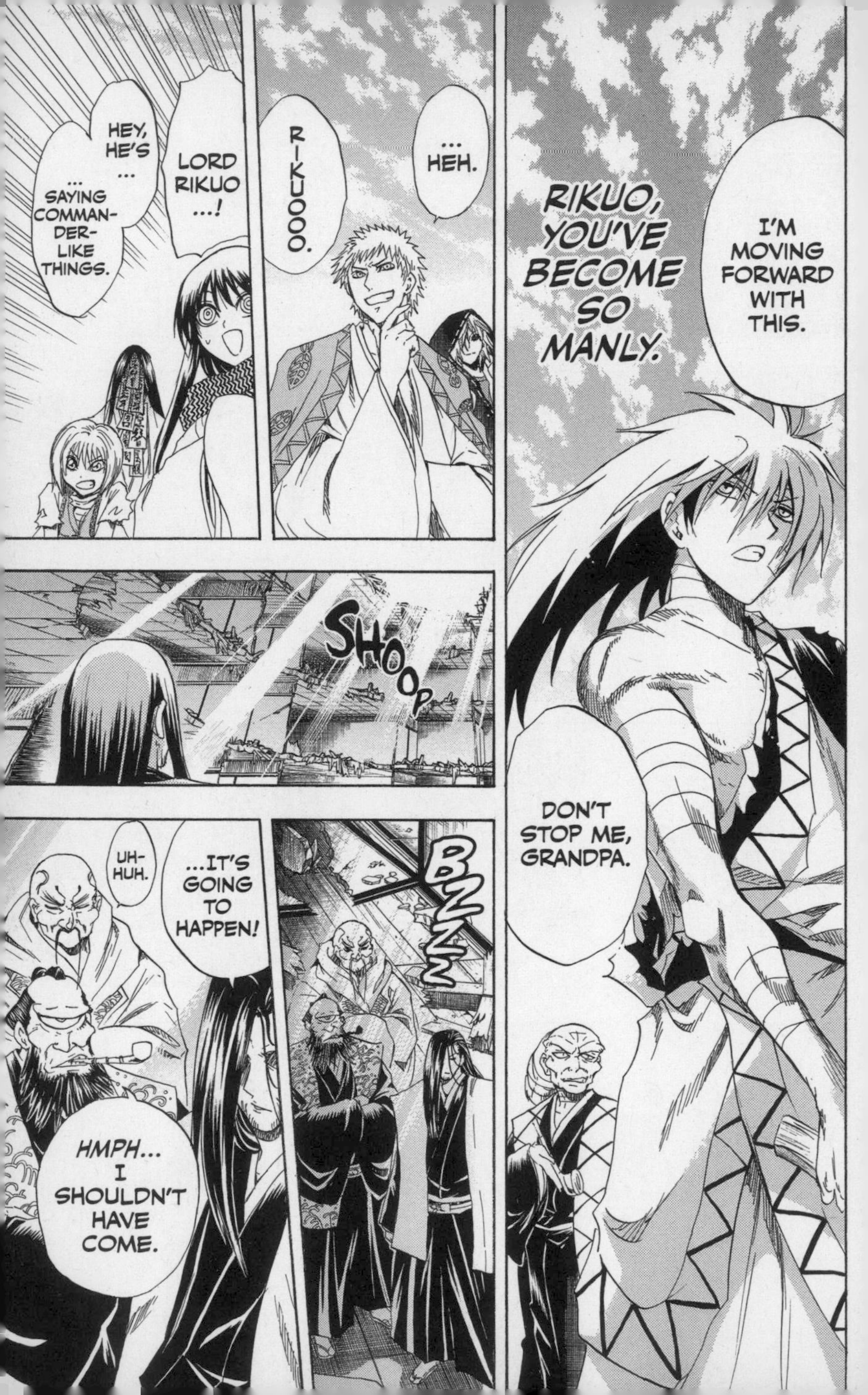
I'M MOVING FORWARD WITH THIS.
RIKUO, YOU'VE BECOME SO MANLY.
DON'T STOP ME, GRANDPA.
... HEH.
RIKUOOO.
LORD RIKUO ...!
HEY, HE'S ... SAYING COMMANDER-LIKE THINGS.
SHOOOP
BZZZ
...IT'S GOING TO HAPPEN!
UH-HUH.
HMPH... I SHOULDN'T HAVE COME.

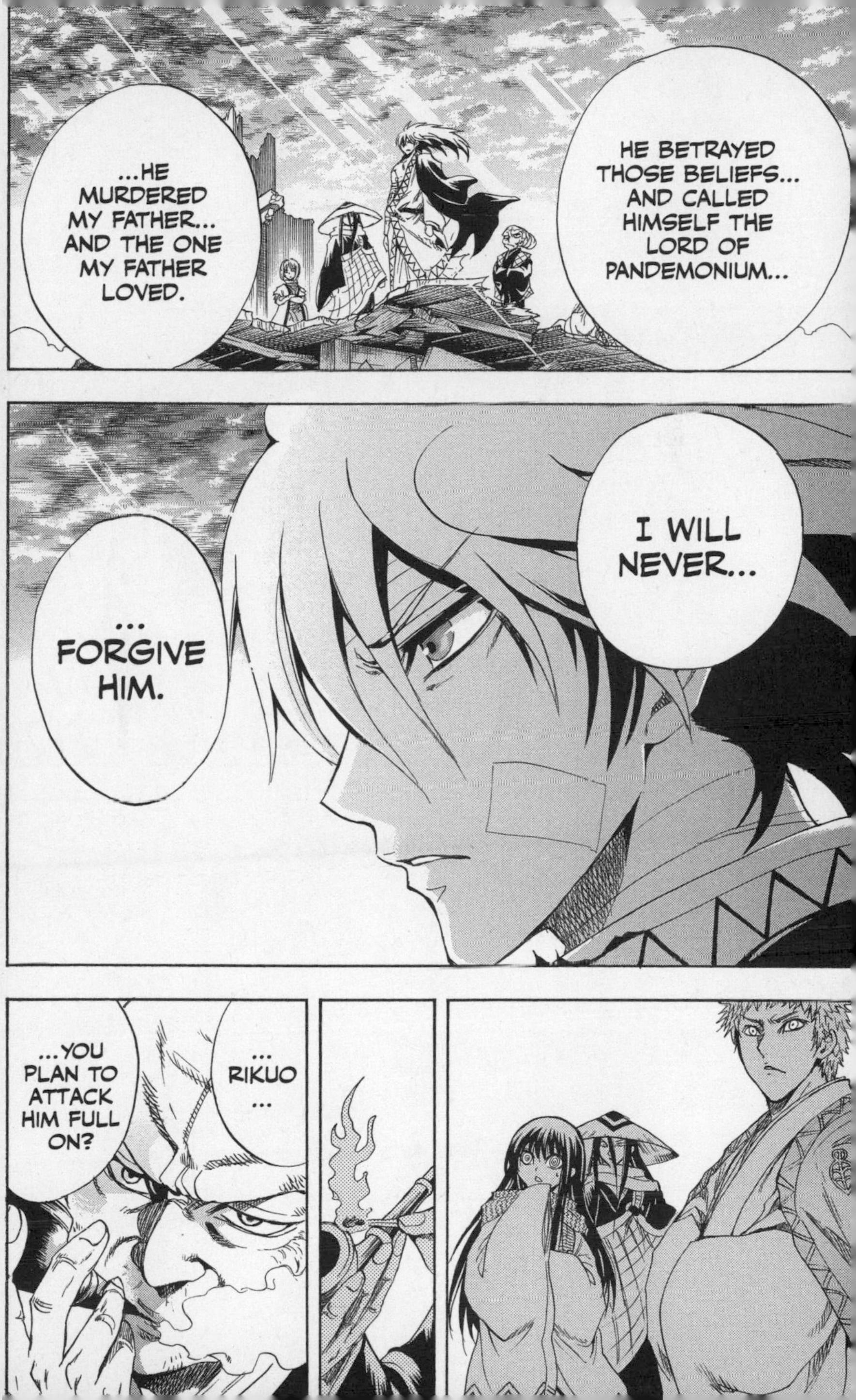
HE BETRAYED THOSE BELIEFS... AND CALLED HIMSELF THE LORD OF PANDEMONIUM...
...HE MURDERED MY FATHER... AND THE ONE MY FATHER LOVED.
I WILL NEVER...
... FORGIVE HIM.
... RIKUO ...
...YOU PLAN TO ATTACK HIM FULL ON?

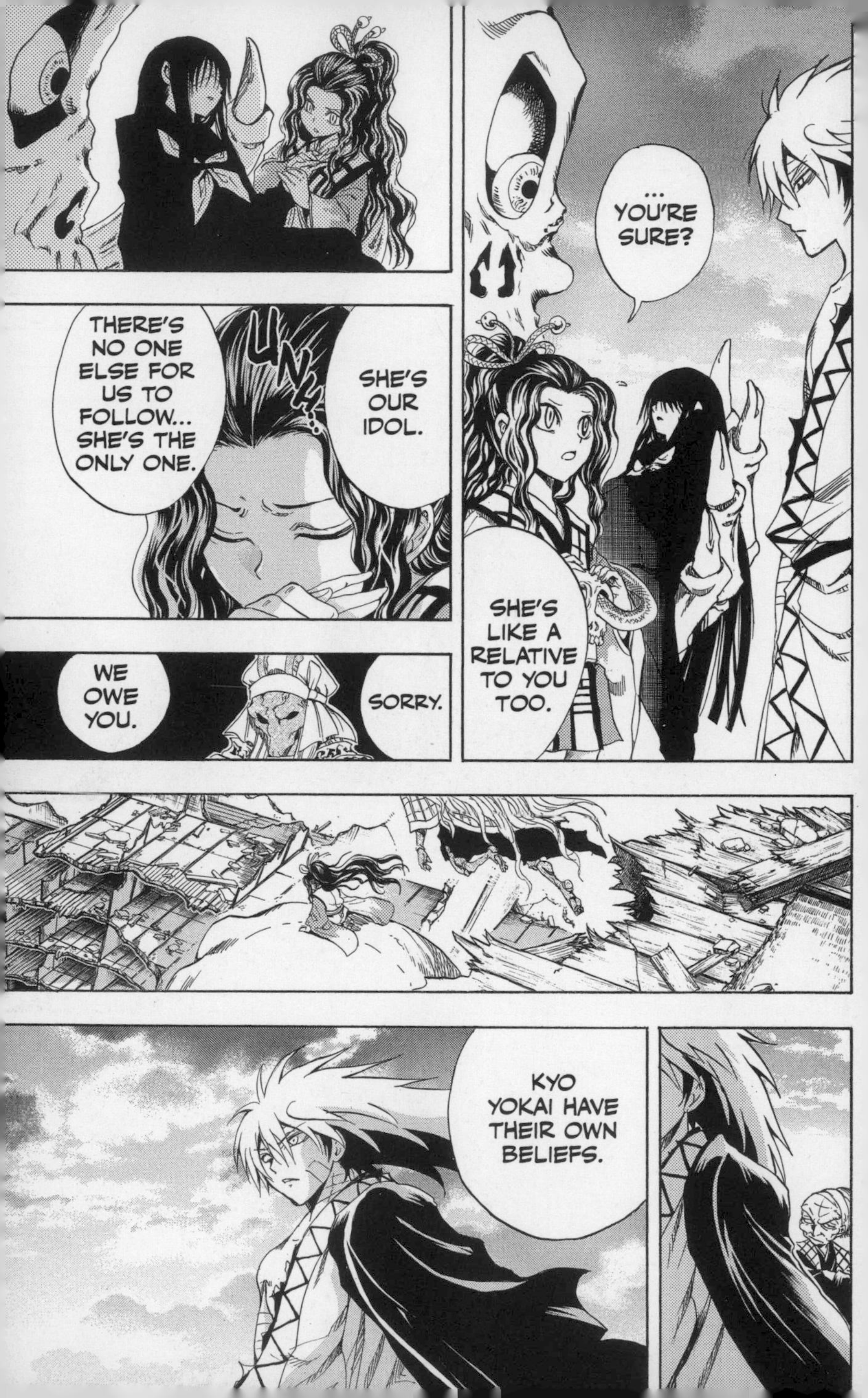

... YOU'RE SURE?
SHE'S LIKE A RELATIVE TO YOU TOO.
SHE'S OUR IDOL.
UNH
THERE'S NO ONE ELSE FOR US TO FOLLOW... SHE'S THE ONLY ONE.
SORRY.
WE OWE YOU.
KYO YOKAI HAVE THEIR OWN BELIEFS.

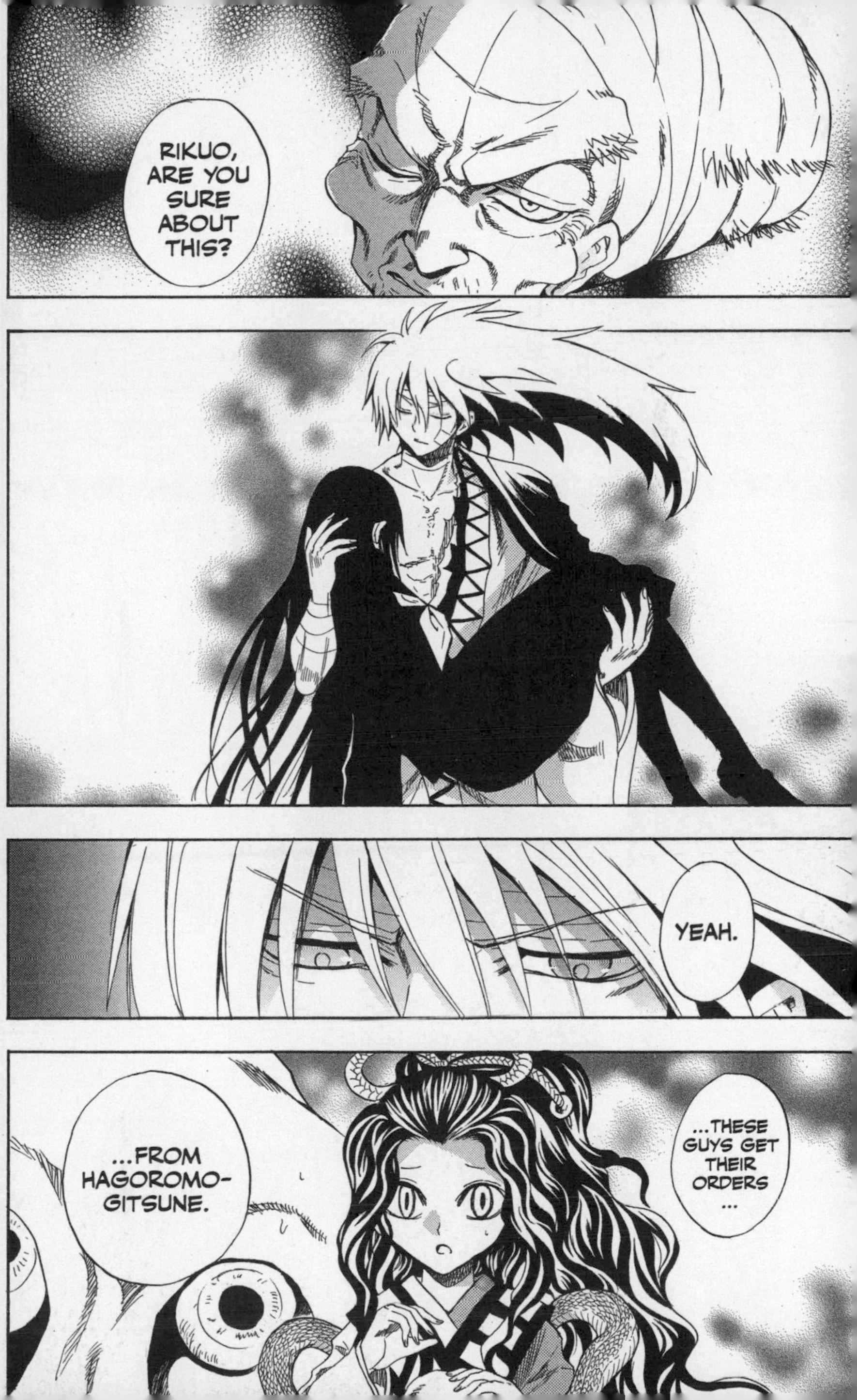
RIKUO, ARE YOU SURE ABOUT THIS?
YEAH.
...THESE GUYS GET THEIR ORDERS ...
...FROM HAGOROMO-GITSUNE.

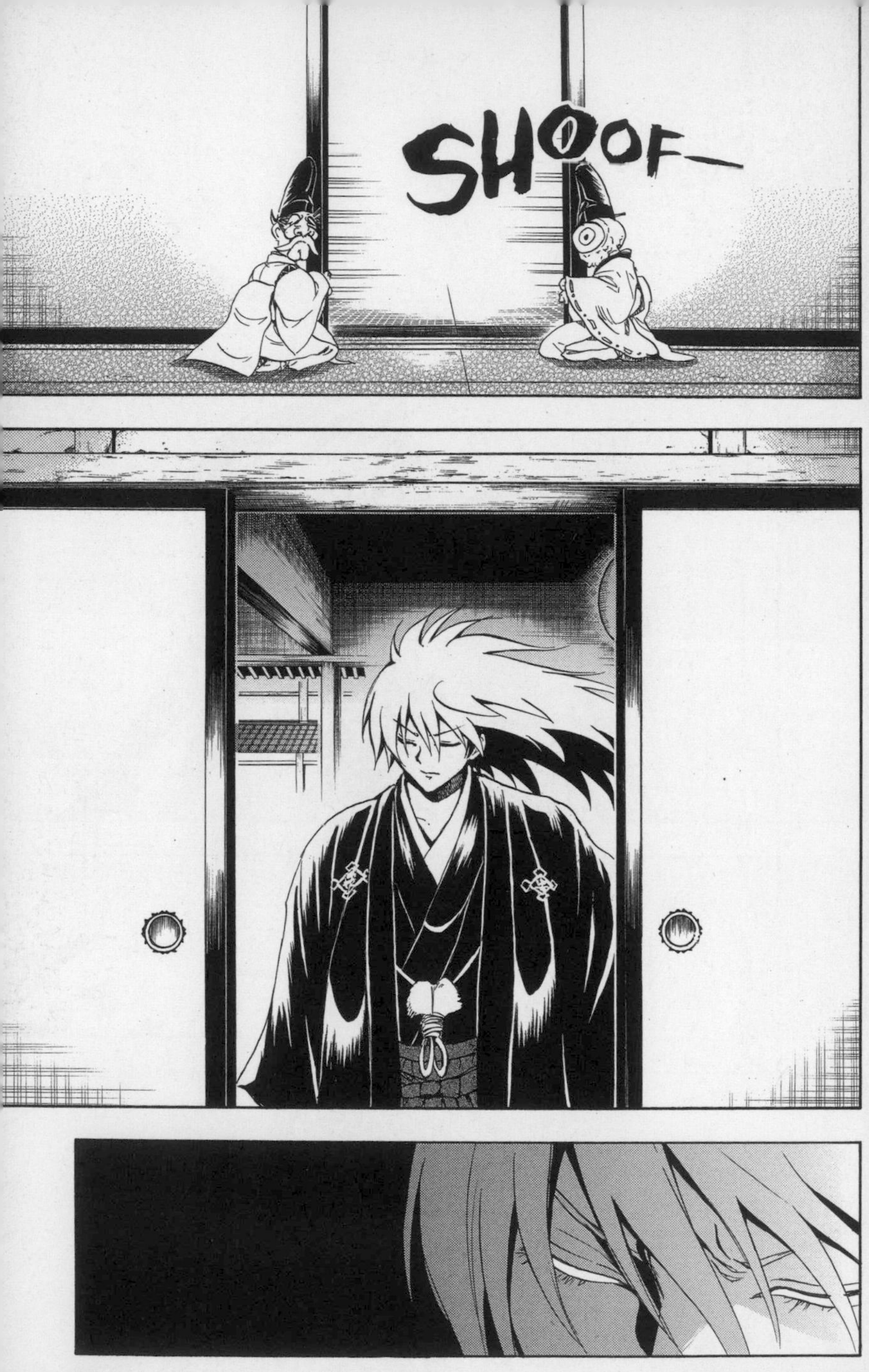
SHOOF—

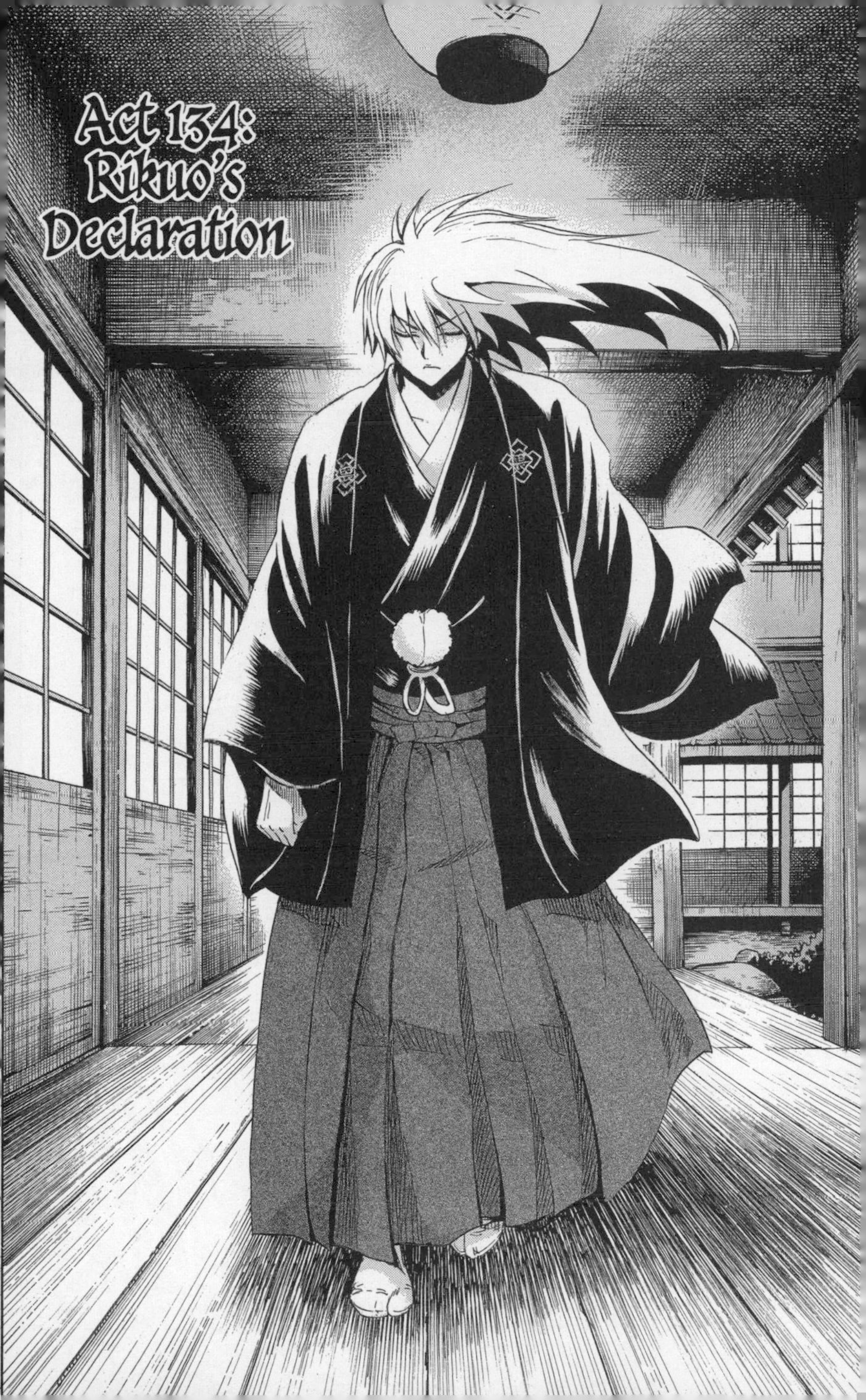
Act 134: Rikuo's Declaration

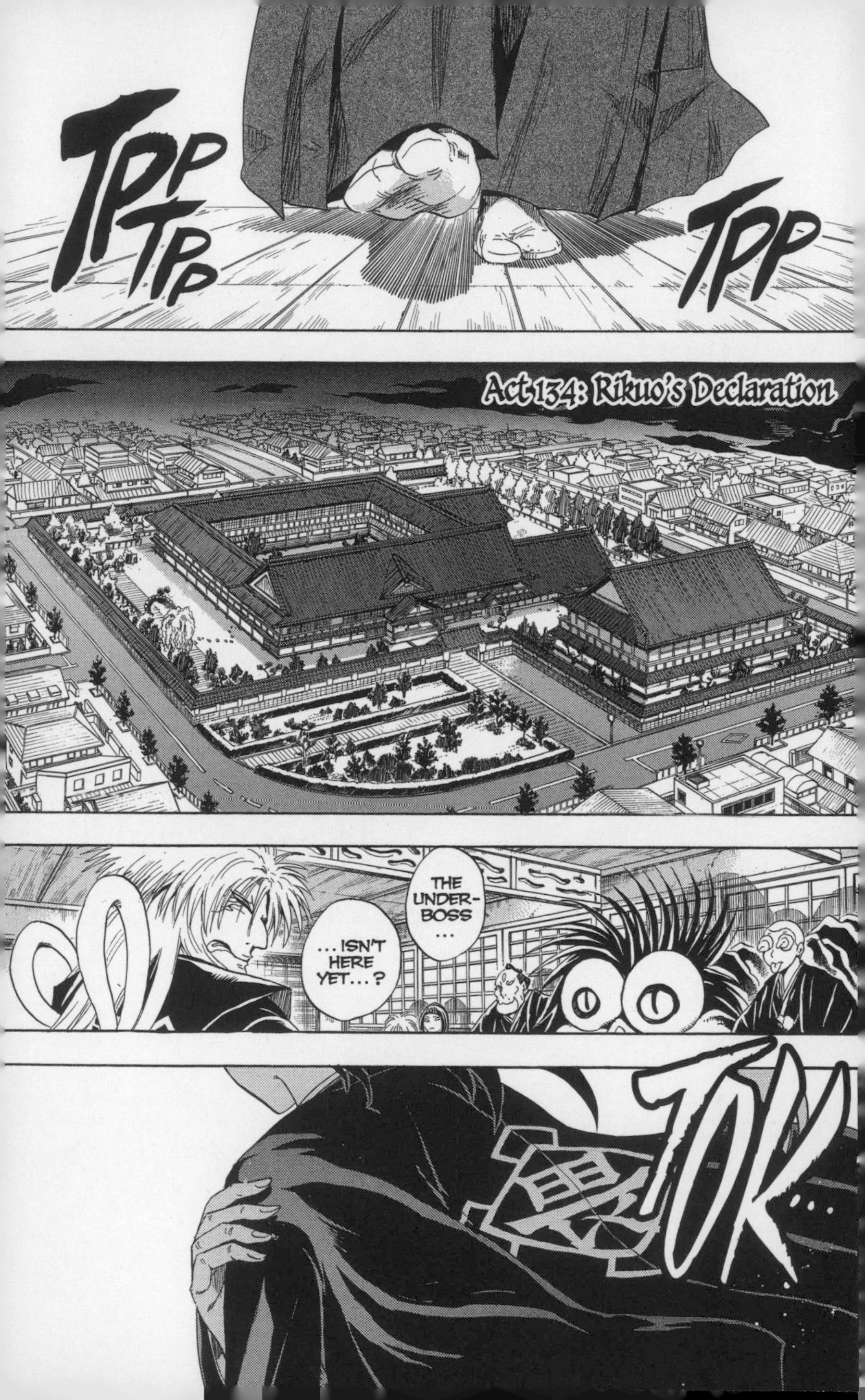
TPP
TPP TPP TPP
Act 134: Rikuo's Declaration
THE UNDER-BOSS...
...ISN'T HERE YET...?
TOK...

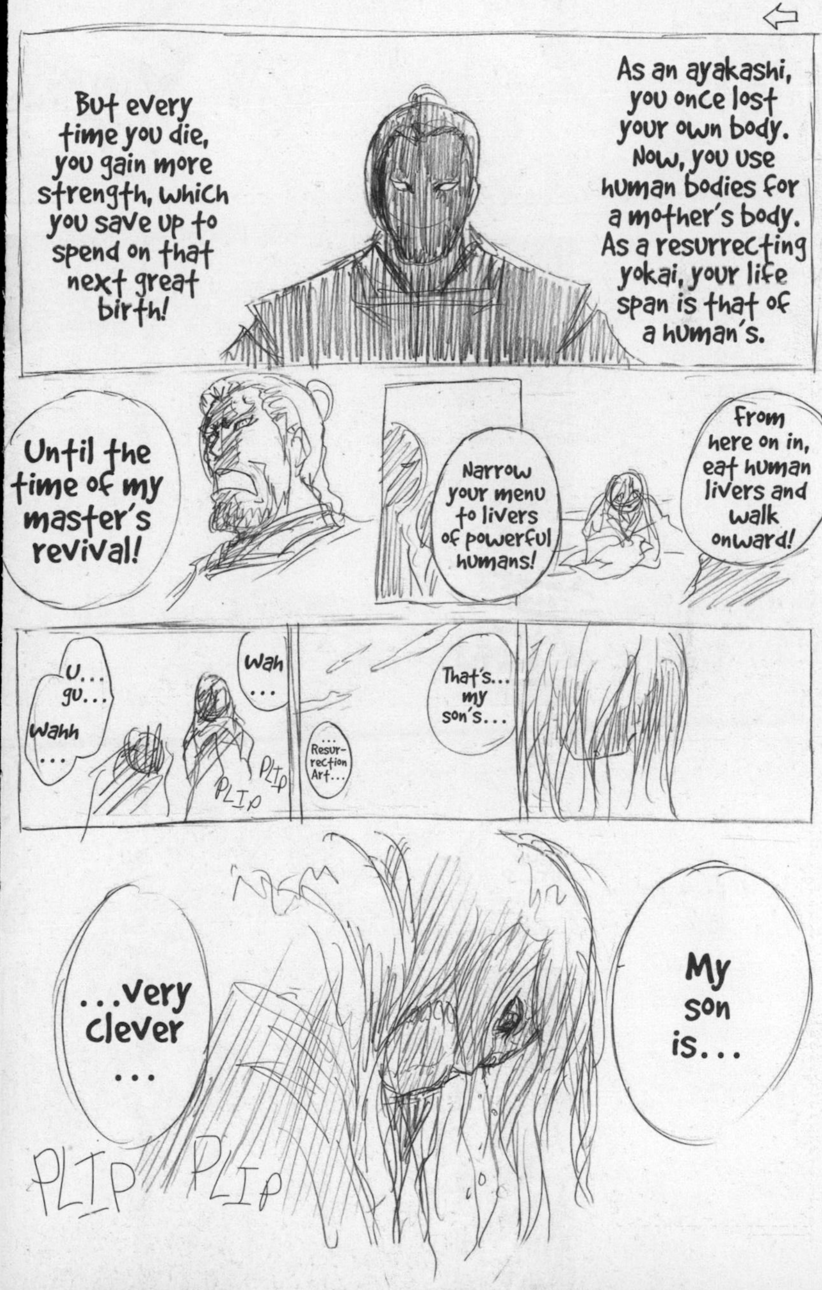
As an ayakashi, you once lost your own body. Now, you use human bodies for a mother's body. As a resurrecting yokai, your life span is that of a human's.
But every time you die, you gain more strength, which you save up to spend on that next great birth!
From here on in, eat human livers and walk onward!
Narrow your menu to livers of powerful humans!
Until the time of my master's revival!
That's... my son's...
...Resurrection Art...
Wah...
U... gu... Wahh...
PLIP
PLIP
My son is...
...very clever...
PLIP
PLIP

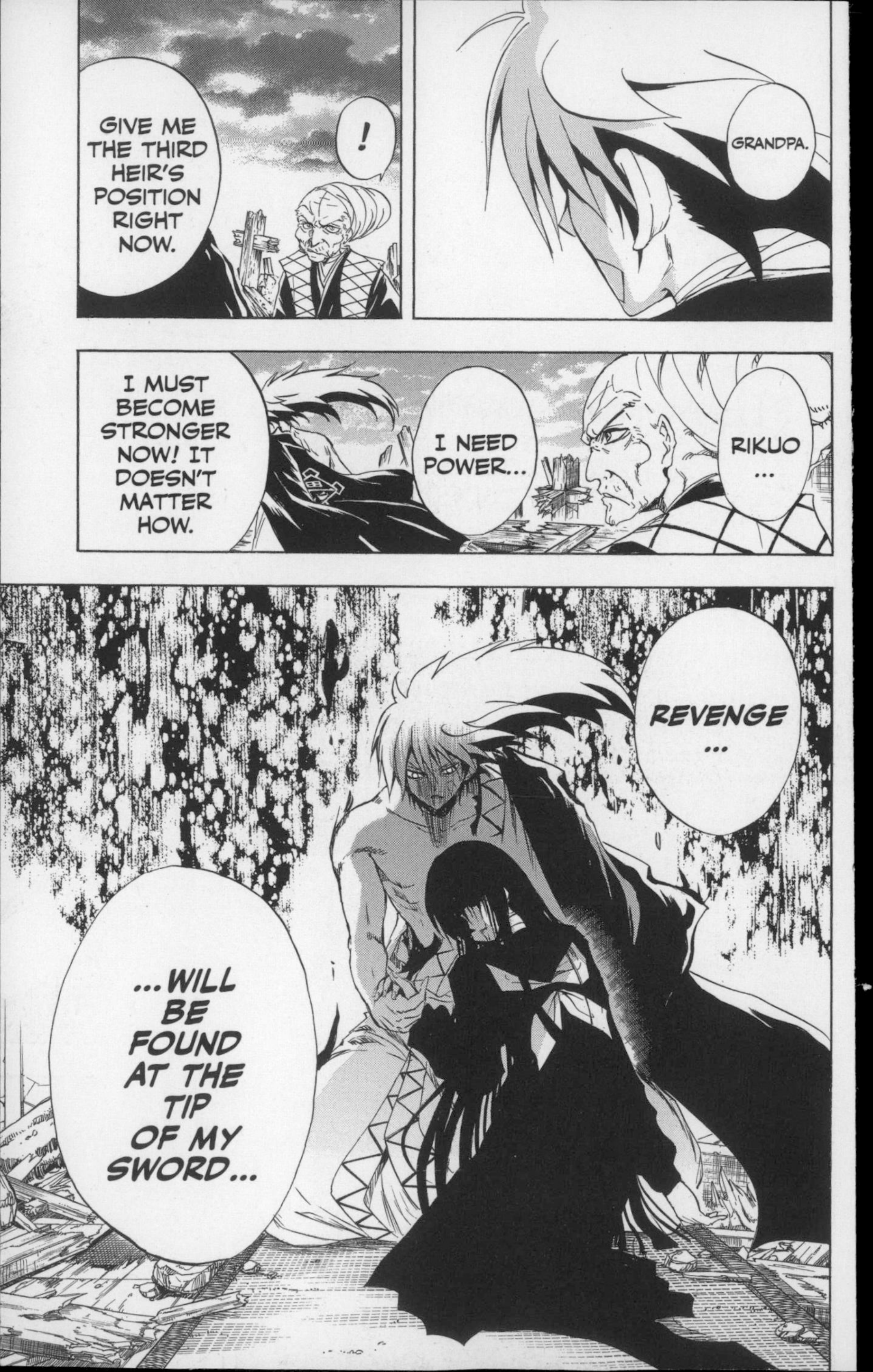
GRANDPA.
!
GIVE ME THE THIRD HEIR'S POSITION RIGHT NOW.
RIKUO ...
I NEED POWER...
I MUST BECOME STRONGER NOW! IT DOESN'T MATTER HOW.
REVENGE ...
...WILL BE FOUND AT THE TIP OF MY SWORD...

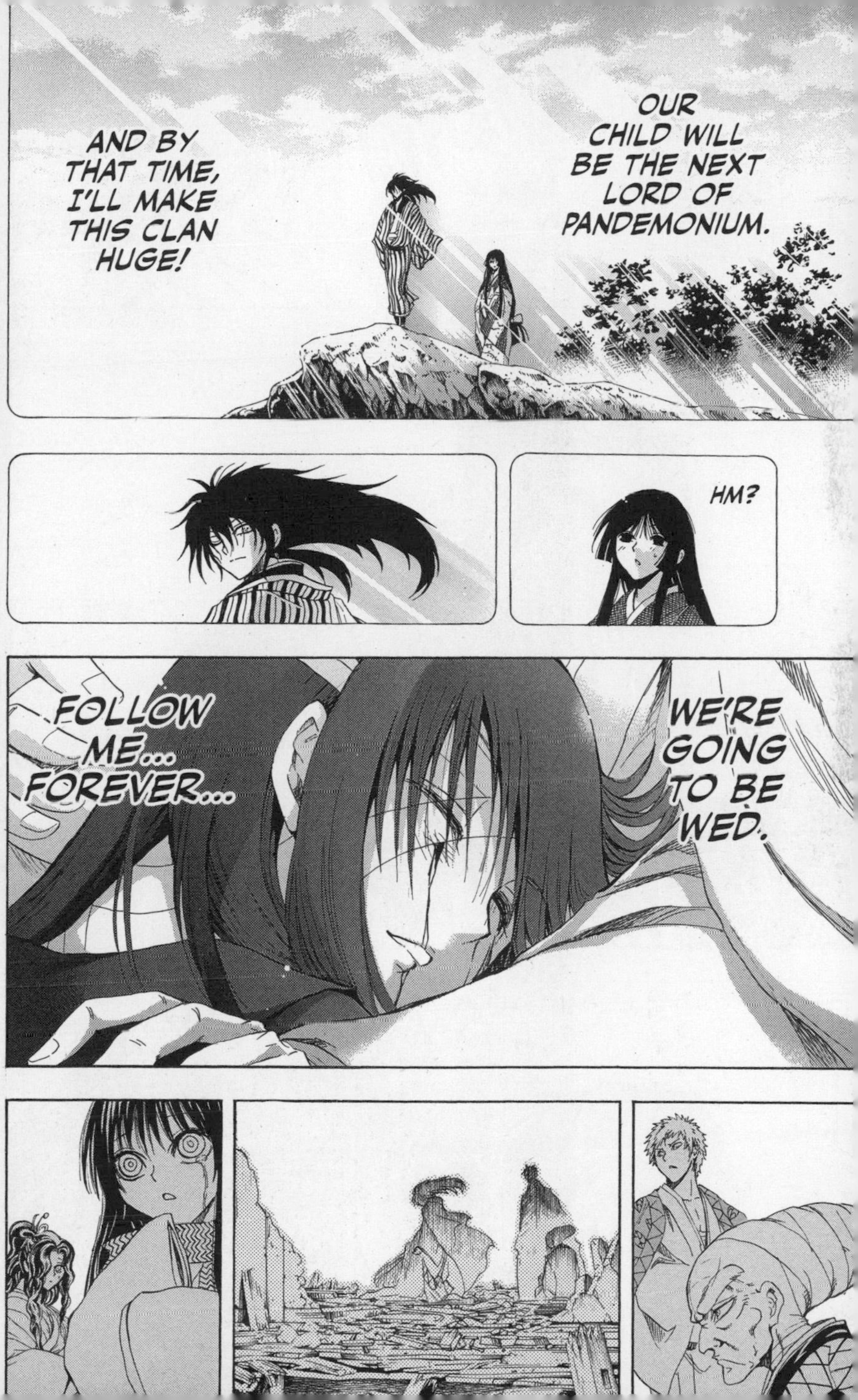
OUR CHILD WILL BE THE NEXT LORD OF PANDEMONIUM.
AND BY THAT TIME, I'LL MAKE THIS CLAN HUGE!
HM?
WE'RE GOING TO BE WED.
FOLLOW ME... FOREVER...

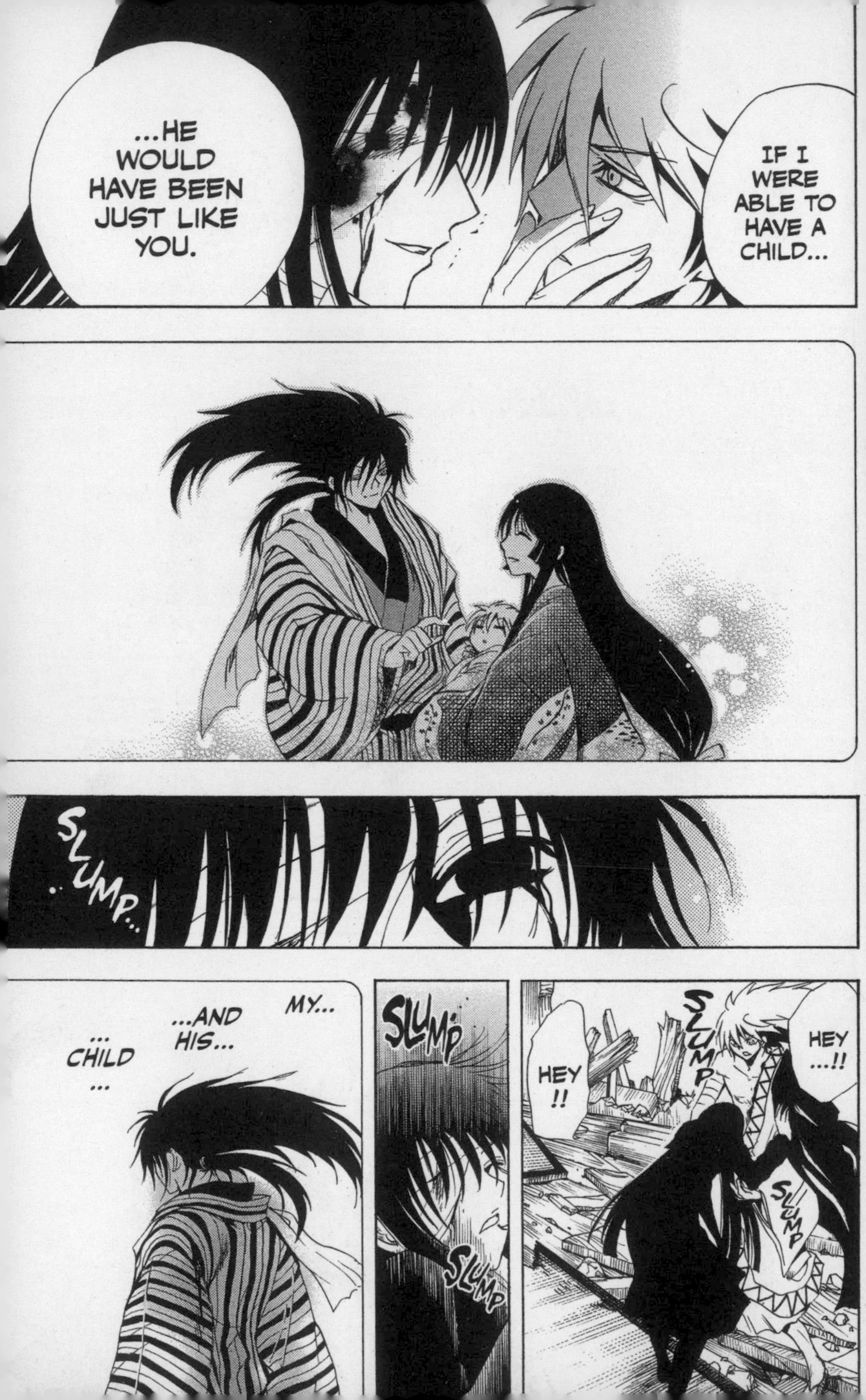
IF I WERE ABLE TO HAVE A CHILD...
...HE WOULD HAVE BEEN JUST LIKE YOU.
SLUMP...
HEY ...!!
SLUMP
HEY !!
SLUMP
SLUMP
SLUMP
MY...
...AND HIS...
... CHILD ...

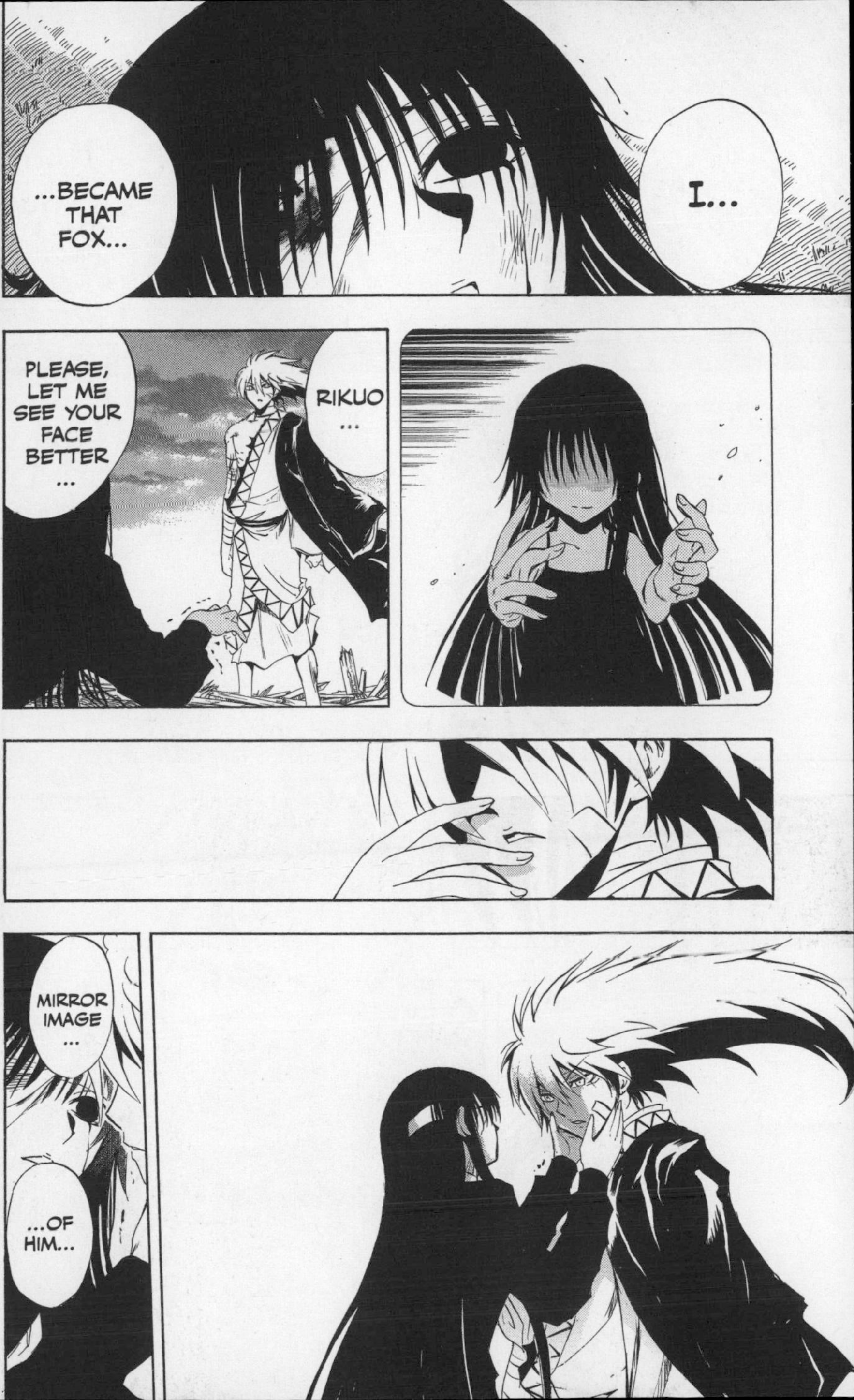
I...
...BECAME THAT FOX...
RIKUO ...
PLEASE, LET ME SEE YOUR FACE BETTER ...
MIRROR IMAGE ...
...OF HIM...

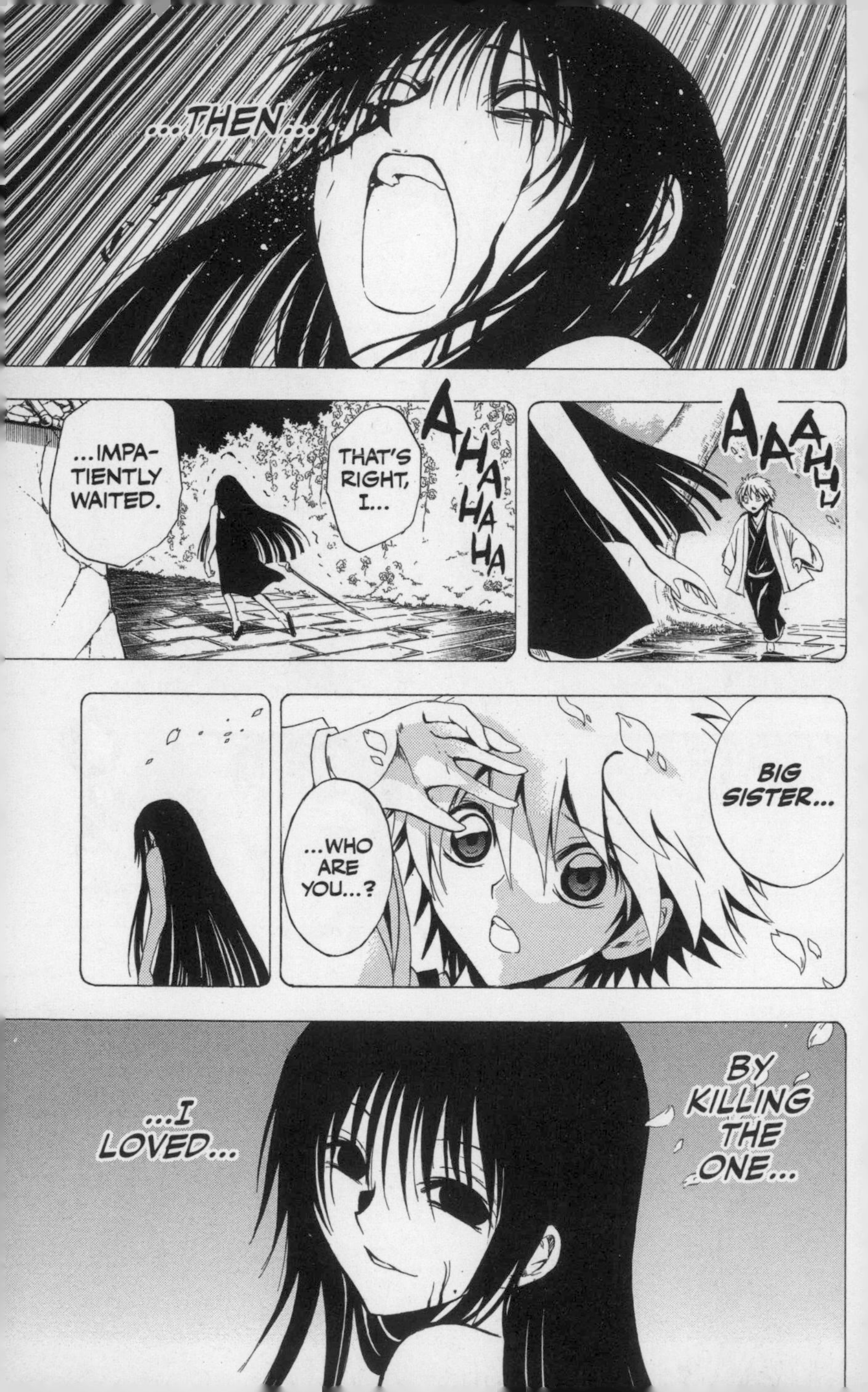
...THEN...
AAAHHH
AHAHAHAHA
THAT'S RIGHT, I...
...IMPATIENTLY WAITED.
BIG SISTER...
...WHO ARE YOU...?
BY KILLING THE ONE...
...I LOVED...

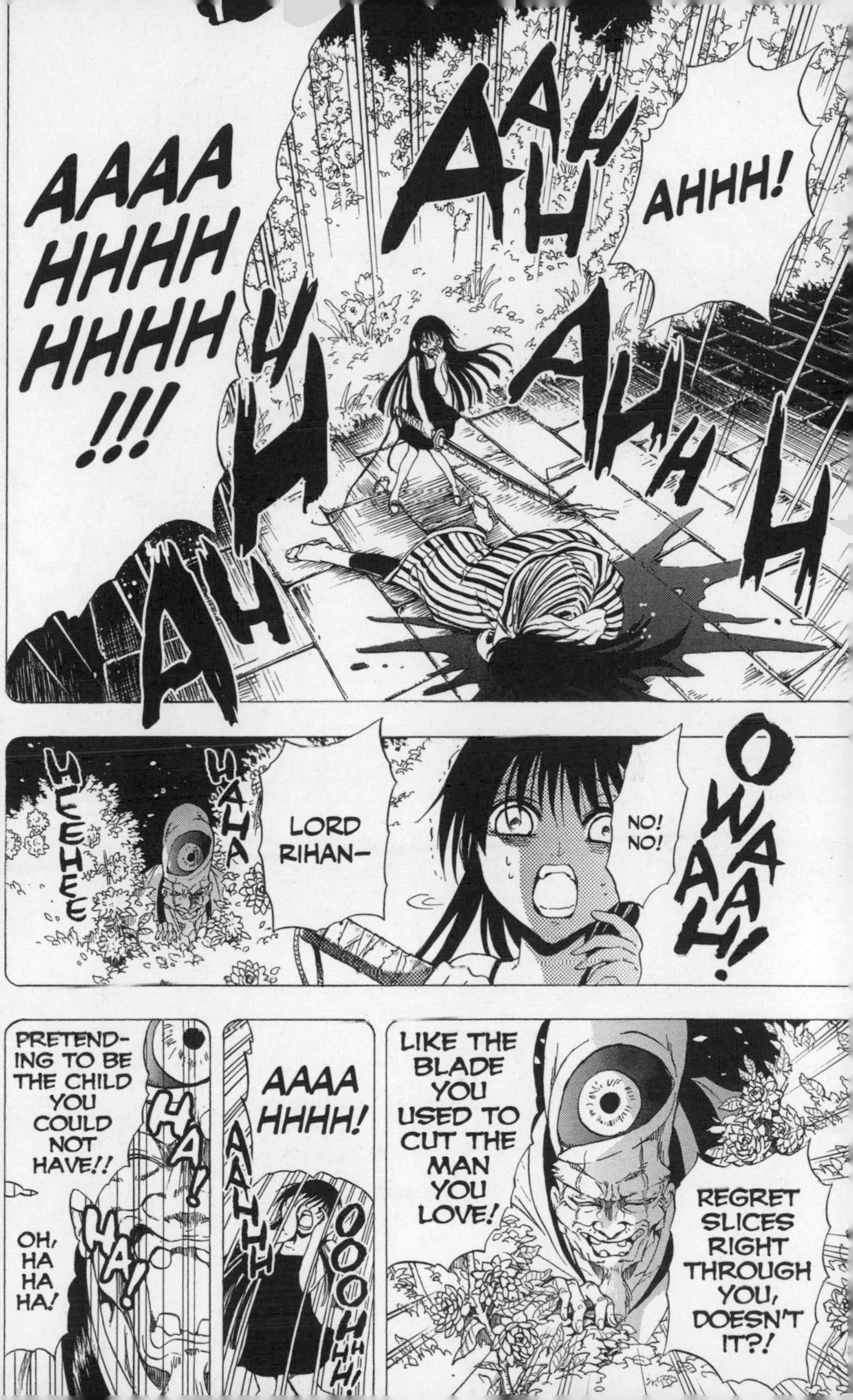
AHHH!
AAAA HHHH HHHH !!!
OWAAAH!
NO! NO!
LORD RIHAN—
HAHAHA
HEEHEE
REGRET SLICES RIGHT THROUGH YOU, DOESN'T IT?!
LIKE THE BLADE YOU USED TO CUT THE MAN YOU LOVE!
AAAA HHHH!
AAHHH
OOOOHHH!
PRETEND-ING TO BE THE CHILD YOU COULD NOT HAVE!!
HA! HA!
OH, HA HA HA!

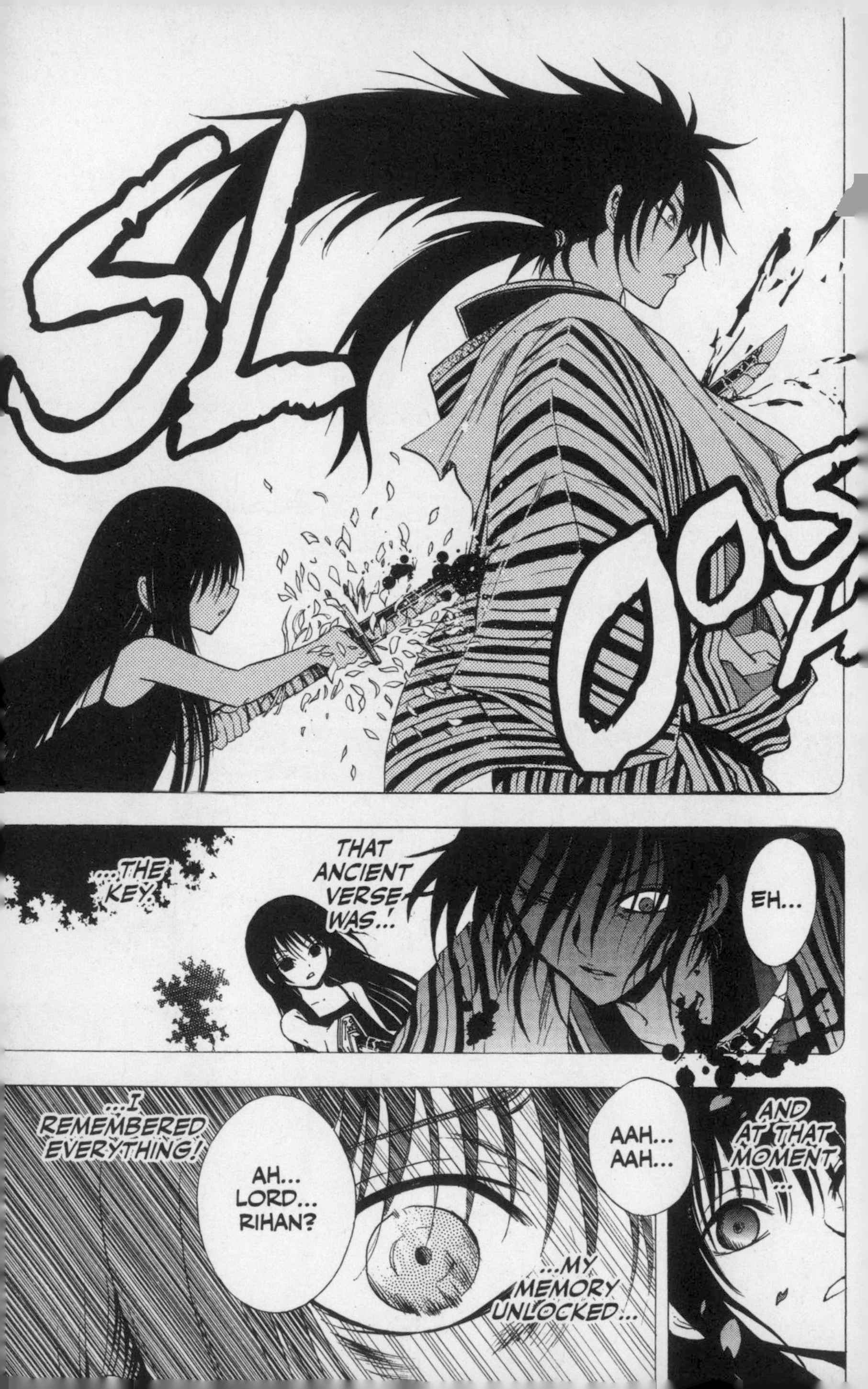
SL
OOS
EH...
THAT ANCIENT VERSE WAS...!
...THE KEY.
AND AT THAT MOMENT...
AAH... AAH...
AH... LORD... RIHAN?
...MY MEMORY UNLOCKED...
...I REMEMBERED EVERYTHING!

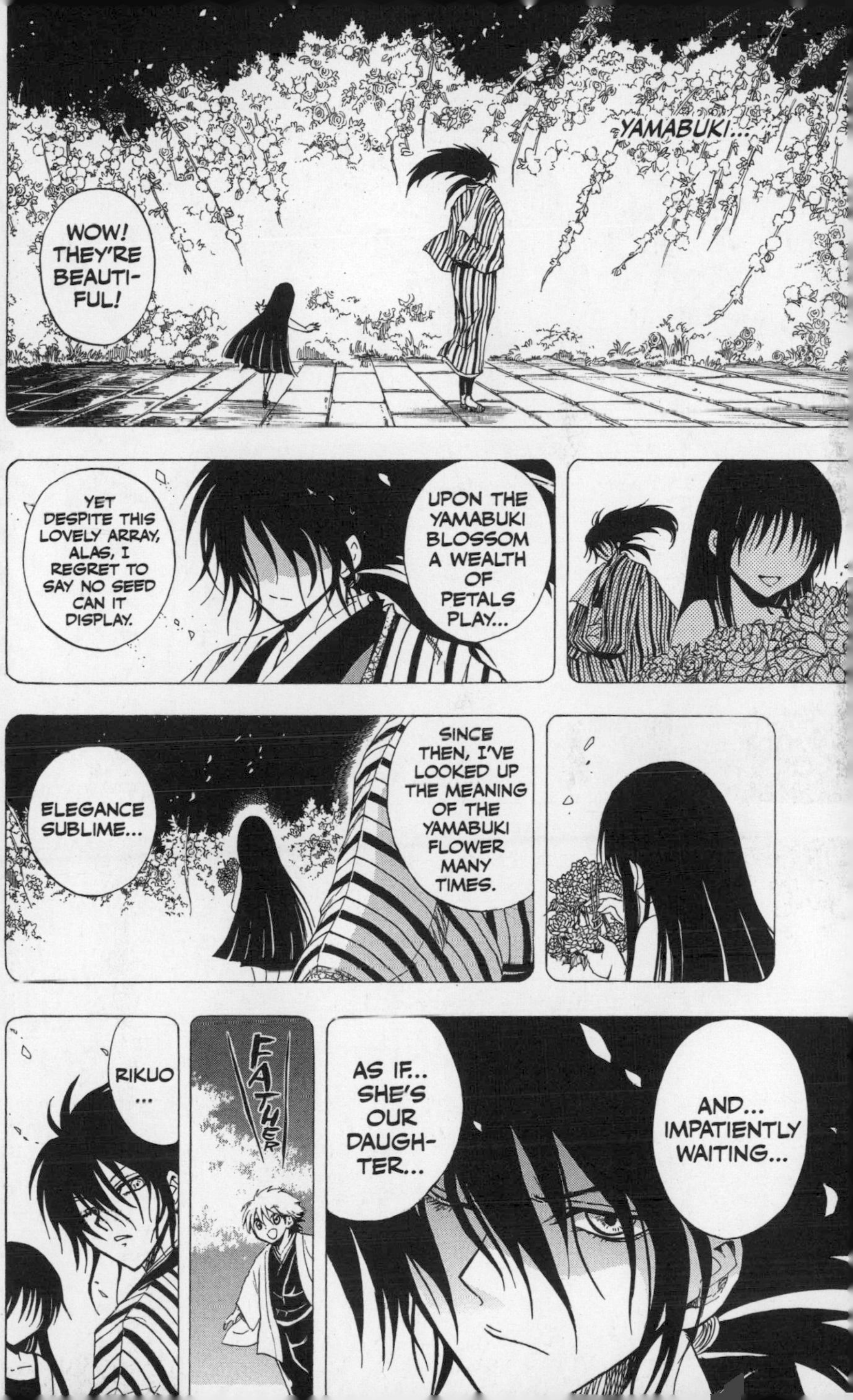
YAMABUKI...
WOW! THEY'RE BEAUTI-FUL!
UPON THE YAMABUKI BLOSSOM A WEALTH OF PETALS PLAY...
YET DESPITE THIS LOVELY ARRAY, ALAS, I REGRET TO SAY NO SEED CAN IT DISPLAY.
SINCE THEN, I'VE LOOKED UP THE MEANING OF THE YAMABUKI FLOWER MANY TIMES.
ELEGANCE SUBLIME...
AND... IMPATIENTLY WAITING...
AS IF... SHE'S OUR DAUGH-TER...
FATHER
RIKUO ...

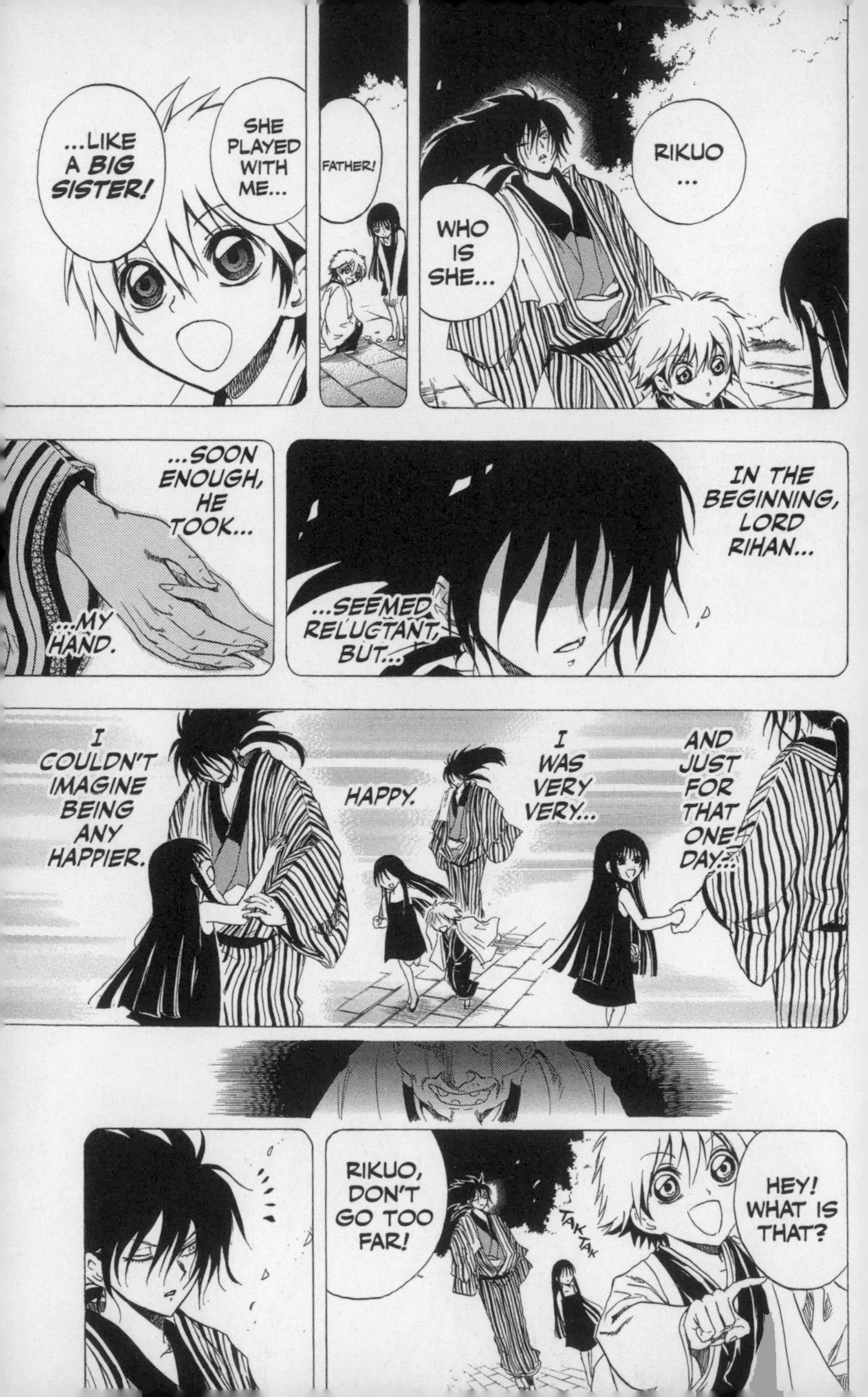
RIKUO ...
WHO IS SHE...
FATHER!
SHE PLAYED WITH ME...
...LIKE A BIG SISTER!
IN THE BEGINNING, LORD RIHAN...
...SEEMED RELUCTANT, BUT...
...SOON ENOUGH, HE TOOK...
...MY HAND.
AND JUST FOR THAT ONE DAY...
I WAS VERY VERY...
HAPPY.
I COULDN'T IMAGINE BEING ANY HAPPIER.
HEY! WHAT IS THAT?
TAK TAK
RIKUO, DON'T GO TOO FAR!

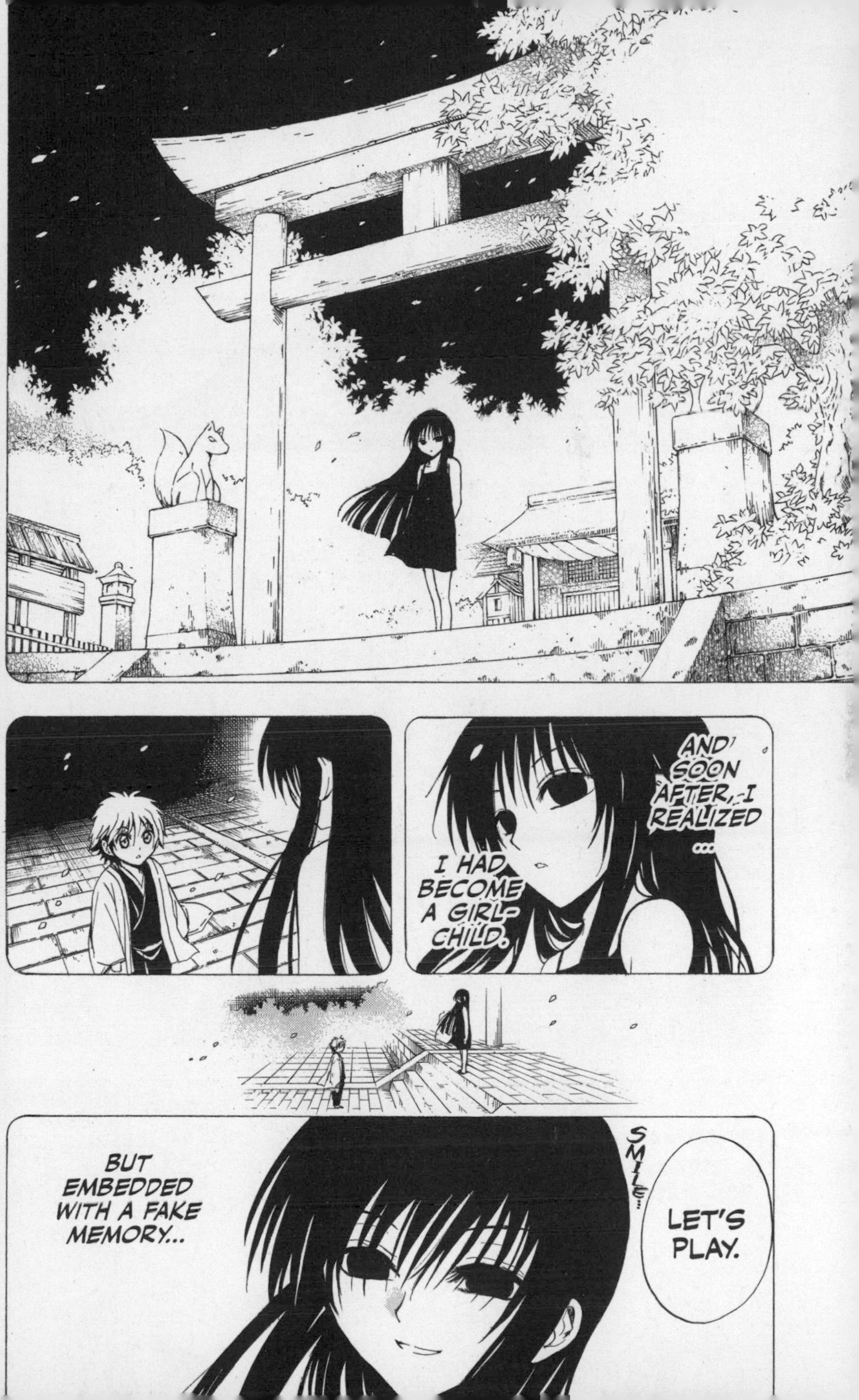
AND SOON AFTER, I REALIZED...
I HAD BECOME A GIRL-CHILD.
SMILE...
LET'S PLAY.
BUT EMBEDDED WITH A FAKE MEMORY...

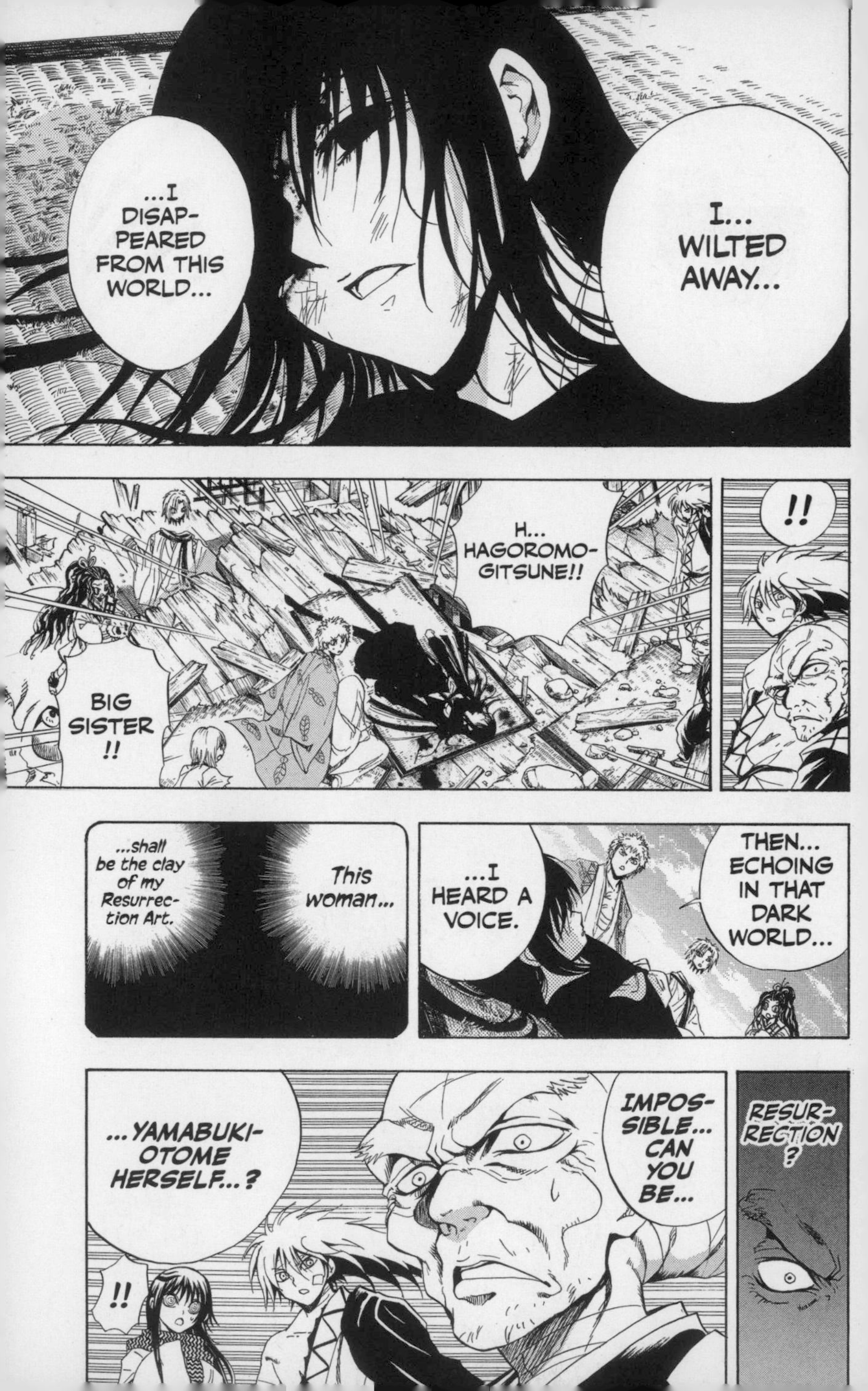
I... WILTED AWAY...
...I DISAPPEARED FROM THIS WORLD...
!!
H... HAGOROMO-GITSUNE!!
BIG SISTER!!
THEN... ECHOING IN THAT DARK WORLD...
...I HEARD A VOICE.
This woman...
...shall be the clay of my Resurrection Art.
RESURRECTION?
IMPOSSIBLE... CAN YOU BE...
...YAMABUKI-OTOME HERSELF...?
!!

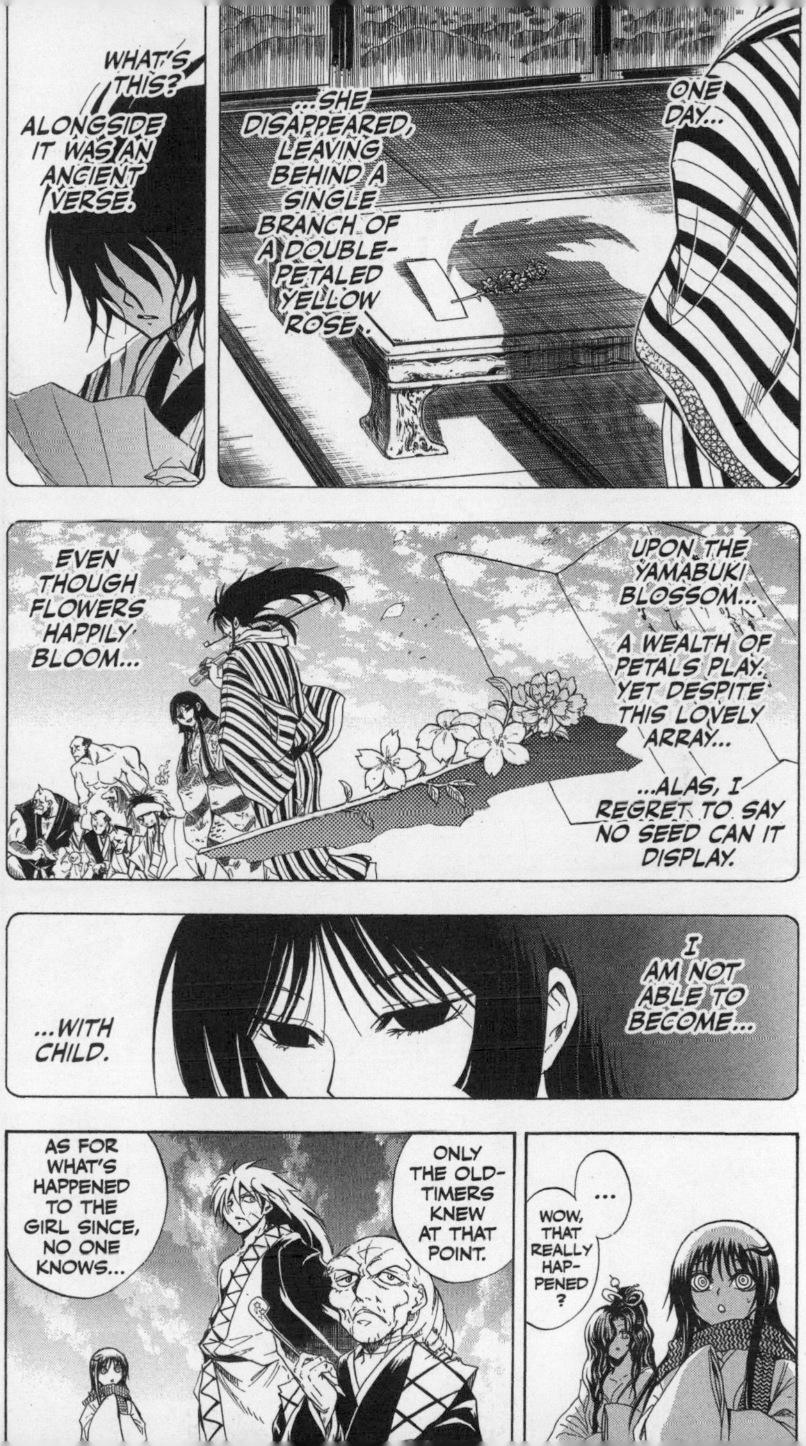

ONE DAY...
...SHE DISAPPEARED, LEAVING BEHIND A SINGLE BRANCH OF A DOUBLE-PETALED YELLOW ROSE...
WHAT'S THIS?
ALONGSIDE IT WAS AN ANCIENT VERSE.
UPON THE YAMABUKI BLOSSOM...
A WEALTH OF PETALS PLAY. YET DESPITE THIS LOVELY ARRAY...
...ALAS, I REGRET TO SAY NO SEED CAN IT DISPLAY.
EVEN THOUGH FLOWERS HAPPILY BLOOM...
I AM NOT ABLE TO BECOME...
...WITH CHILD.
...
WOW, THAT REALLY HAPPENED?
ONLY THE OLD-TIMERS KNEW AT THAT POINT.
AS FOR WHAT'S HAPPENED TO THE GIRL SINCE, NO ONE KNOWS...

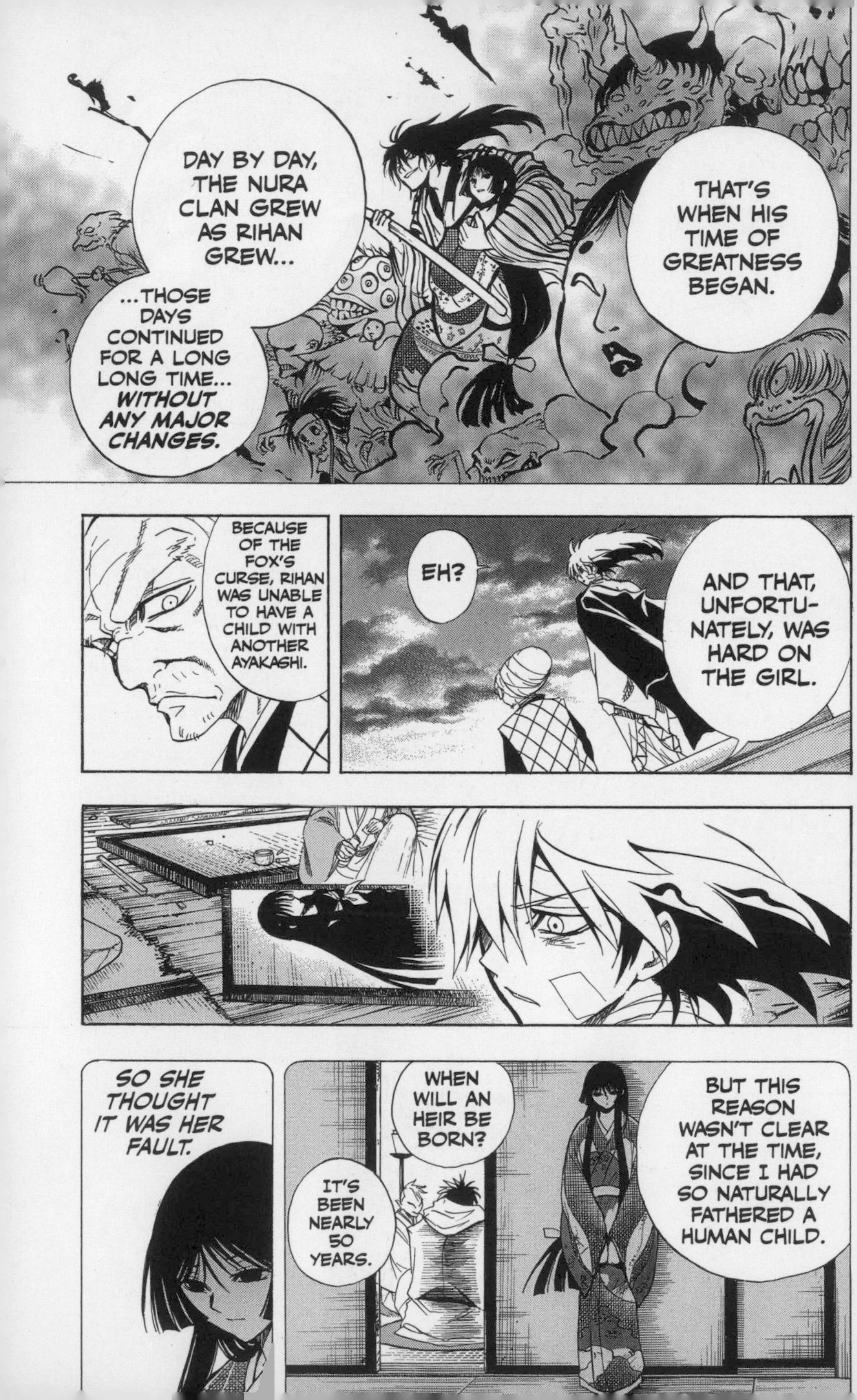
THAT'S WHEN HIS TIME OF GREATNESS BEGAN.
DAY BY DAY, THE NURA CLAN GREW AS RIHAN GREW...
...THOSE DAYS CONTINUED FOR A LONG LONG TIME... *WITHOUT ANY MAJOR CHANGES.*
AND THAT, UNFORTUNATELY, WAS HARD ON THE GIRL.
EH?
BECAUSE OF THE FOX'S CURSE, RIHAN WAS UNABLE TO HAVE A CHILD WITH ANOTHER AYAKASHI.
BUT THIS REASON WASN'T CLEAR AT THE TIME, SINCE I HAD SO NATURALLY FATHERED A HUMAN CHILD.
WHEN WILL AN HEIR BE BORN?
IT'S BEEN NEARLY 50 YEARS.
SO SHE THOUGHT IT WAS HER FAULT.

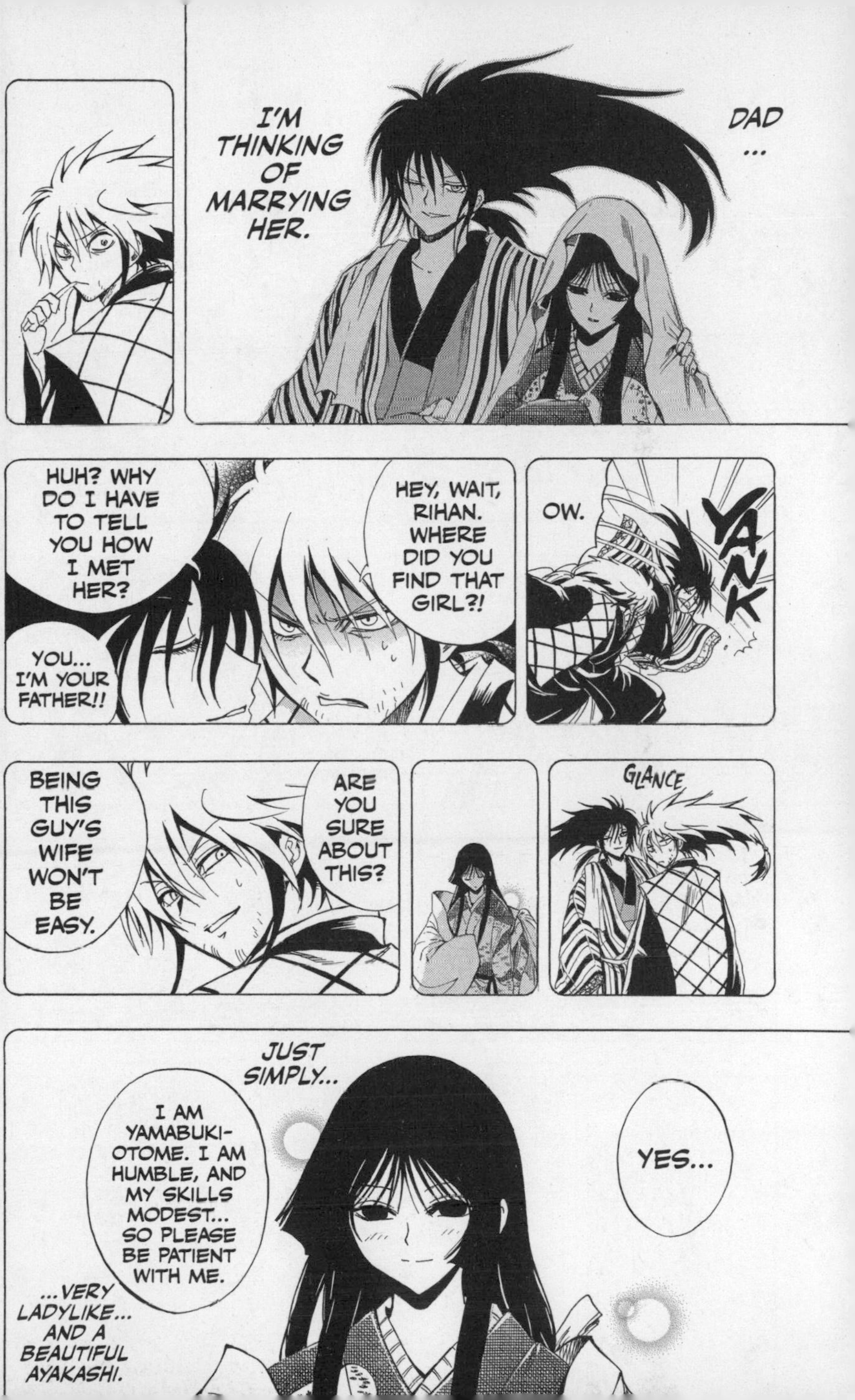
DAD ...
I'M THINKING OF MARRYING HER.
OW.
YANK
HEY, WAIT, RIHAN. WHERE DID YOU FIND THAT GIRL?!
HUH? WHY DO I HAVE TO TELL YOU HOW I MET HER?
YOU... I'M YOUR FATHER!!
GLANCE
ARE YOU SURE ABOUT THIS?
BEING THIS GUY'S WIFE WON'T BE EASY.
YES...
JUST SIMPLY...
I AM YAMABUKI-OTOME. I AM HUMBLE, AND MY SKILLS MODEST... SO PLEASE BE PATIENT WITH ME.
...VERY LADYLIKE... AND A BEAUTIFUL AYAKASHI.

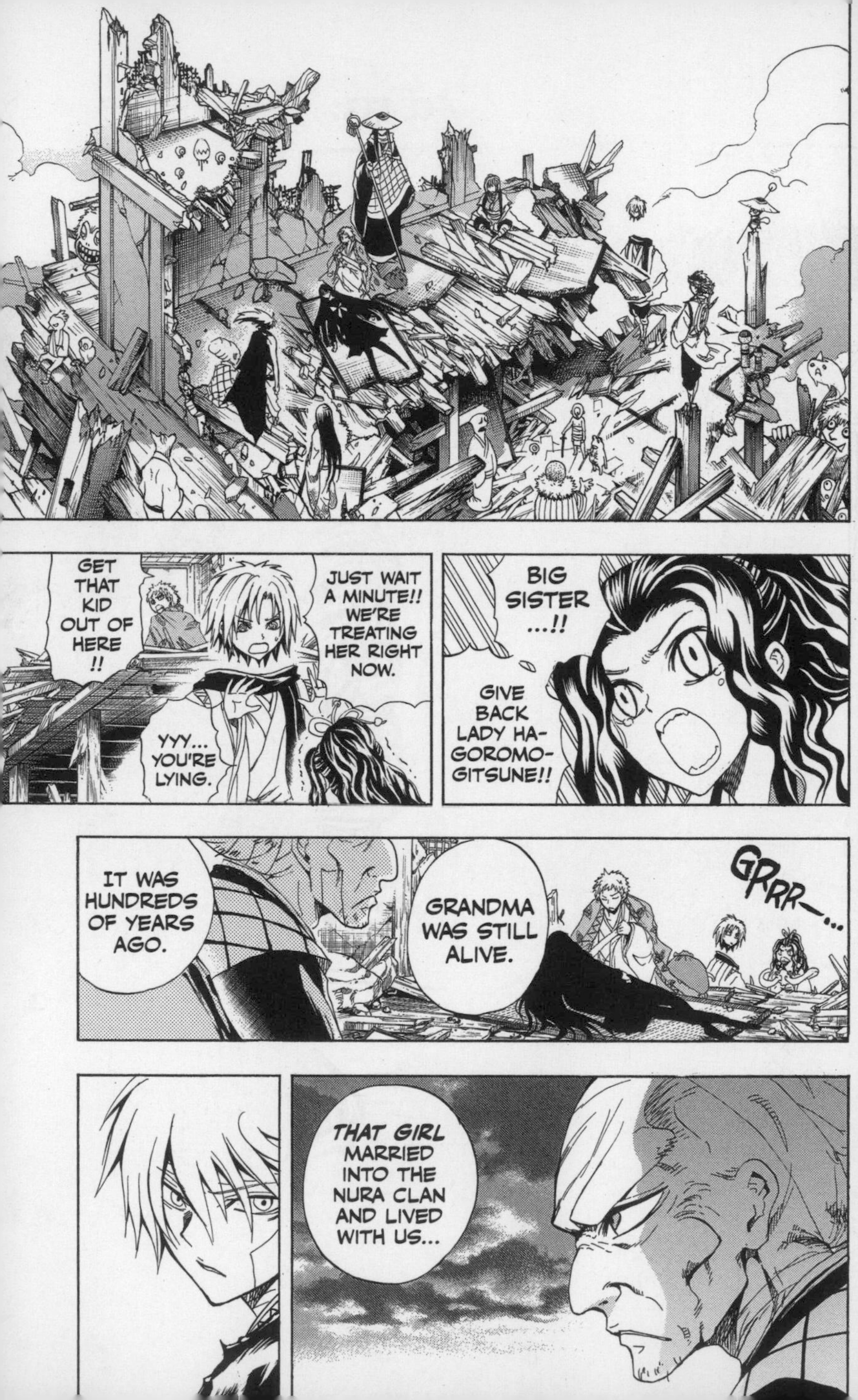
BIG SISTER ...!!
GIVE BACK LADY HAGOROMO-GITSUNE!!
JUST WAIT A MINUTE!! WE'RE TREATING HER RIGHT NOW.
GET THAT KID OUT OF HERE!!
YYY... YOU'RE LYING.
GRRR—...
GRANDMA WAS STILL ALIVE.
IT WAS HUNDREDS OF YEARS AGO.
THAT GIRL MARRIED INTO THE NURA CLAN AND LIVED WITH US...

Act 133: Mirror Image

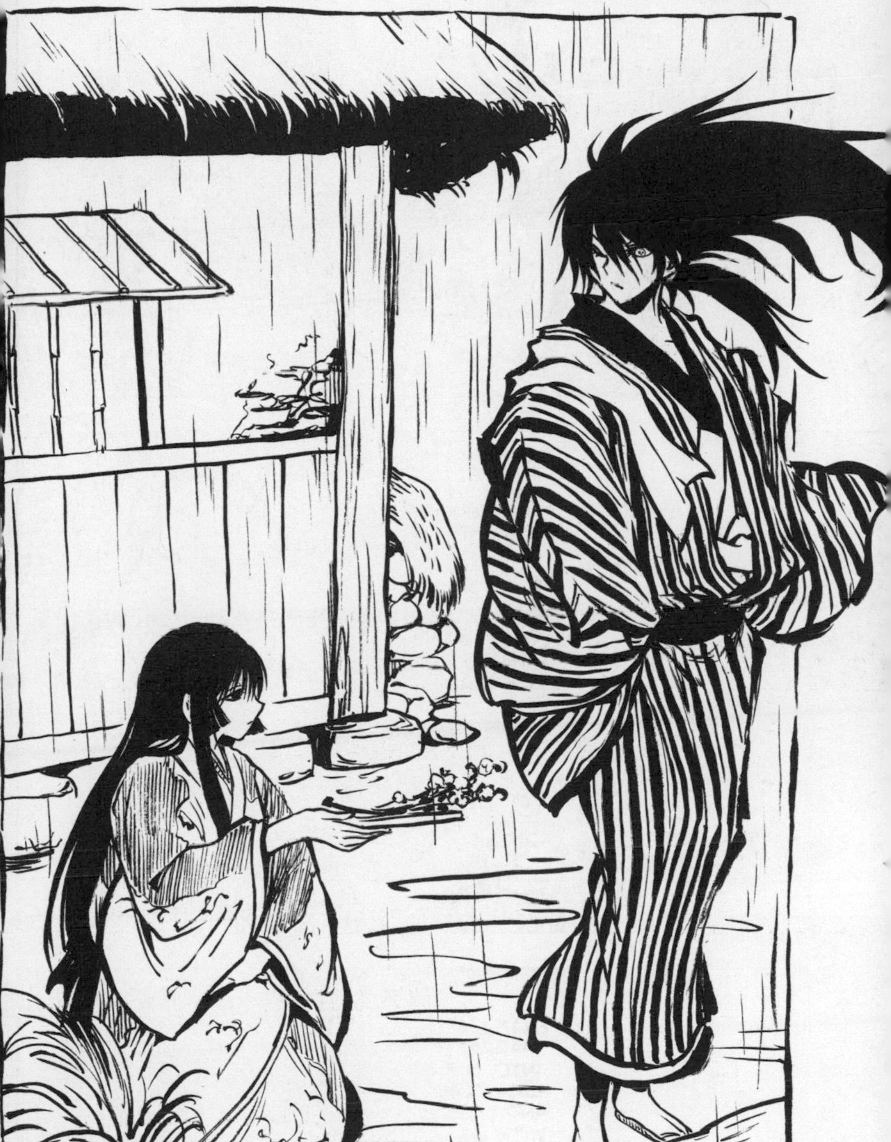

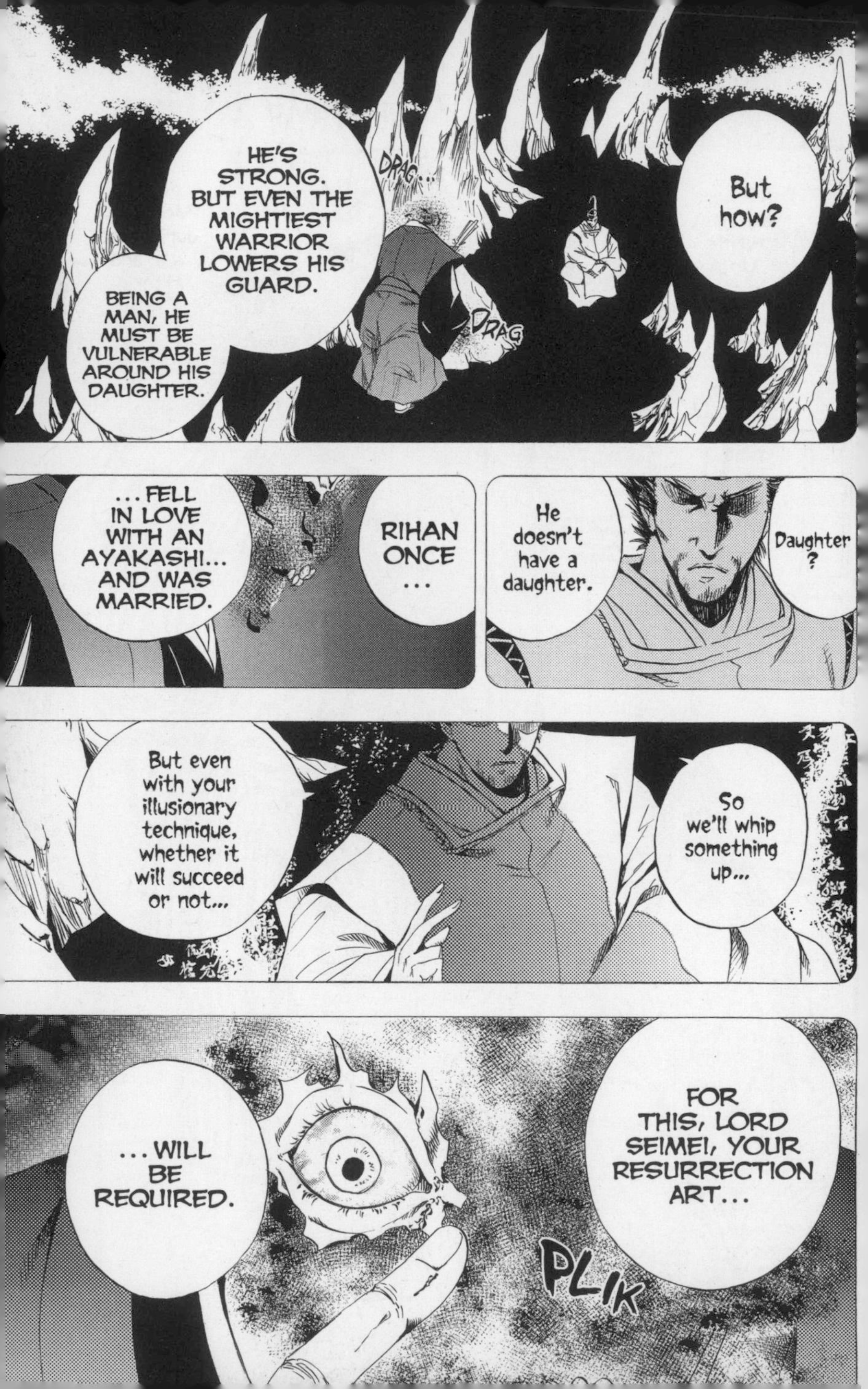
But how?
DRAG...
HE'S STRONG. BUT EVEN THE MIGHTIEST WARRIOR LOWERS HIS GUARD.
DRAG
BEING A MAN, HE MUST BE VULNERABLE AROUND HIS DAUGHTER.
Daughter?
He doesn't have a daughter.
RIHAN ONCE...
...FELL IN LOVE WITH AN AYAKASHI... AND WAS MARRIED.
So we'll whip something up...
But even with your illusionary technique, whether it will succeed or not...
FOR THIS, LORD SEIMEI, YOUR RESURRECTION ART...
...WILL BE REQUIRED.
PLIK

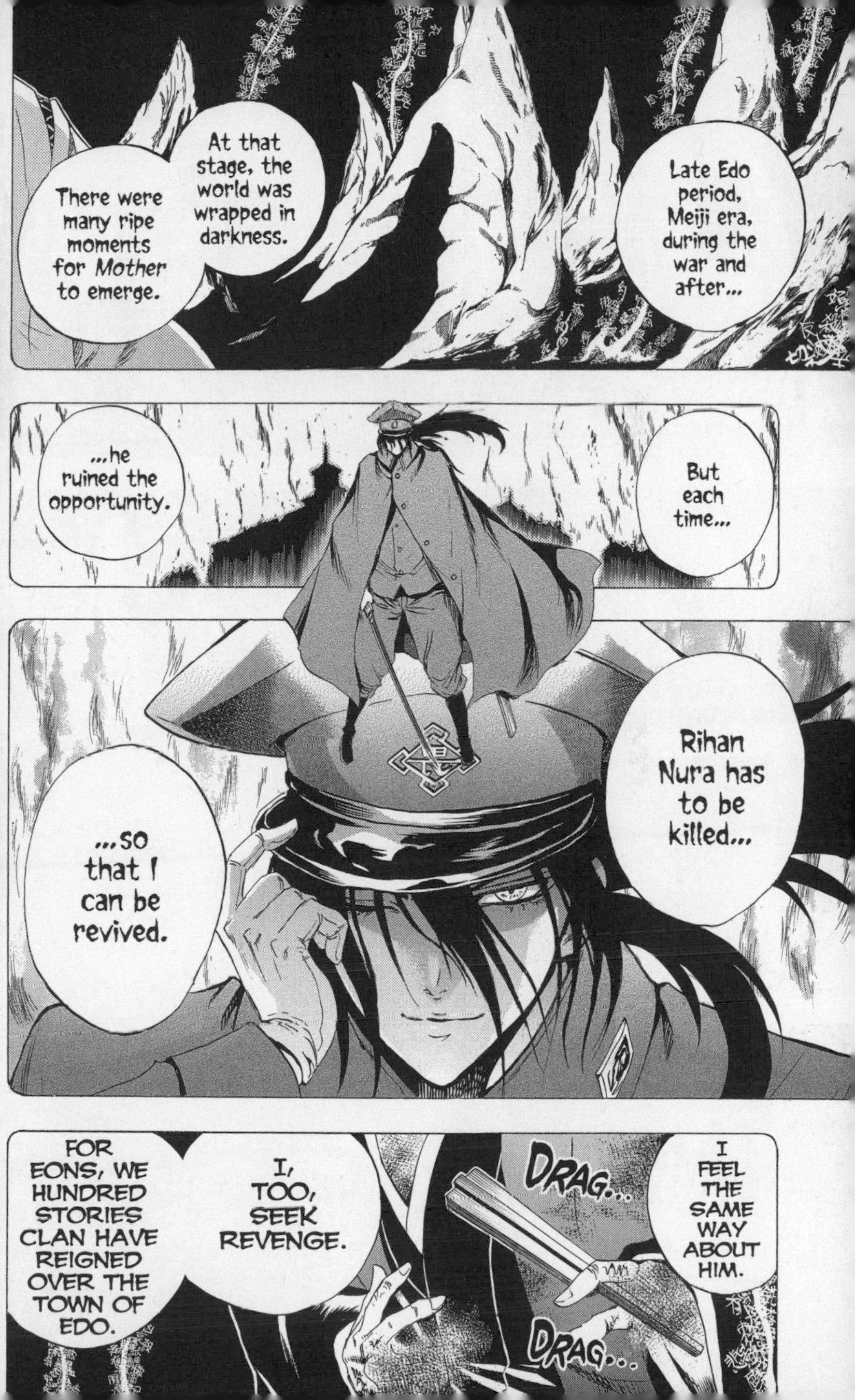
Late Edo period, Meiji era, during the war and after...
At that stage, the world was wrapped in darkness.
There were many ripe moments for *Mother* to emerge.
But each time...
...he ruined the opportunity.
Rihan Nura has to be killed...
...so that I can be revived.
I FEEL THE SAME WAY ABOUT HIM.
DRAG...
I, TOO, SEEK REVENGE.
FOR EONS, WE HUNDRED STORIES CLAN HAVE REIGNED OVER THE TOWN OF EDO.
DRAG...

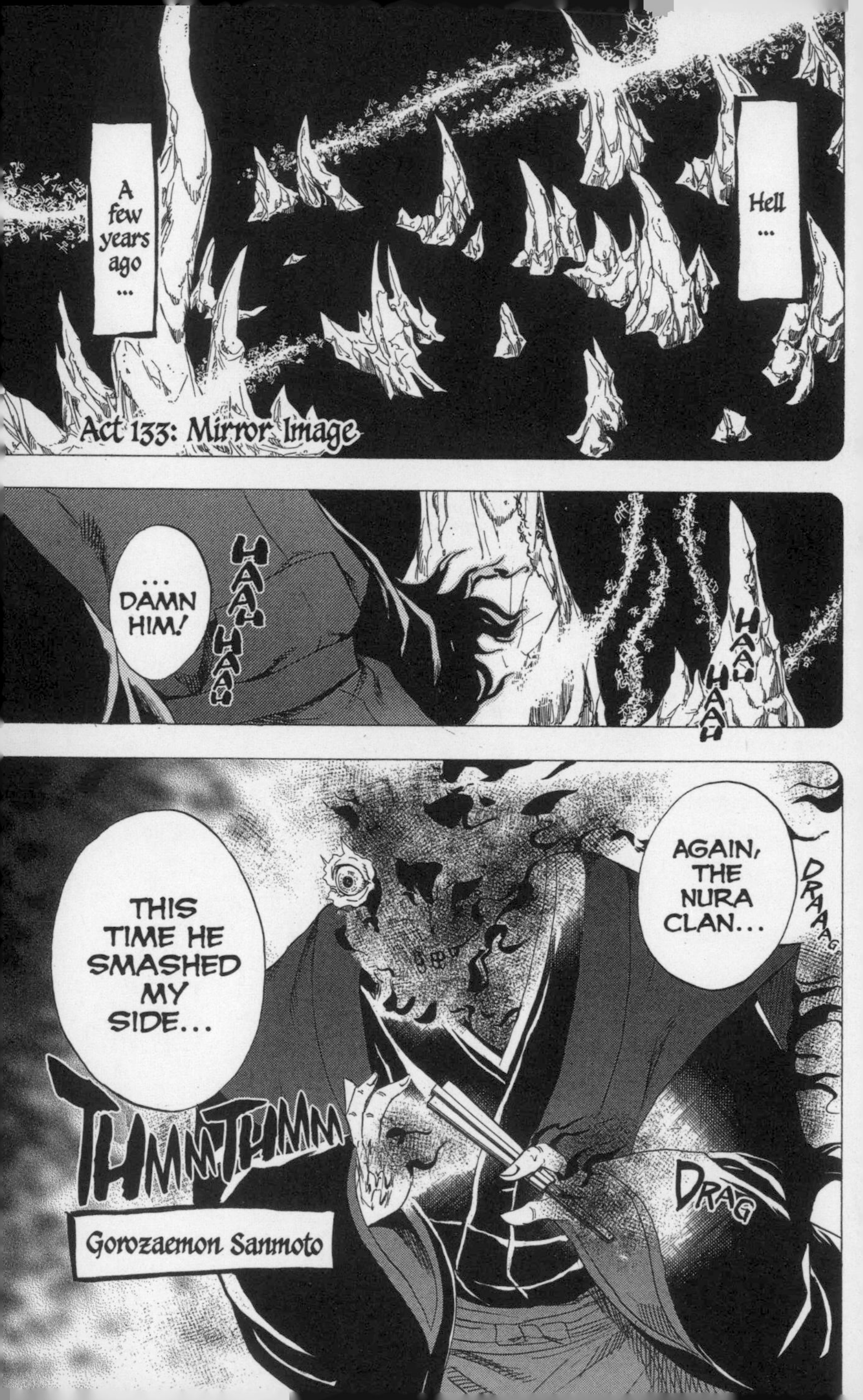
Hell...
A few years ago...
Act 133: Mirror Image
HAAH HAAH
...DAMN HIM!
HAAH HAAH
DRAAAAG
AGAIN, THE NURA CLAN...
THIS TIME HE SMASHED MY SIDE...
DRAG
THMMTHMM
Gorozaemon Sanmoto

Continued from the last act

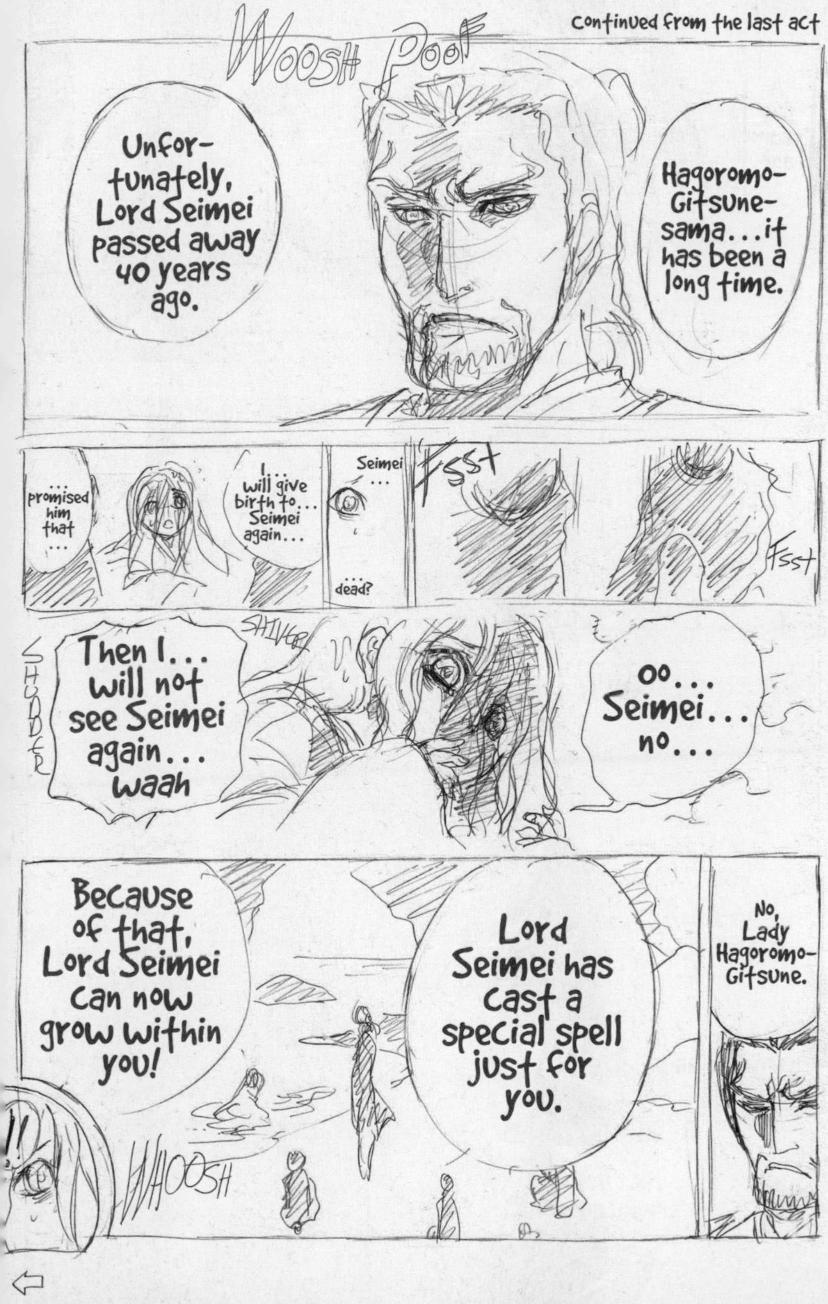
WOOSH POOF
Hagoromo-Gitsune-sama... it has been a long time.
Unfortunately, Lord Seimei passed away 40 years ago.
Fsst
Fsst
Seimei...
...dead?
I... will give birth to... Seimei again...
...promised him that...
oo... Seimei... no...
SHIVER
Then I... will not see Seimei again... waah
SHUDDER
No, Lady Hagoromo-Gitsune.
Lord Seimei has cast a special spell just for you.
Because of that, Lord Seimei can now grow within you!
WHOOSH
!!

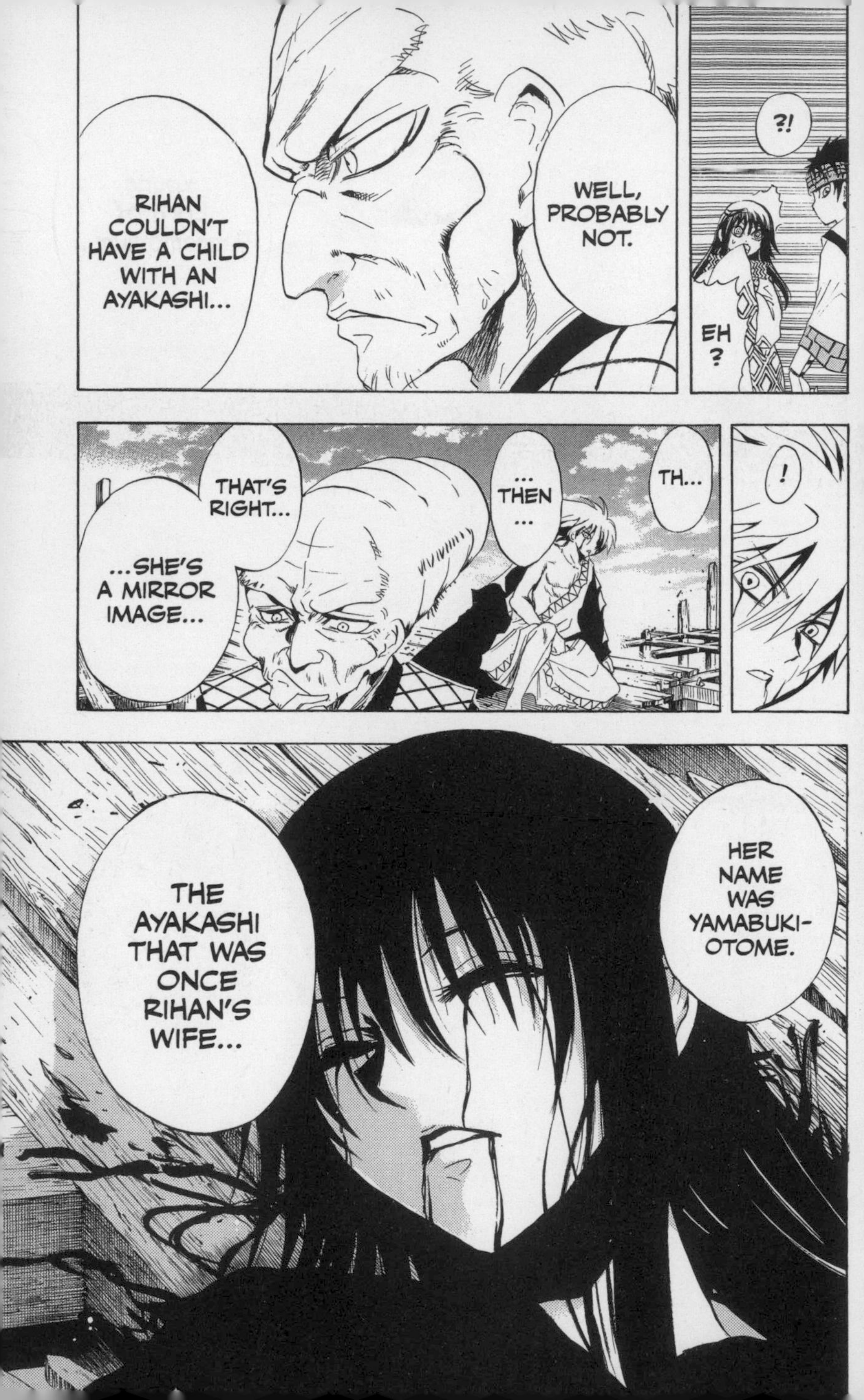
?!
EH ?
WELL, PROBABLY NOT.
RIHAN COULDN'T HAVE A CHILD WITH AN AYAKASHI...
!
TH...
... THEN ...
THAT'S RIGHT...
...SHE'S A MIRROR IMAGE...
HER NAME WAS YAMABUKI-OTOME.
THE AYAKASHI THAT WAS ONCE RIHAN'S WIFE...

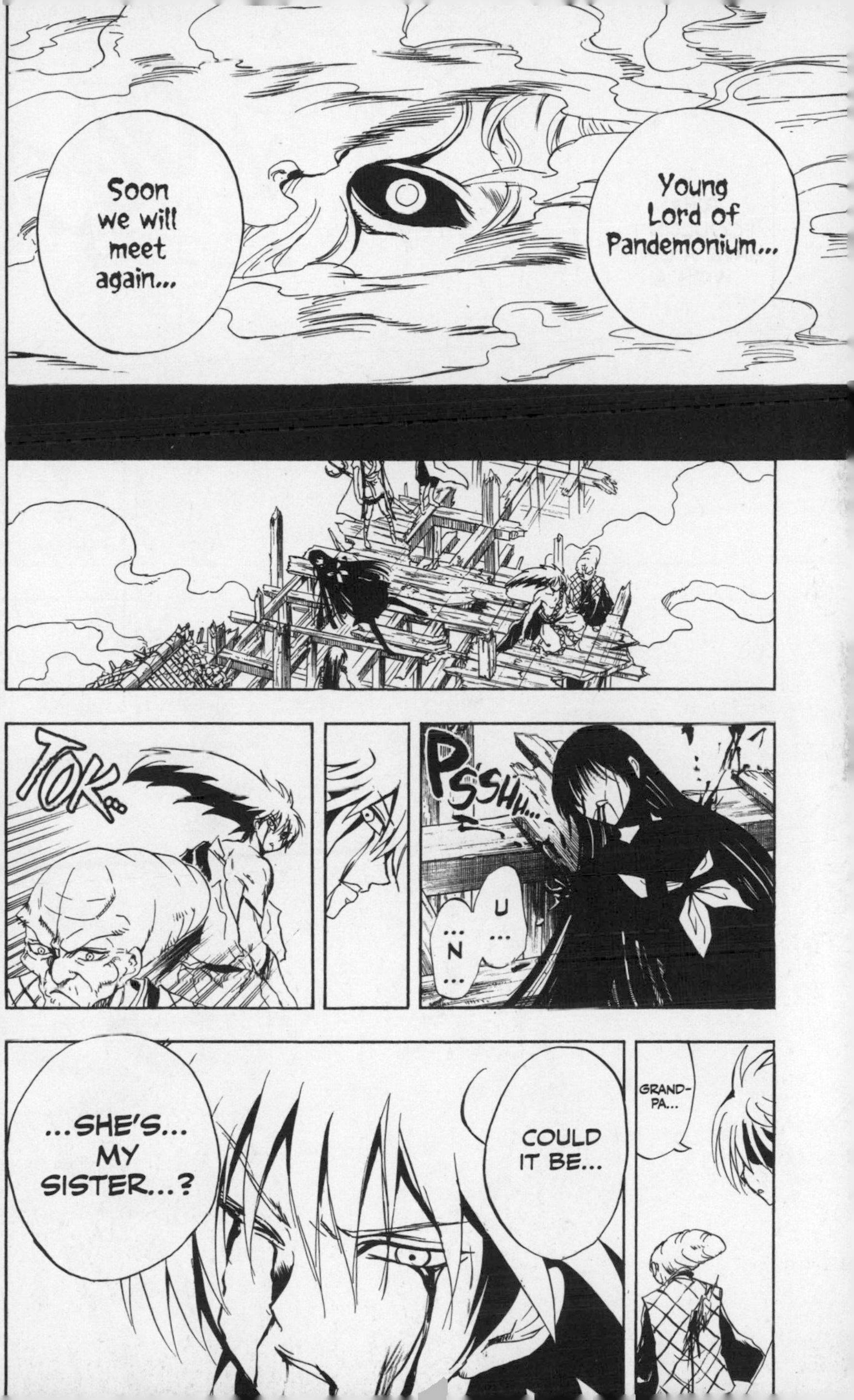
Young Lord of Pandemonium...
Soon we will meet again...
PSSHU...
U... N...
TOK..
GRAND-PA...
COULD IT BE...
...SHE'S... MY SISTER...?

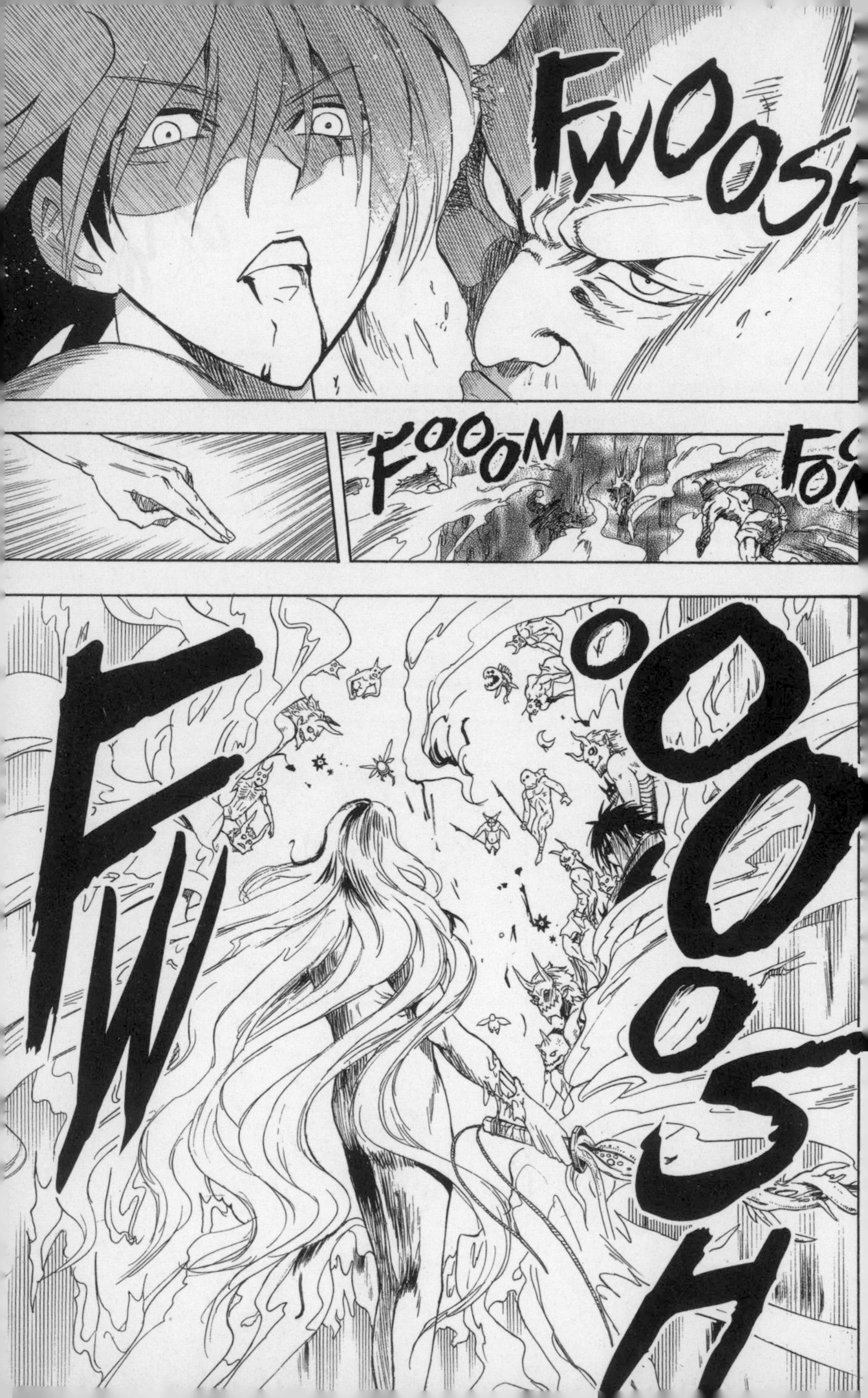
FWOOS
FOOOOM
FWOOOOSH

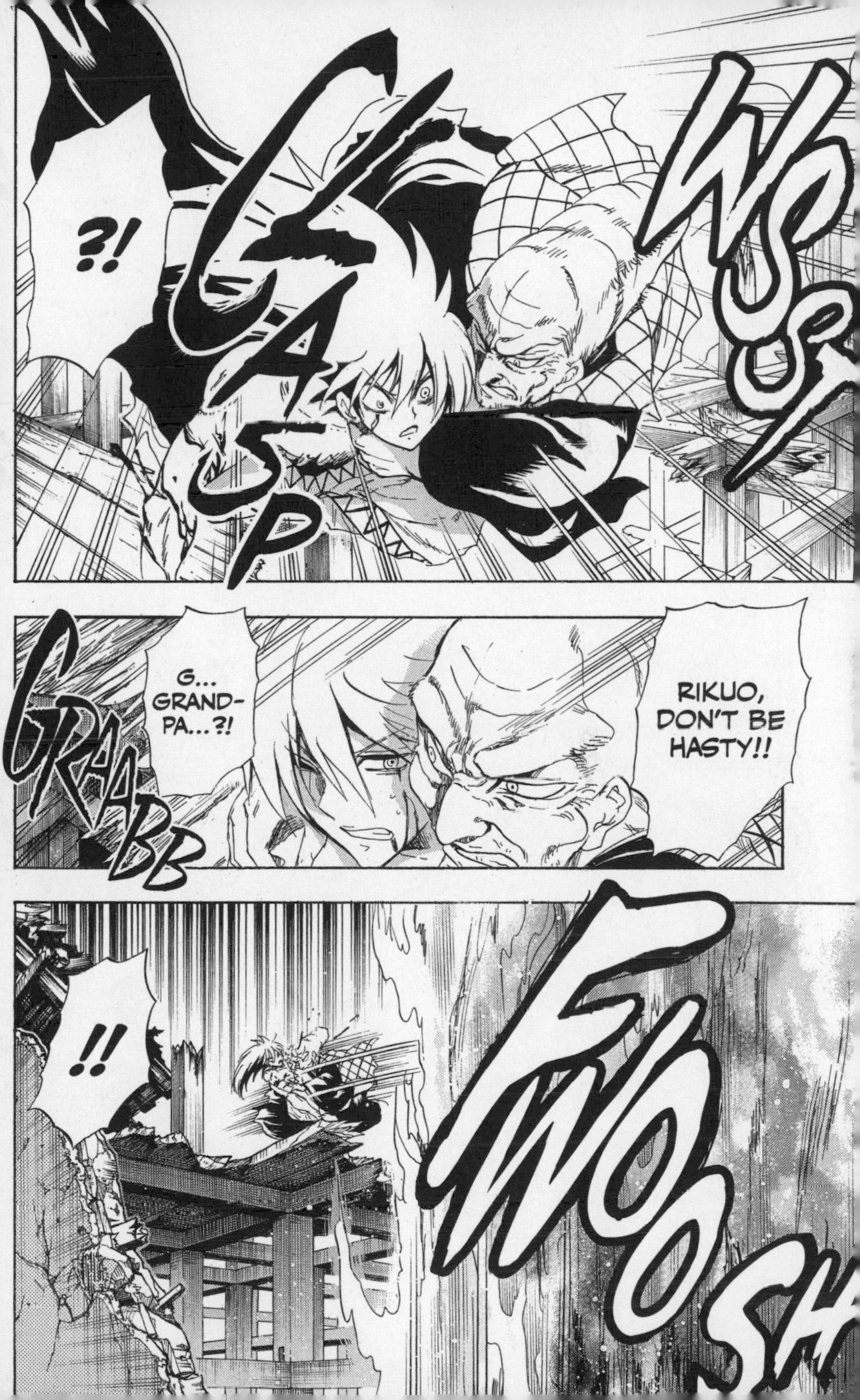
CLASP
?!
RIKUO, DON'T BE HASTY!!
G... GRAND-PA...?!
GRAABB
FWOOSH
!!

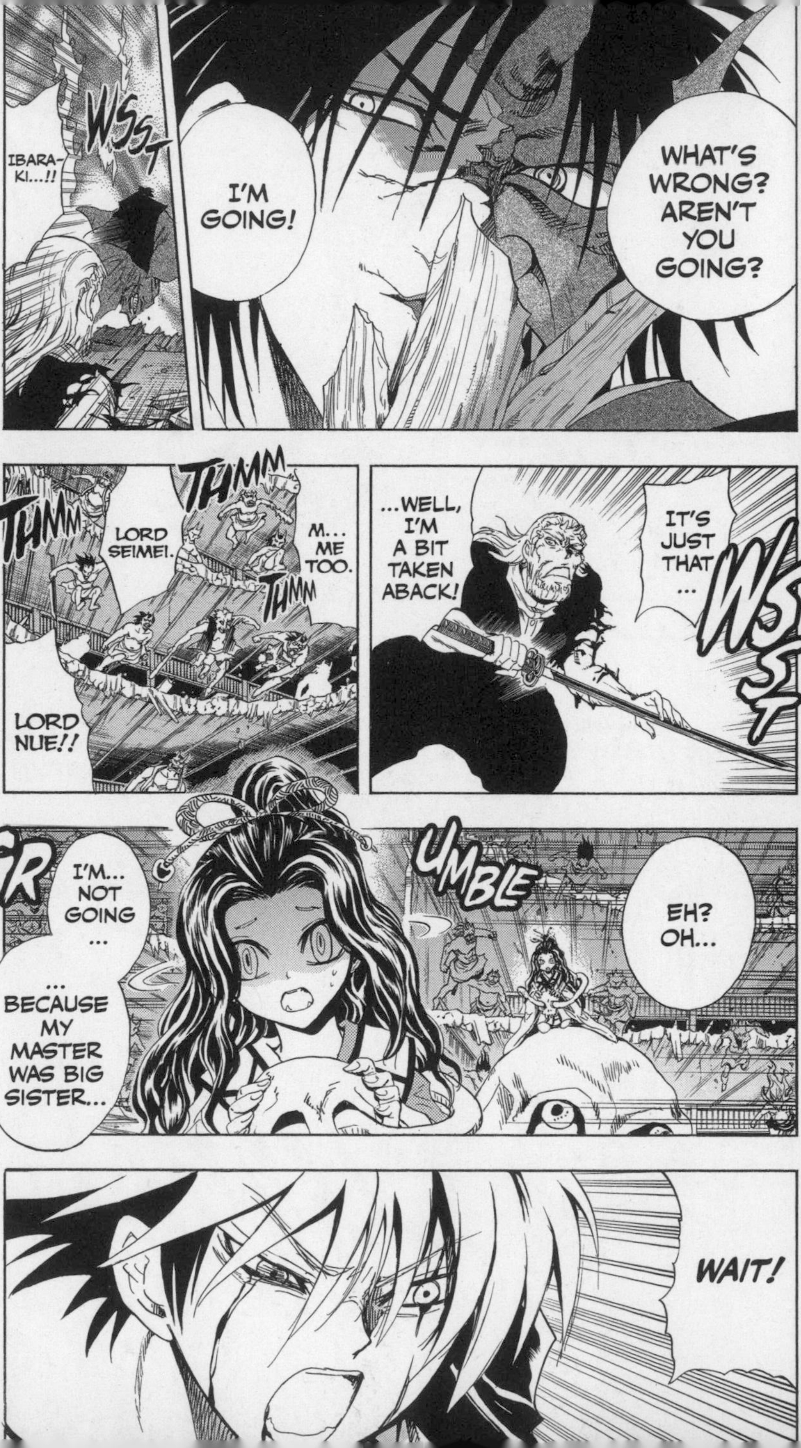
WHAT'S WRONG? AREN'T YOU GOING?
I'M GOING!
WSST
IBARAKI...!!
IT'S JUST THAT ...
WSST
...WELL, I'M A BIT TAKEN ABACK!
THMM
M... ME TOO.
LORD SEIMEI.
THMM
THMM
LORD NUE!!
EH? OH...
UMBLE
I'M... NOT GOING ...
... BECAUSE MY MASTER WAS BIG SISTER...
GR
WAIT!

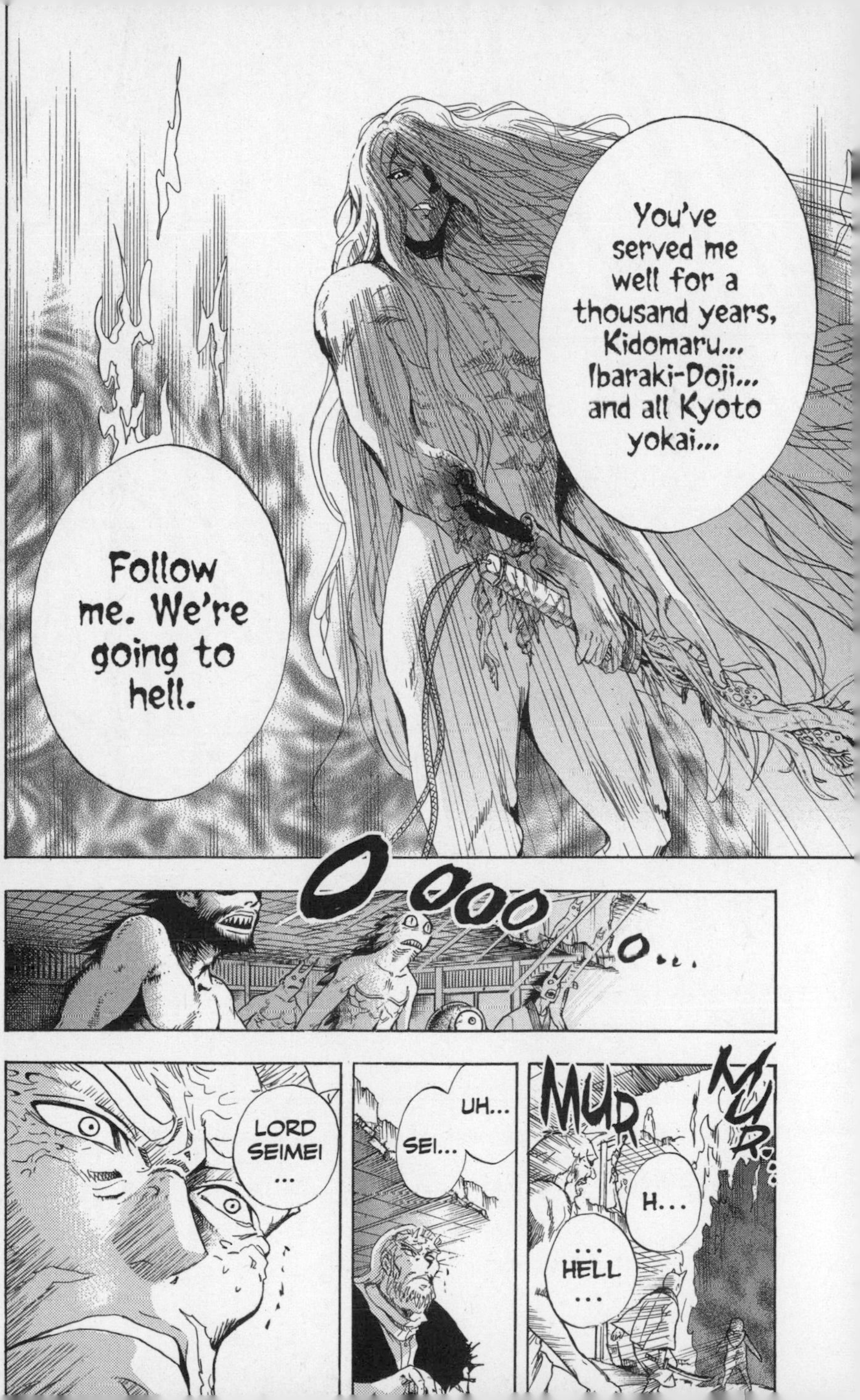
You've served me well for a thousand years, Kidomaru... Ibaraki-Doji... and all Kyoto yokai...
Follow me. We're going to hell.
OOOOO...
MUR MUR...
H...
...HELL...
UH...
SEI...
LORD SEIMEI...

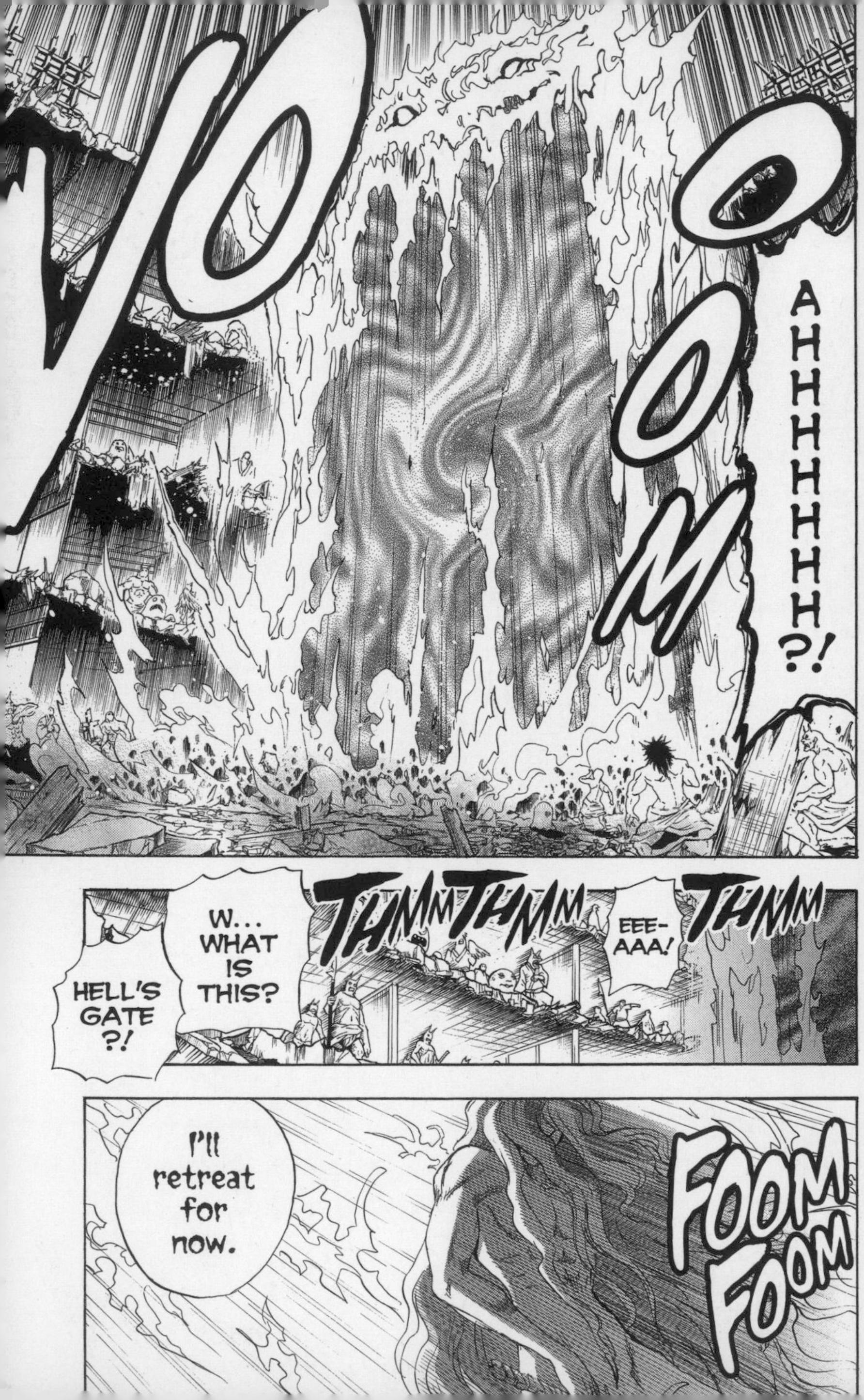
AHHHHHHH?!
OOOM
THMM
EEE-AAA!
THMM THMM
W... WHAT IS THIS?
HELL'S GATE ?!
FOOM FOOM
I'll retreat for now.

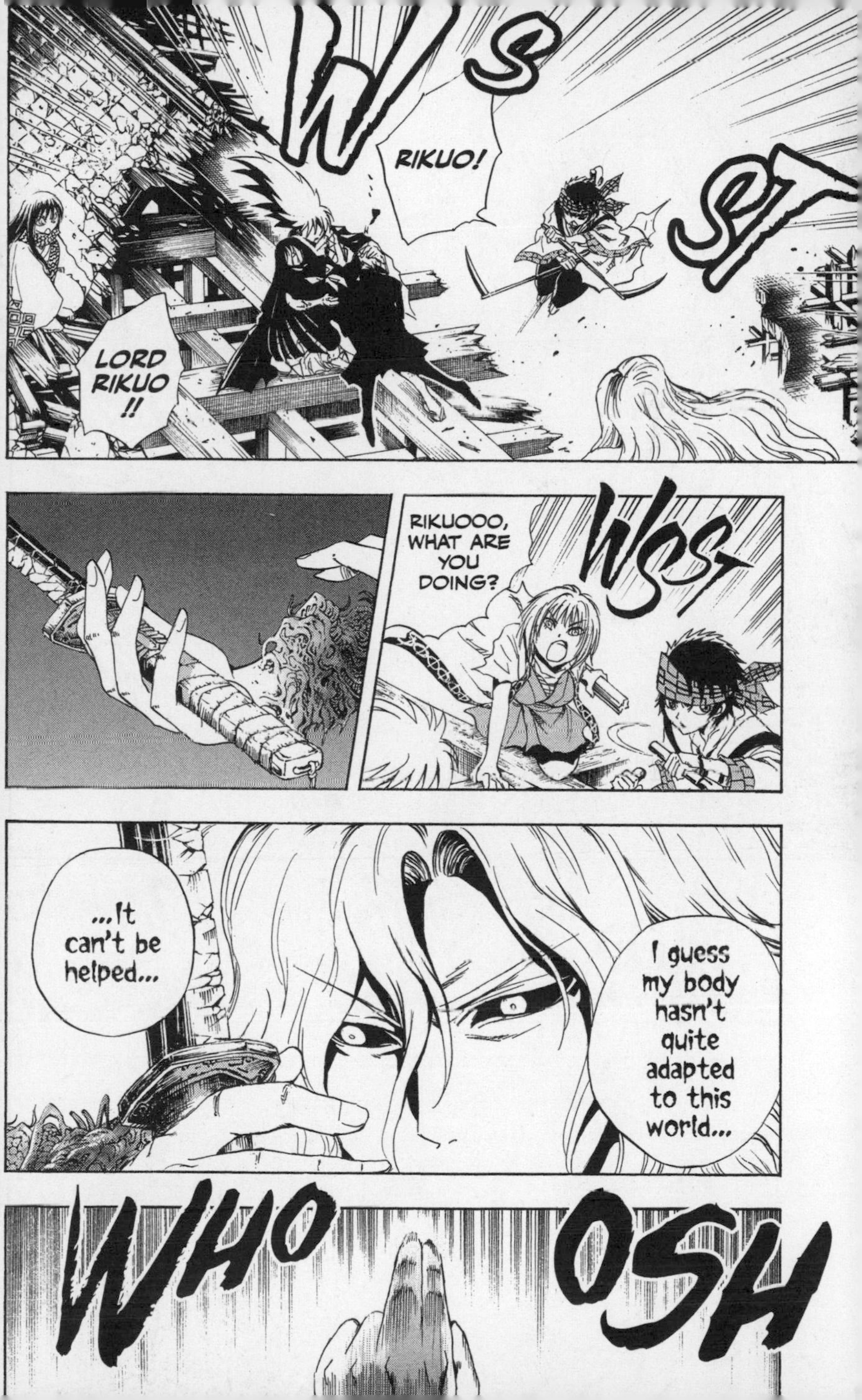
RIKUO!
LORD RIKUO !!
RIKUOOO, WHAT ARE YOU DOING?
I guess my body hasn't quite adapted to this world...
...It can't be helped...
WHOOSH

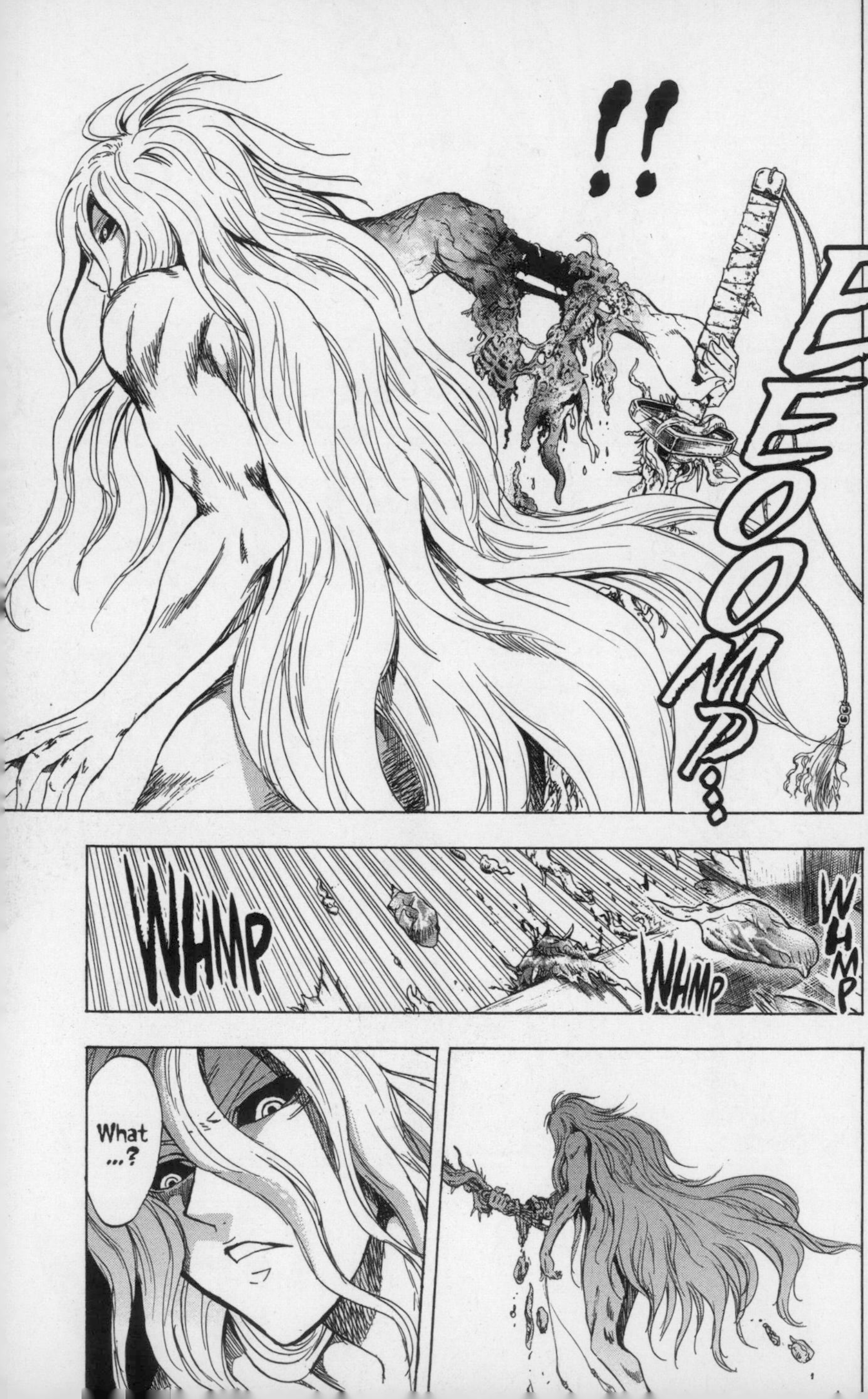
!!
BLEOOOMP...
WHMP
WHMP
WHMP
What ...?

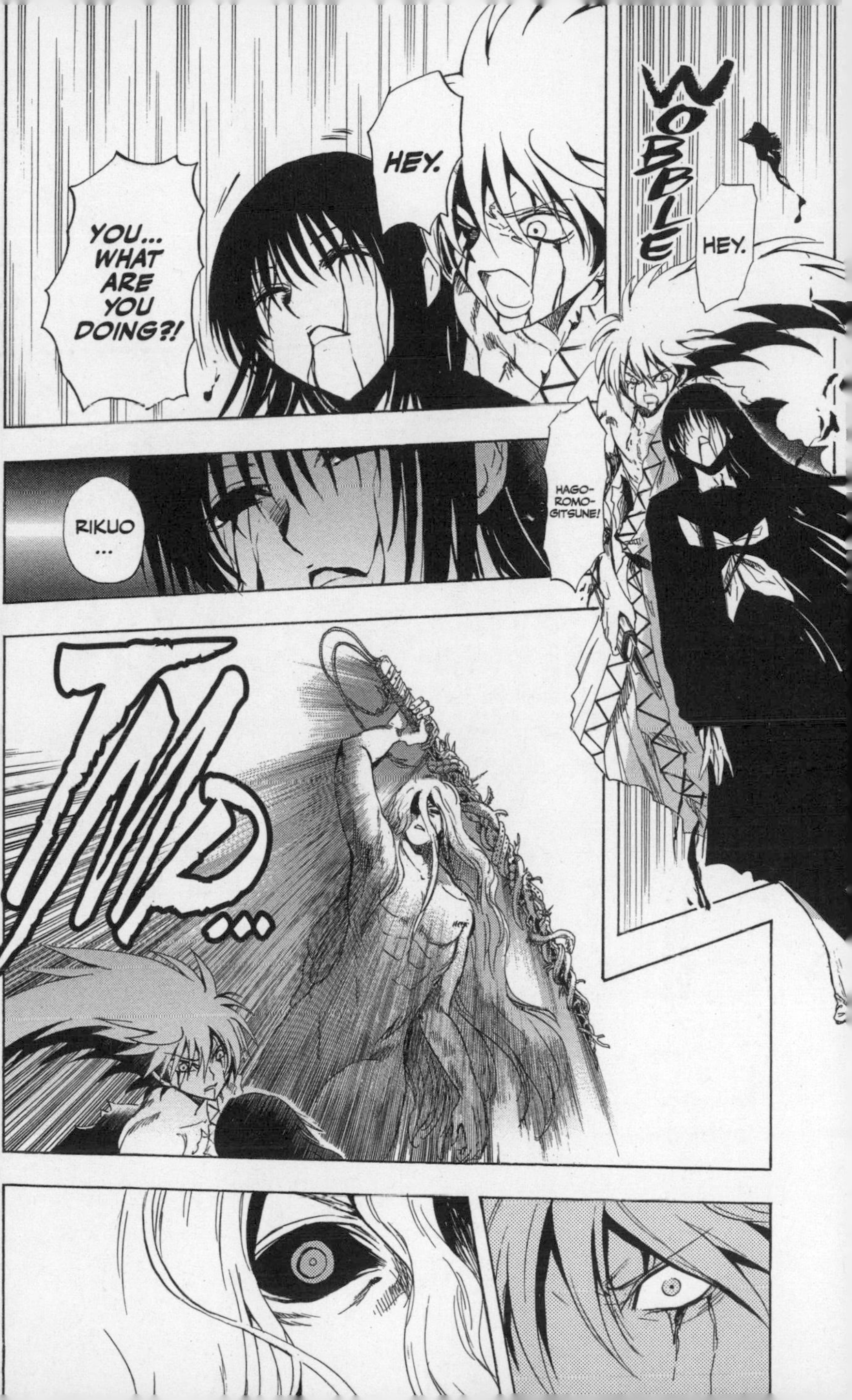
WOBBLE
HEY.
HAGO-ROMO-GITSUNE!
HEY.
YOU... WHAT ARE YOU DOING?!
RIKUO ...

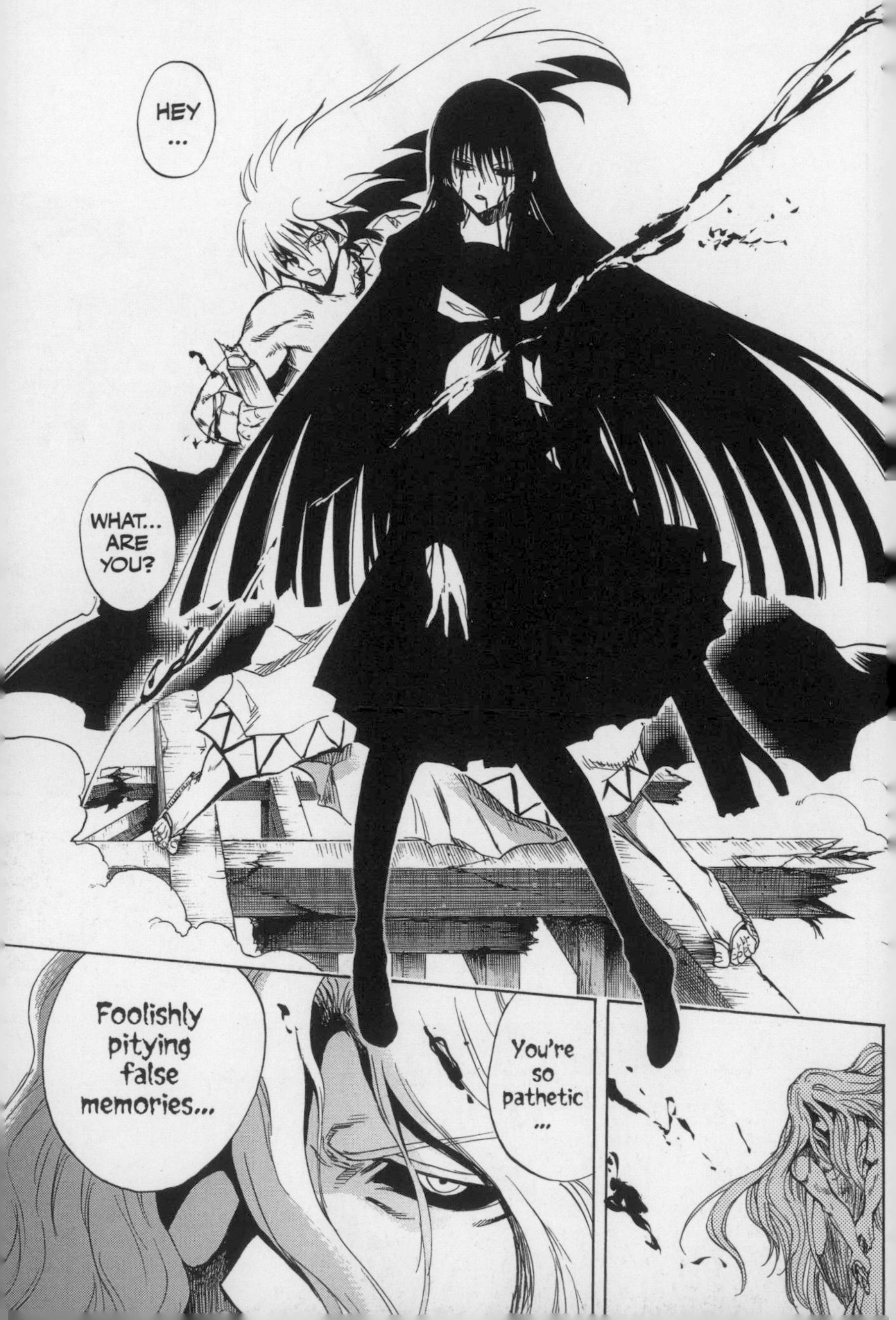
HEY ...
WHAT... ARE YOU?
You're so pathetic ...
Foolishly pitying false memories...

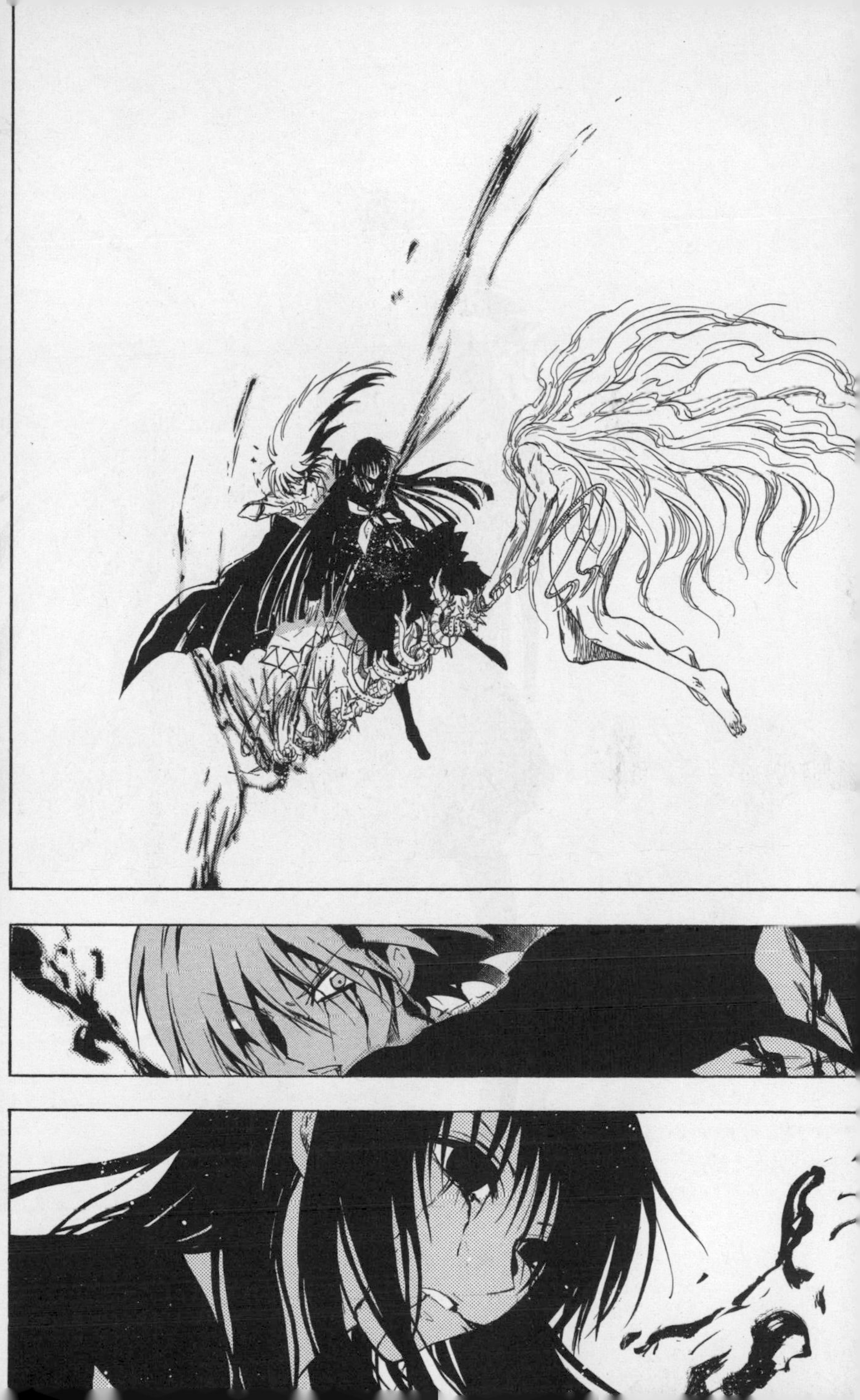

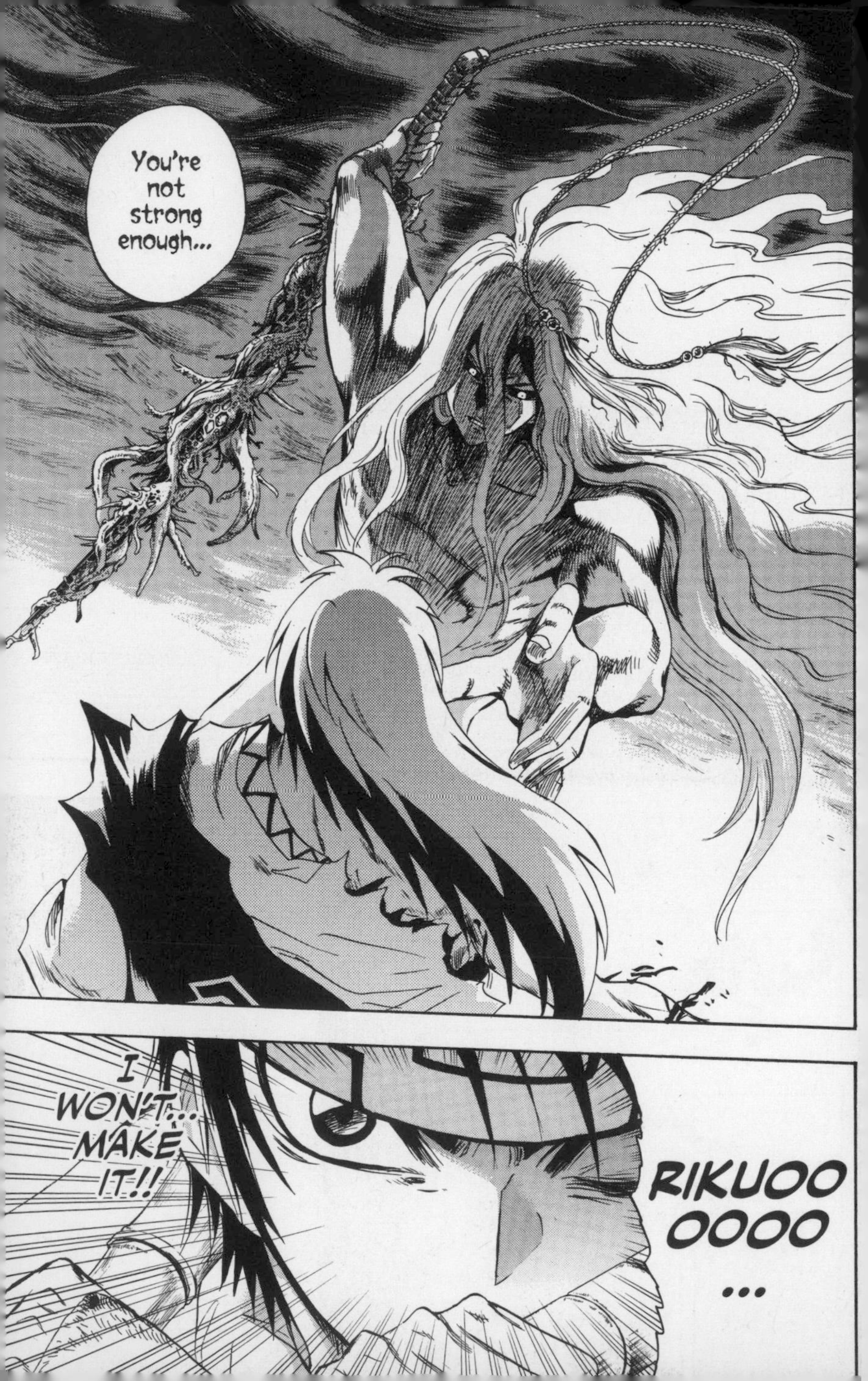
You're not strong enough...
RIKUOO OOOO ...
I WON'T... MAKE IT!!

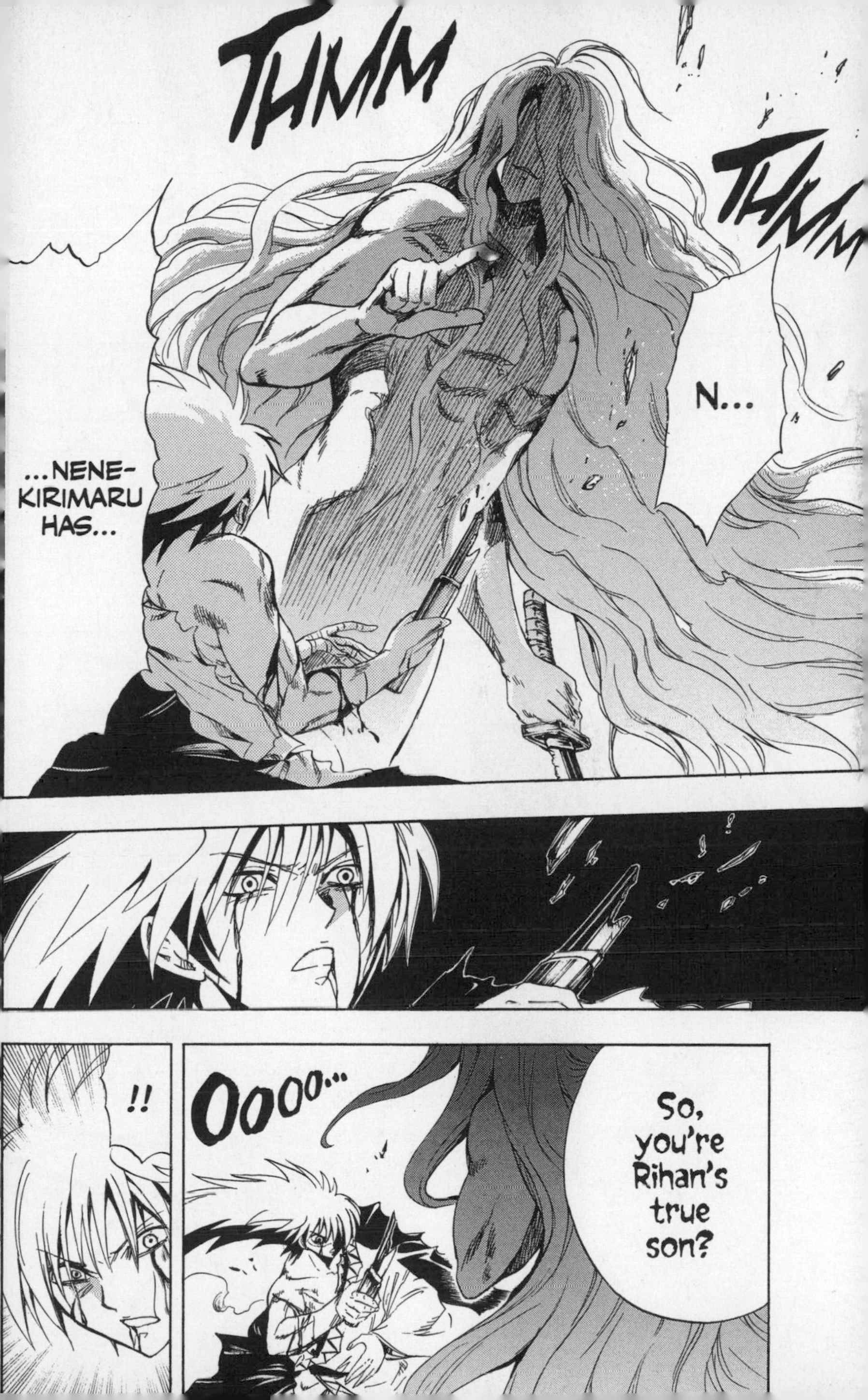
THMM
THMM
N...
...NENE-KIRIMARU HAS...
So, you're Rihan's true son?
OOOO...
!!

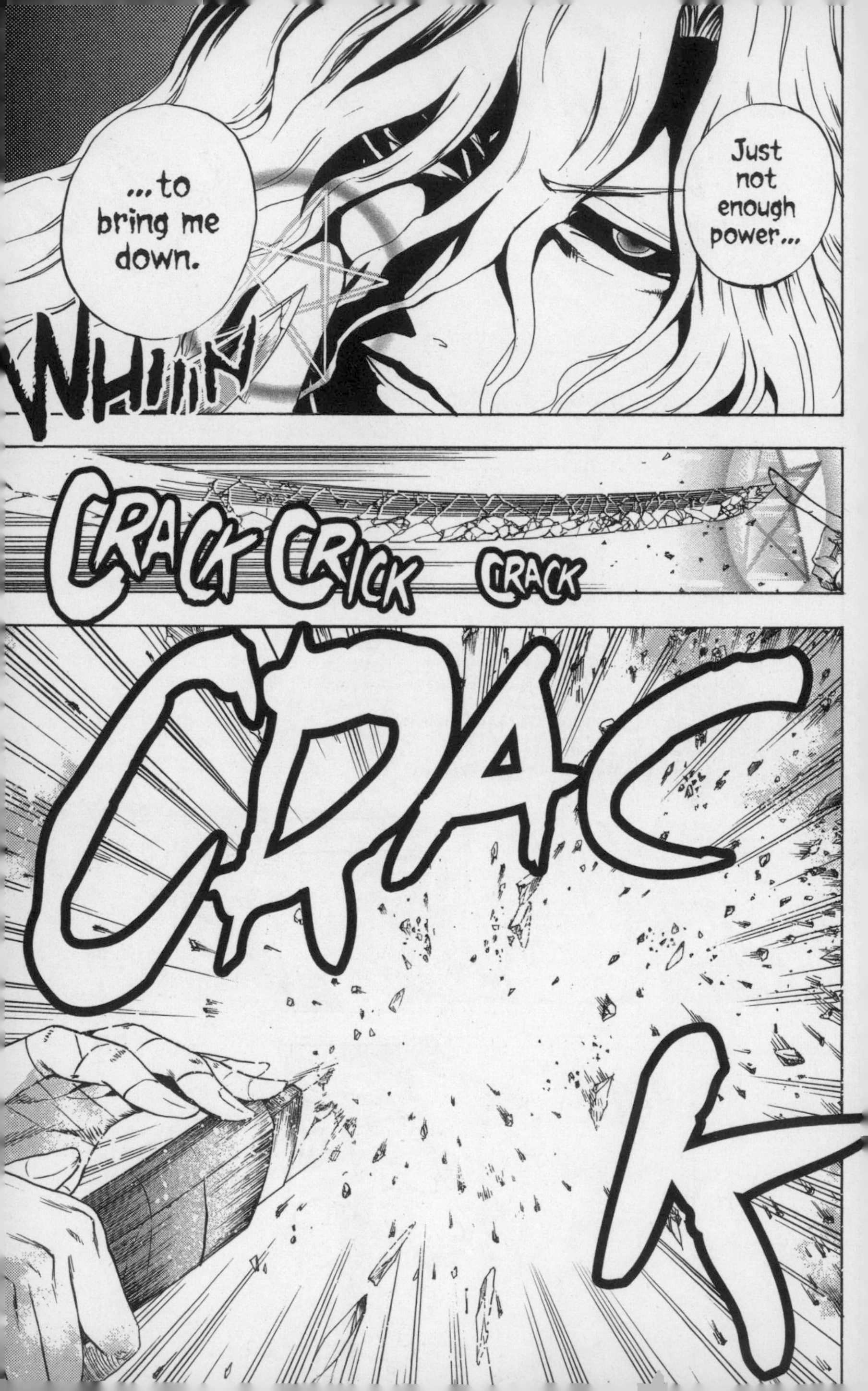
Just not enough power...
...to bring me down.
WHIIIN
CRACK CRICK CRACK
CRACK

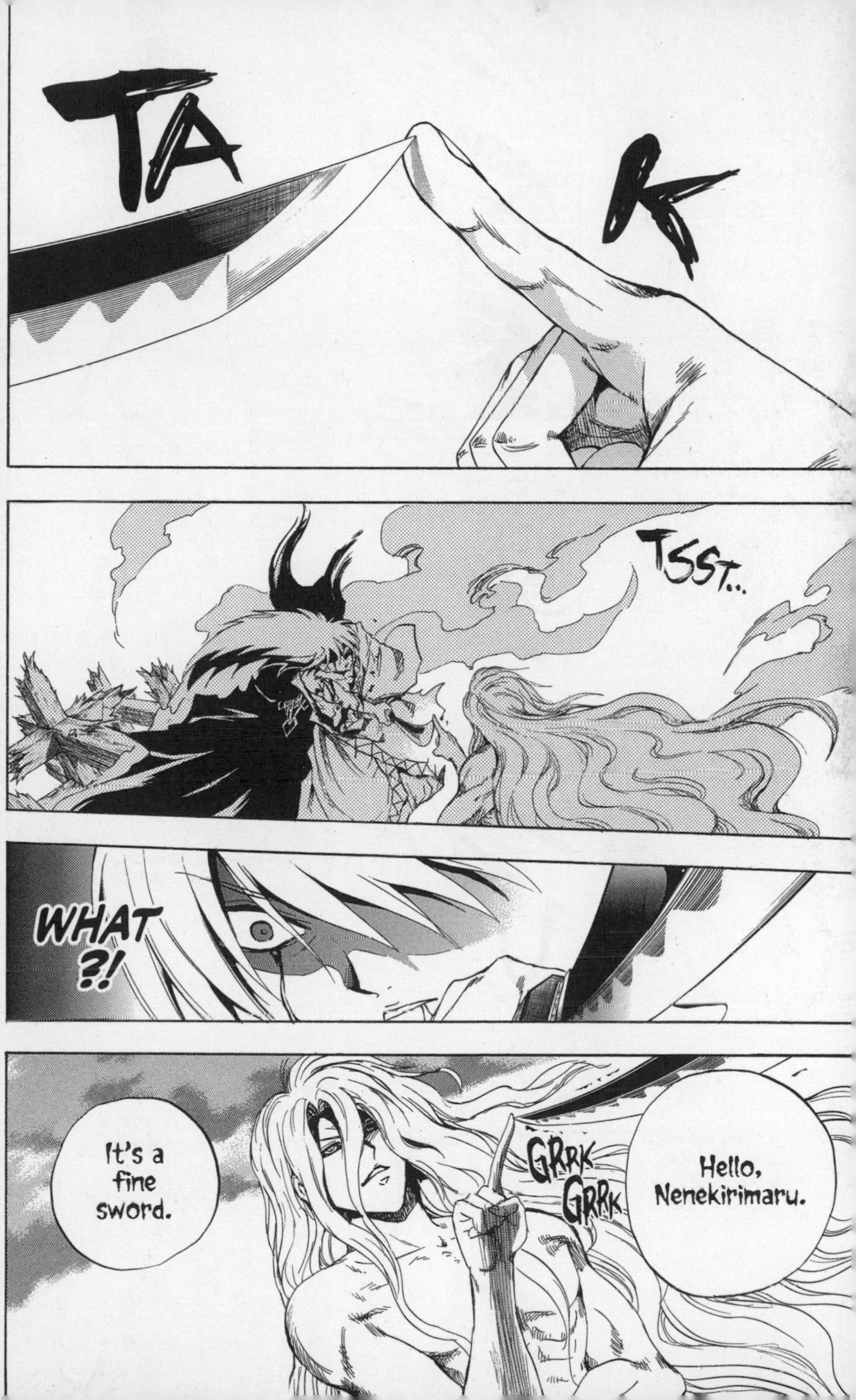
TAK
TSST...
WHAT?!
Hello, Nenekirimaru.
GRRK GRRK
It's a fine sword.

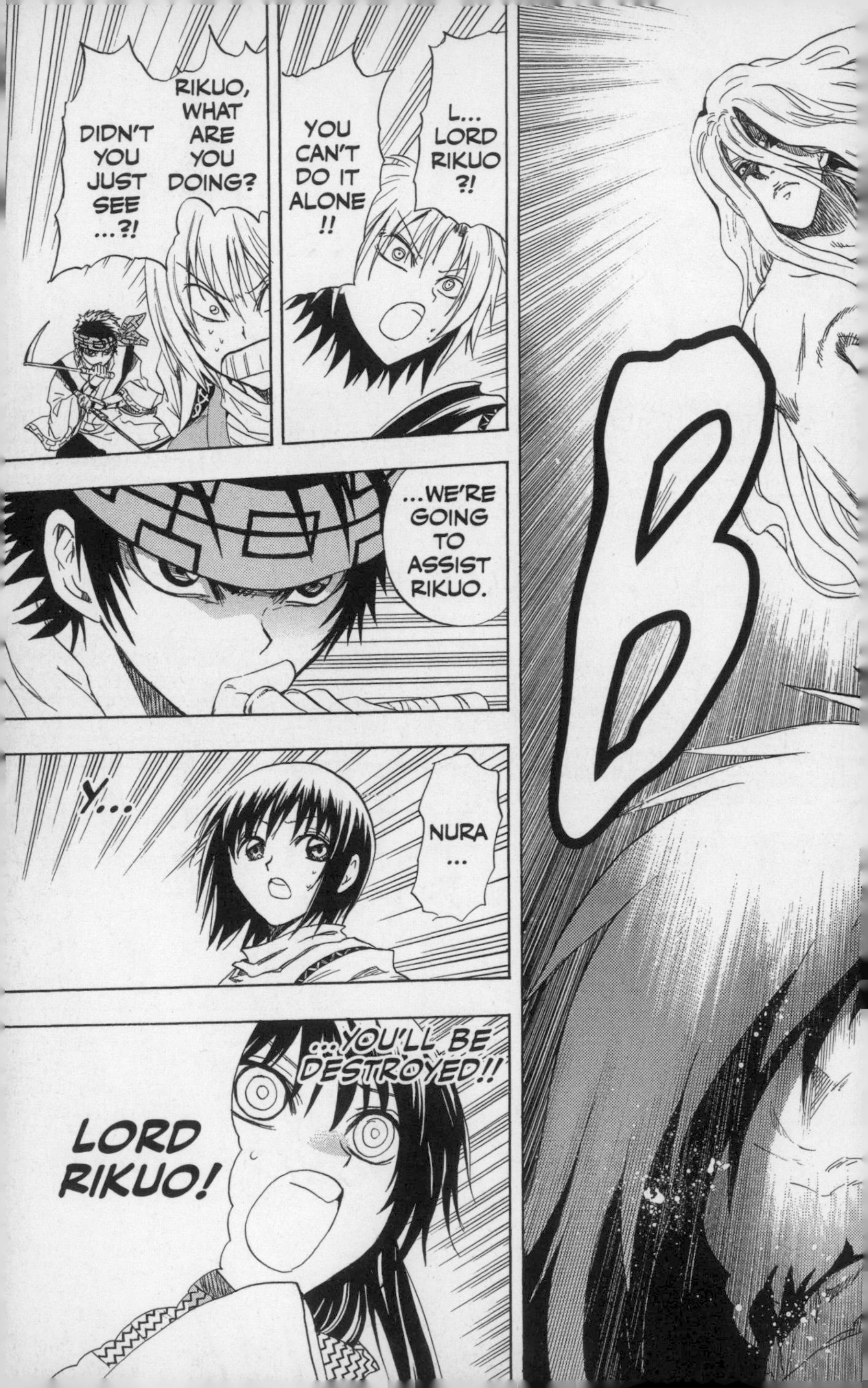
B
L... LORD RIKUO ?!
YOU CAN'T DO IT ALONE !!
RIKUO, WHAT ARE YOU DOING?
DIDN'T YOU JUST SEE ...?!
...WE'RE GOING TO ASSIST RIKUO.
NURA ...
Y...
...YOU'LL BE DESTROYED!!
LORD RIKUO!

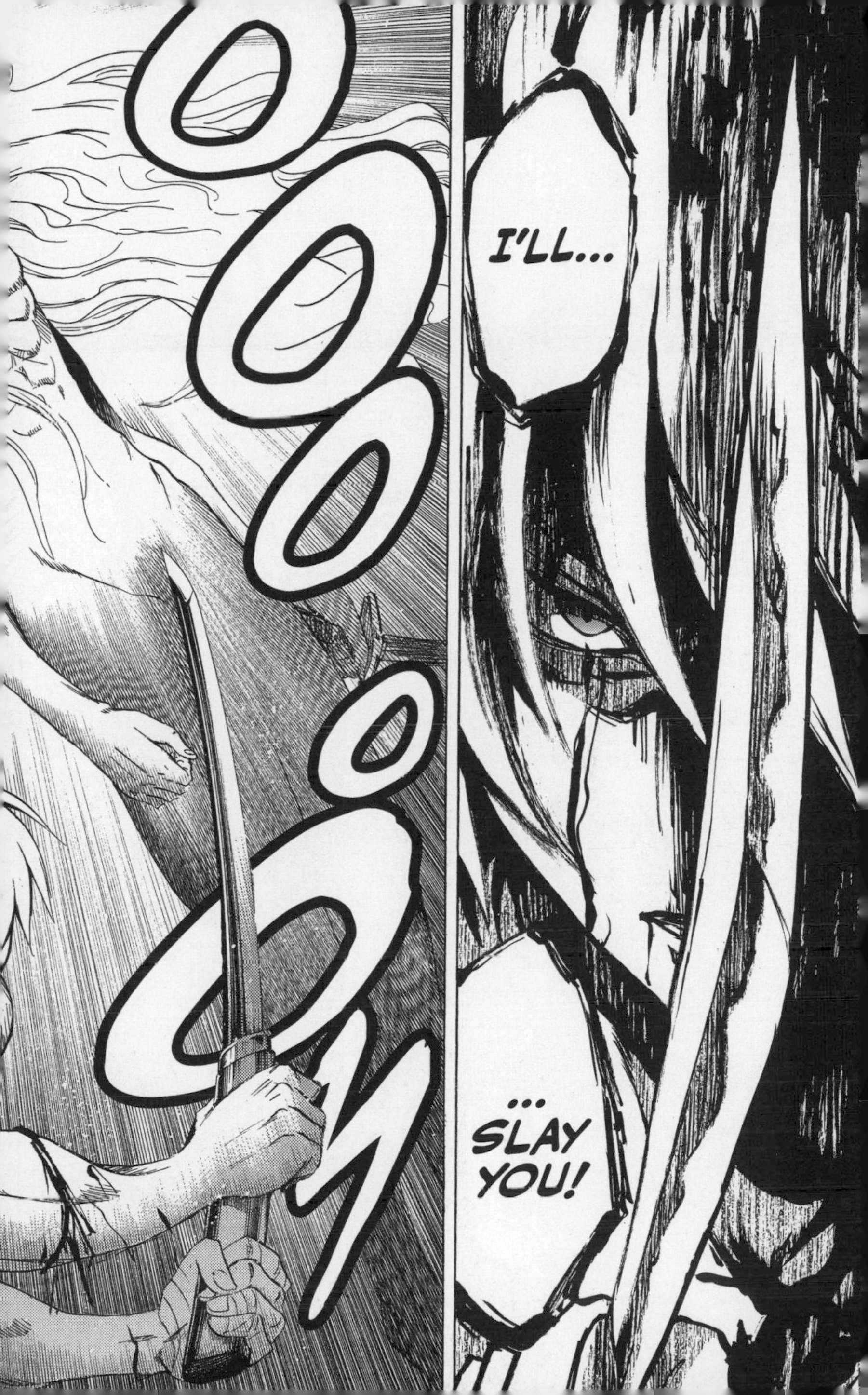
I'LL...
...SLAY YOU!

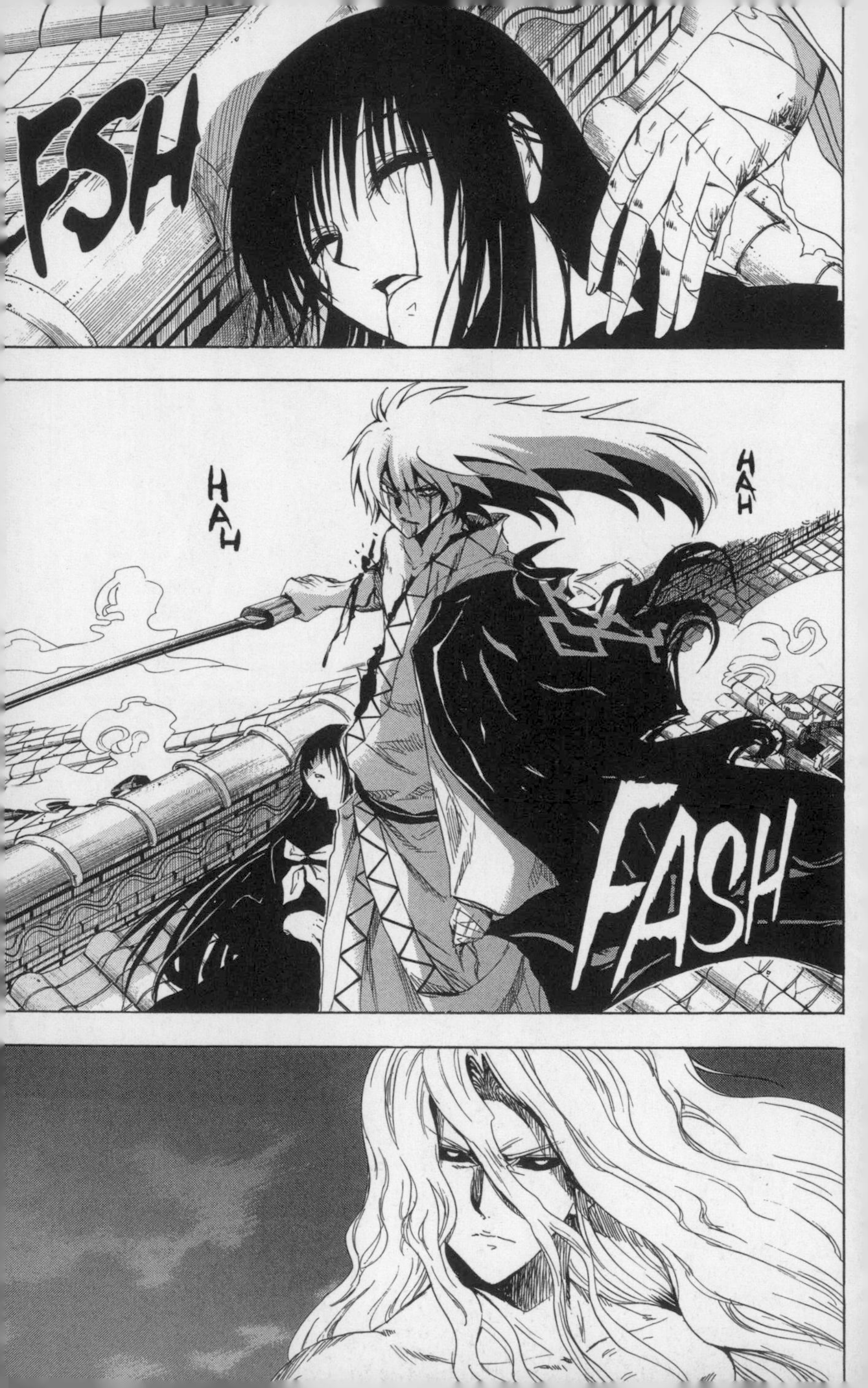
FSH
HAH
FASH
HAH

Act 132: Kyoto in Flames

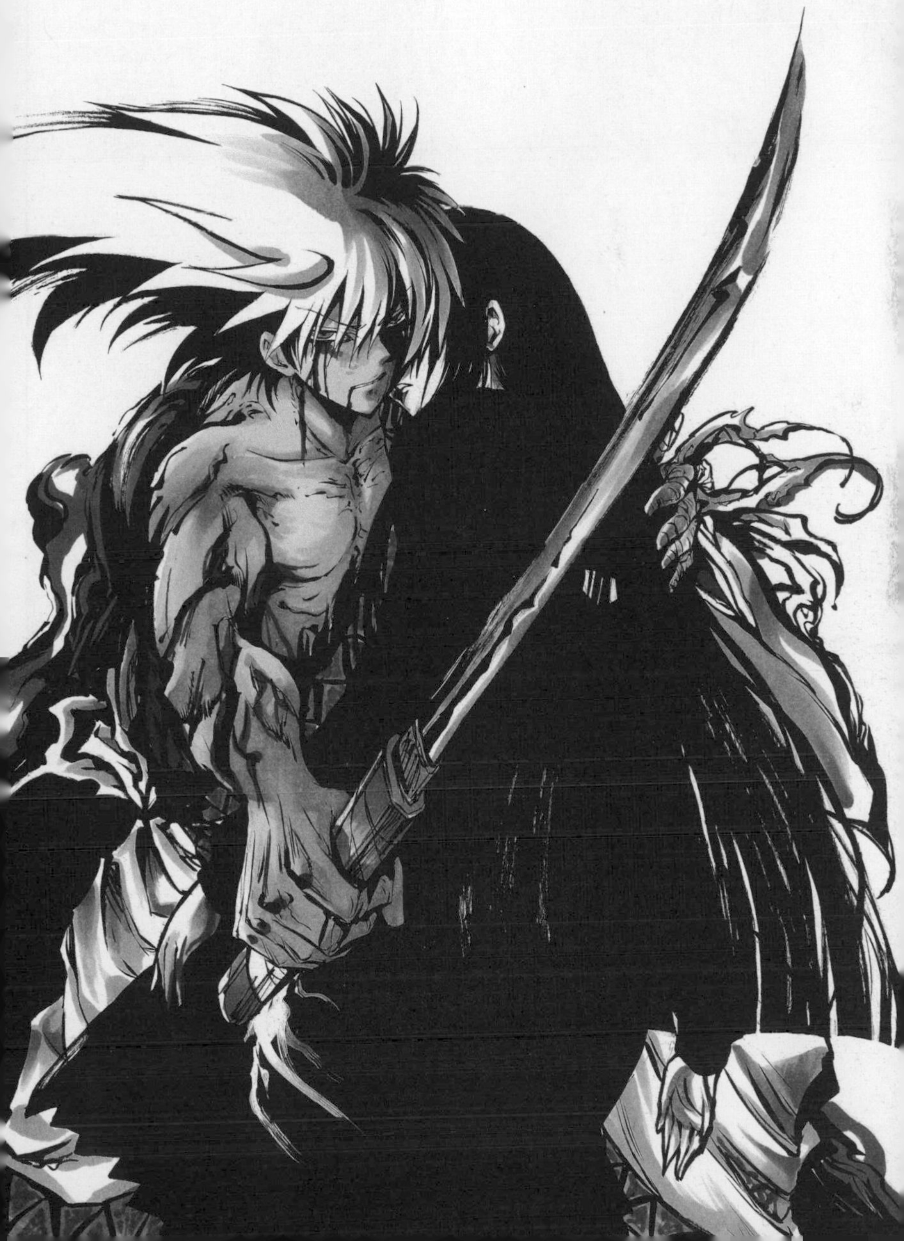

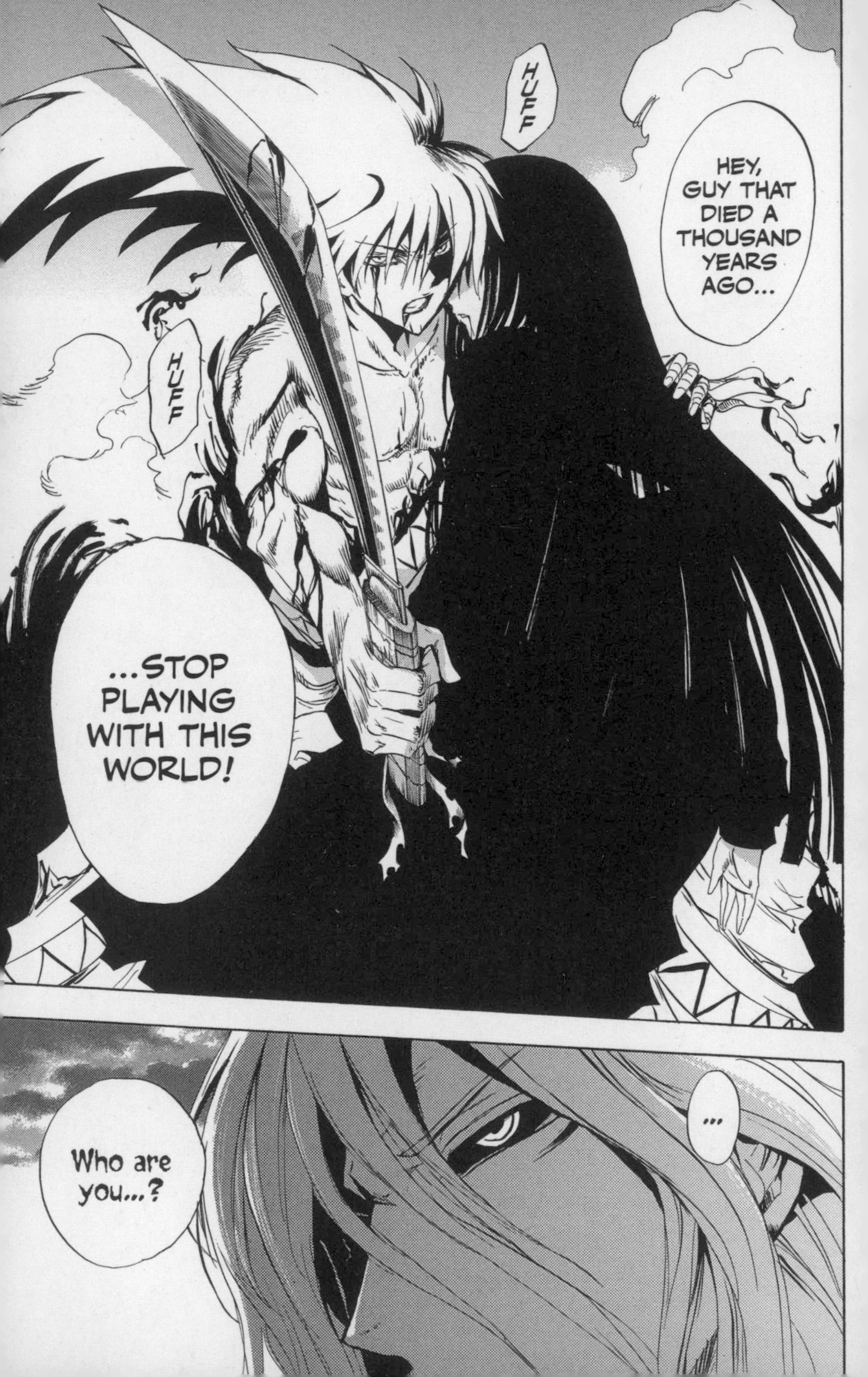
HEY, GUY THAT DIED A THOUSAND YEARS AGO...
HUFF
HUFF
...STOP PLAYING WITH THIS WORLD!
...
Who are you...?

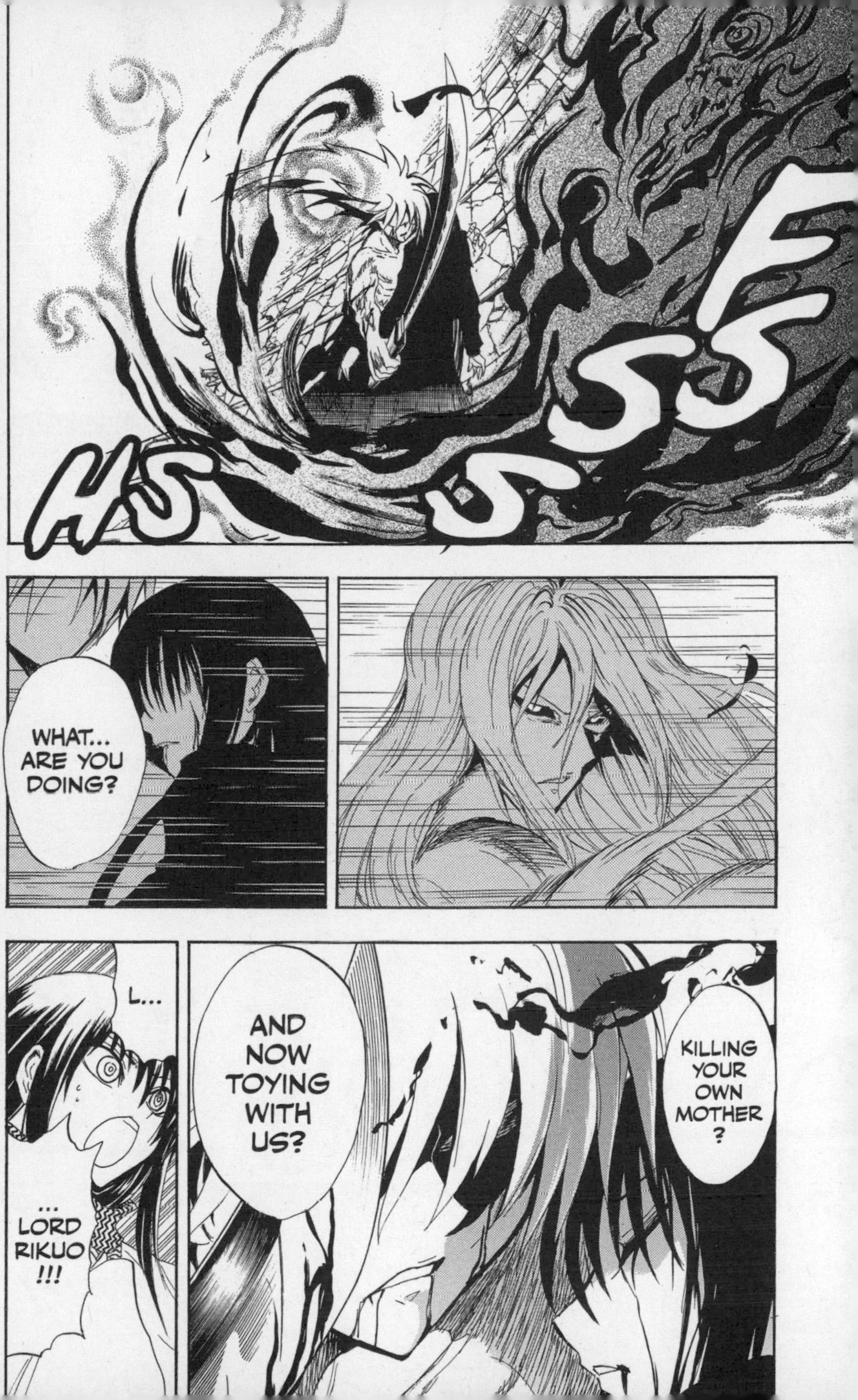
WHAT... ARE YOU DOING?
KILLING YOUR OWN MOTHER?
AND NOW TOYING WITH US?
L...
...LORD RIKUO!!!

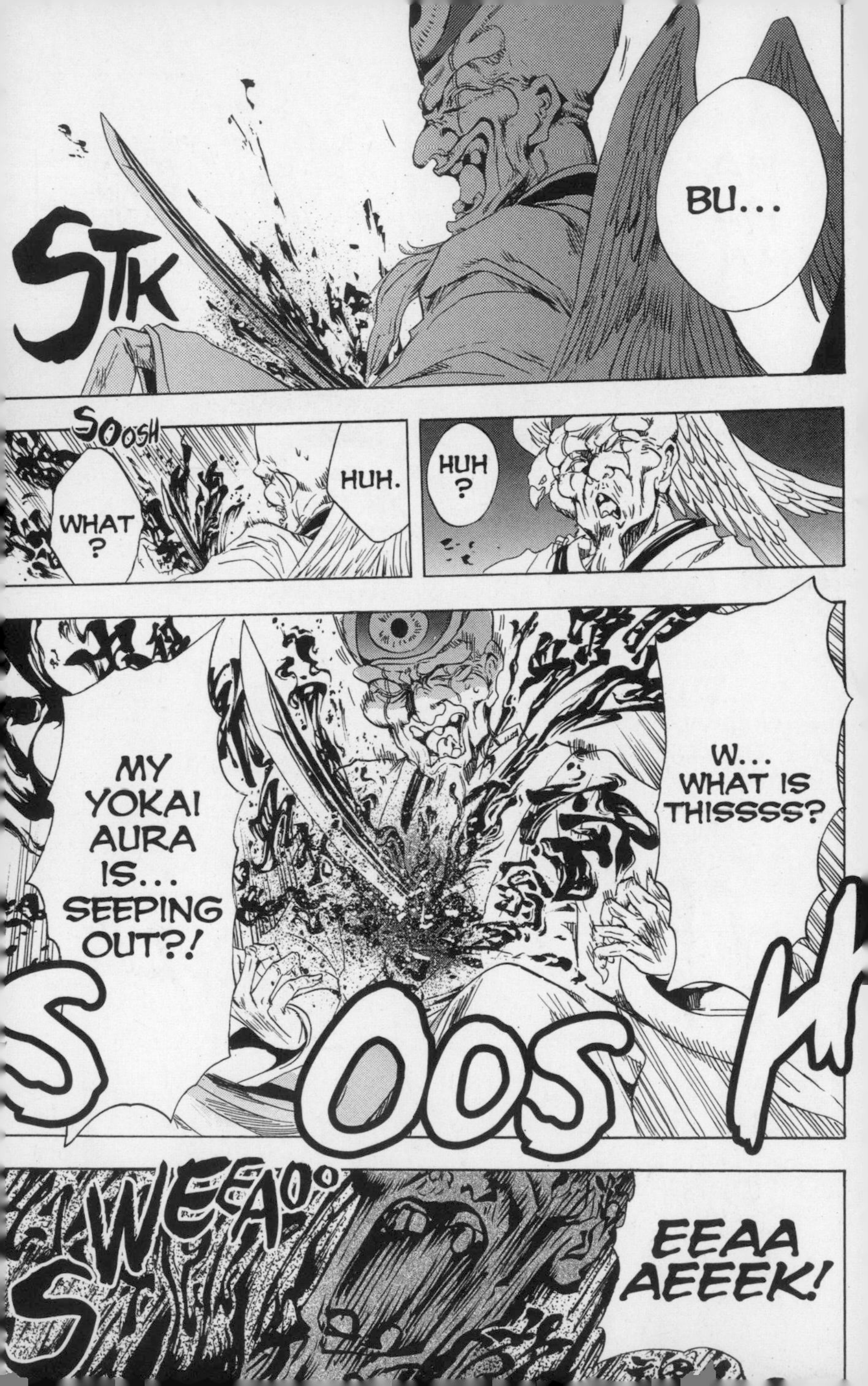
BU...
STK
HUH ?
HUH.
SOOSH
WHAT ?
W... WHAT IS THISSSS?
MY YOKAI AURA IS... SEEPING OUT?!
SOOSH
EEAA AEEEK!
SWEEA

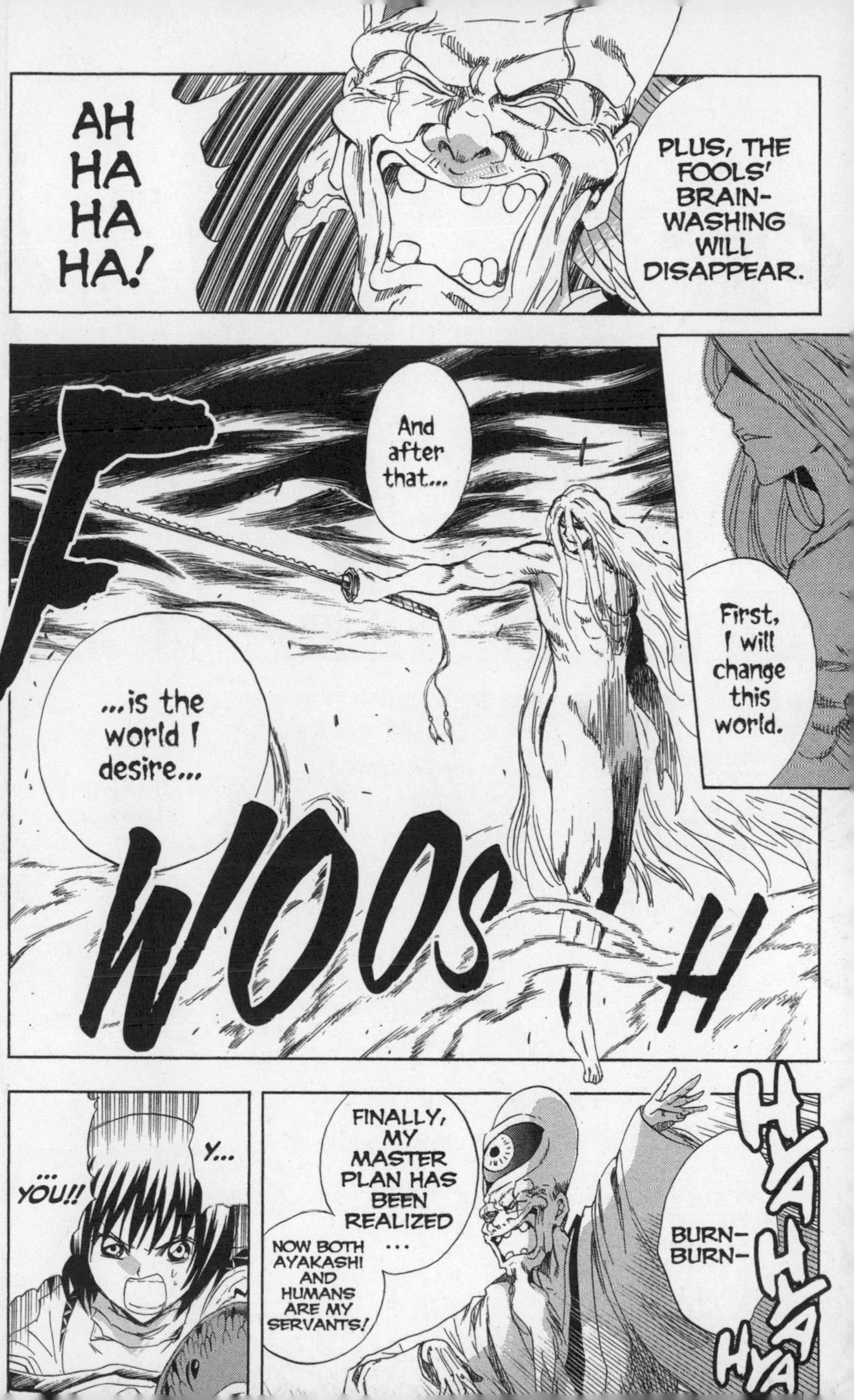
PLUS, THE FOOLS' BRAIN-WASHING WILL DISAPPEAR.
AH HA HA HA!
First, I will change this world.
And after that...
...is the world I desire...
WOOSH
HYA HYA HYA
BURN-BURN-
FINALLY, MY MASTER PLAN HAS BEEN REALIZED ...
NOW BOTH AYAKASHI AND HUMANS ARE MY SERVANTS!
Y...
...YOU!!

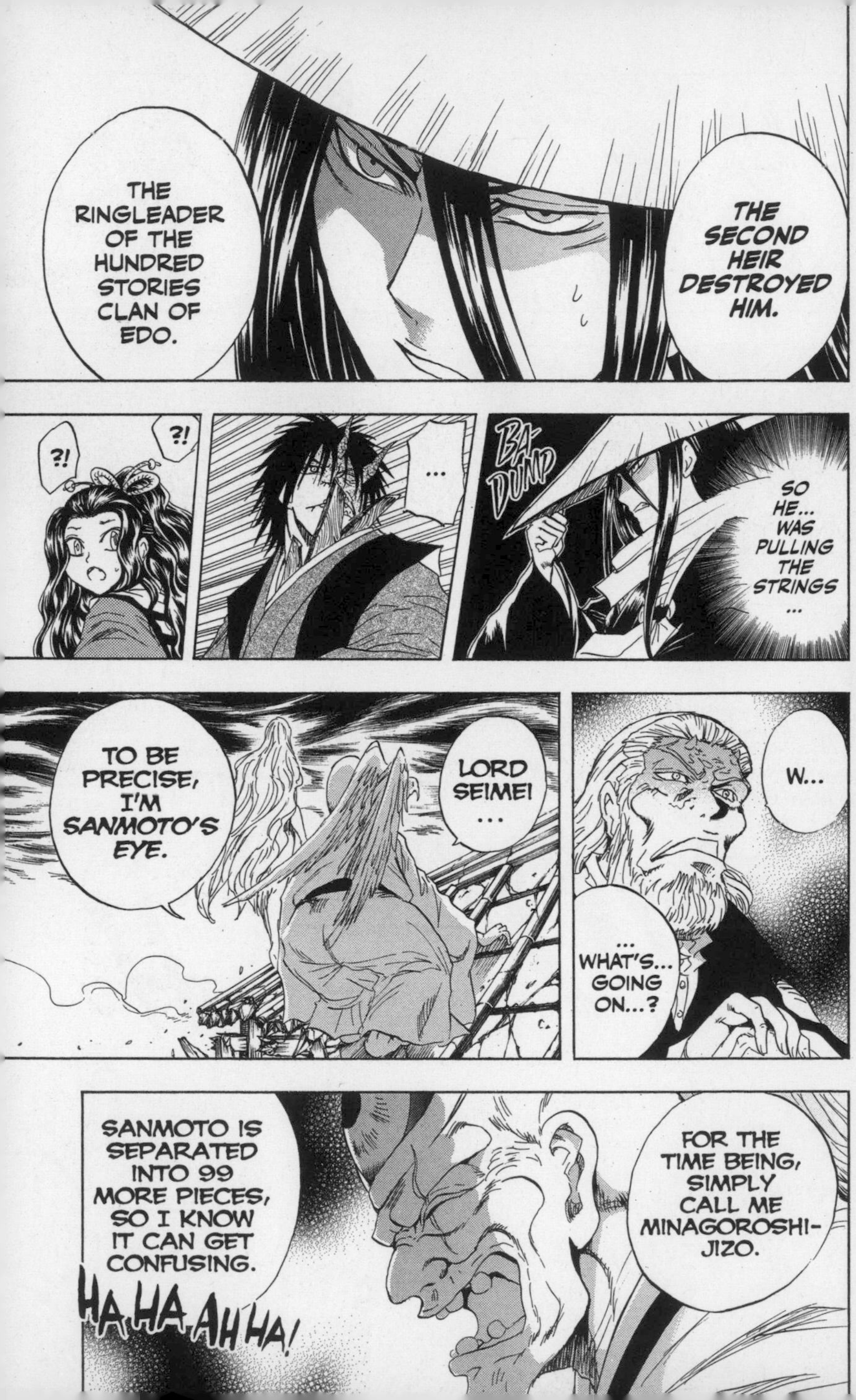
THE RINGLEADER OF THE HUNDRED STORIES CLAN OF EDO.
THE SECOND HEIR DESTROYED HIM.
BA-DUMP
SO HE... WAS PULLING THE STRINGS ...
...
?!
?!
W...
... WHAT'S... GOING ON...?
LORD SEIMEI ...
TO BE PRECISE, I'M SANMOTO'S EYE.
FOR THE TIME BEING, SIMPLY CALL ME MINAGOROSHI-JIZO.
SANMOTO IS SEPARATED INTO 99 MORE PIECES, SO I KNOW IT CAN GET CONFUSING.
HA HA AH HA!

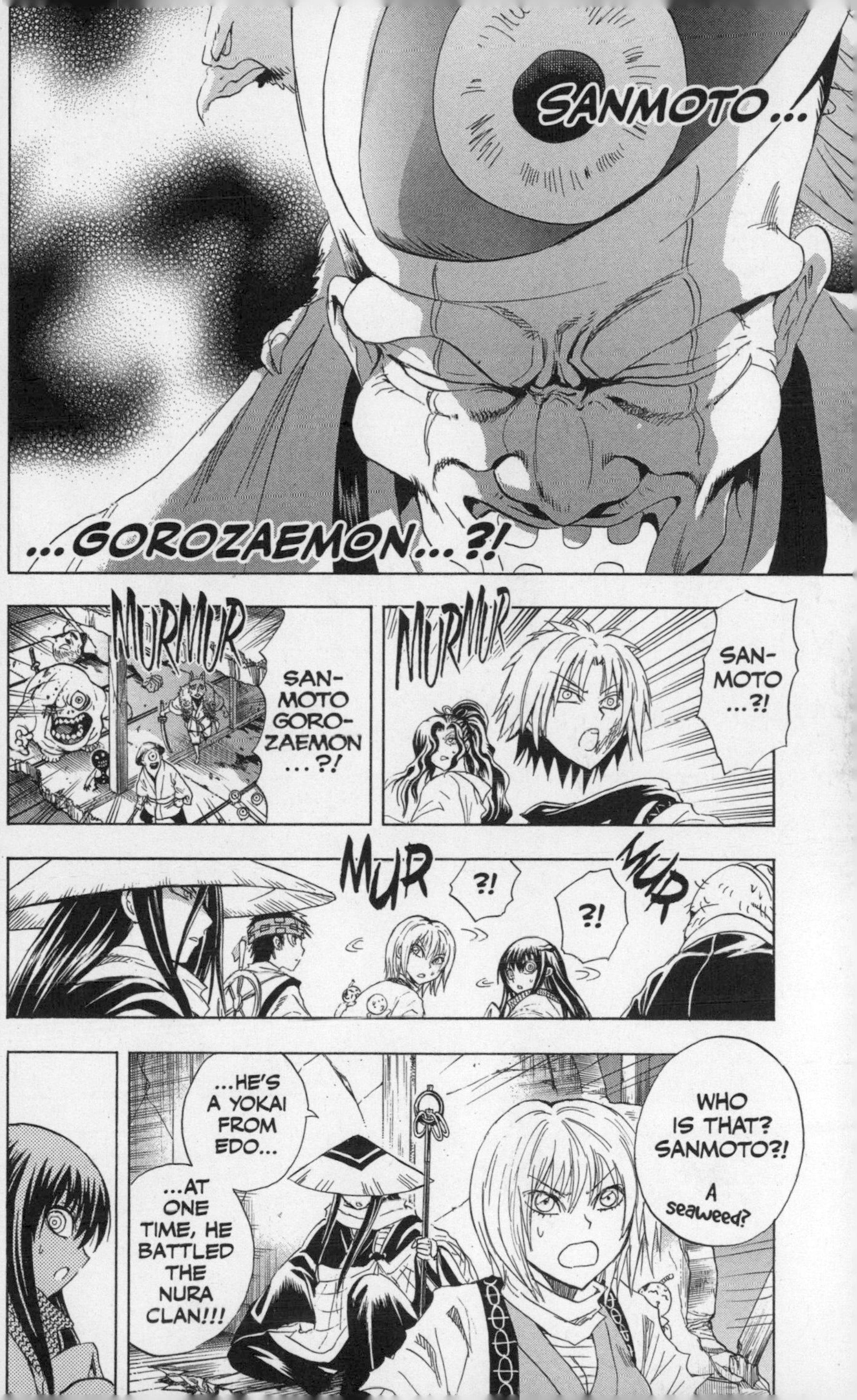
SANMOTO...
...GOROZAEMON...?!
MURMUR
SAN-MOTO ...?!
MURMUR
SAN-MOTO GORO-ZAEMON ...?!
MUR
?!
?!
MUR
WHO IS THAT? SANMOTO?!
A seaweed?
...HE'S A YOKAI FROM EDO...
...AT ONE TIME, HE BATTLED THE NURA CLAN!!!

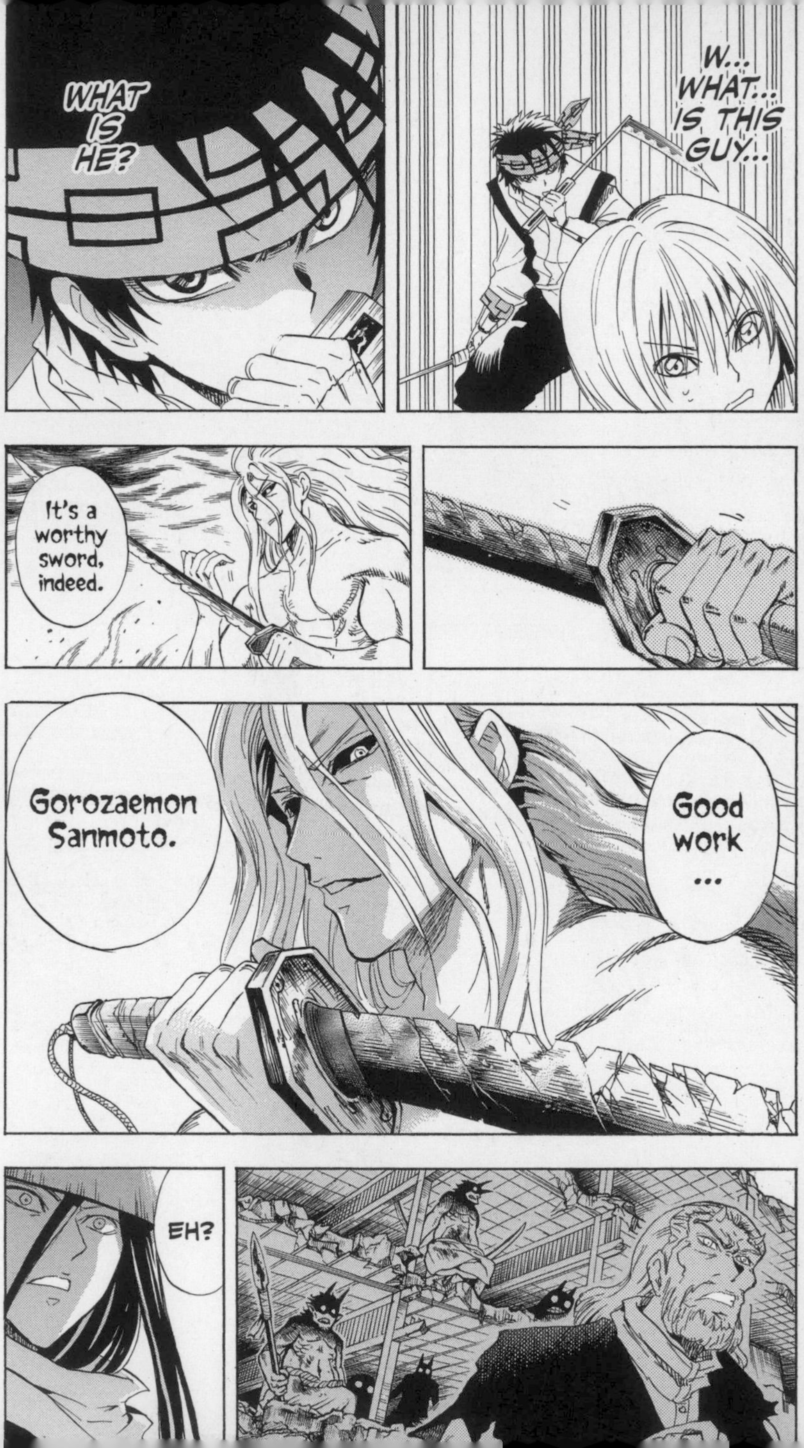
W... WHAT... IS THIS GUY...
WHAT IS HE?
It's a worthy sword, indeed.
Good work ...
Gorozaemon Sanmoto.
EH?

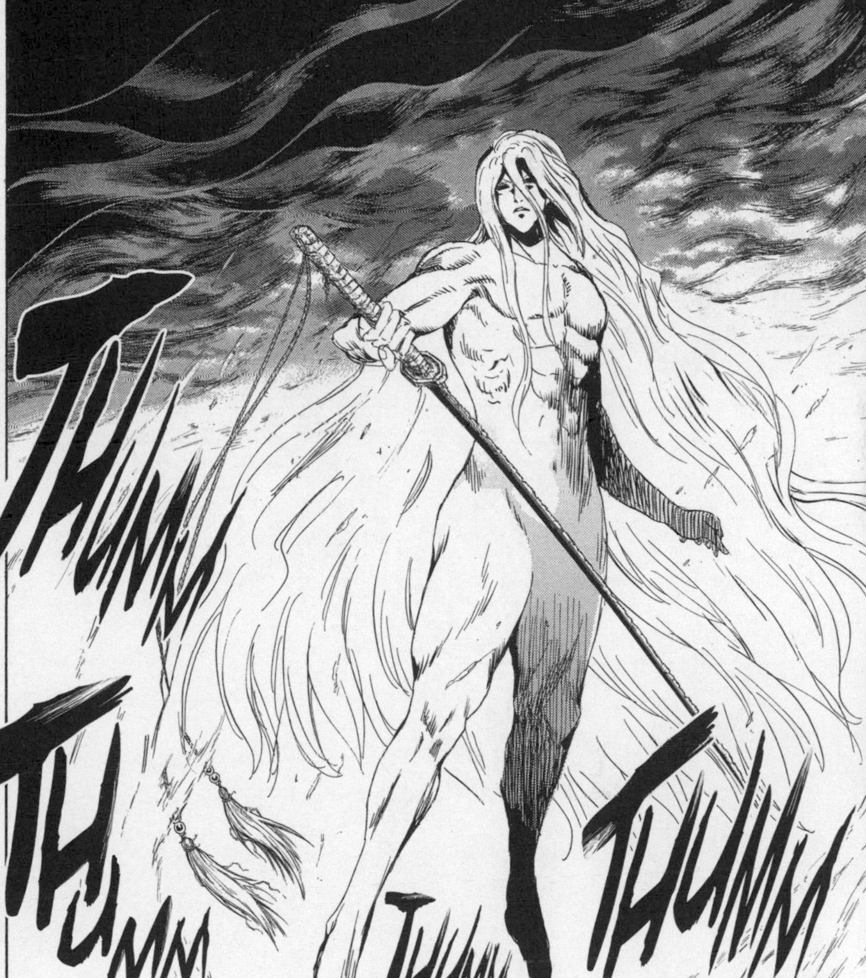
THUMM
THUMM
THUMM
THUMM
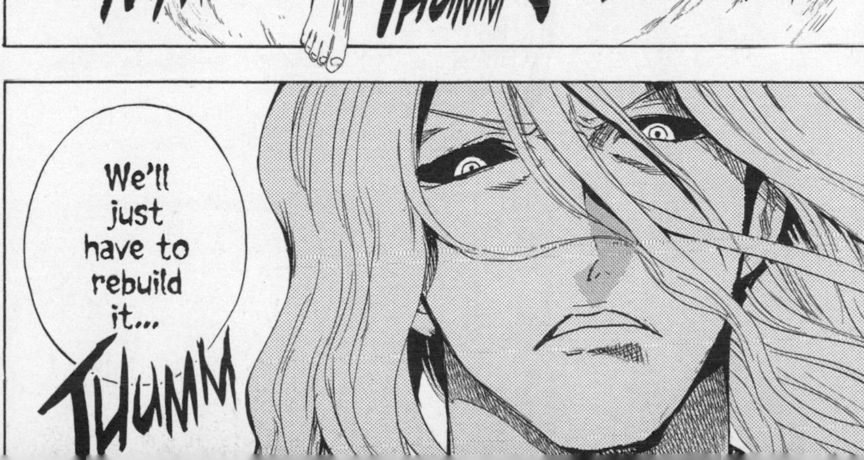
We'll just have to rebuild it...
THUMM

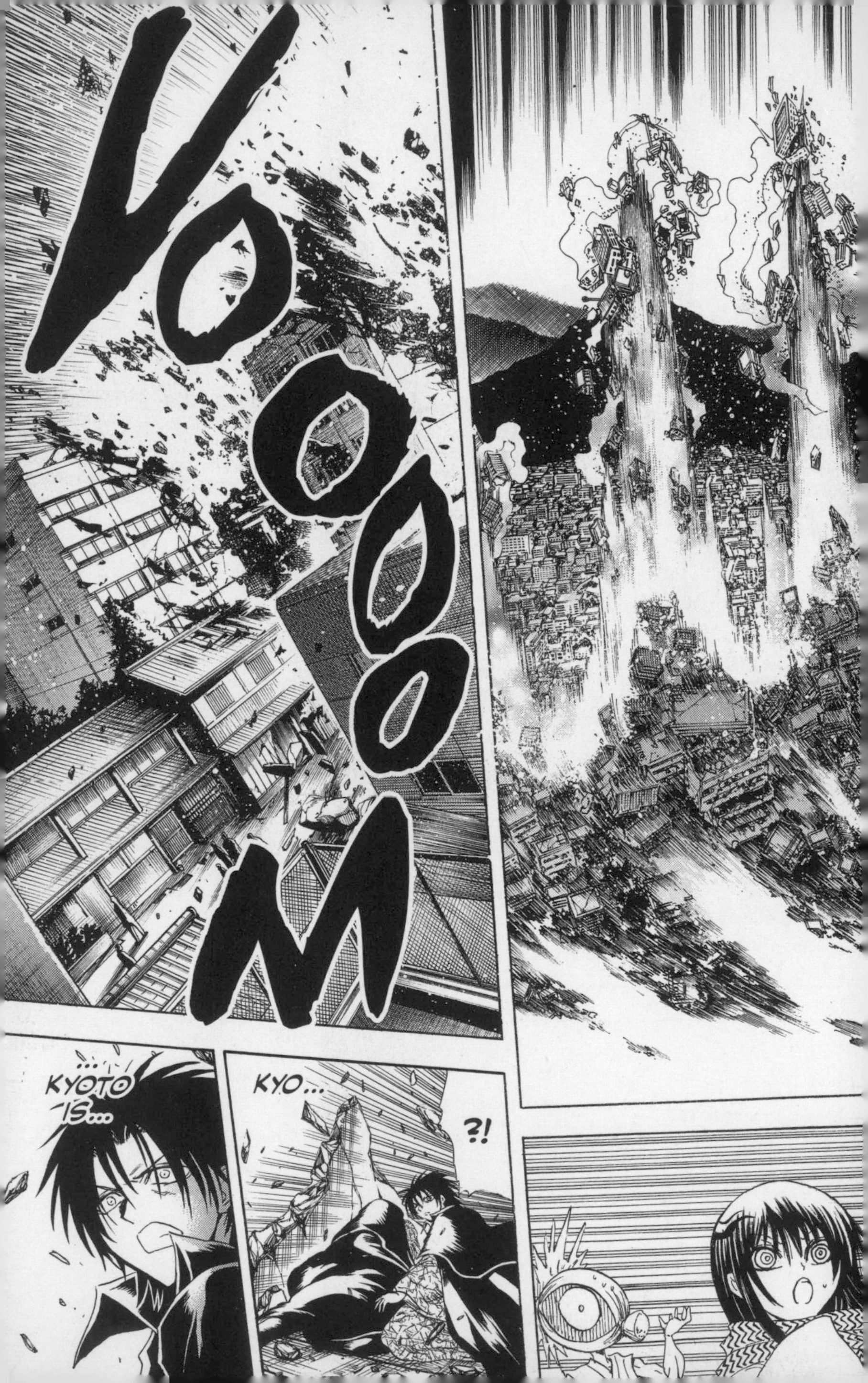
VOOOOM
KYO...
?!
...KYOTO IS...

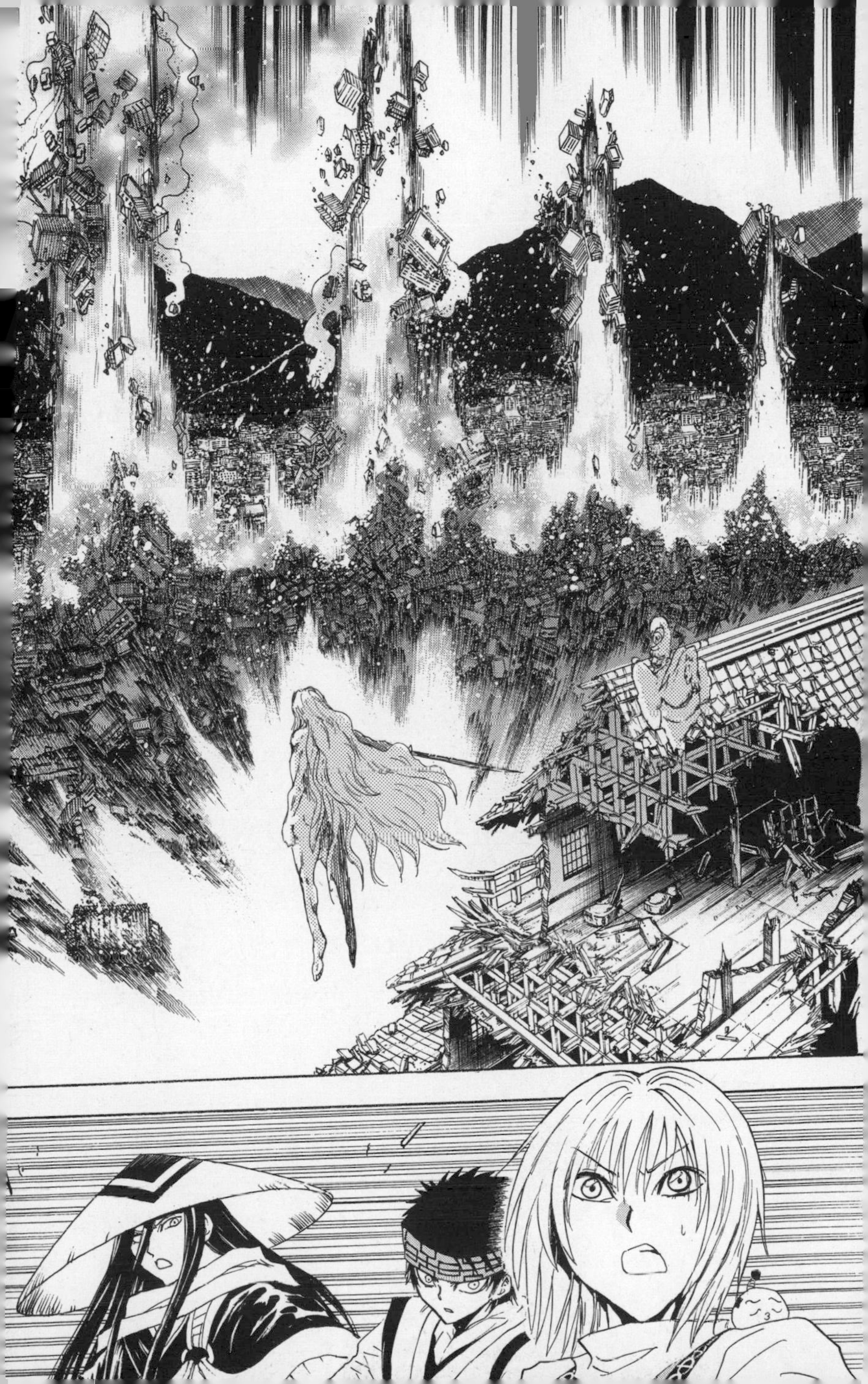

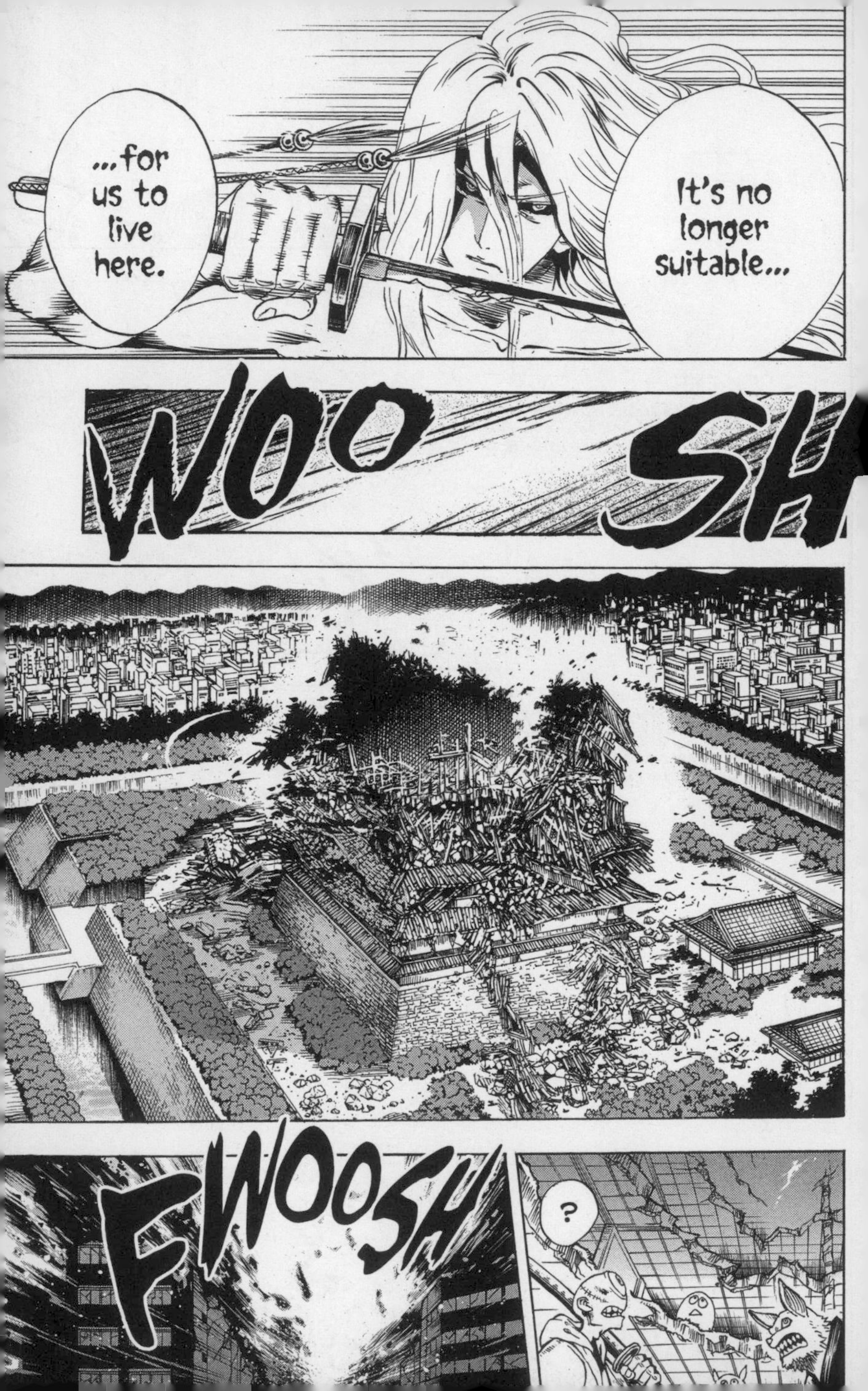
It's no longer suitable...
...for us to live here.
WOOSH
?
FWOOSH

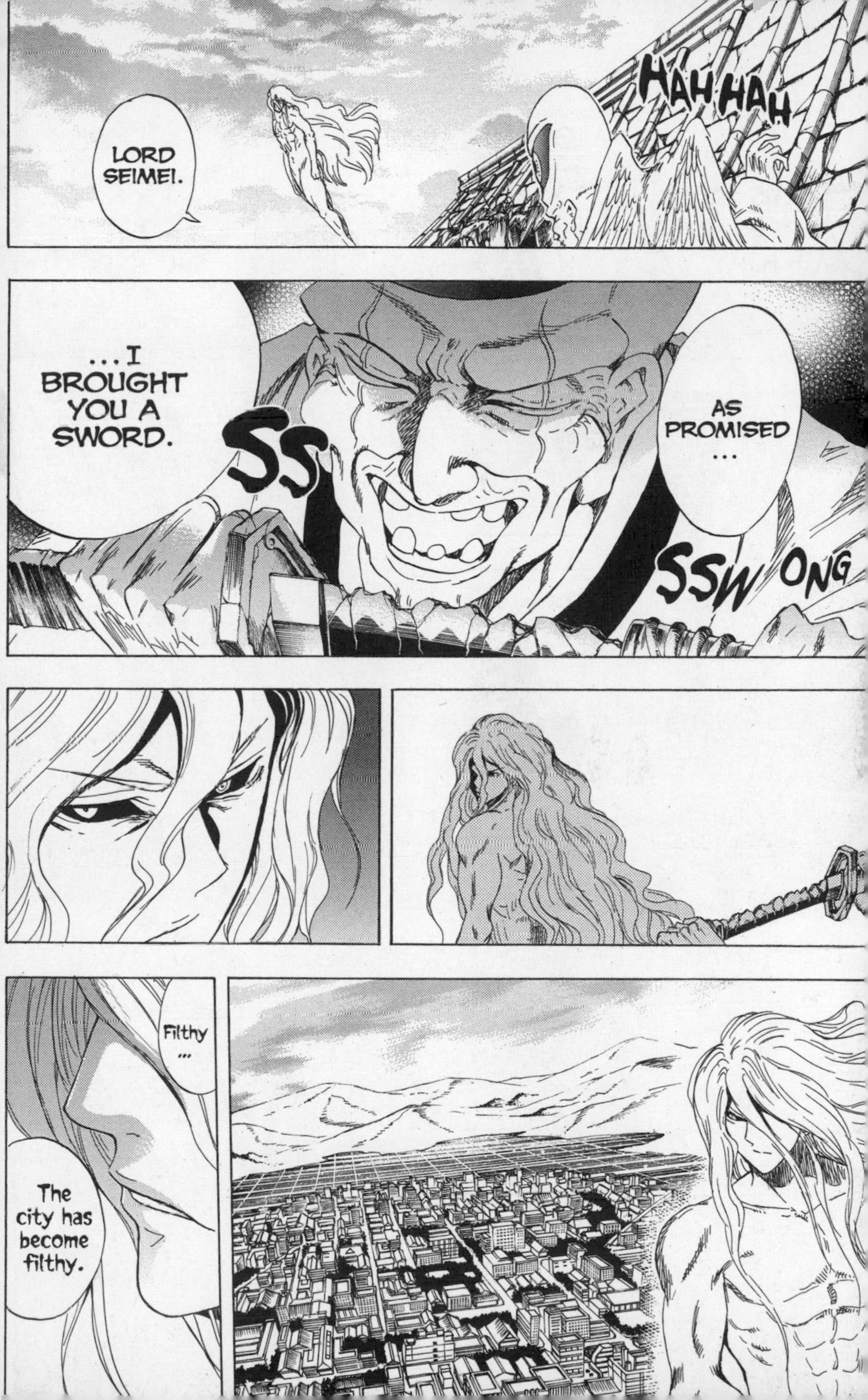
HAH HAH
LORD SEIMEI.
AS PROMISED ...
SSW ONG
... I BROUGHT YOU A SWORD.
SS
Filthy ...
The city has become filthy.

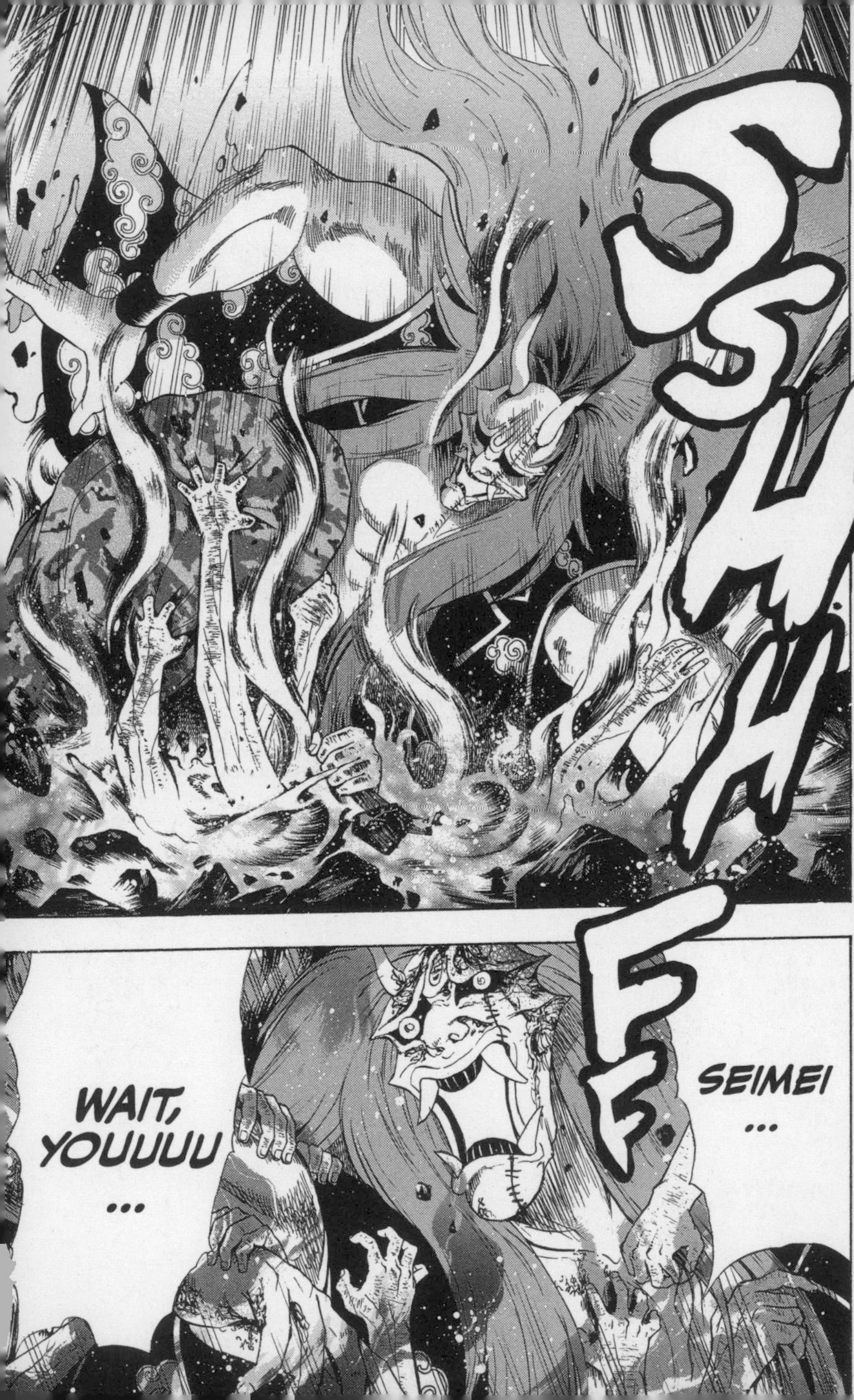
SSHHFF
SEIMEI ...
WAIT, YOUUUU ...

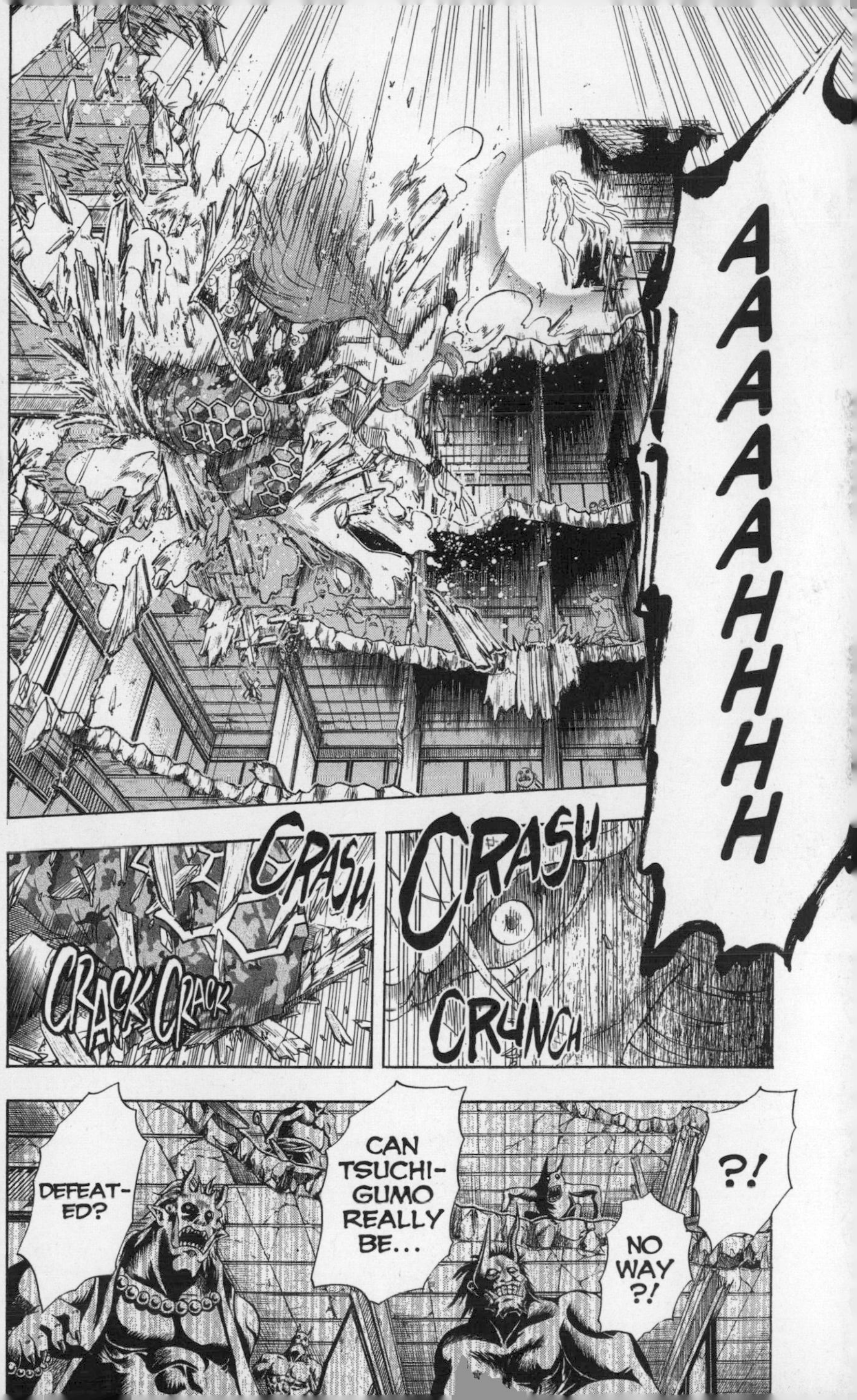
AAAAAHHHH
CRASH
CRASH
CRUNCH
CRACK CRACK
?!
NO WAY?!
CAN TSUCHI-GUMO REALLY BE...
DEFEAT-ED?

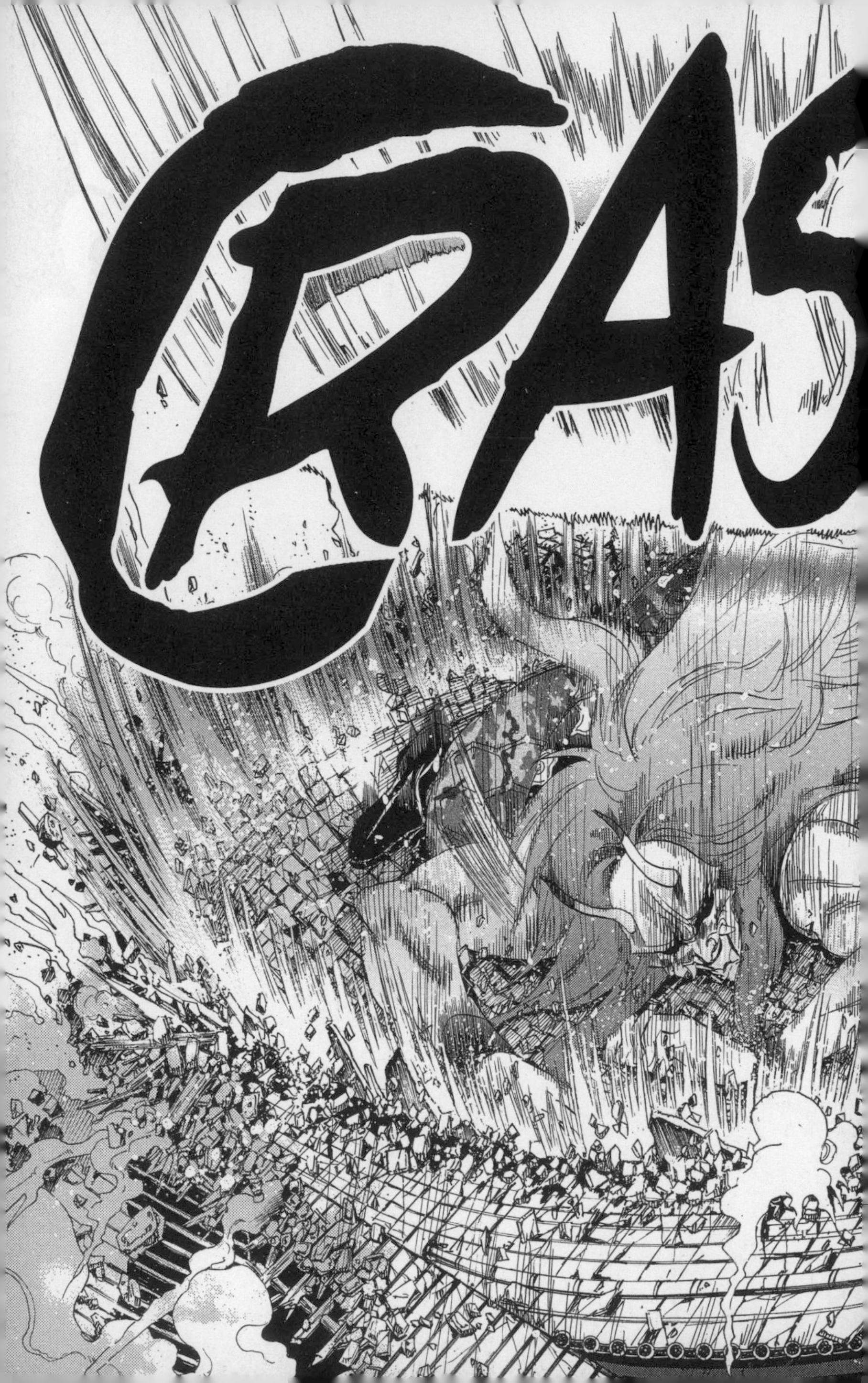
CRAS

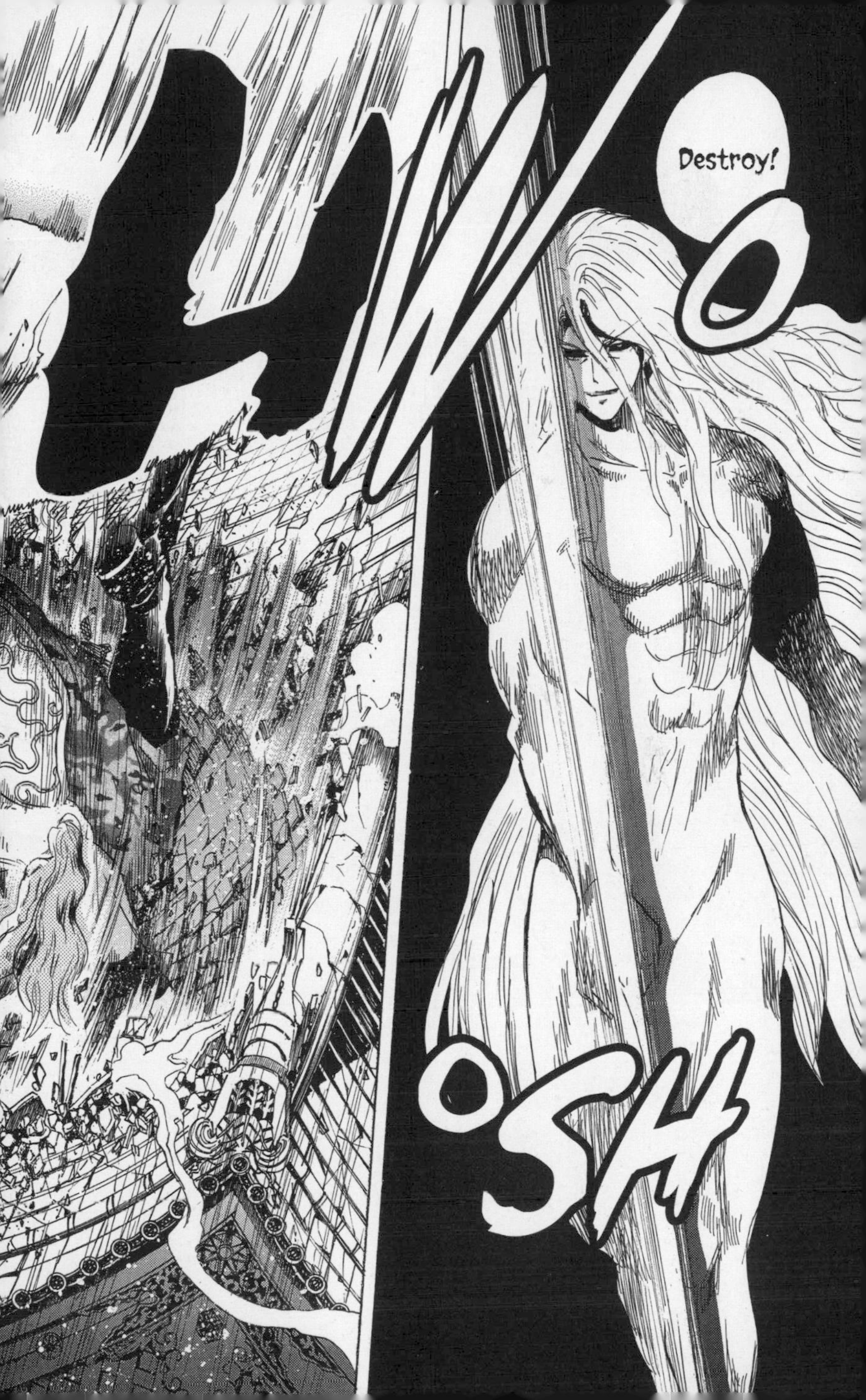
Destroy!
WOOSH

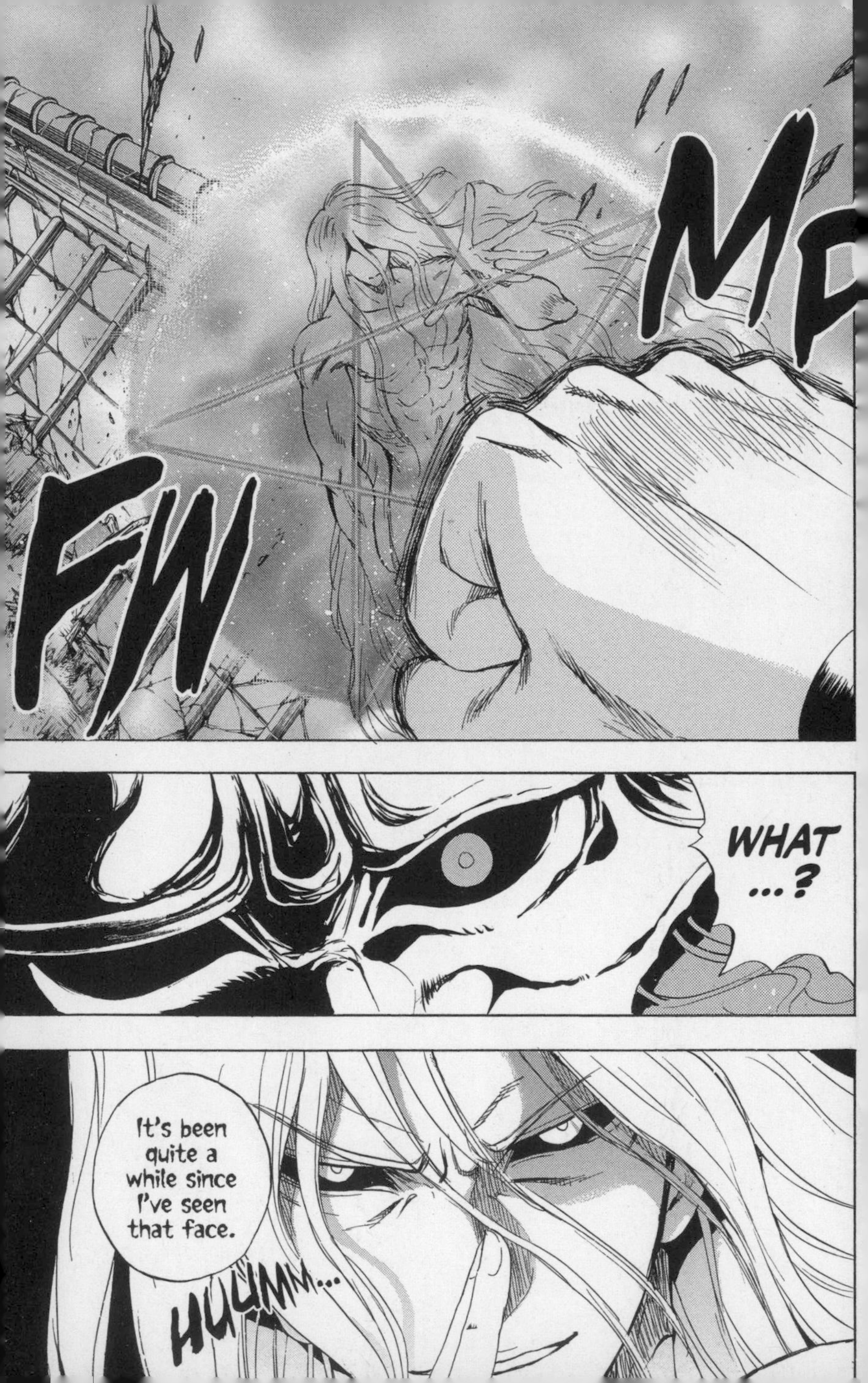
MP
FW
WHAT ...?
It's been quite a while since I've seen that face.
HUUMM...

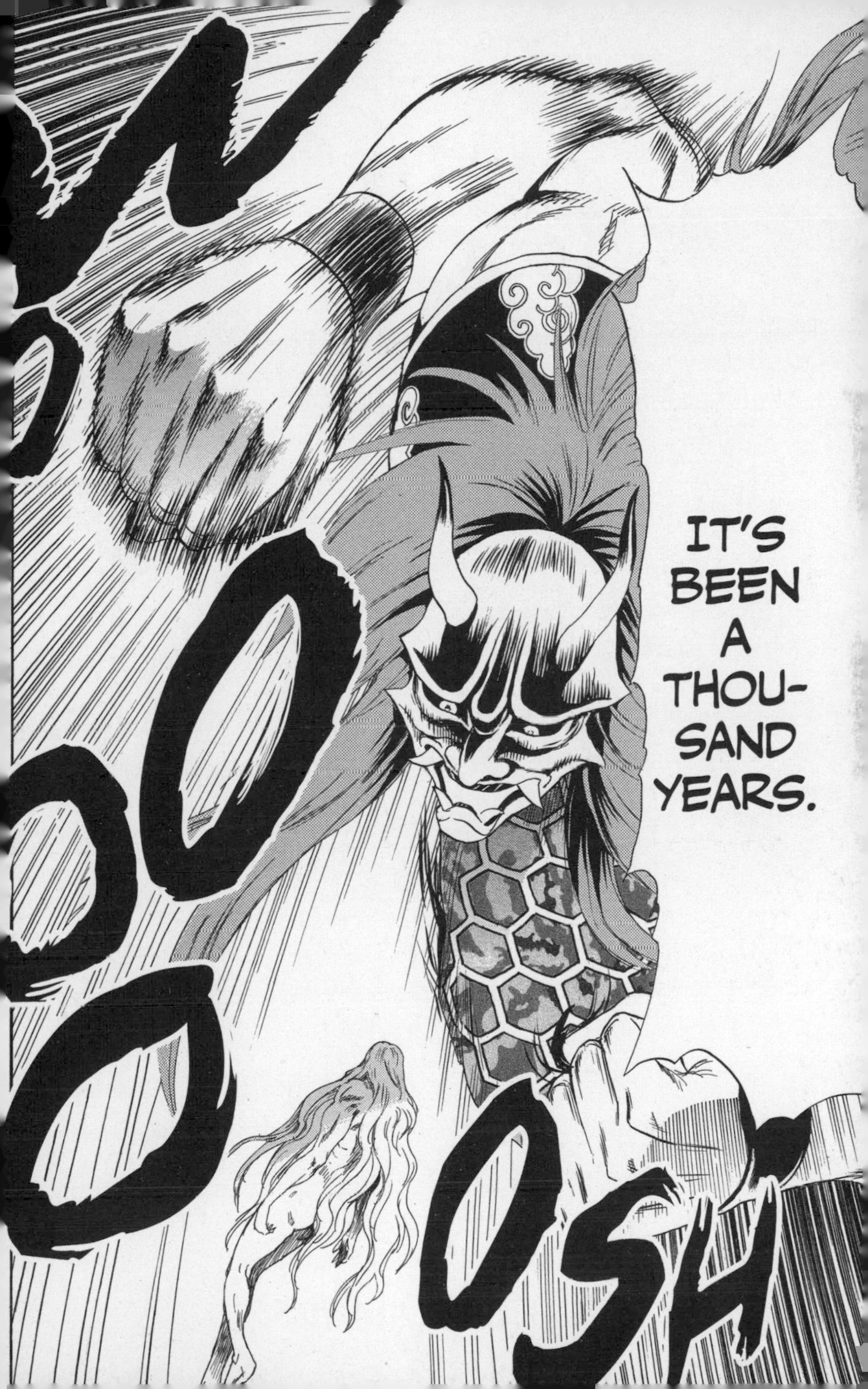
IT'S BEEN A THOU-SAND YEARS.

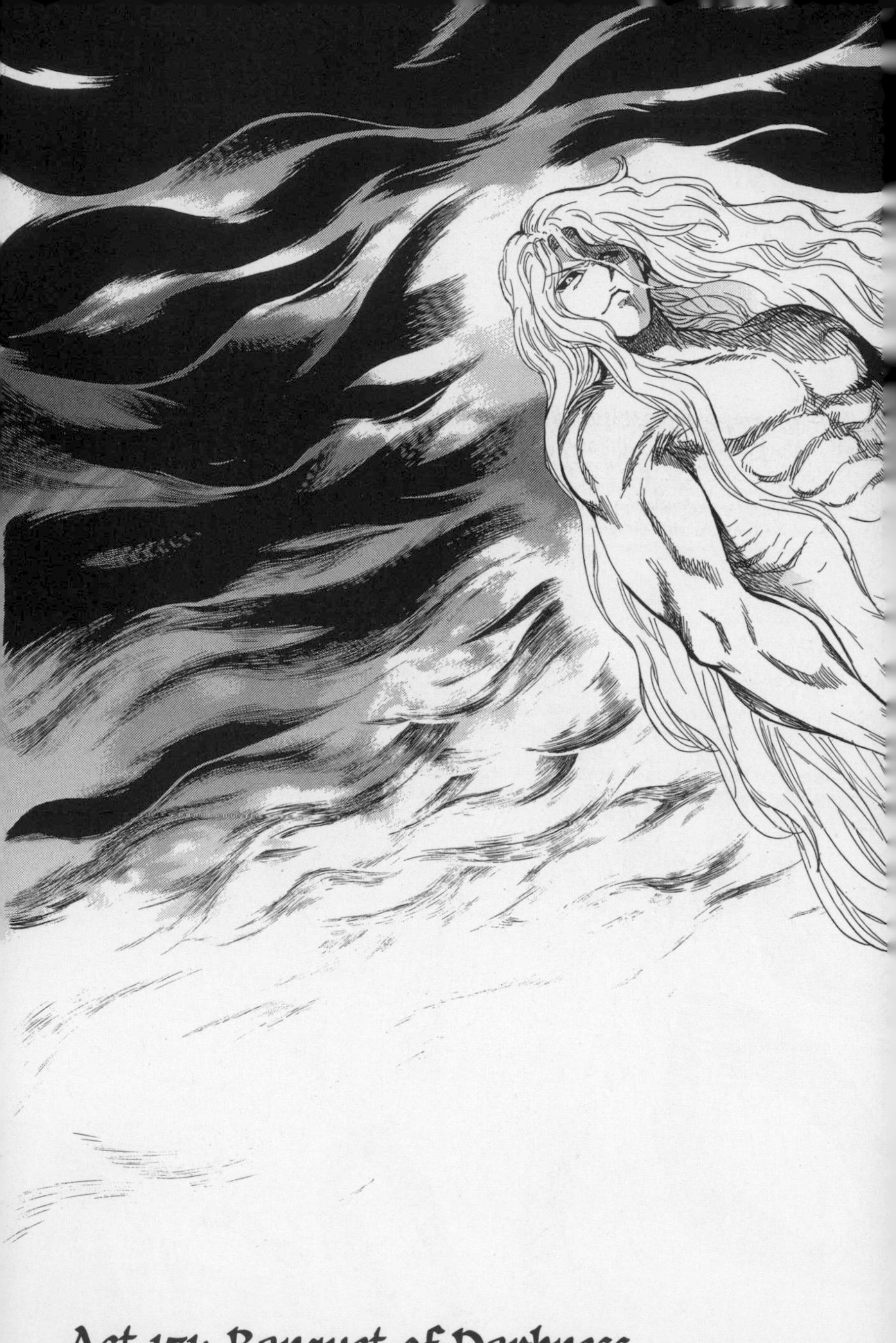

Act 131: Banquet of Darkness

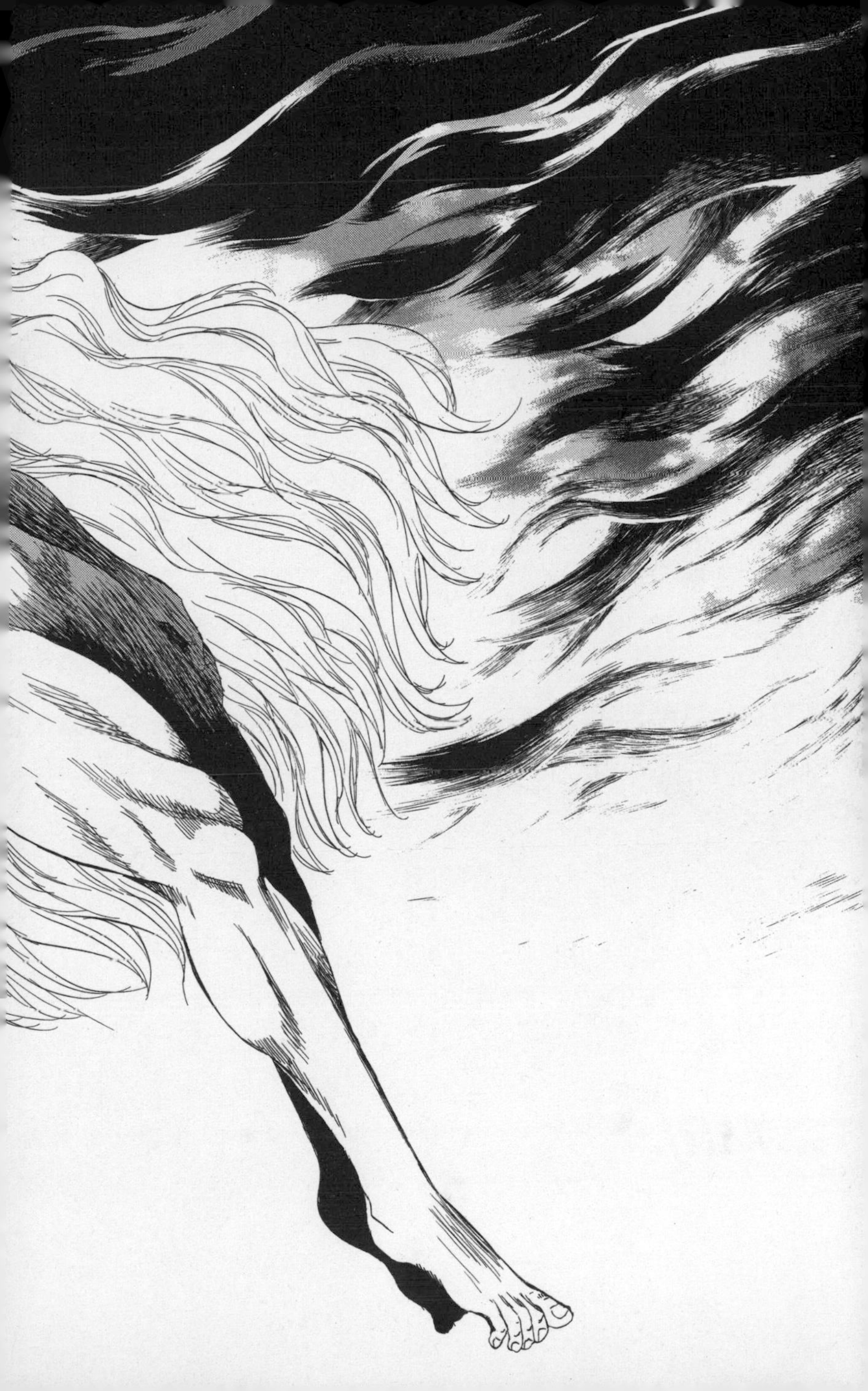

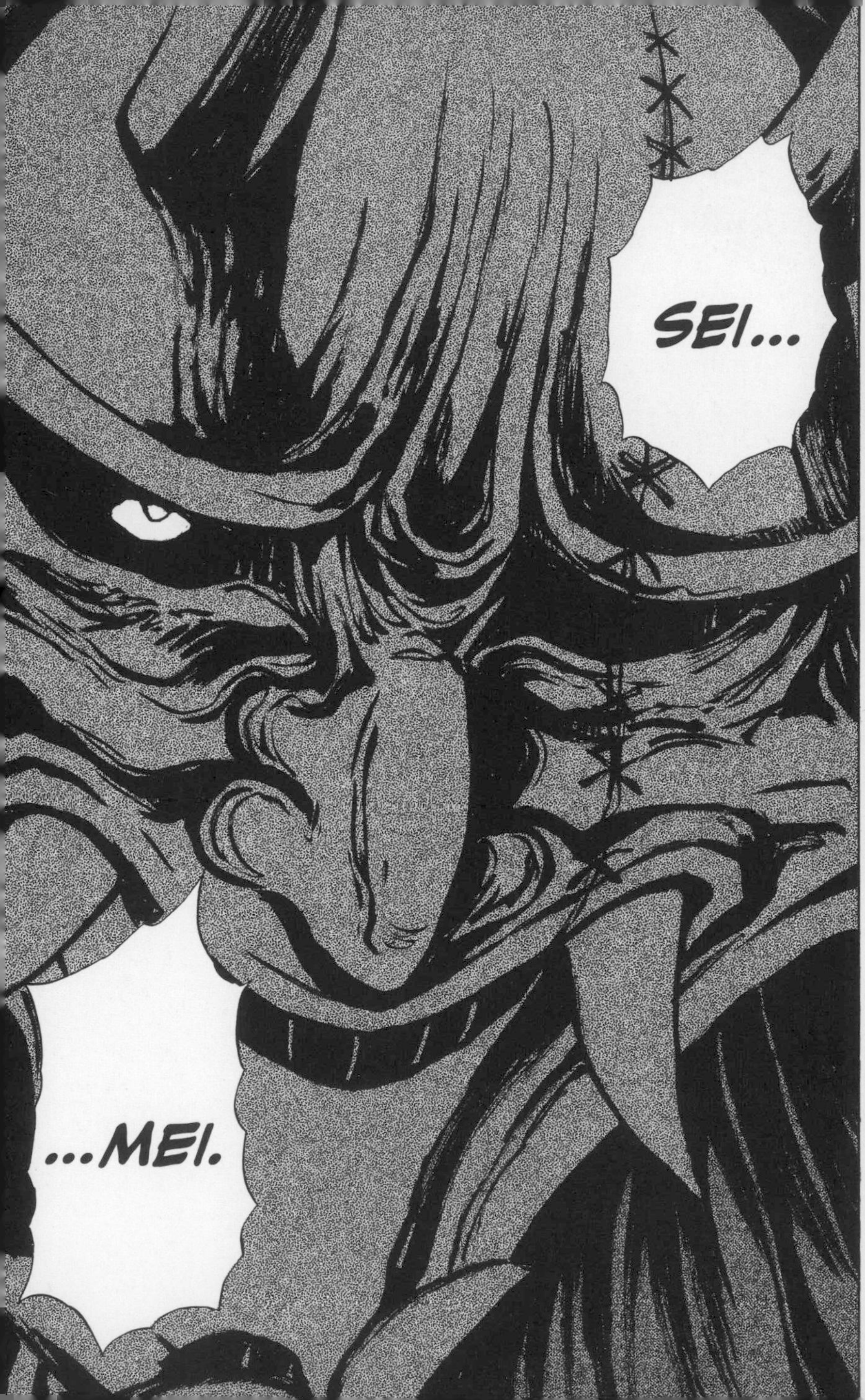
SEI...
...MEI.

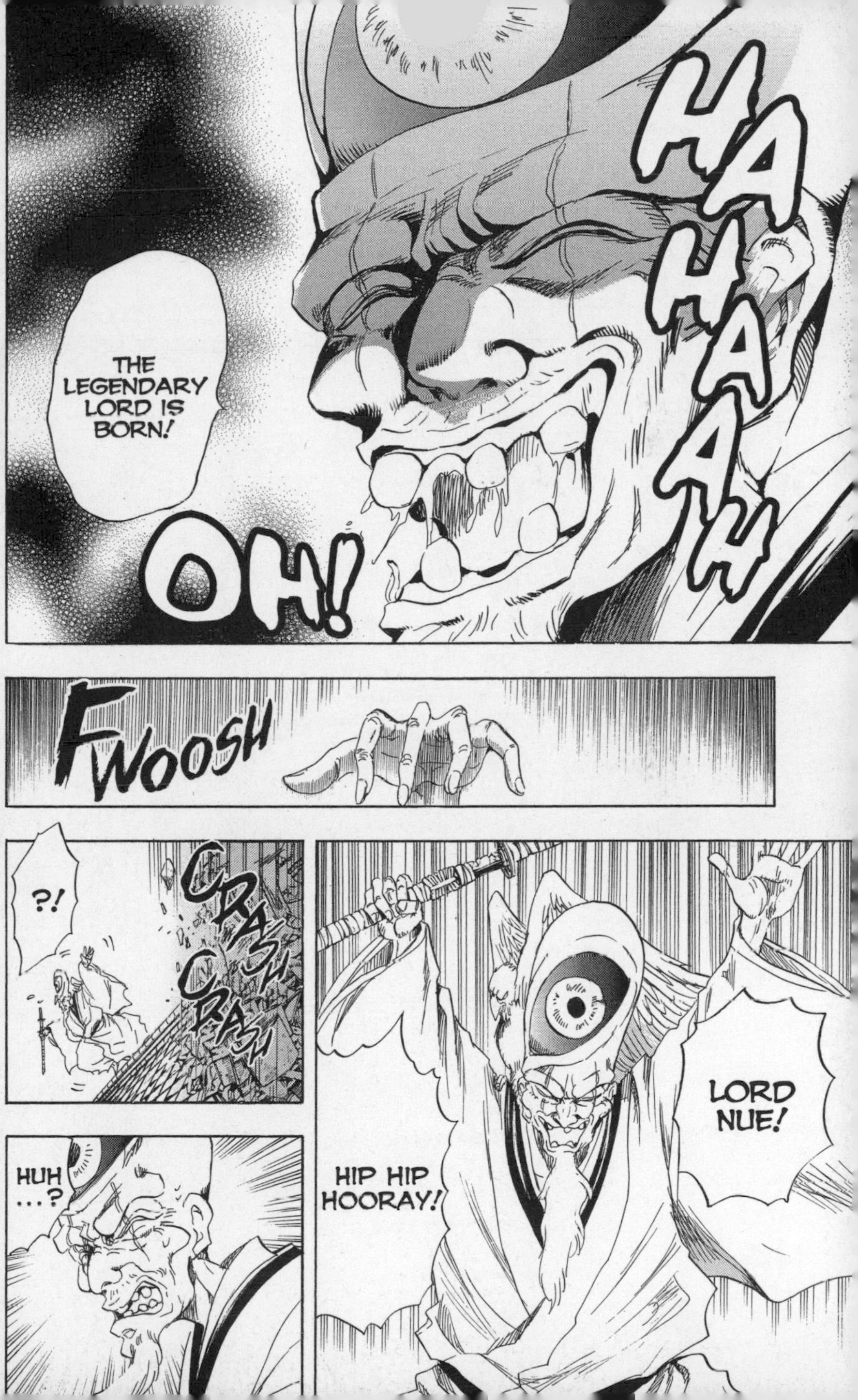
HA HA HA AH
THE LEGENDARY LORD IS BORN!
OH!
FWOOSH
LORD NUE!
HIP HIP HOORAY!
CRASH CRASH
?!
HUH ...?

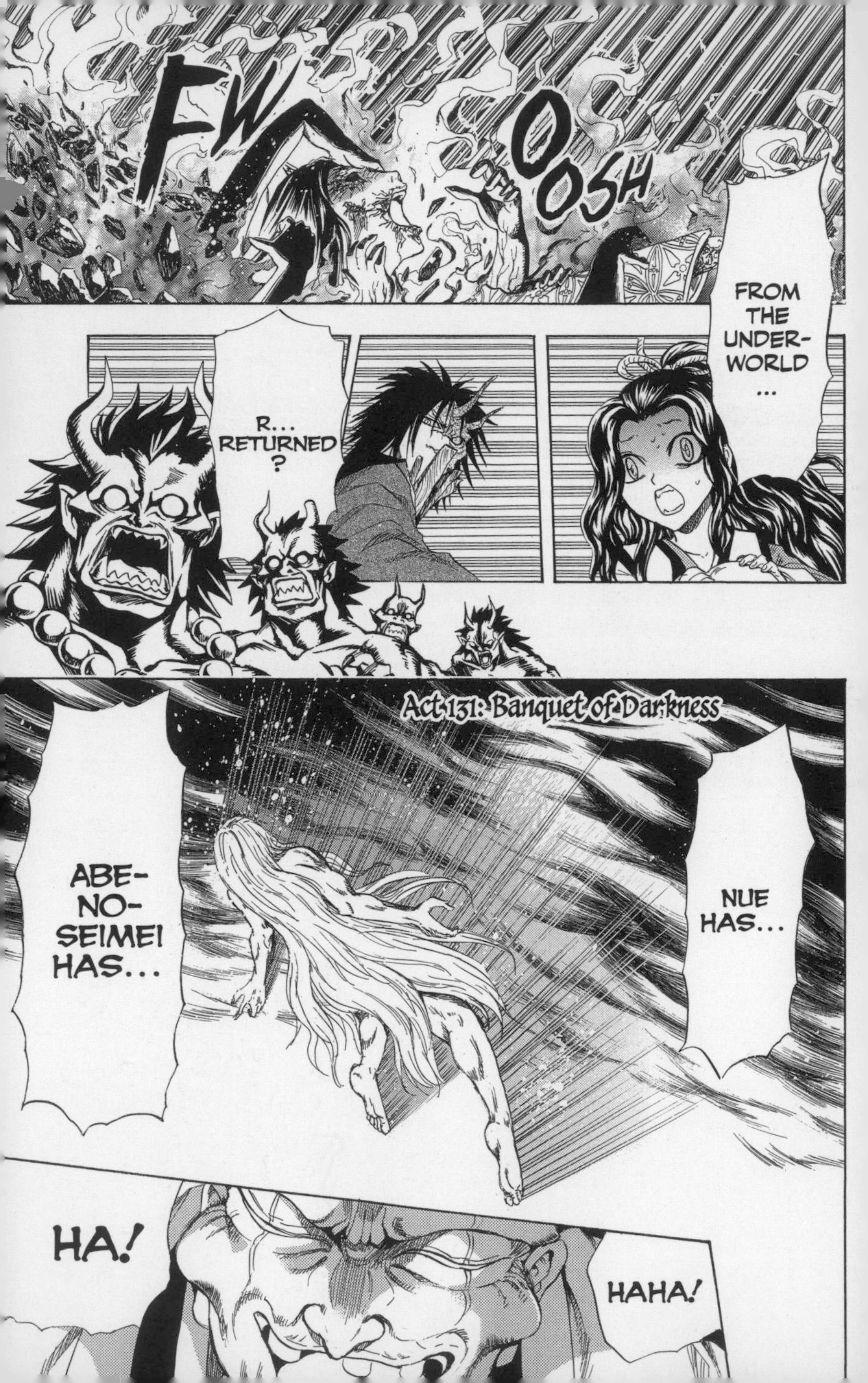
FWOOOSH
FROM THE UNDER-WORLD...
R... RETURNED?
Act 131: Banquet of Darkness
NUE HAS...
ABE-NO-SEIMEI HAS...
HAHA!
HA!

NURA: RISE OF THE YOKAI CLAN

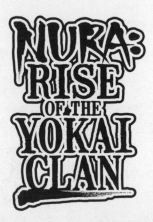

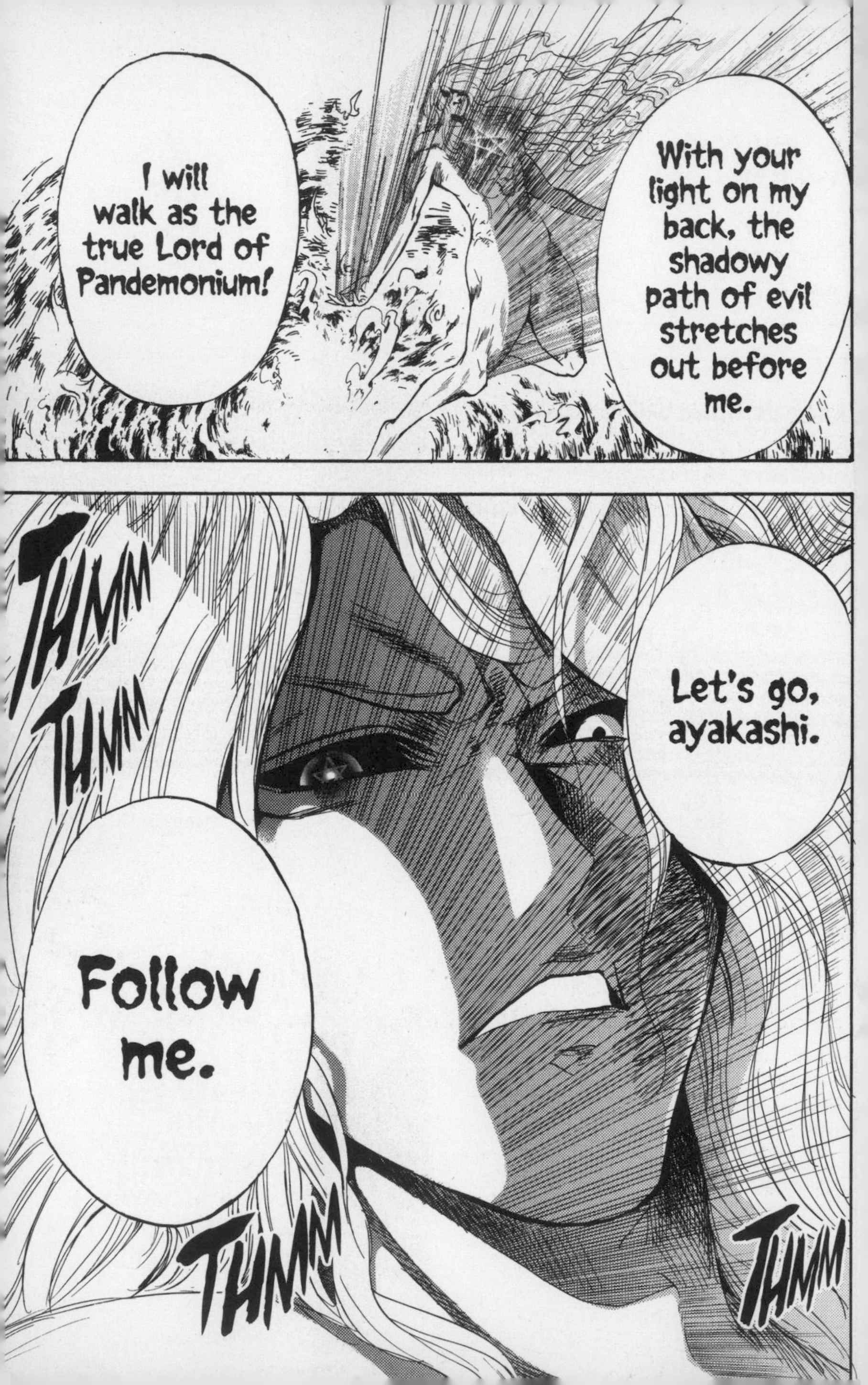
With your light on my back, the shadowy path of evil stretches out before me.
I will walk as the true Lord of Pandemonium!
Let's go, ayakashi.
THMM
THMM
Follow me.
THMM
THMM

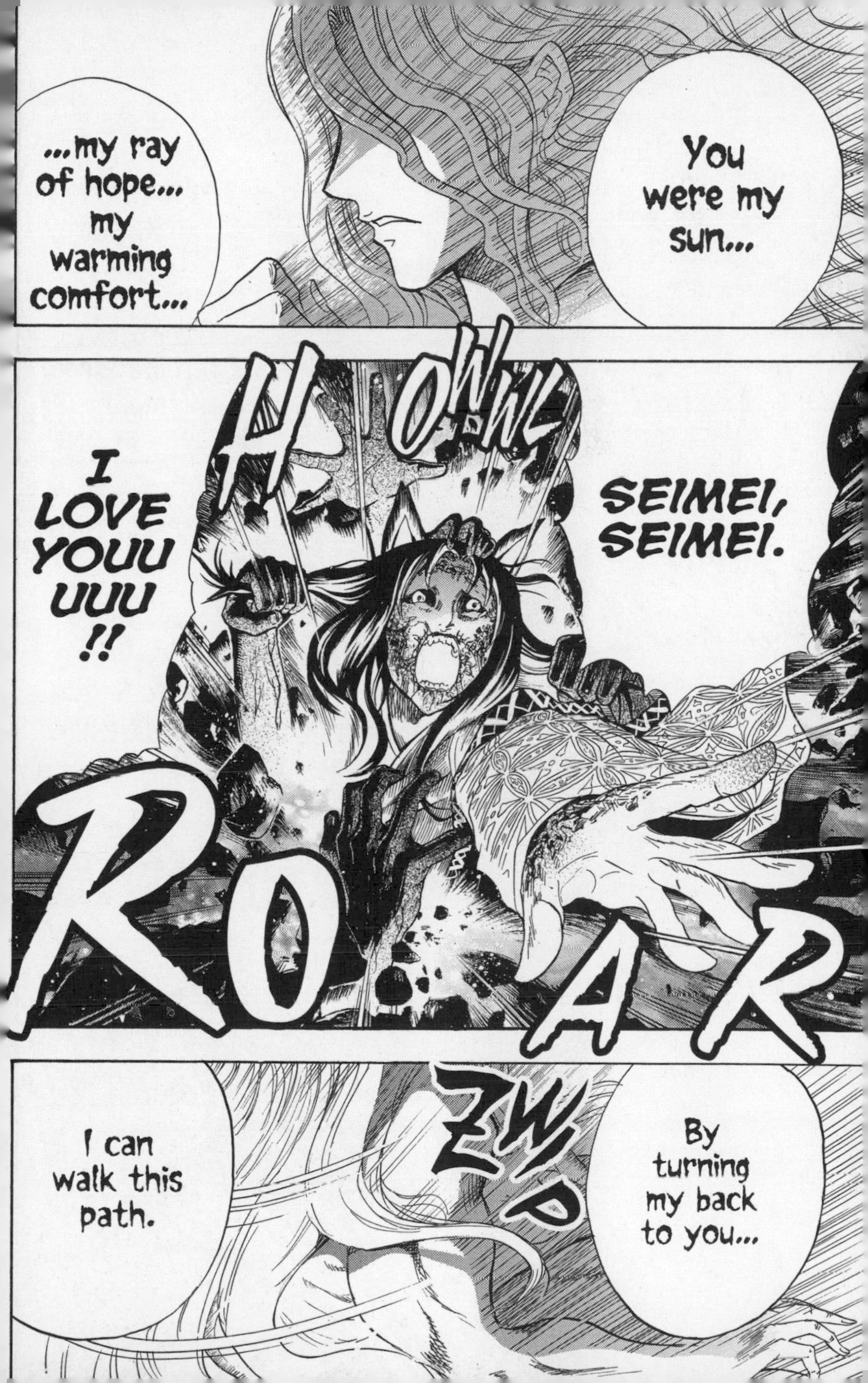
You were my sun...
...my ray of hope... my warming comfort...
HOWL
SEIMEI, SEIMEI.
I LOVE YOUUUUU!!
ROAR
ZWIP
By turning my back to you...
I can walk this path.

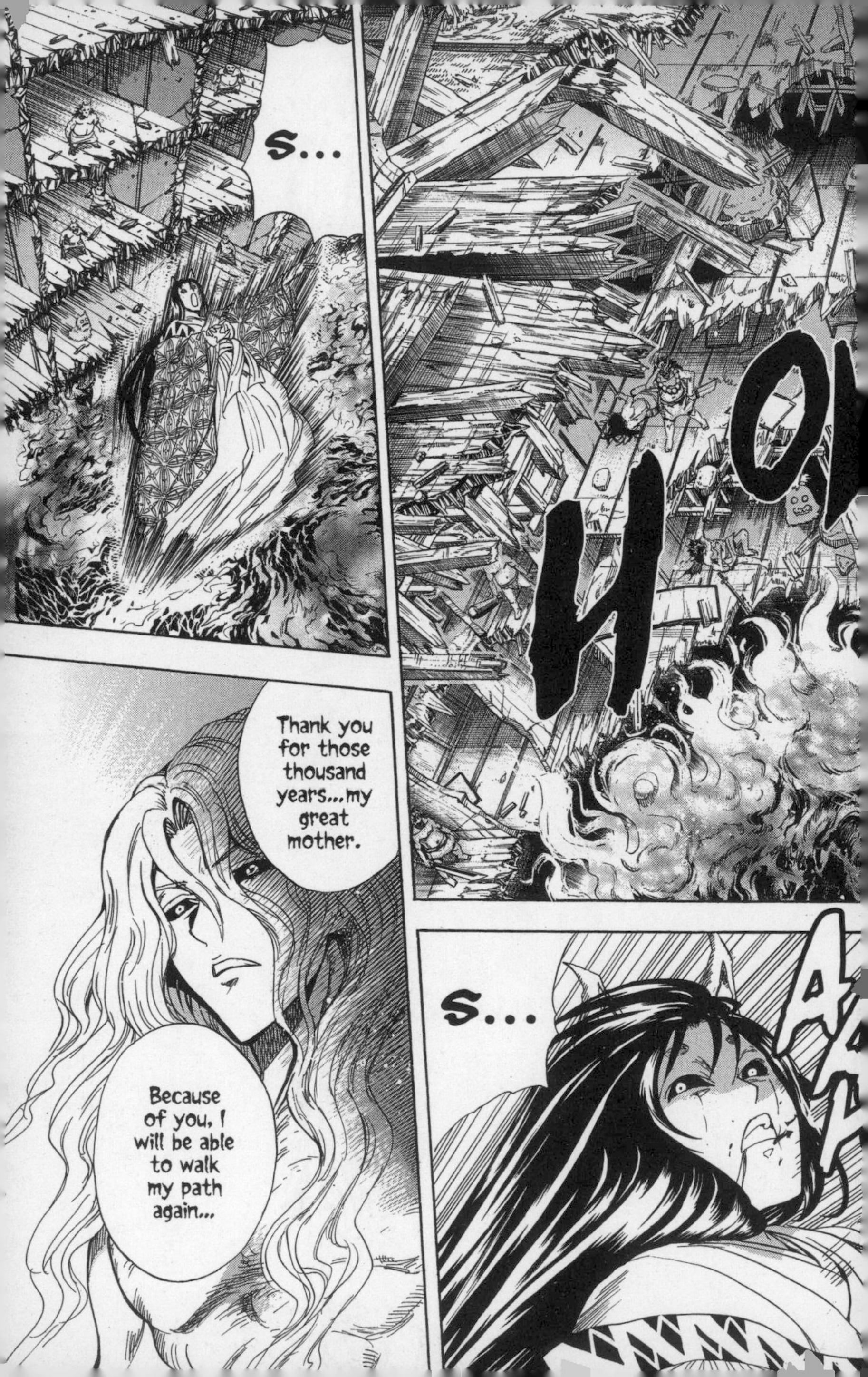
S...
S...
Thank you for those thousand years...my great mother.
Because of you, I will be able to walk my path again...

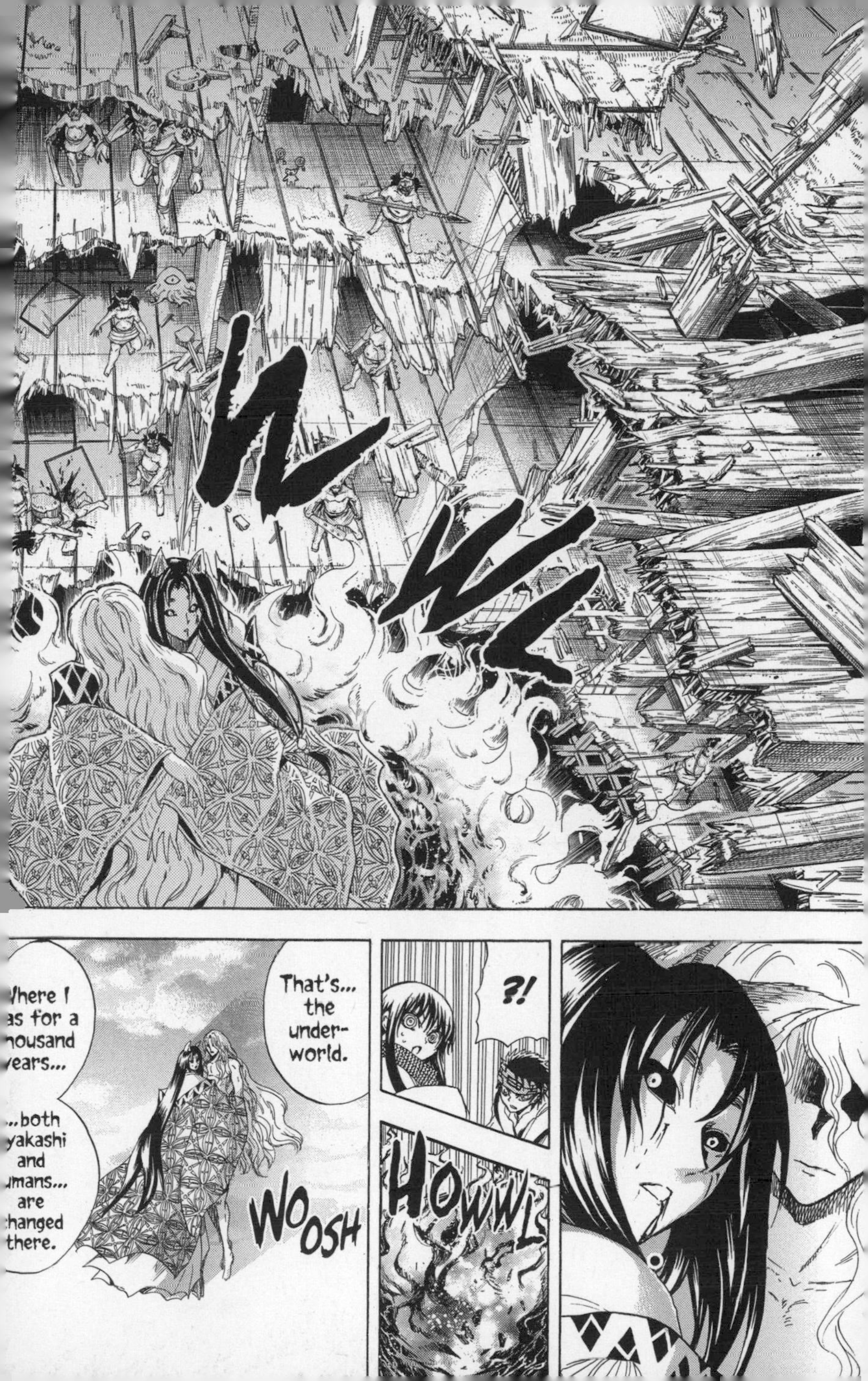
?!
HOWWL
That's... the under-world.
Vhere I as for a housand ears...
...both yakashi and umans... are hanged there.
WOOSH

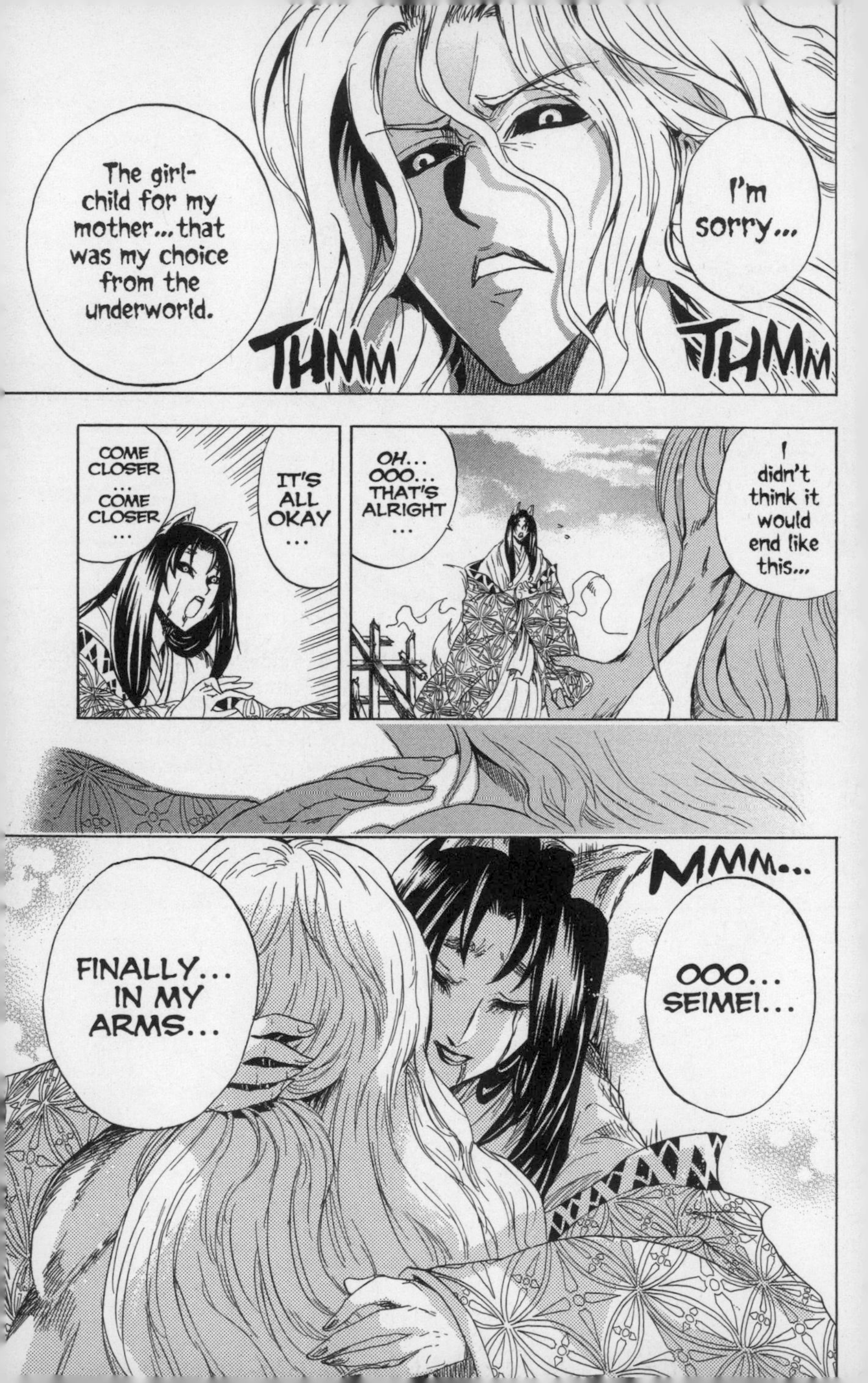
I'm sorry...
THMM
The girl-child for my mother... that was my choice from the underworld.
THMM
I didn't think it would end like this...
OH... OOO... THAT'S ALRIGHT...
IT'S ALL OKAY...
COME CLOSER... COME CLOSER...
MMM...
OOO... SEIMEI...
FINALLY... IN MY ARMS...

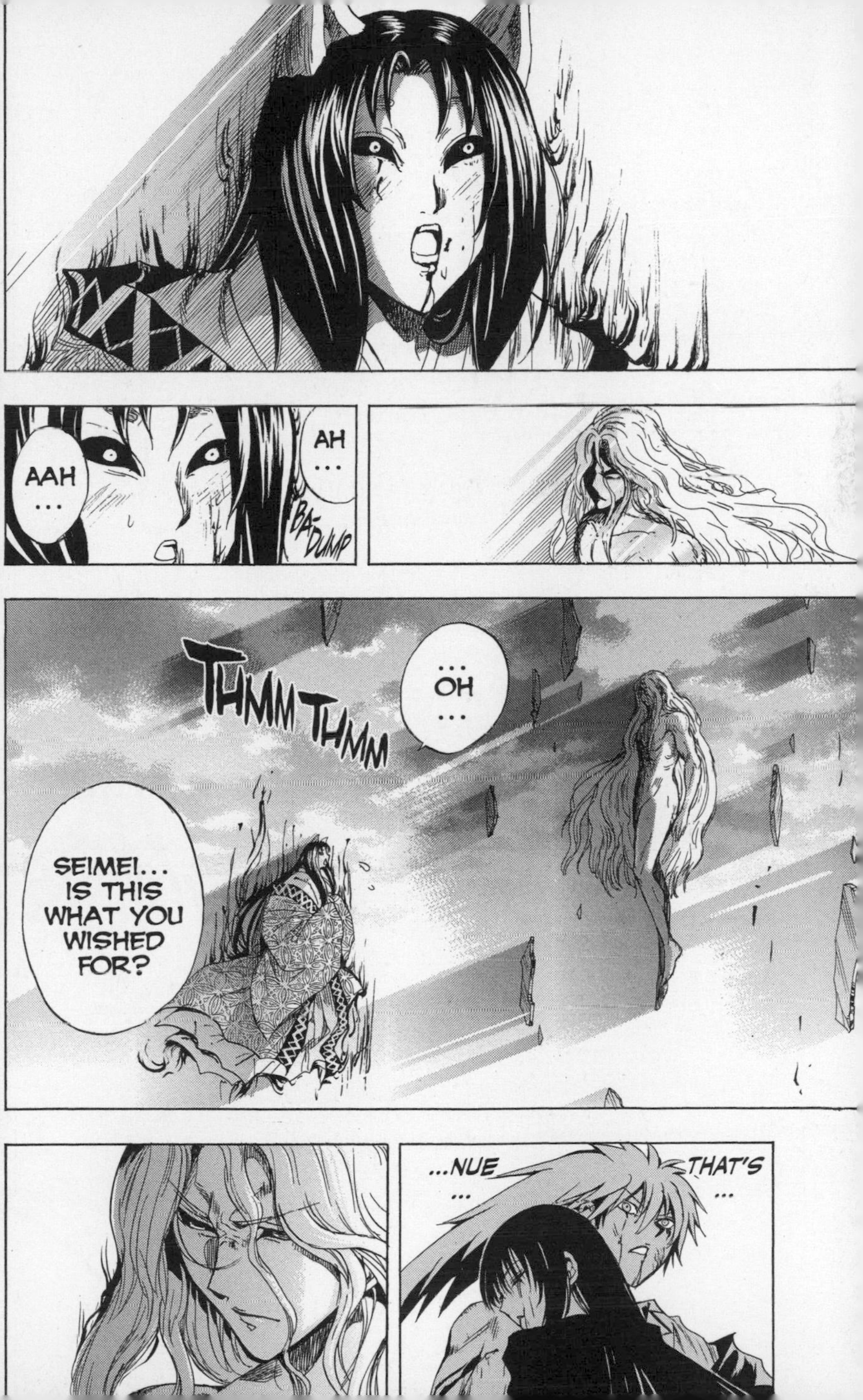
AH ...
AAH ...
BA-DUMP
... OH ...
THMM THMM
SEIMEI... IS THIS WHAT YOU WISHED FOR?
THAT'S ...
...NUE ...

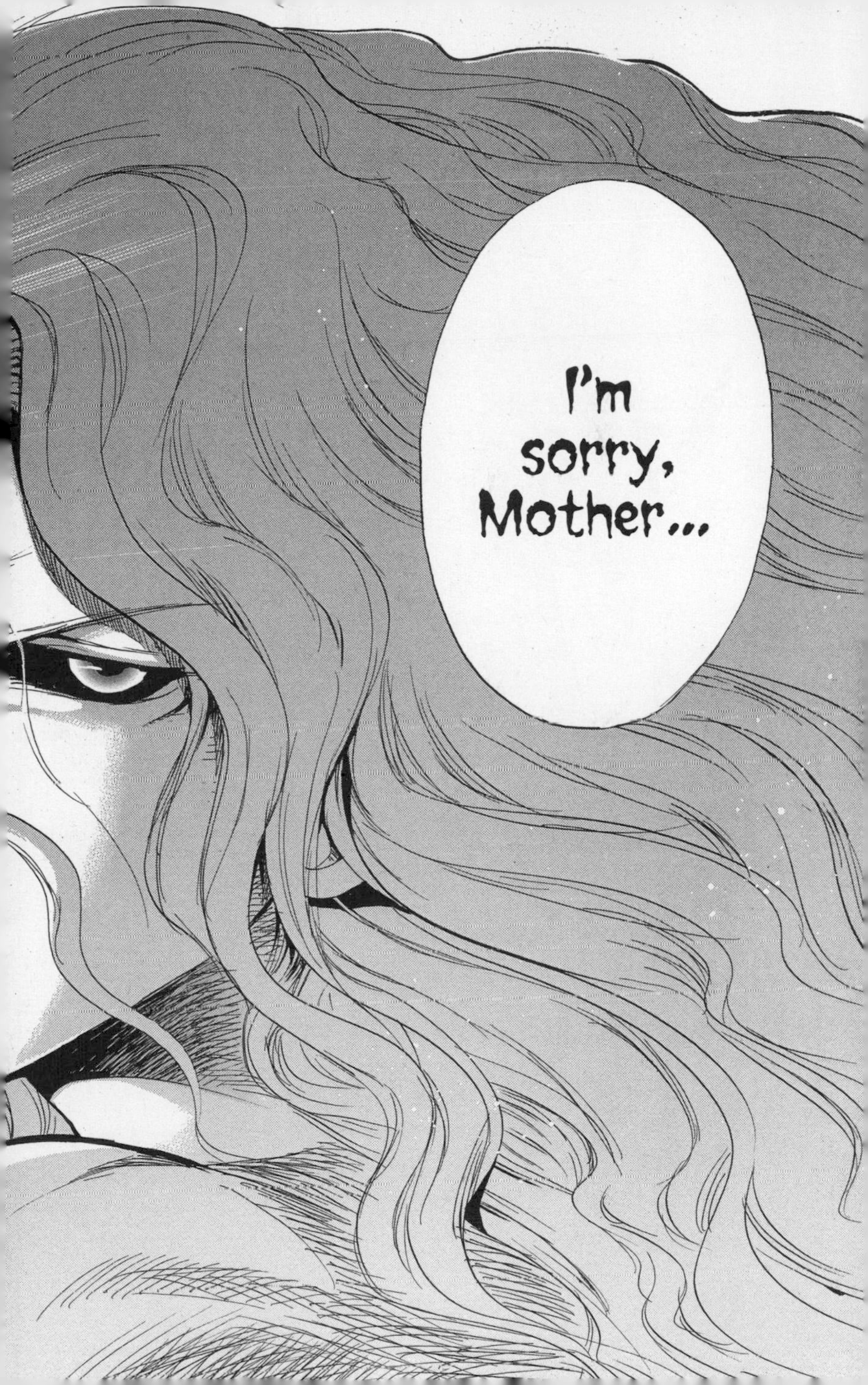
I'm sorry, Mother...

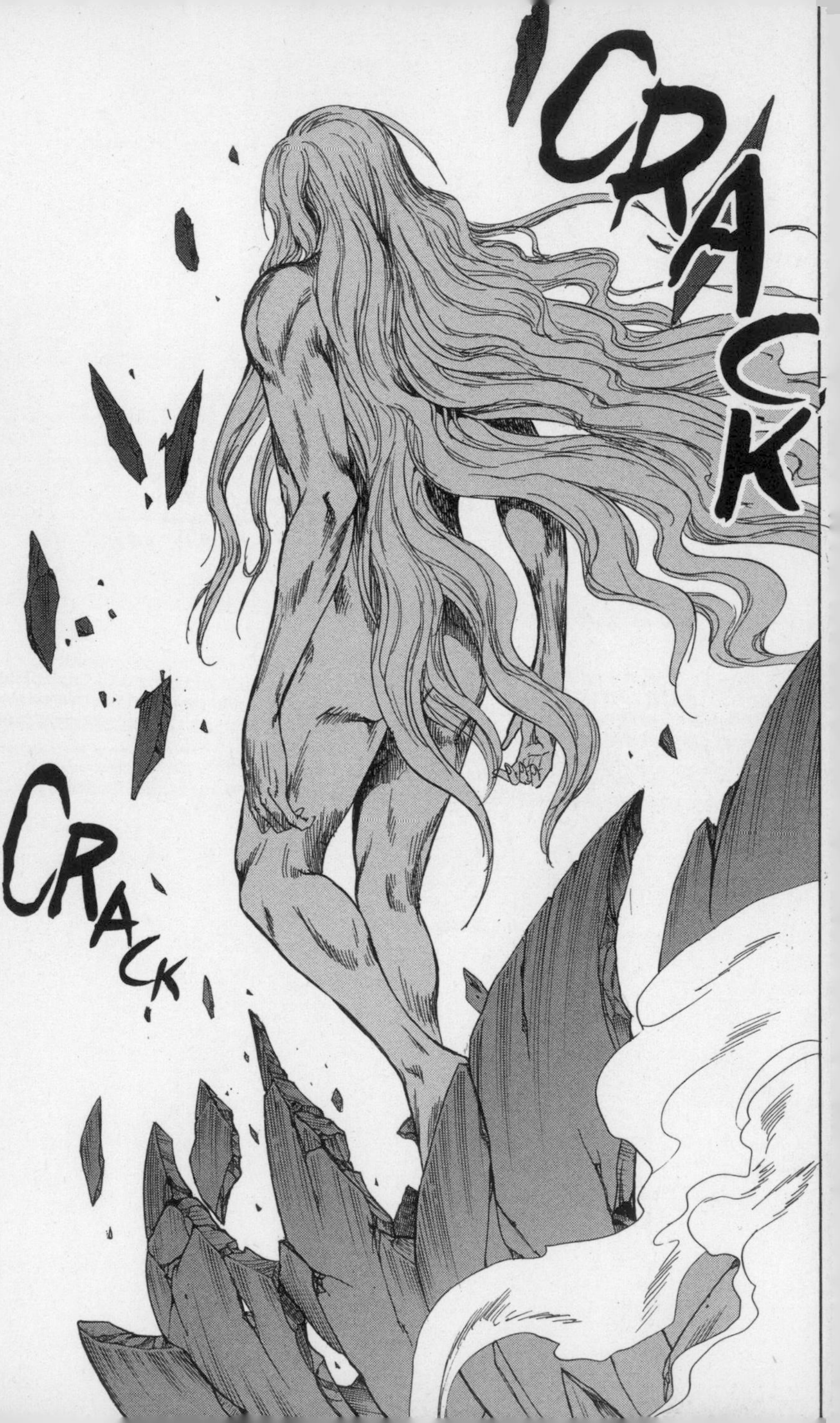
CRACK
CRACK

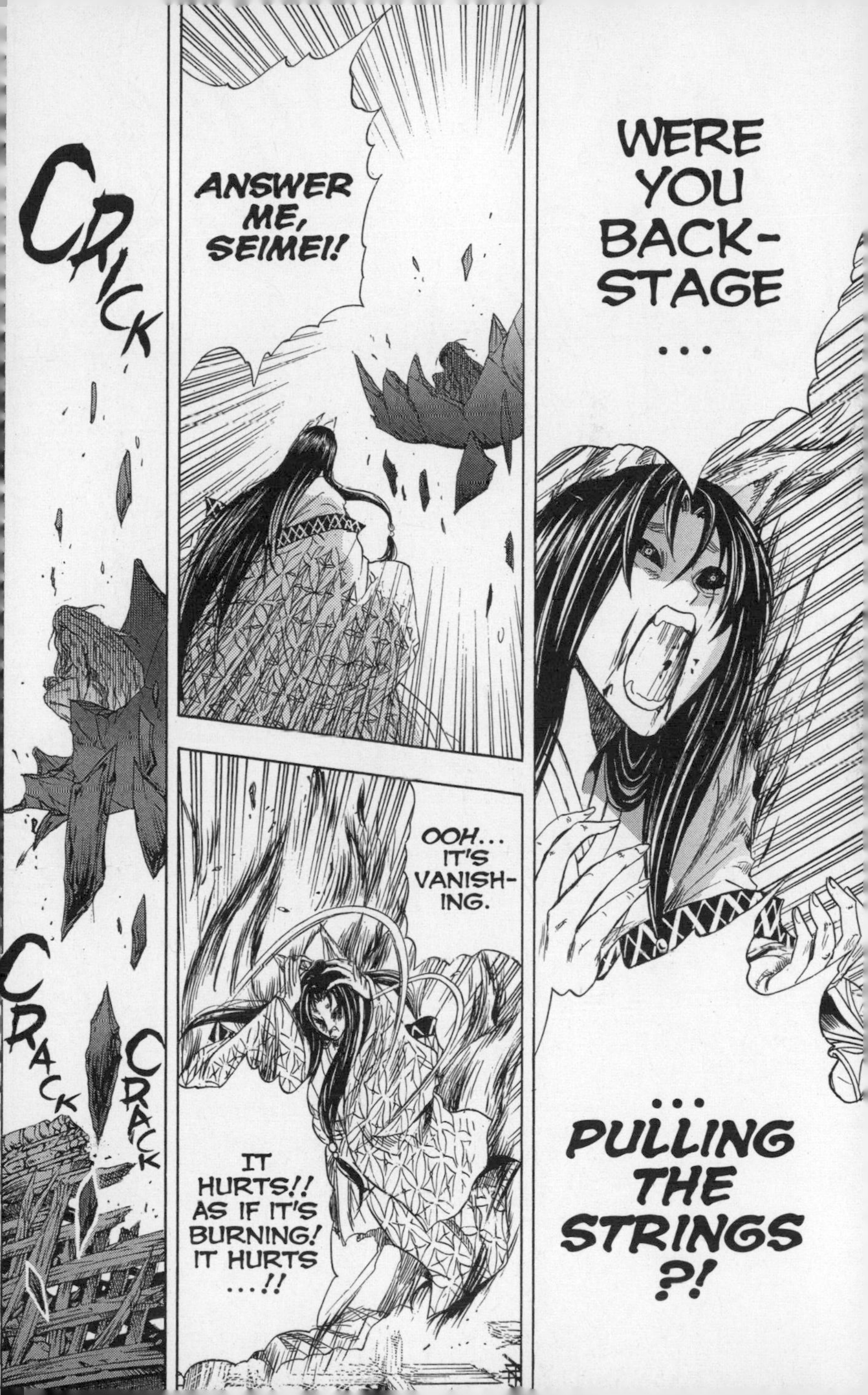
WERE YOU BACKSTAGE...
...PULLING THE STRINGS?!
ANSWER ME, SEIMEI!
OOH... IT'S VANISHING.
IT HURTS!! AS IF IT'S BURNING! IT HURTS...!!
CRICK
CRACK
CRACK

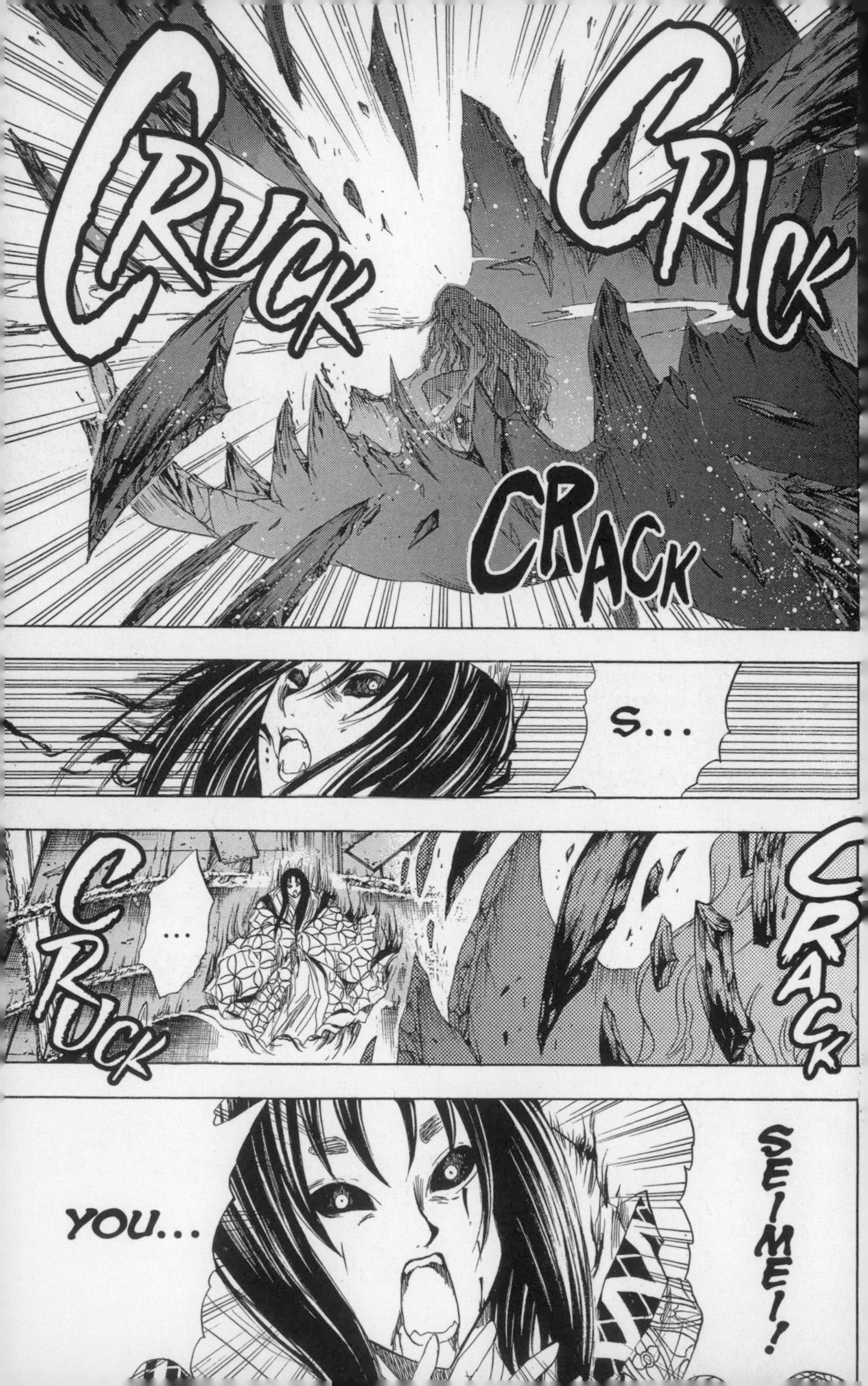
CRICK
CRUCK
CRACK
S...
CRACK
...
CRUCK
SEIMEI!!
YOU...

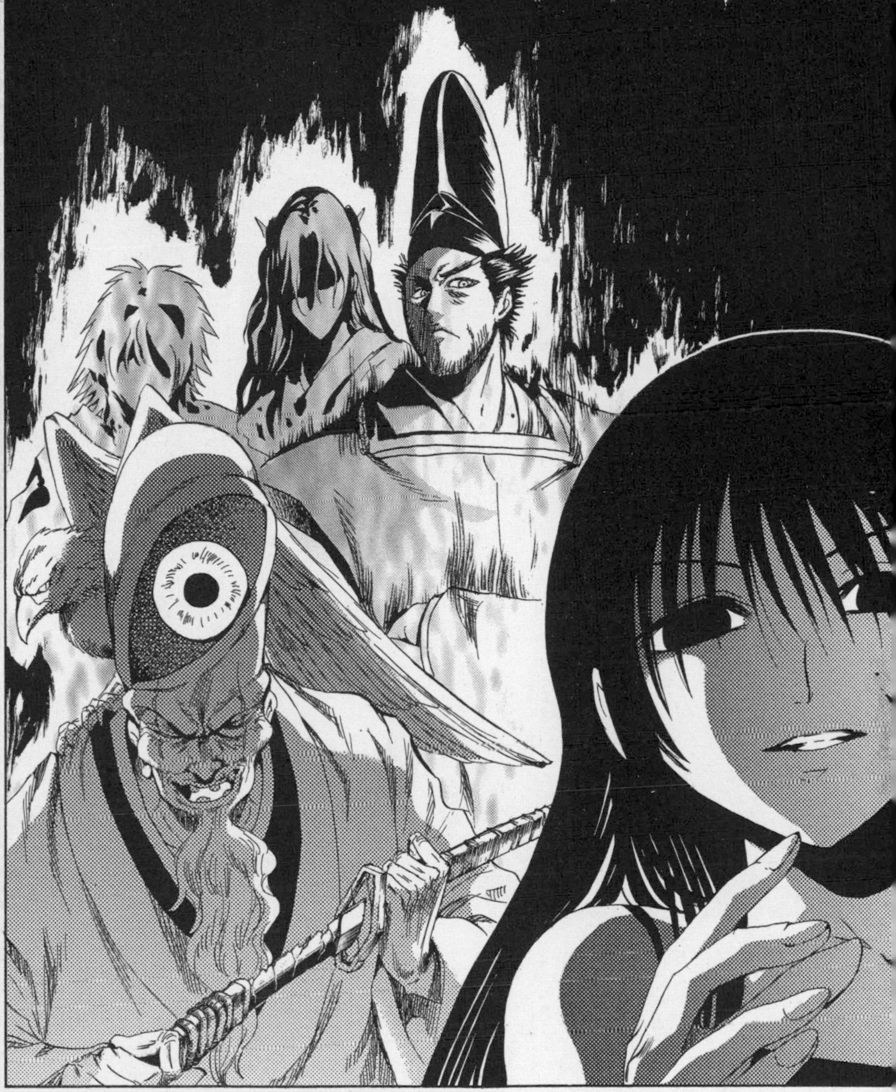

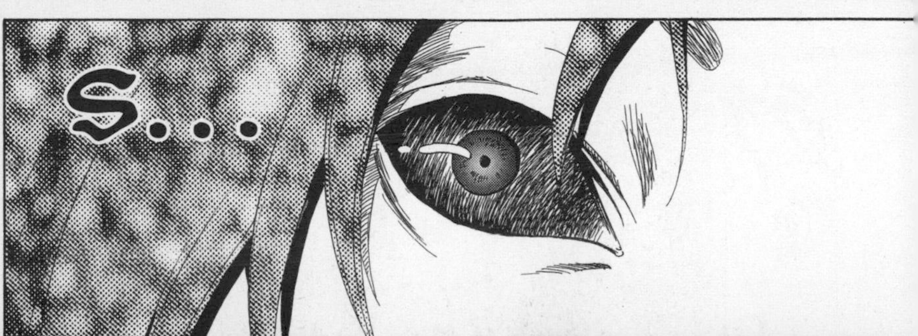
S...

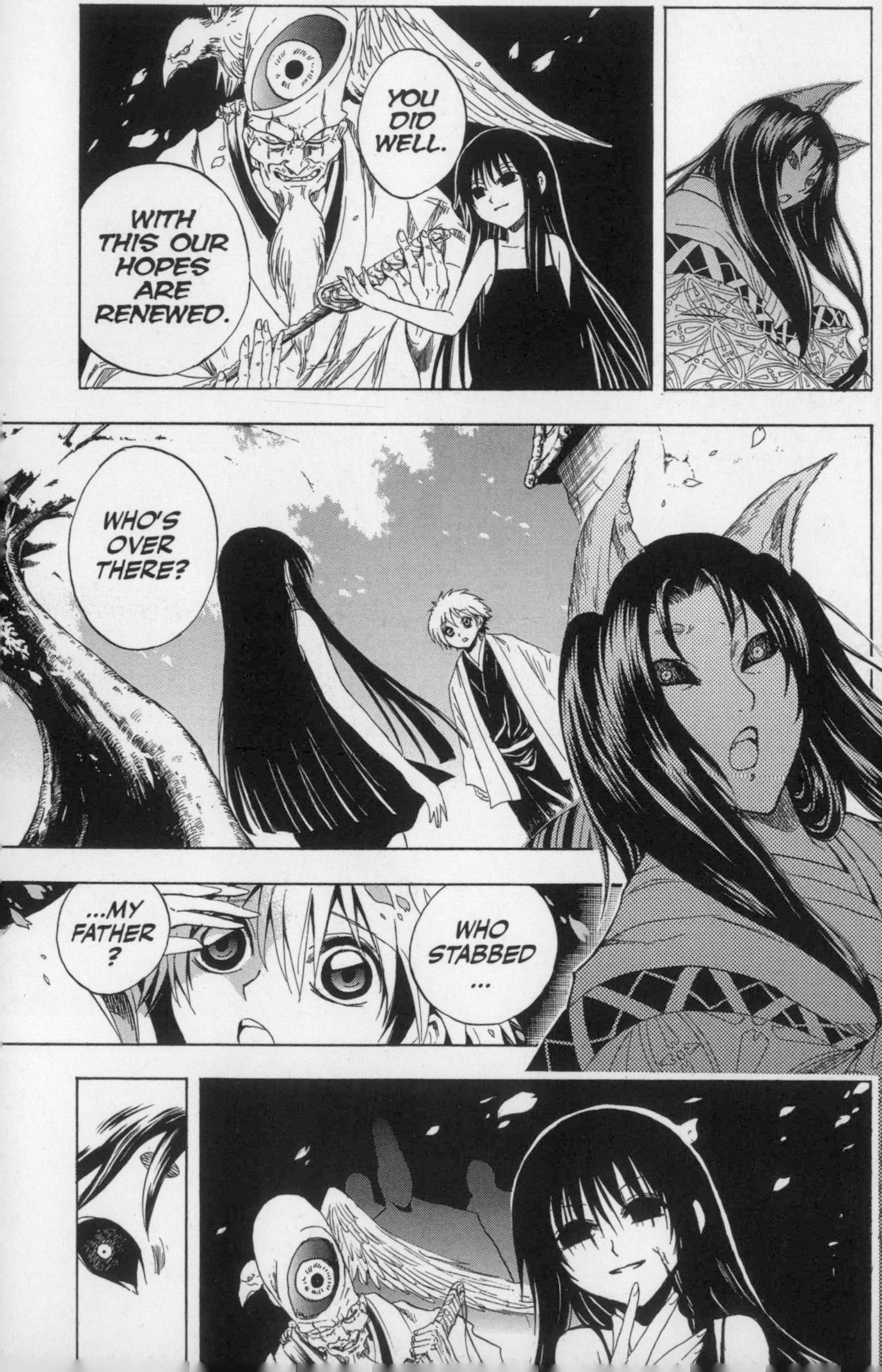
YOU DID WELL.
WITH THIS OUR HOPES ARE RENEWED.
WHO'S OVER THERE?
WHO STABBED ...
...MY FATHER ?

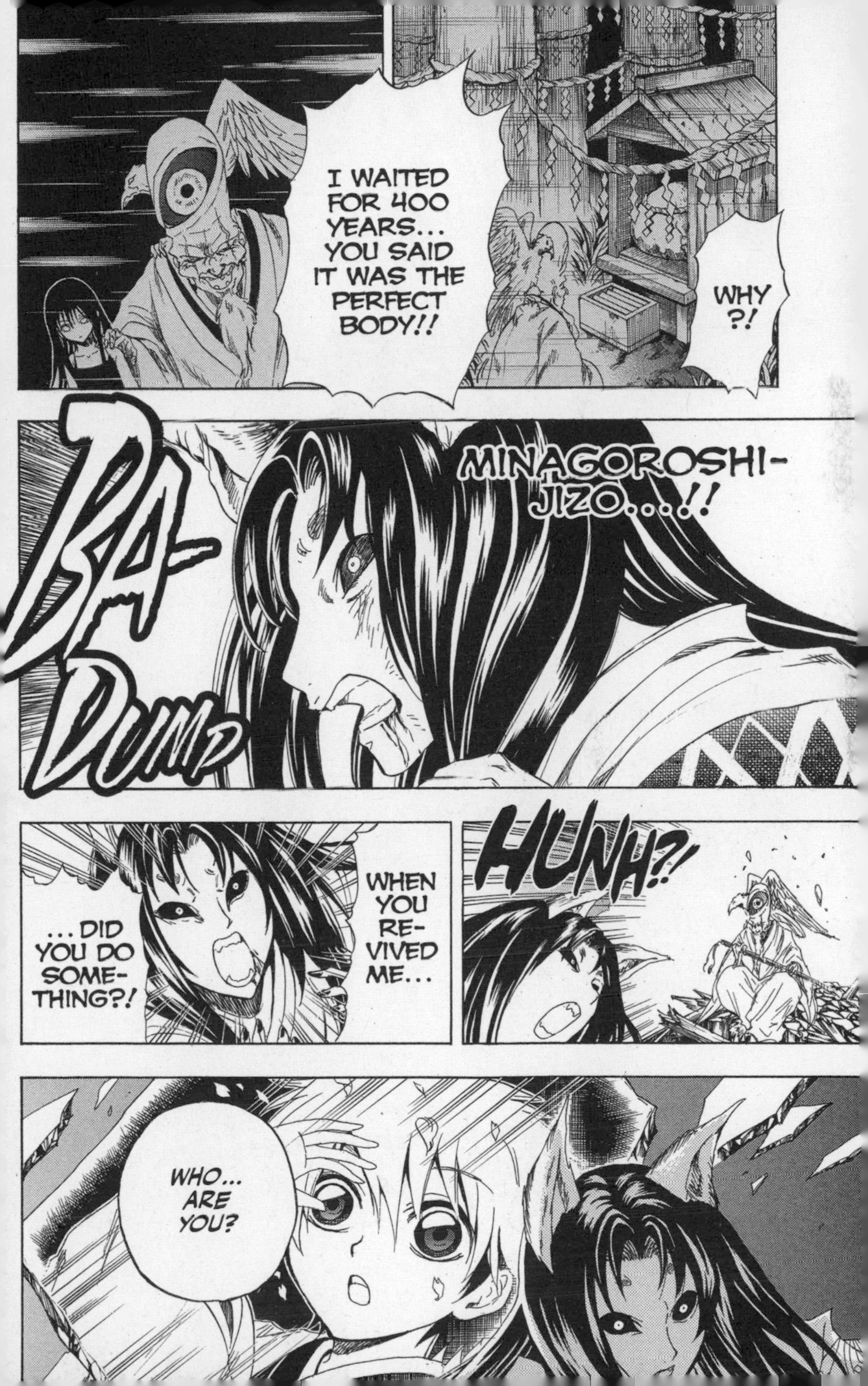
I WAITED FOR 400 YEARS... YOU SAID IT WAS THE PERFECT BODY!!
WHY?!
MINAGOROSHI-JIZO...!!
BA-DUMP
HUNH?!
WHEN YOU RE-VIVED ME...
...DID YOU DO SOME-THING?!
WHO... ARE YOU?

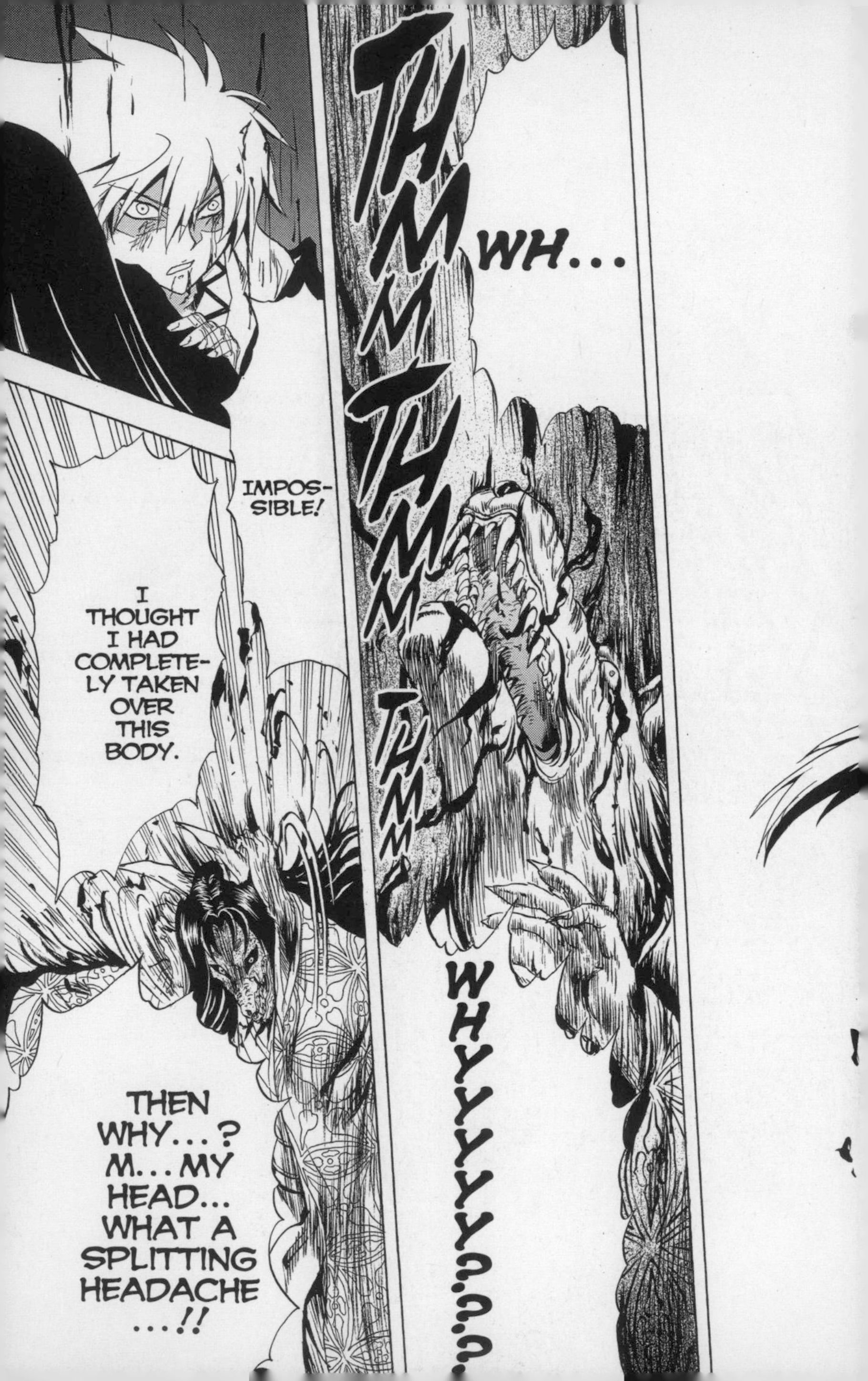
THMM THMM THM
WH...
WHYYYYY???
IMPOS-
SIBLE!
I THOUGHT I HAD COMPLETE-LY TAKEN OVER THIS BODY.
THEN WHY...? M...MY HEAD... WHAT A SPLITTING HEADACHE ...!!

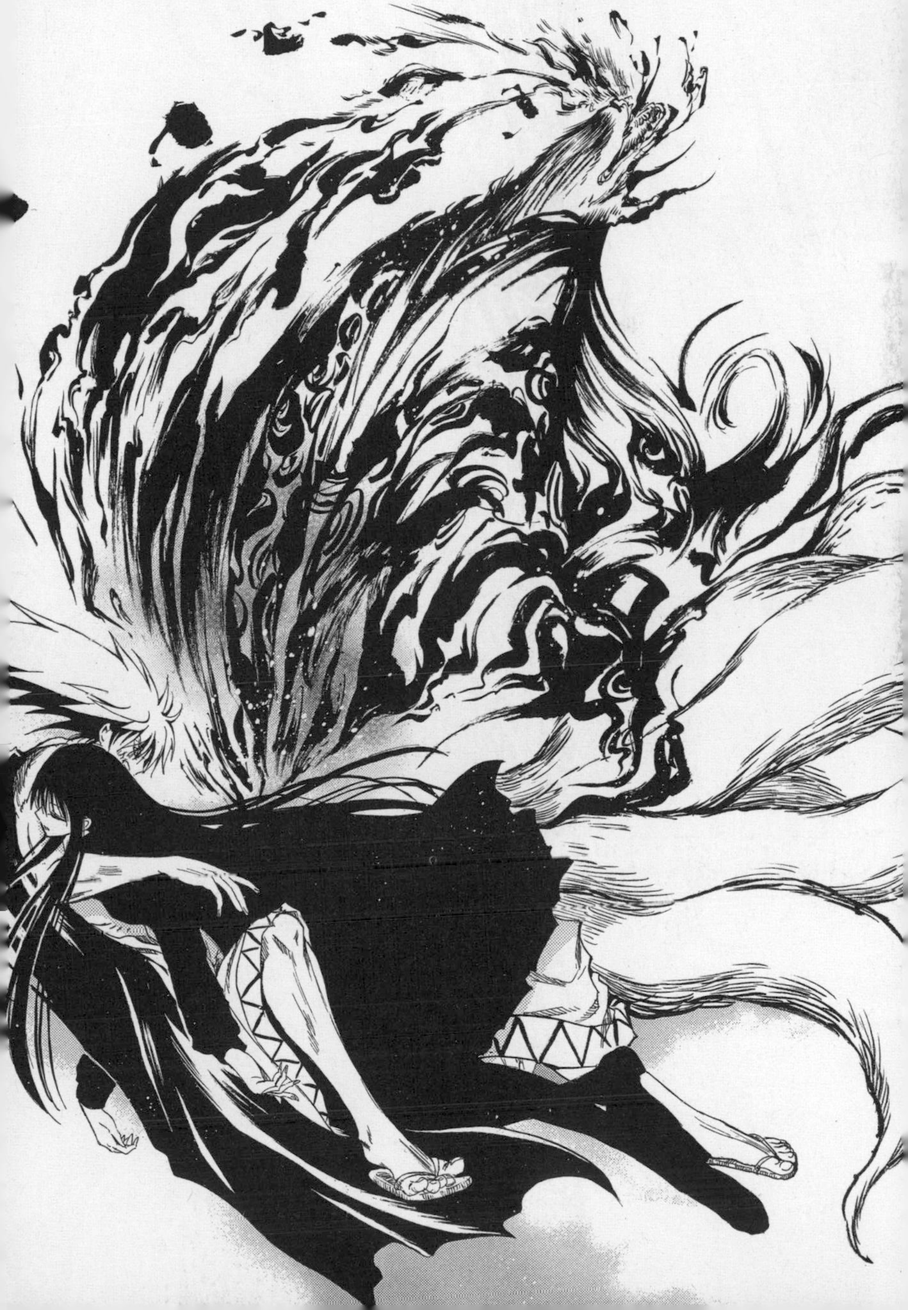

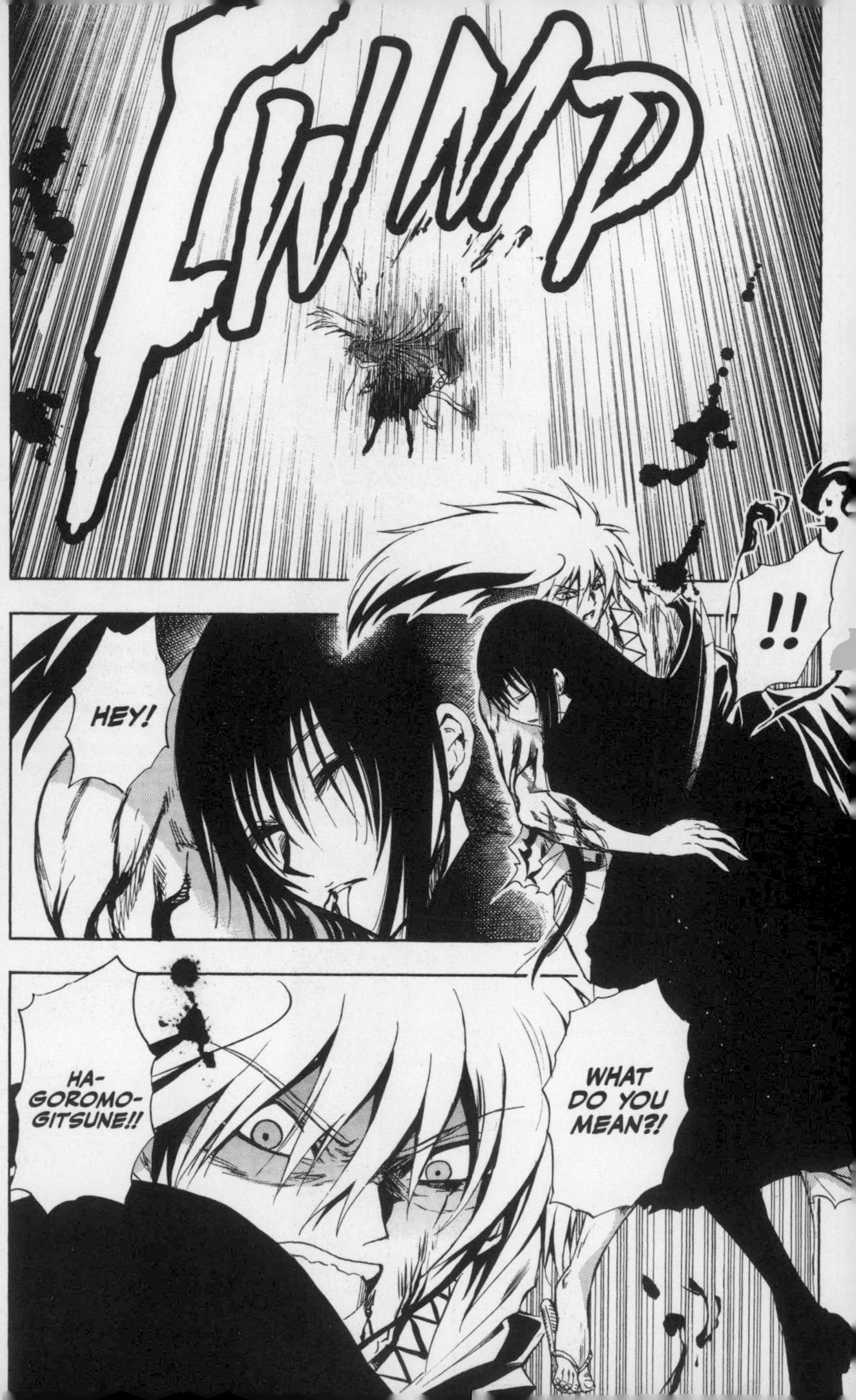
!!
HEY!
WHAT DO YOU MEAN?!
HA-GOROMO-GITSUNE!!

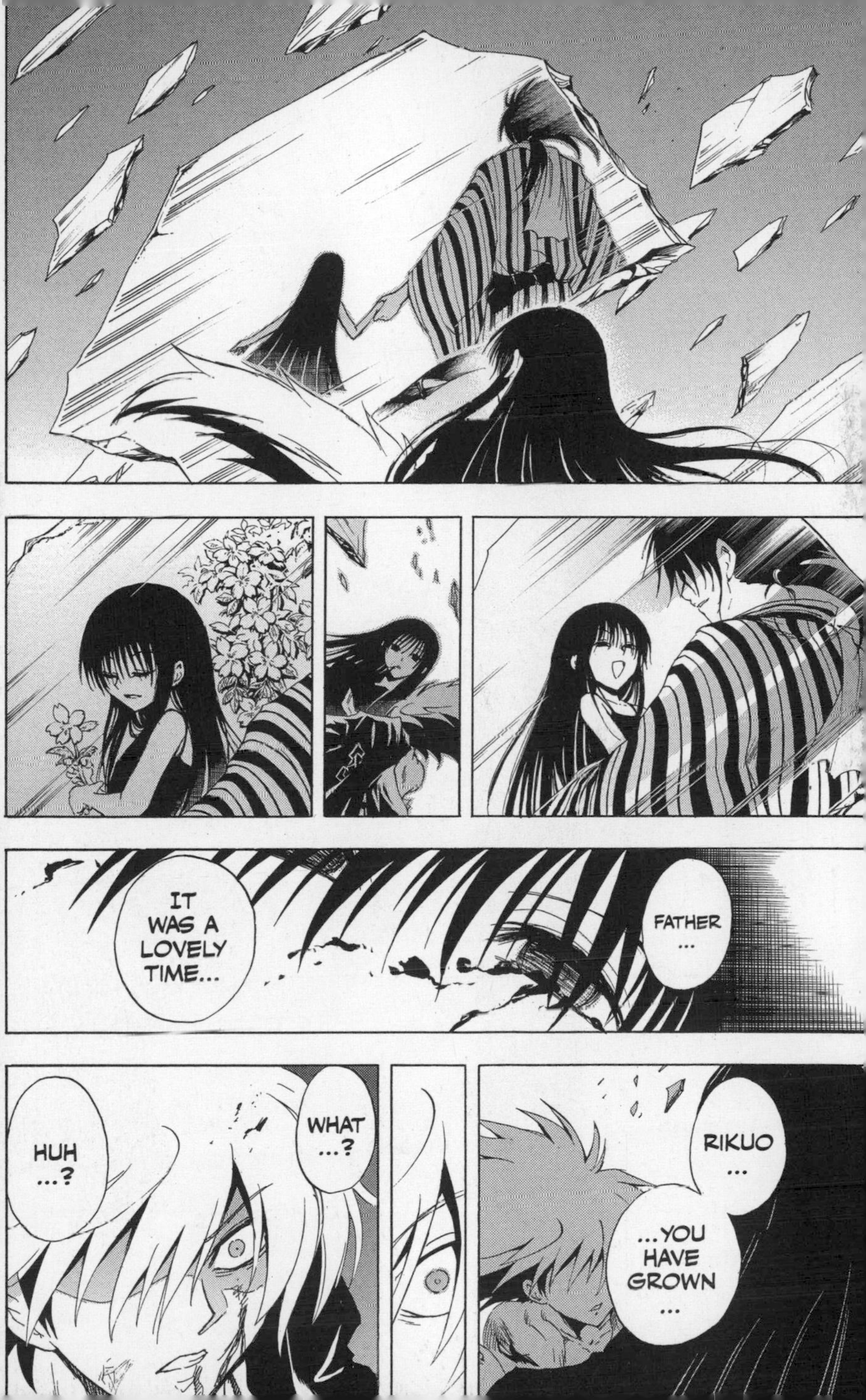
FATHER...
IT WAS A LOVELY TIME...
RIKUO...
...YOU HAVE GROWN...
WHAT...?
HUH...?

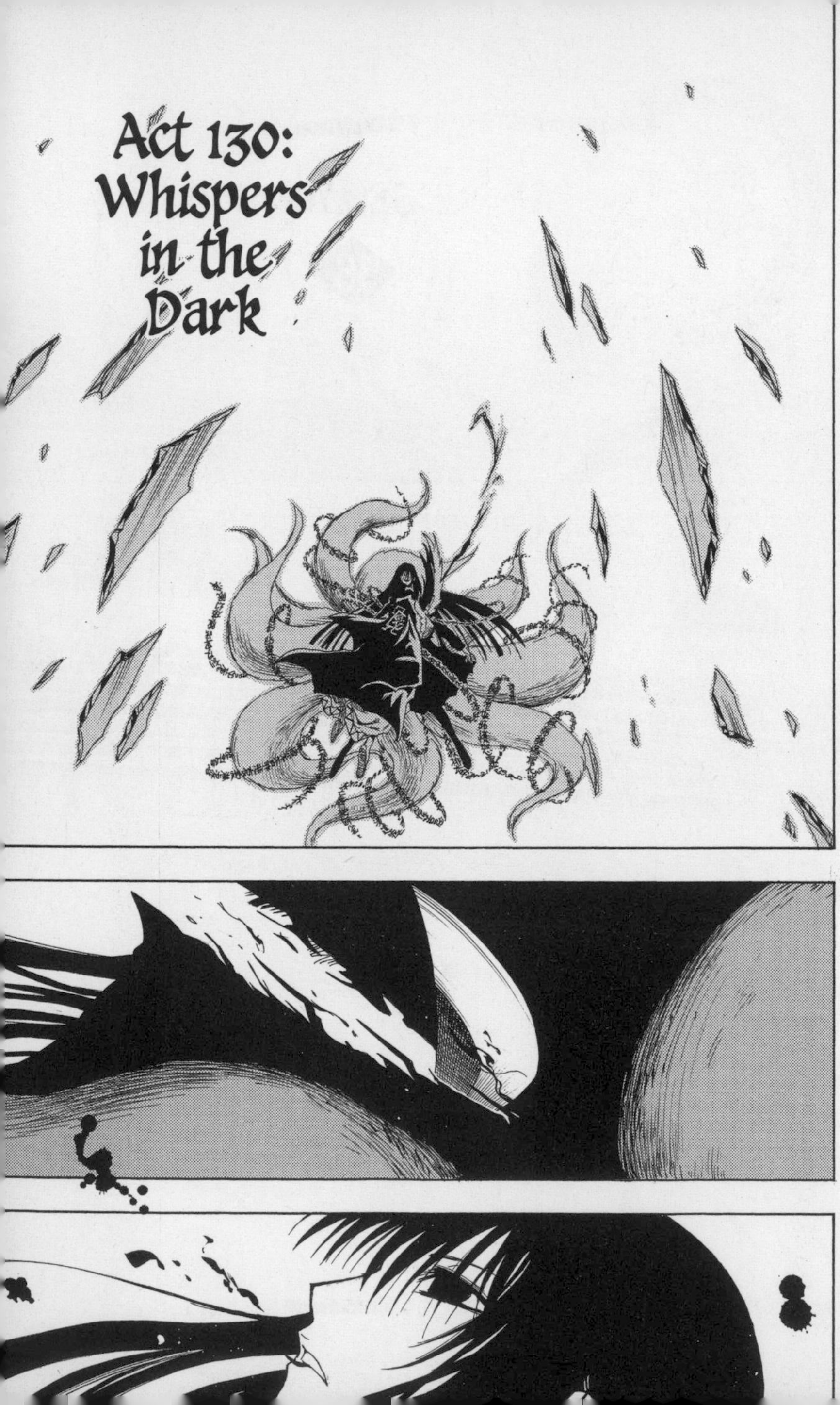
Act 130: Whispers in the Dark

TABLE OF CONTENTS

NURA: RISE OF THE YOKAI CLAN

KIDOMARU

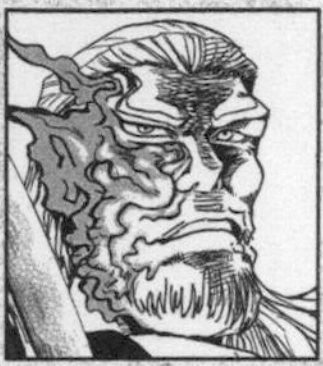

An executive of Kyoto yokai who's been serving Abe no Seimei since the Heian period. Hence, he strongly desires Nue's revival.

HAGOROMO-GITSUNE

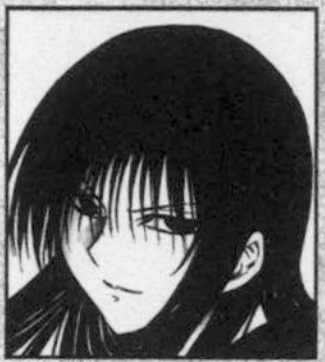

A great Kyoto yokai who has a fateful connection to both Nurarihyon and the Keikain family. She possesses humans and forces them to do evil things. She has returned to life after a 400-year absence.

MINAGOROSHI-JIZO

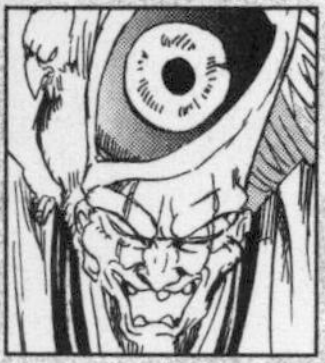

A Kyoto yokai who attends to Hagoromo-Gitsune in an advisory position. He can enter the bodies of humans who carry darkness in their hearts. This is how he controls them.

TSUCHIGUMO

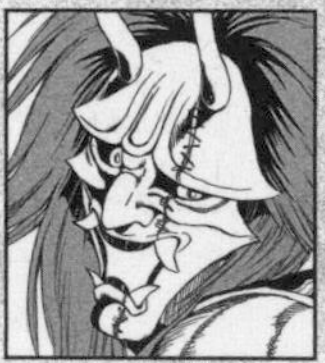

A rogue-minded Kyoto yokai who won't bow to Hagoromo-Gitsune. He's so powerful, he's known as an ayakashi to avoid.

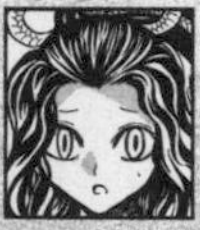

KYOKOTSU

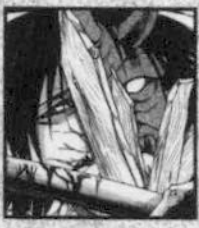

IBARAKI-DOJI

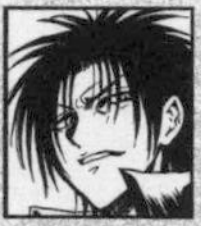

RYUJI

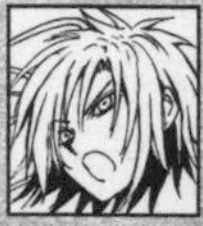

KUBINASHI

STORY SO FAR

Rikuo Nura is a seventh-grader at Ukiyoe Middle School. At a glance, he appears to be just another average, normal boy. But he's actually the grandson of the yokai Overlord Nurarihyon and is now the Underboss of the Nura clan, leaders of the yokai in the region. He is expected to become a great Overlord like his grandfather, but in the meantime he lives his days as a human being.

Rikuo charges into Nijo Castle, but Kidomaru gets in his way. Kurotabo assists in the battle by teaching Rikuo a new way of using the Equip technique: it's called Meld, and it combines the fears of two different individuals, doubling their fear power! With this technique, Rikuo goes on the offensive against Kidomaru. Meanwhile, Hagoromo-Gitsune gives birth to Nue, the reincarnated Abe no Seimei. Rikuo perceives Nue's vulnerability in this transitional state, so Ryuji takes the opportunity to seal away the fetal-like Nue. But Tsuchigumo stops him as Rikuo and Hagoromo-Gitsune face off against each other! Rikuo seems to be losing the fight, but in the midst of the battle, the memories from within the body Hagoromo-Gitsune currently possesses flicker in her mind, causing her to lose balance. Taking advantage of this momentary weakness, Yura uses her Hagun move to stop Hagoromo-Gitsune in her tracks. Rikuo stabs Hagoromo-Gitsune with his spirit sword, Nenekirimaru. As Hagoromo-Gitsune loses consciousness, she utters prophetic last words, the meaning of which is still unclear.

CHARACTERS

NURARIHYON

Rikuo's grandfather and the Lord of Pandemonium. He intends to pass leadership of the Nura clan—a powerful yokai consortium—to Rikuo. He's a mischievous sort who enjoys slipping out of diners without paying his bill.

RIKUO NURA

Though he appears to be a human boy, he's actually the grandson of Nurarihyon, a yokai. His grandfather's blood makes him one-quarter yokai, and he transforms into a yokai at times.

YURA KEIKAIN

Rikuo's classmate and a descendant of the Keikain family of onmyoji. She transferred into Ukiyoe Middle School to do field training in yokai exorcism. She has the power to control her shikigami and use them to destroy yokai.

KIYOTSUGU

Rikuo's classmate. He has adored yokai ever since Rikuo saved him in his yokai form, leading him to form the Kiyojuji Paranormal Patrol.

KUROTABO

A Nura clan yokai, also known as the Father of Destruction. One of the clan's best warriors, he hides a healthy arsenal of lethal weapons under his priest's robe. He teaches Rikuo an Equip technique called Meld.

YUKI-ONNA

A yokai of the Nura clan who is in charge of looking after Rikuo. She disguises herself as a human and attends the same school as Rikuo to protect him from danger. When in human form, she goes by the name Tsurara Oikawa.

NURA: RISE OF THE YOKAI CLAN

16

RIKUO'S DECLARATION

STORY AND ART BY
HIROSHI SHIIBASHI

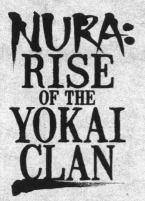

NURA: RISE OF THE YOKAI CLAN
VOLUME 16
SHONEN JUMP Manga Edition

Story and Art by HIROSHI SHIIBASHI

Translation — Yumi Okamoto
English Adaptation — Ross Anthony
Touch-up Art and Lettering — Annaliese Christman
Graphics and Cover Design — Fawn Lau
Editors — Joel Enos, Megan Bates

NURARIHYON NO MAGO © 2008 by Hiroshi Shiibashi. All rights reserved. First published in Japan in 2008 by SHUEISHA Inc., Tokyo. English translation rights arranged by SHUEISHA Inc.

Printed in the U.S.A.

Published by VIZ Media, LLC
P.O. Box 77010
San Francisco, CA 94107

10 9 8 7 6 5 4 3 2 1
First printing, August 2013

www.viz.com   www.shonenjump.com

I usually photograph my color illustrations and keep the prints close by.
I use them to check color consistency. Copies from a machine take up too
much space, and scanning can misrepresent the color.

They're about the size of a postcard, and it's fun to collect them—sort
of a hobby!

—HIROSHI SHIIBASHI,
2011

HIROSHI SHIIBASHI debuted in BUSINESS JUMP
magazine with *Aratama*. NURA: RISE OF THE YOKAI CLAN
is his breakout hit. He was an assistant to manga artist Hirohiko Araki,
the creator of *Jojo's Bizarre Adventure*. *Steel Ball Run* by Araki is one of
his favorite manga.